Liberty for the Twenty-First Century

Studies in Social, Political, and Legal Philosophy
General Editor: James P. Sterba, University of Notre Dame

This series analyzes and evaluates critically the major political, social, and legal ideals, institutions, and practices of our time. The analysis may be historical or problem-centered; the evaluation may focus on theoretical underpinnings or practical implications. Among the recent titles in the series are:

Moral Rights and Political Freedom
　by Tara Smith, University of Texas at Austin
Democracy and Social Injustice
　by Thomas Simon, Illinois State University
Morality and Social Justice: Point/Counterpoint
　by James P. Sterba, University of Notre Dame; Tibor Machan, Auburn University; Alison Jaggar, University of Colorado, Boulder; William Galston, White House Domestic Policy Council; Carol C. Gould, Stevens Institute of Technology; Milton Fisk, Indiana University; and Robert C. Solomon, University of Texas
Faces of Environmental Racism: Confronting Issues of Global Justice
　edited by Laura Westra, University of Windsor, and Peter S. Wenz, Sangamon State University
Plato Rediscovered: Human Value and Social Order
　by T. K. Seung, University of Texas at Austin
Punishment as Societal-Defense
　by Phillip Montague, Western Washington University
Liberty for the Twenty-First Century: Contemporary Libertarian Thought
　edited by Tibor R. Machan, Auburn University, and Douglas B. Rasmussen, St. John's University
Capitalism with a Human Face: The Quest for a Middle Road in Russian Politics
　by William Gay, University of North Carolina at Charlotte, and T. A. Alekseeva, Institute of Philosophy and Moscow State University

Liberty for the Twenty-First Century

Contemporary Libertarian Thought

edited by
Tibor R. Machan
and
Douglas B. Rasmussen

ROWMAN & LITTLEFIELD, INC.

ROWMAN & LITTLEFIELD PUBLISHERS, INC.

Published in the United States of America
by Rowman & Littlefield Publishers, Inc.
4720 Boston Way, Lanham, Maryland 20706

3 Henrietta Street
London WC2E 8LU, England

Copyright © 1995 by Rowman & Littlefield Publishers, Inc.

All rights reserved. No part of this publication may be reproduced, stored in a retrieval system, or transmitted in any form or by any means, electronic, mechanical, photocopying, recording, or otherwise, without the prior permission of the publisher.

The first part of Tibor R. Machan's "The Nonexistence of Basic Welfare Rights" has been reprinted from *Individuals and Their Rights* by Tibor R. Machan by permission of Open Court Publishing Company, La Salle, Illinois. © by Open Court Publishing Company.
"The Right to Welfare and the Virtue of Charity" by Douglas Den Uyl was originally published in *Social Philosophy and Policy*, vol. 10, No. 1 (Winter 1993). Reprinted with the permission of Cambridge University Press. © 1993 by Cambridge University Press.
"Political Legitimacy and Discourse Ethics" by Douglas Rasmussen was originally published in the *International Philosophical Quarterly*, vol. 32, pp. 17–34. Reprinted with permission.
"Moral Basis for National Defense" by Eric Mack was originally published in *Defending a Free Society* by Robert W. Poole Jr. Reprinted with permission.

British Cataloging in Publication Information Available

Library of Congress Cataloging-in-Publication Data

Liberty for the 21st century : contemporary libertarian thought / edited by Tibor R. Machan and Douglas B. Rasmussen.
p.   cm.—(Studies in social, political, and legal philosophy)
Includes bibliographical references (p.   ) and index.
1. Libertarianism.   I. Machan, Tibor R.   II. Rasmussen, Douglas B.   III. Series.
JC585.L427   1995   320.5'12—dc20   95-19310   CIP

ISBN 0-8476-8057-6 (cloth: alk. paper)
ISBN 0-8476-8058-4 (pbk.: alk. paper)

 The paper used in this publication meets the minimum requirements of American National Standard for Information Sciences—Permanence of Paper for Printed Library Materials, ANSI Z39.48—1964.

To the memory of

David L. Norton
and
Murray N. Rothbard

*David's vision of ethical individualism
inspired us and Murray's courage
in defense of liberty sustained us.*

Contents

Introduction   xi

Part 1. Libertarian Basics

Introduction   3
What Libertarianism Is
  John Hospers   5
Contracting for Liberty
  Jan Narveson   19
Moral Individualism and Libertarian Theory
  Eric Mack   41
"Rights" as MetaNormative Principles
  Douglas J. Den Uyl and Douglas B. Rasmussen   59
The Anarchism Controversy
  Aeon J. Skoble   77

Part 2. Social Problems in a Free Society

Introduction   99
Rights, Just War, and National Defense
  Eric Mack   101
"Righting" Civil Wrongs: Toward a Libertarian Agenda
  Steven Yates   121
Business Ethics in a Free Society
  Tibor R. Machan   143
Environmentalism Humanized
  Mike Gemmell   157
Education in a Free Society
  J. E. Chesher   175
The Repeal of Prohibition
  Mark Thornton   187

Part 3. Answering Critics and Responding to Other Views

Introduction	207
The Nonexistence of Basic Welfare Rights	
Tibor R. Machan	209
Capitalism, Socialism, and Equity Ownership	
N. Scott Arnold	227
Liberal Obituary?	
Loren E. Lomasky	243
Community versus Liberty?	
Douglas B. Rasmussen	259
Liberalism and Libertarianism: Narrowing the Gap	
Daniel Shapiro	289
The Right to Welfare and the Virtue of Charity	
Douglas J. Den Uyl	305
Against Moral Minimalism	
Gregory R. Johnson	335
Political Legitimacy and Discourse Ethics	
Douglas B. Rasmussen	351
Recommended Readings	375
Index	379
About the Contributors	387

A century that has witnessed the Holocaust and the Gulag is not one which can be aptly characterized as paying too much heed to basic rights.

—*Loren E. Lomasky*

Introduction

This is not perhaps the happiest of times for champions of the right to individual liberty. Despite the glaring failures of all types of regimes that amounted to official permission to violate individual rights—Nazi Germany, Fascist Italy, the socialist Soviet Union, and racist South Africa—intellectuals and politicians around the globe, as well as millions of those who either support or tolerate them, deride the ideal of a polity of uncompromised individual rights to life, liberty, and property. Even in the United States of America, and the country from which it learned much of its political philosophy, Great Britain, the notion that the best government is that which has its authority firmly restricted to defensive and retaliatory functions has been almost forgotten. That a politically just community is one in which the lives and creative energies and products of free men and women are for no one other than themselves and those whom they choose is more and more in dispute. Now that communism and socialism have had to go on the defensive, new incarnations of quasi- or semi-collectivist theories such as communitarianism, market socialism, and less systematic versions of anti-individualism are being erected and offered as the solution to human social problems.

Yet there are those, too, who remain confident that individual human beings who are not coerced into involuntary servitude—via doctrines of universal service, positive rights, solidarity, and the like—offer the best chance for building a just and decent human community. Whatever may differentiate groups of people around the globe—and many of the facts that make for the differences are benign and thoroughly welcome to the libertarian—the one thing that is unacceptable is that some people deem it their prerogative to run the lives of others, to deprive these others of their sovereignty, and of their full authority to govern themselves.

There are books available in which various ideas defending the rights of individuals are collected. Ours is an addition to this group. These ideas have, of course, a history. Indeed, one of us has collected similar essays in the past.* Our aim, however, is to present to readers the most novel and fully developed arguments for the libertarian alternative. Most of the pieces are original and not only address problems pertinent to the present, but also show the promise of libertarian thought for dealing with the issues of the next century. Nevertheless, this is not primarily a topical book. Mainly, it concerns perennial questions of human political life and offers principled answers to these. We discuss questions regarding human nature, morality, society, and knowledge—even aspects of the question of whether libertarianism's attempt to find basic answers to these questions can be well-grounded.

The essays in this volume are interrelated. Together, they are meant to provide insight into the depth and breadth of the libertarian political perspective. They have been grouped together, however, to form three different parts within this work. Each part has a goal. The goal of part one is to introduce the reader to what libertarianism is and outline some approaches by which it might be justified. The goal of part two is to address the question of how a society that embraces libertarian political principles might deal with various social problems, especially those that seem to require government intervention into people's lives, energies, and resources. The goal of part three is to answer some of the criticisms of libertarianism from other political perspectives, as well as to respond to those perspectives themselves. Though each essay serves the goal of the part to which it belongs, some essays offer insights that are relevant to the aim of other parts of this work. Thus, the division of this work is not intended to isolate each part from the others.

Though this volume of libertarian thought addresses many issues and questions, these essays are by no means exhaustive. Thus, the curious reader should examine other sources. Besides the notes at the end of each essay, there is a list of recommended readings at the end of this volume that anyone interested in libertarianism should consult.

We wish to thank all the contributors for their hard work. They are a diverse lot (not, perhaps, unusual for people who find individualism a sound social framework). Still, in these essays they clearly share a concern for identifying various libertarian political and social solutions as right, indeed, as right as such solutions can ever be. Producing these pieces is not usually done for immediate pay-off, either in terms of monetary gain or career advancement. It shows dedication to the work of the political philosopher, period.

---

*See, Tibor R. Machan, ed., *The Libertarian Alternative* (Chicago, Illinois: Nelson-Hall Co., 1973), and Tibor R. Machan, ed., *The Libertarian Reader* (Totowa, New Jersey: Rowman & Littlefield, 1982).

We also wish to thank the editors of Rowman & Littlefield, especially Professor James Sterba, who were kind enough to encourage the project through its several stages. We also wish to thank the anonymous reviewers who gave us suggestions and criticism, both of which made the final result better than it would otherwise have been.

Finally, we wish to thank Lucille Hartmann, who assisted in preparation of the manuscripts, and to acknowledge the permission to reprint all or part of the following: Eric Mack, "The Moral Basis of National Defense," *Defending a Free Society*, ed. Robert W. Poole Jr. (Lexington, Mass.: D.C. Heath and Los Angeles: The Reason Foundation, 1984), 1–31; Tibor R. Machan, "The Nonexistence of Basic Welfare Rights," *Individuals And Their Rights* (LaSalle, Illinois: Open Court, 1989), 100–111; Loren E. Lomasky, "Liberal Obituary?" *Ethics* 102 (1991): 140–154; Douglas J. Den Uyl, "The Right to Welfare and the Virtue of Charity," *Social Philosophy & Policy* 10 (Winter 1993): 192–224; and Douglas B. Rasmussen, "Political Legitimacy and Discourse Ethics," *International Philosophical Quarterly* 32 (March 1992): 17–34.

Part One

Libertarian Basics

Introduction

This section contains five essays. The first one explains the nature of libertarianism. However, we may note here that "libertarianism" designates a group of positions concerning political institutions stressing the primacy of individual liberty. With more and more confusion about what is liberalism—so that the term is used alternatively to refer to nearly diametrically opposed sociopolitical systems—the term "libertarianism" has come to mean the sort of polity in which the right of every individual to life, liberty, and property is fully and consistently protected. Libertarianism is the political-economic theory whereby a *political* community is just if and only if each member has his or her basic negative rights (that is, not to be murdered, coerced, assaulted, kidnapped, robbed, defrauded, raped by other persons) respected and protected.

If all this appears familiar, the reason is that libertarianism is mostly the purified version of the political, legal, and economic system established in the United States of America. Libertarians would maintain that they are carrying out to its rational implications the political ideal identified by the Declaration of Independence or, more precisely, as found in the political, legal and economic works of John Locke, Adam Smith, and other classical liberals. Accordingly, libertarians either propose a government that is required to protect, maintain, and promote the basic negative rights of all members of society or a system of competing law enforcement and adjudication that has the same objective.

Libertarians hold that everyone in a community must be accorded his or her sovereignty regarding choices, decisions, and actions that do not violate the same rights of anyone else. A legal system must prevail in which everyone's civil liberties, including the rights to free expression, religious affiliation, commercial associations, and procedural justice in the case of litigation are to be upheld. In short, regardless of their (peaceful) goal, none may be made subject to involuntary servitude. Even the funding of government must be secured by means of voluntary payment, not coercive taxation.

There are, however, different arguments in support of the libertarian political/legal system. Some libertarians embrace a utilitarian moral foundation in their defense of the free society, holding that the free society, especially the free market, will best promote the greatest happiness of the greatest number. Yet others eschew all reference to ethics or morality and hold that libertarianism most faithfully reflects the natural, evolutionary, development of human social life. There are also those who defend libertarianism because of its supposed concordance with a religious idea of human existence. Some libertarians rely on a thoroughgoing moral skepticism, following, for example, the Chinese philosophical school of Taoism (mainly Lao Tzu), claiming that since nothing about right and wrong is knowable, no one could ever justify exercising any inherent authority over another.

The next three essays in this section do not take any of the above approaches to justifying liberty. Rather, they offer, respectively, a contractarian, a deontological, and a virtue ethics approach to the claim that people have a basic negative right to liberty. These essays are but outlines of more well-developed statements, but each constitutes a serious argument for the libertarian political perspective. Together, they provide insight into how the libertarian political view might be defended and a good place to start for anyone seeking to understand the intricacies of this position.

Libertarians argue that government ought to concern itself primarily with protecting individual rights to life, liberty, and property. Libertarian anarchists find even this objectionable, claiming that a single governmental authority would itself amount to a violation of such rights. The final essay in this section introduces the reader to this viewpoint.

What Libertarianism Is

John Hospers

1. Liberty

The word "libertarianism," as the name implies, has something to do with liberty, or freedom. But until more is said, one cannot know just what the term means in a given situation. If you overheard someone exclaim, "I'm free!" you would not know whether she had just been released from jail, gone off her diet, obtained a divorce, or solved the free-will problem. Does a person have liberty if he is doing what he wants to do, regardless of later consequences? Does he have liberty when he is in jail, but prefers to remain there? Does a woman have liberty when she is in thrall to a man who mesmerizes her and orders her to do things that she does not want to do, but always obeys him? Does an army officer have liberty if he can give orders to enlisted men, but is himself subject to orders of those above him in the chain of command? Apparently, the word "liberty" is not always used with the same meaning; the meanings overlap and intertwine. It is not necessary to go through all the subtleties of meaning to explain the libertarian use of the term. First, however, one must make an important distinction.

Negative liberty, or freedom-*from*, exists when one is not coerced by other human beings, and can make one's own decisions and act on them. One need not be uninfluenced by the acts or words of others, but to be free, one must not act under threat of force in case one fails to act as ordered. We also use the term to refer to *positive* liberty or freedom-*to*: in this sense, the degree of one's liberty is proportional to one's range of choices. A wealthy person is free to do many things, such as spend winters in the south of France, that a person of lesser means can't do. It is not only financial means that make one free to do many things: a condition of nature is equally

5

essential. A person who is paralyzed is not free to walk; she cannot walk even if she tries. A person is not free to fly through the air like a bird, since no attempt by human beings to do so will succeed.

It has been alleged that the inability to walk or fly is not really a restriction on one's liberty—that (for example) if I am unable to afford air fare or bus fare across the country, this is no restriction of my freedom, but a law passed prohibiting me from traveling is.[1] However, this limitation seems quite arbitrary. We do constantly use the term in both ways: a lack of freedom can refer to the imposition of others' will upon us and also to inabilities that prevent us from doing what we desire. If a person's lifelong dream is to fly through the air, it is certainly felt to be a limitation on his freedom that he cannot do this—as limiting as if the inability was the result of coercion.

The two senses are, of course, related: if man is free from his chains, he is free to walk about. However, the two are also relatively independent of each other: one can have freedom-from and yet have a very limited range of choices. If Robinson Crusoe has to choose between remaining forever on his island and embarking in a leaky rowboat in the hope of finding another island, his choices are negligible and unenviable, but no one is coercing him. If you are caught in a fire, your choices may be to either stay and burn or try to escape and run a 50–50 chance of getting out alive.

For the libertarian, the fundamental sense of "liberty" is the freedom-from. If people are free from the coercive dictates of others, they can exercise their choices in countless ways that would have been impossible before; they can grow crops, build, invent, sell, and exchange new things, and reap the rewards of their ingenuity, while at the same time others have goods available that they would not otherwise have. The early American pioneers were relatively free from coercion, but they were not free to obtain antibiotics, anesthetics, telephones, or cars. Today, with the accumulation of knowledge from generation to generation, we are free to do countless things that no king or emperor was free to do in all the preceding centuries. No monarch in past ages was able to go to a drugstore or supermarket.

Why is freedom-from the more fundamental meaning of liberty for libertarians? To answer this question, we must explain the central concept in libertarian thought, human rights. Only then can liberty be more precisely defined.

2. Rights

When I claim a right, I carve out a niche (as it were) in my life, saying in effect, "This activity I must be able to perform without interference from others. For you and everyone else, this activity of mine is off-limits." Claiming a right is in effect putting up a "no trespassing" sign in relation to everyone else. I may not encroach on another's domain any more than he upon mine, without my consent. For example, I have no right to decide how you should spend your money. I may deplore your choice of life-style, and I may remonstrate you about it, provided you are willing to listen. But I have no right to force you to change it.

Not, that is, unless your activity violates *my* right, or mine yours. If I rob you (take what is yours without your consent), I am violating your right, and there is no right to violate rights. Every right of one person entails a duty of others not to interfere with the exercise of that right—the duty is one of noninterference or forbearance. A person is not free to do whatever he likes, for doing so may interfere with the rights of others. Herbert Spencer formulated this principle in his Law of Equal Freedom: Each person should be free to do as he will, provided that in so doing he does not interfere with the equal right of others to do as they will. The moment he does, the "no trespassing sign" is up.

What is the basis of this right against forcible interference?

Each kind of entity in nature has a distinct set of properties, which are called its "nature." Every chemical element or compound has a specific nature: oxygen supports combustion, hydrogen is combustible, and water, a compound of the two, extinguishes combustion. Iron acts in one way, chlorine in another, uranium in a third. Each species of living creature also has a distinct nature; cats behave in ways that dogs do not. The human species—man in the generic sense of that word—also has a specific nature. Unlike all other species of living things, man is not controlled (or not entirely controlled) by his natural instincts; he is not genetically programmed to do most of the things he does, as other creatures are. Man's actions are mediated through his *mind*: people can think, deliberate, weigh alternatives, and decide what actions to undertake. A wild creature can survive without thought or deliberation by following its inborn instincts. Man can survive only by using his mind—or sometimes by imitating those who do. To survive and prosper, a human being must be free to develop his faculties, to acquire knowledge, and to act upon that knowledge. Ayn Rand writes:

> Stand on an empty stretch of soil in a wilderness unexplored by men and ask yourself what manner of survival you would achieve and how long you would last if you refused to think, with no one around to teach you the motions, or, if you chose to think, how much your mind would be able to discover—ask yourself how many independent conclusions you have reached in the course of your life and how much of your time was spent on performing the actions

you learned from others—ask yourself whether you would be able to discover how to till the soil and grow your food, whether you would be able to invent a wheel, a lever, and induction coil, a generator, an electronic tube. . . .[2]

The essential ingredient in all this is freedom from coercion by others. This is one's basic and inalienable right. It is the key to human survival and development. "Those who hold that life is valuable, hold, by implication, that men ought not to be prevented from carrying on life-sustaining activities," wrote Spencer. "The conception of 'natural rights' originates in recognition of the truth that if life is justifiable, there must be a justification for the performance of acts essential to its preservation; and, therefore, a justification of those liberties and claims which make such acts possible."[3]

What are these liberties and claims? The right to life, liberty, and the pursuit of happiness, wrote Thomas Jefferson in the Declaration of Independence. But what precisely do they mean? The right to life is the right not to be killed or otherwise harmed against one's will. The right to liberty is the right to live one's life in accordance with one's own voluntary choices, as long as one does not, in doing so, violate the equal rights of others. The right to the pursuit of happiness is the right to pursue happiness in a way that does not violate rights—it does not include the right to plunder others even if one might be happier doing so. And there is the right to property, which is the right to earn whatever is required to be an owner of material goods. None of these is the right to be given something by others; they are all rights to take certain actions in order to further one's life. Ayn Rand takes care to explain what these rights do and do not include:

> The right to property means that a man has the right to take the economic actions necessary to earn property, to use it and dispose of it; it does *not* mean that others must provide him with property.
> The right of free speech means that a man has the right to express his ideas without danger of suppression, interference, or punitive action by the government. It does not mean that others must provide him with a lecture hall, a radio station, or a printing press through which to express his ideas.
> Any undertaking that involves more than one man requires the *voluntary* consent of every participant. Every one of them has the *right* to make his own decision; but none has the right to force his decision on the others.[4]

"No person's life should be a nonvoluntary mortgage on the life of another. Slavery is the total denial of the rights of the person who is enslaved." But even to be enslaved in part of one's life is a violation of one's rights. I cannot claim the products of your labor as mine. The fruit of one person's labor should not be fair game for anyone who comes along and demands it as his right. What a person should do with the products of his labor is for him to decide, not for others to determine on the basis of their wants or even their needs.

"Other people's lives are not yours to dispose of." A hundred men might gain so much pleasure from beating and killing one person that, in the calculation of pleasures and pains advocated by some utilitarians, the total benefits to the aggressors outweigh the costs to the victim. But this, of course, is a violation of the victim's right; other people's lives are not anyone else's to dispose of. Do you want to occupy, rent-free, the mansion that someone else has worked for twenty years to buy? But other men's lives are not yours to dispose of. "In order to achieve the worthy goals of the next five-year plan, we must forcibly collectivize the peasants. . . ." but other men's lives are not yours to dispose of.

3. Property Rights

The "liberal establishment" has usually defended the right of free speech, but denigrated the right to property. But the right to freedom of speech is impossible without property rights. What does your right to a free press come to if the government owns all the newsprint? What does your right to free speech come to if the government owns all the lecture halls? A person has no right to a free advertisement in a newspaper if the owner of the paper declines to run it, and no right to radio time if the station decides not to air his message. A person has the right to rent a lecture hall or run an ad if the owner agrees; if the owner were forced to run it, he could not make his own decision in the matter, and would be owner in name only. What if nobody will run your ad? You can distribute mimeographed handbills, or rent space elsewhere (this is almost always possible, unless the government owns all property and will not permit dissenting views), or become an owner yourself, which may take time but gives you in turn the right to refuse to air the views of others. In any society in which the government does not monopolize the channels of communication, dissenting opinions of whatever stripe can be publicized.

The old question, "Do you have a right to yell 'Fire!' falsely in a crowded theater?" is often taken to be a free-speech issue, but it is a property-rights issue. The answer is no, you have no such right, because you are on the theater-owner's property, and the owner will not usually permit yelling, screaming, defacing the walls, or other disturbances—if he did he would soon lose his paying audience. For the same reason, you cannot go into a cathedral and scream obscene epithets. Free-speech issues cannot be analyzed apart from the issue of property rights.

Government always has been the principal enemy of property rights. Officials of government, always attempting to increase their own power, find the seizure of other people's wealth an effective way to bring this about. The person who gains that wealth is always insecure under such a predatory government; he always runs the risk of confiscation. The government may tax or regulate him to death, inflate the currency so as to make his earnings worthless, or nationalize the whole enterprise overnight. In such an atmosphere, people who produce goods and services lose their incentive to continue, and poverty sweeps across the land. Depriving people of property is depriving them of the ability to plan their lives for the long range. Property rights are what make long-range planning possible—how can one sustain his life if he cannot plan ahead?

> Without property rights, no other rights are possible. If one is not free to use that which one has produced, one does not possess the right of liberty. If one is not free to make the products of one's work serve one's chosen goals, one does not possess the right to the pursuit of happiness. And—since man is not a ghost who exists in some nonmaterial manner—if one is not free to keep and to consume the products of one's work, one does not possess the right to life. In a society where men are not free privately to own the material means of production, their position is that of slaves whose lives are at the absolute mercy of their rulers. It is relevant here to remember the statement of Trotsky: "Who does not obey shall not eat."[5]

Indeed, one can plausibly assert that *all* rights are actually property rights. First, one has property in one's own person. John Locke said, "Every man has a property in his own person. This nobody has a right to but himself." And second, said Locke, one has the right, through his labor, to own material things: "The labor of his body and the work of his hands . . . are properly his. Whatsoever, then, he removes out of the state that nature hath provided and left it in, he hath mixed his labor with it, and joined to it something that is his own, and thereby makes it his property."[6]

A discussion of property rights soon becomes lengthy and intricate, involved as it is in questions such as, who owns the underground aquifer on which one depends for water? Who owns land that no one wishes to claim? Who owns the Colorado River? Who has the right to build a dam that affects many people's property? and so on. But the main thrust is clear enough: (1) as self-owners we each have property rights in our own bodies, and it is up to each of us what to do with our own bodies; (2) we are also owners of material things, such as our clothes, books, and other possessions, and sometimes also land; we have the right to the use and disposal of these material things, but cannot use them in such a way as to violate the rights of others, for example, by polluting a stream so that the owner downstream can no longer use it for his purposes. If a person assaults you, this is a violation of your property right in yourself, and if he steals from you, this is a violation of your property right in things.

At this point, freedom can be defined in terms of property rights: "Freedom is a condition in which a person's ownership rights in his own body and his legitimate material property are not invaded, are not aggressed against."[7]

4. Alleged Rights

Today there is an endless array of claimed rights. People claim as their right whatever they happen to want or need. "I have a right to free medical care"; "I have a right to be educated at state expense," and countless others. These are all claims to *positive* rights.

The rights set forth in the Declaration of Independence and the Bill of Rights are all negative rights; if one person has the right, others have only the duty of noninterference with the exercise of the right. You have a duty not to assault someone who asks you for money (he has a right to engage in this noncoercive act), but you need not give him the help he requests; to say yes or no to his request is *your* right.

> Jobs, food, clothing, recreation, homes, medical care, education, etc. do not grow in nature. They are man-made values—goods and services produced by men. *Who* is to provide them?
>
> If some men are entitled *by right* to the products of the work of others, it means that those others are deprived of rights and condemned to slave labor.
>
> Any alleged right of one man, which necessitates the violation of the rights of another, is not and cannot be a right.
>
> No one can have a right to impose an unchosen obligation, an unrewarded duty or an involuntary servitude on another man. There can be no such thing as *the right to enslave*.
>
> A right does not include the material implementation of that right by others; it includes only the freedom to earn that implementation by one's own effort.[8]

A positive right is one that requires not only noninterference, but also some positive action on the part of others. If one person has a positive right to receive assistance in some endeavor, others are duty-bound to render the assistance, no matter how it may interfere with their plans for their own lives. The only positive rights, according to libertarianism, are contractual ones: if I have borrowed $100 from you and promised to return it on March 1, then on March 1 you have a right to the return of the money. The duty is one that the borrower has chosen. There are (on this view) no unchosen duties. Parents have positive duties to their children, but these duties were incurred when they decided to have the children. But there are no positive *general* rights, rights that can be claimed by everyone as "the rights of man." Michael Levin explains why:

> Any conception of rights that exceeds noninterference must play favorites. . . . If you have a right to a portion of the total product of society, I am excluded from having a right to that portion. Such systems not only play favorites, they lead to a Kantian absurdity when pressed toward full generalization. The tendency of such a system to self-destruct is hidden by our tendency to imagine people continuing to work when basic positive rights are invented, and so to imagine that there is always enough for those who claim their rights. But if the claim that people have a fundamental right to (say) subsistence is to mean anything at all, it must mean that you and everyone else can do nothing and yet rightfully demand enough food to stay alive. After all, you don't have to *do* anything, beyond refraining from aggression, to claim a right to free speech. That is what makes free speech a basic right. But there can be sufficient food for some only if others continue to produce, and do not simply throw down their hoes and get in line for their own share of society's product.
>
> A system of subsistence rights, if acted on by everybody, would annihilate itself. The government could enforce the subsistence rights of some only by compelling others to work, and it would be a poor joke to tell farmers that while they, too, had a categorical right to subsistence, they did not have the right to *act* on that right. Communism plays the poorer joke of promising everyone a subsistence portion of the social product and, then, making everyone work to insure that a social product exists. A system of positive subsistence rights need not come to this in practice, since some people will work no matter what, out of habit or pride or ignorance of their entitlement, but that just makes my point all over again: a system of positive rights to the social product requires that some do not claim these rights. It presupposes a distinction between recipient grasshoppers and worker ants. . . .
>
> No system of positive rights can avoid this result. If the state decides to enrich Paul with money it must take the money from Peter or run the printing presses for Paul (decreasing Peter's purchasing power). Such a system can function only when there are not as many takers as there are entitled to be.[9]

To survive and prosper, every person requires freedom from coercive interference by others, and such coercive interference violates each person's fundamental right. This central tenet of libertarianism is often viewed as cold, hard-hearted, and cruel. This impression, however, arises, as is so often the case in the economic area, from a failure to make Frederic Bastiat's famous distinction between *what is seen* and *what is not seen*. What is seen is millions of people, some disabled and some not, receiving their entire income from the government. What is seen is that high taxes are exacted from the citizenry to pay for this, as well as to keep a huge bureaucracy in office. What is not seen is the millions of business enterprises that *would* have come into existence if the government did not take so much of people's income (the average American works from January 1 to sometime in May just to support the government). What is not seen is how many people now unemployed *would* have been employed if their employers had not gone bankrupt trying to survive in the face of endless taxes and regulation. What is not seen is how much better off people (all except for bureaucrats and politicians) *would* be, how many dreams they could realize that must now remain unrealized, if the government did not take, by force or threat of force, such a life-destroying part of the fruits of one's labor.

But what of the disabled, the sick, the unemployable? "Would you let them all starve?" is the question often asked. People now pay (and vote for) high taxes for the welfare of other citizens. By conservative estimates, at least half of this money disappears into the ever-expanding government bureaucracy. What if this money, or even a portion of it, were to go to the poor as voluntary gifts from private citizens? They would have far more than they have now, in part because there would be so many fewer poor. If Native Americans received everything allotted to them in taxes, each would get over $50,000 a year and not be semistarving in dismal windswept reservations. Most of the money is absorbed by the poverty industry, with its administrative assistants and assistant administrators.

Many people feel secure in receiving an income from the government (that is, from taxpayers). But they are secure only as long as the money continues to be appropriated, as long as the currency remains stable, as long as no natural or man-made catastrophe overtakes them, as long as the waste and corruption in the present system are not brought home to voters, angering them to the point of throwing the spenders out. In fact, they are much less secure than they would be in an economy in which the right to production and trade was totally unimpeded. Few people can easily imagine the degree of economic well-being that would exist if people could create new enterprises, employ more people, offer new goods and services, and bring into existence new technology that could treble our standard of living in a generation.

The government's promise of economic security is illusory. Trusting the ingenuity of enterprising people is much safer. But there is no *right* to security; there is only the right to take the actions required to increase one's chances of security. Rose Wilder Lane makes the point eloquently:

> Anyone who says that economic security is a human right has been too much babied. While he babbles, other men are risking and losing their lives to protect him. They are fighting the sea, fighting the land, fighting diseases and insects and weather and space and time, for him, while he chatters that all men have a right to security and that the State must give it to them. Let the fighting men stop fighting this inhuman earth for one hour, and he will learn how much security there is.
>
> Let him get out on the front lines. Let him bring one slow freight through a snowstorm in the Rockies. Let him drive one rivet to hold his apartment roof over his head. Let him keep his own electric light burning through one quiet cozy winter evening when the mist is freezing to the wires. Let him make, from seed to table, just one slice of bread, and we will hear no more about the human right to security.
>
> No man's security is greater than his own self-reliance. If every man and woman worth living did not stand up to the job of living, did not take risk and danger and exhaustion and go on fighting for one thin hope of victory in the certainty of death, there would not be a human being alive today.[10]

5. Government

Government is the institution that wields a monopoly on the use of force within a defined geographical area. One is not required to consent to its existence or its policies; one must obey it or go to jail. It is because government acts coercively, using force and the threat of force to make people obey its edicts, that libertarians have such a problem with government.

> A group is composed of a number of individuals. If it is morally wrong for one individual to aggress against another, then it is also morally wrong for any group of individuals to do so—even if the group calls itself the government....
>
> Suppose an aggressor, A, is one of a gang of ten aggressors. He conducts a hold-up in a place of business and takes the proprietor's cash.... Suppose, however, the gang had conducted a vote by secret ballot before the holdup, for the purpose of selecting their hatchet man. Does the fact that these nine people previously approved of the robber's actions justify them? Does the fact that a secret ballot was conducted make the robbery or intimidation moral? Suppose instead of nine people in the gang there were 999. Would this justify the robbery? Would 90 million people justify it? It is apparent the immorality is not changed by numbers....[11]

"But it isn't forced on me, I *consented* to it—I voted for it!" Even being beaten up *with* one's consent is no violation of one's rights—it is not the use of force, but one's consent to it that is all-important. Doesn't government, at least in democratic countries, operate with the consent of the governed?

What exactly is it, however, to which we consented? Let us assume that the person consented to be taxed; since he consented, there is no aggression against him. But would he consent to be taxed unless *all the others* were also taxed? Isn't he "consenting" for himself *and everyone else* to be taxed? And how can he consent on behalf of others? Can *I* consent for *you* to be beaten or robbed? Would I say yes to being taxed if everyone else were not similarly taxed? But then I would be "consenting" for all those others to be victims of aggression.

One wing of the libertarian movement then draws the conclusion that government is always a violator of rights, always the initiator of aggression against individuals, and that as such, it should be abolished entirely. In its place would arise a series of private courts, private police, and so on—there would still be a need for safety, but it would be fulfilled on the market, as is the need for food and housing in a free economy. Instead of calling up the police, you would call up your defense agency, which would be connected with arbitration agencies (private courts) to arbitrate disputes.[12]

The other wing of the libertarian movement is the "limited government" wing. There can be competing business organizations, but no competing governments in the same geographical area; an organization designed to keep the peace must have a monopoly on the use of force in order to achieve this end—if there were two or more claimants to be the sole jurisdiction within the area, this would be tantamount to civil war.

According to this view, government should be a "night watchman." It takes over the job of defending you against aggression so that you don't have to try doing it yourself. But it may not engage in aggression itself. Its function must be purely defensive; it defends your rights against anyone who would violate them, and punishes those who do, but it does not itself *initiate* aggression against any citizen or any other government. It does not take from one citizen to give to another, as in the welfare state; it takes a little from everybody in order to secure their defense against aggression and the peaceful arbitration of their disputes.

The Founding Fathers of the United States were (though not in every respect) advocates of limited government; that is what they attempted to bring into existence in America. However, there are problems with it that are difficult to reconcile with libertarian theory. (1) Money is required to sustain the police, army, and courts. Can this money be secured on a voluntary basis? Won't there always be people who say, "I'll be defended anyway, so I just won't put my share in the kitty?" (the problem of freeloaders). But if the contribution is compulsory, then isn't this a violation of one's fundamental right against coercion? (2) In any enterprise involving more than one person, said Ayn Rand, the voluntary consent of all parties is required. Does government have the voluntary consent of all those who are subject to it? One is not required to belong to any club, church, or fraternity—one can belong or not belong according to one's judgment. But with government, one is forced to belong. Herbert Spencer described the problem as follows, on the issue that, more than any other, is in contention among libertarians:

> We cannot choose but admit the right of the citizen to adopt a condition of voluntary outlawry. If every man has freedom to do all that he wills, provided he infringes not on the equal freedom of any others, then he is free to drop his connection with the State—to relinquish its protection and to refuse paying toward its support . . . In so behaving he in no way trenches upon the liberty of others, for his position is a passive one, and while passive he cannot become an aggressor . . . Government being simply an agent employed in common by a number of individuals to secure them certain advantages, the very nature of the connection implies that it is for each to say whether he will employ such an agent or not. If any one of them determines to ignore this mutual-safety confederation, nothing can be said except that he loses all claim to its good offices and exposes himself to the danger of maltreatment—a thing he is quite at liberty to do if he likes. He cannot be coerced into political combination without breach of the Law of Equal Freedom: he can withdraw from it without committing any such breach, and he has therefore a right so to withdraw.[13]

Notes

1. George Reisman, *The Government Against the Economy* (Ottawa, Illinois: Caroline House, 1979).
2. Ayn Rand, *Atlas Shrugged* (New York: Random House, 1957), 1048–9.
3. Herbert Spencer, *The Man versus the State* (1884; reprint, Caldwell, Idaho: Caxton Press, 1940), 191.
4. Ayn Rand, "Man's Rights," in *The Virtue of Selfishness* (New York: Signet Books, 1964), 97.
5. Nathaniel Branden, *Who Is Ayn Rand?* (New York: Random House, 1962), 43.
6. John Locke, *Second Treatise of Civil Government* (1690), Chapter 5.
7. Murray Rothbard, *For a New Liberty* (New York: Macmillan, 1973), 43.
8. Ayn Rand, "Man's Rights," in *The Virtue of Selfishness*, 96–7.

9. Michael Levin, "Negative Liberty," in *Human Rights* edited by Ellen Paul et al. (New York: Blackwell, 1989), 90–1.

10. Rose Wilder Lane, *The Discovery of Freedom* (New York: Arno Press, 1943), 60.

11. Richard and Ernestine Perkins, *Rational Anarchy*. (Privately printed, 1971) 72–3.

12. For example, see David Friedman, *The Machinery of Freedom* and others.

13. Herbert Spencer, *Social Statics* (1845; reprint, abridged and revised together with *The Man versus the State*, NY: D. Appleton, 1896), 95.

Contracting for Liberty

Jan Narveson

Politics and Reason

Many have found the political outlook now generally known as "libertarianism" attractive, but most of them have held it in much the same way as most who adhere strongly to any other political outlook: they regard it as *obviously* true—scarcely in need of argument. They might even hold that no argument at this level is possible—just what people often say about religious beliefs. And in both cases, there is the same result: they are virtually barred from convincing anyone who doesn't already incline toward their outlook. Only nonrational methods are possible—not rational discourse, but maneuvering for power, if not by naked force of arms, then by conspiring to wield the arm of the law against all rivals.

It would be nice if we could do better than that. It may even be of genuine practical importance that the basic tenets of a political society should be amenable to reasoned discussion instead of war, soap-box rhetoric, or back-room machinations. The present essay is a brief defense of the proposal that there are actually good reasons for adopting the libertarian program above any other, and that these reasons can be explicated in a plausible way. I am proposing, then, that there actually are reasonable "foundations" for this political theory.

Talk of foundations is unpopular today. Innumerable arguments exist in the realm of politics, and of the many devoted to theories as general as this one, most are certainly found wanting. Political writers reach sympathetic ears nowadays when they infer from this that foundations are impossible and the whole idea of supplying them for any highly general theory is a mistake. Those who write thus do not, I suspect, appreciate the implications of their view. Or perhaps they do, but think that war and politics are more *fun* than peace. Still, with the stakes so high, the boring truth is nevertheless preferable. Better, then, to keep trying, even if only to learn. Still, the following arguments are intended to be persuasive, not just to the converted, but to any who will attend.

The Other Views

Political and moral theories have been argued for on such bases as ideals of virtue, the will of God, self-evidence, and, in one way or another, nature. Why reject all these? Actually, as we will see, we needn't reject them all, quite: the contractarian view may be aligned with one kind of "natural law."

Meanwhile, we can say something about the inadequacy of such theories. *Virtue theories* fail because their ideas of virtue are never shared by *all*, and are unprovable to those who disagree. Appeals to *authority* are useless because they are circular: What the Authority says is right, we are told. And why? Well, because he knows what is right. His commands are a fifth wheel. And if we appeal to "self-evidence," what do we do about those who, alas, do not "see" the self-evident? The usual answer—kick 'em!—lacks cogency.

Morals are for people: if a theory is to work, it must be shown that it appeals to people. Those who propose that politics are based on "natural law" or "nature" may be obscurely appreciating this point. But the claim that some view is "based on the nature of things" or on "human nature" is unclear. Talk of "conforming to nature" makes no literal sense; nature simply *is*. It sets limits to what is possible, but can prescribe nothing.

Can the idea of natural law be given a useful interpretation? I suggest this: a natural law theory should say, in the end, that in view of the way things and people are, subscribing to *this* set of rules or virtues is our *best* means of accommodating them.

So, what *makes* it best, then? People make choices. To say that nature *determines* which choice to make is pointless: *we* must choose. But given that I *want* this or that, then with good information I can see that *this* is the thing to do. And so we might adapt the terminology of natural law for this purpose and suggest that a rule or a value is "natural" when it is one's rationally best response to one's circumstances. In just that spirit, Hobbes proposed his Laws of Nature. And he got them right: modern decision-theoretic arguments confirm Hobbes' basic moral ideas, even as they fail to support his argument for the State.

The Contractarian Idea

John Stuart Mill declared that "society is not founded on a contract, and . . . no good purpose is answered by inventing a contract in order to deduce social obligations from it"—yet he adds the remarkably contract-like suggestion that "everyone who receives the protection of society owes a return for the benefit, and the fact of living in society renders it indispensable that each should be bound to observe a certain line of conduct toward the rest."[1] To any who envisage a need to justify the ways of their fellows to themselves, or vice versa, that line of argument is inevitable. There is no alternative.

Rational Action

Practical rationality consists in selecting one's actions with a view to realizing as best one can the objects of one's interests. This is an intentionally "thin" notion of rationality, to be sure. Precisely because it is so thin, if we can establish rational motivation for moral constraints on its basis, we shall have appealed to the widest possible audience.

Where would such a thing as morality come from, then? A morality is a set of internally monitored controls on one's behavior as it relates to other people. The problem is that other people are also possessed of concerns and interests, which they pursue independently of one's own pursuits. Their actions are likely to cross paths with one's own—for better or worse. Sometimes there is an inherent harmony with others, from the nature of our respective interests; but often, indeed typically, there is some degree of conflict. Friends or enemies, associates or strangers, some of their actions are likely to lead to results we would prefer to avoid, and others to results we would welcome. As rational persons, we want to maximize the desirable interactions and minimize the undesirable ones. How do we bring about the preferred profile of actions on *their* part? How do we maximize the likelihood of their acting in ways that are either positively desirable from our point of view, or at least not undesirable?

Some might ask, why get hung up about rationality? After all, ordinary people are only moderately rational. True: but it does not follow that we should be unconcerned to find rational solutions to important problems. For one thing, a rational solution to human problems takes into account the likelihood that some of those concerned will be less than fully rational. But mainly, we ask what is rational because we are trying to decide what to do. There is simply no sense in the notion of "irrational solutions,"—surely an oxymoron, for rationality consists in doing our best to get what we value, whatever it is. It is not some special project that you can take or leave. We may value spontaneity, say: but we can hardly value the habit of "trying" to achieve what we regard as *less* valuable. And those who say we should assume ordinary people to be irrational are probably out to exploit those people: if Jones is irrational, then of course he can't do his *own* thinking, can he?

Go it Alone? Or Work with Others?

One way to respond to the presence of others of differing minds is to try to ignore them altogether. How this option would go is in any case puzzling—how do you ignore someone who is about to knife you, for instance? But it is easy to see that for virtually anyone, general adherence to that option would be, even if possible at all, completely irrational. For people react. We may classify these reactions under two headings. First, one might hope to overcome any difficulties their contrary actions may present by sheer force or cunning—the unilateral exercise of one's own powers: say, by trying to push them out of the way or disable them. That is the *parametric* response profile: the agent takes the other persons in his environment as fixed entities, not amenable to rational influence.

Second is the "strategic" outlook: we attempt to improve the situation by establishing some kind of communication with the other parties, in the course of which we supply information to them about our likely response to possible actions of theirs, and they in turn communicate an intention to respond to your response in one way or another.

For any recognizably human agent, the second profile is immensely preferable to the first. No person's powers are equal to getting his way against all and sundry by superior force. The familiar Hobbesian reasons for this are persuasive, beginning with his astute observation that, "as to strength of body, the weakest hath enough to kill the strongest."[2]

But a further distinction is needed, and one that is immensely more difficult to come adequately to grips with. We may distinguish two kinds of response, or "strategy." First, there is the type which consists either in outrightly using force or at least in threatening it: that is, in attempting to influence the decisions of those you interact with by proposing to bring about situations that are, from their point of view, undesirable, unless they choose some alternative more agreeable to oneself. This is the strategy of the Stick. On the other hand, there is the Carrot: proposing to do something that from their point of view is desirable, but proffering it conditionally on their selecting alternatives more agreeable to you than those they might otherwise select. Which shall we generally employ? If we choose the former, we make enemies of all we encounter. If we choose the latter, on the other hand, we invite all to be, if not actually friends, at least neutral or better. The former, the libertarian holds, is to be excluded from the list of publicly permissible options: we may require all to refrain from using those. And we encourage people to adopt the latter, along with the option of engaging in actions that have no significant detriments *or* benefits. In the process, so the contractarian argument runs, we may expect to do very much better, especially in any longish run.

Some find this whole way of talking offensive. They suppose that there are further options not even considered in my division. Can't we engage our fellows in dialogue, resulting in a new joint outlook? Or take them to be brothers or sisters under some or other layer of epidermis? The answer is that of course we sometimes can, and where we can, we sometimes should: when the assumptions underlying them are accurate, we can act effectively along those lines. But when, as often, they are not, we are headed for trouble. And in a case where dialogue gets you nowhere, there is the prospect of an interminable stretch of discourse. Meanwhile, however, there are things you'd really prefer to be getting on with. Then the appearance that this was a "third alternative" vanishes. If the proponents of this view mean that you shall be *forced* to engage in that dialogue, and denied the option of sitting this one out or trying to do your best on your own, that is actually the stick again. If, on the other hand, it is meant merely as a suggestion, and the proposed dialogue, the supposedly third alternative, would be nice for all, then it is being viewed as a species of carrot. Similarly for the siblings-under-the-skin approach: if the other party really *is* such a sibling, he or she will act, you suppose—assuming that you had a fairly happy childhood—in ways generally agreeable to you. But life, alas, does not support the conclusion that all are siblings. Besides, some siblings are the nasty type—Cain vs. Abel—while most others just don't fit the 'sibling' description at all. As *general* responses to the human situation, therefore, they are of limited utility; nor do they differ fundamentally from the options already listed.

There is, then, simply no alternative. We shall deal with the probable disharmonies in our relations to others by making the best proposals we can in response to, or in anticipation of, the range of expected actions on their part. These are proposals which, we hope, will have the effect of altering for the better their strategies for action relating to us. There is, to repeat, no alternative. Moral theories alleging otherwise assume what reality constantly refutes.

Contract

Why "contract"? And especially, why the "social" contract? Does the idea of a "contract" at the universal level we contemplate here make any sense? We need a characterization sufficiently general to capture what is in common both to the many explicit arrangements normally so-called in ordinary life, and to that pattern or principle of interactions, *not* the result of explicit negotiations, that the social-contract theorist proposes as the basis of morals and politics.

The answer has been identified plausibly by Hobbes and Hume, and latterly, in a more precise and general form, by David Gauthier.[3] In contracts, people make their behavior *conditional on each other's performance*. In so doing, at least one of them typically makes himself vulnerable to the other's decision not to carry through on it.[4] An inward impetus of the will is required to make it work. That is morality. Now and again, one of the parties concerned may lack the necessary inner commitment. We may then have to resort to external imposition, sometimes to force.

A contract in the relevant sense is *social* when it is a conditional arrangement of *each with all*. The building block of such a contract is an arrangement between oneself and whomever comes to treat them thus-and-so *provided* they do likewise. "Social contract" does not refer to anything not analyzable into the plans of action of particular individuals. And if, as is likely, we fall short of unanimity, near-unanimity contract will somehow have to serve. That problem will be carefully considered below. Meanwhile, though, the prospect of mutual benefit is what underwrites social reinforcement of contracts generally, and in particular the commitment to refrain from force in the pursuit of one's goals. We rationally expect all to adhere to that rule: it is a rational commitment.

Commitment is rational only where one can expect reciprocity—which in turn can only be expected if the other party can expect it from you. Can either really expect it, though? Here we must make an obvious and familiar distinction, between two senses of "expect": (1) to *predict*, and (2) to *insist*, that is, to feel entitled to performance. As to (1), whether we can expect others to perform depends on their characters, and we sometimes know enough of that to form reliable predictions, and sometimes not. But (2) we can always *insist* on others' keeping the terms of any particular promise, provided that we do our share and provided that it was made in a suitably well-informed and uncoerced fashion. In so insisting, we invoke the support of anyone and everyone in the social environment—not just that of our interactee. This social element is a substantial reinforcer, if applied consistently and carefully. Being the general object of disapprobation, with accompanying withdrawal of assorted amenities of civilized exchange, is a heavy price to pay for displaying a tendency to renege, and those who are motivated to avoid getting caught at their reneging pay a price in having to devote effort to covering their tracks and avoiding detection. They can and sometimes do succeed, more or less, and just what that shows is debatable—certainly that morality is imperfect, but not that it is irrational nor even that it is less than fully rational. Any doctrine that made immorality incomprehensible would be convicted of unreality on that account. My claim is only that rational people will give weight to morality as here explained, in the form of a disposition to abide by agreements and to refrain from trying to get one's way by sheer force.

The "social contract" has in common with all contracts that (1) it is the reciprocal conditionalizing of behavior and (2) it involves commitment from those concerned. But it is, of course, an unspoken understanding, a *non*-negotiated agreement—an agreement in action, not in words nor preceded by words. Each party adopts a disposition to respond in ways that make the resulting interaction mutually preferable to its alternatives. Such dispositions are moral virtues: dispositions we do well to have. But the contractarian view differs from theories claiming to found morals on a prior discernment of what is virtuous, independently of interaction. On the view defended here, we can *show* that this disposition is a virtue. It isn't a matter of what's "in the eye of the beholder."

The Libertarian Idea[5]

It cannot be too strongly emphasized that libertarianism is not a view about the same thing as contractarianism. The latter is a *metatheory* of morals and politics. It holds that the principles of morals, whatever they may turn out to be, are those we all do have reason to agree on provided all others accept them as well. The reason for agreeing is simple: we do better in the condition where all comply with the proposed principles. But only if others agree too; absent agreement, we revert to the unsatisfactory condition in which no one can trust anyone else. Libertarianism is a view about the substance of that agreement.

That substance is the principle that force—the stick, as I call it—ought to be restricted, in human affairs, to countering those who would or do employ force without that restriction: namely, to the initiators of violence, those who propose to make their way by removing the human obstacles to it by brute force or threat of same. The libertarian strategy, then, is *to resort to force only to counter the aggression of others*. And the libertarian theory is contractually *grounded* only if (1) libertarianism is the best rule for everybody in the way of general restrictions on behavior, and (2) no other way of arriving at the virtue in question is plausible. Our argument is that the Universal Social Contract, the agreement of all with all, calls for nothing more nor less than to refrain from the use of force to attain one's goals. In Hobbes' words, it is to "seek peace, and follow it," which, together with its famous corollary, that when peace is unattainable, one may then use "all the helps and advantages of war"⁶ constitute his First Law of Nature, and really the only one, if he is right in holding that all the others flow from it. The job is to show that it is indeed the only reasonable candidate for the role of fundamental principle of morality, and showing that is not a purely a priori matter. The argument may not only be difficult, but varyingly plausible under different conditions.

Why is this 'libertarian'? To be at liberty, in general, is to have no obstacles impeding one's efforts. To be at *social* liberty, liberty in relation to one's fellows, is for them to refrain from impeding one's efforts. For people in general to have social liberty is for all to refrain from impeding each other's efforts—that each person, A, has no obstacles to A's efforts imposed by the voluntary actions of A's fellow persons. Of course the expectation of liberty at the hands of others is unreasonable if it is not reciprocal: A won't impede B, but only on condition that B in turn will not impede A. The social contract is necessary for liberty. But is it sufficient? That is the big question.

Liberty cannot sensibly be regarded as an *intrinsic* value. One values liberty because there are things that one values, and liberty is necessary for getting them by one's own efforts. But what if we can get it by somebody else's efforts? Terrific—if we can. But how can we? Perhaps by happenstance appeal to the goodness of their hearts—which, no doubt, will sometimes work and sometimes not. But if not, then what? The answer, as we have already seen, is by force or fraud—means that the person against whom they are used has the strongest reason for objecting to. Universal agreement precludes use of those methods.

Others will talk of "positive" liberty, perhaps. Of what use to a paraplegic is the liberty to walk, it will be asked? The answer to that is easy: none, until he becomes equipped with devices to move him around; and then it's plenty of use, just as it is for the rest of us. But those who propose to equip him at our expense, involuntarily incurred, need to tell *us* why *we* should accept that imposition. To look myopically at the paraplegic alone is absurd, and it is dishonest. "We" do *not* prefer supposed positive liberty, which must always be at the expense of others, to negative liberty, which can be had by all. Only *some* prefer that.

Liberty and Property

Liberty is the absence of impediments, and thus of impositions. What constitutes an "impediment" must, then, be one of the first questions on our conceptual agenda. The libertarian has a specific view about this. He proposes that general nonimpediment entails respecting *property*, broadly speaking. Explicating this idea carefully and plausibly is our first conceptual task. If we don't know what constitutes impediment, then we don't know what constitutes liberty, and if we don't know that, we don't know what we are advocating under the banner of libertarianism. If we do know what it is, however, then we can also understand how to formulate a workable notion of property.

The libertarian holds, in effect, that *liberty* = *property*. To own something is to have the right to do with it as one pleases: the disposition of that thing is up to you, not someone else. Take the special case in which the "something" is the person himself, and it follows immediately that liberty consists in self-ownership. Locke's confidence that a man owns himself was, therefore, correct. To act is to make use of one's own capacities, one's own equipment and abilities—limbs, memory, pianistic talents, the works. Too many talk as though property were not only entirely distinct from but perhaps antithetical to liberty. That is nonsense. If one's tongue is not one's own, what means freedom of speech? If one's mind isn't, what sense is there in freedom of thought?

The large question about this must concern external property: land, amplifiers, hotels, metal-working machines. Many writers seem to think that there is a terrible problem about extending a right of personal freedom to the use of items in the external world. While too large an issue for this essay to deal with completely,[7] the basic idea is simple: just as we can do what we wish with the natural parts of our own person, bodily and psychological, so we may do what we wish with bits of external nature, so long only as we do not thereby damage or impede the uses by others of such objects. In particular, it as not an impediment that if A acquires x, B is thereby unable to do so. The implication of an argument along those lines is that nobody may use anything—a strange doctrine of *liberty*! The correct view is that you can use *whatever* you find if nobody else already has it. Once you begin to use it, then anyone else who comes along will interfere with your already-commenced train of action if he renders it impossible for you to continue. To own x is to have control over the further disposition of x. Once we acquire hitherto unowned nature, all further acquisition of property must be via agreement: that is, by voluntary exchange, of things for things, things for services, or services for services. Liberty = property. If we have no property rights, we have no rights. Period.

Liberalism and Conservatism in Moral Theory

Any decent theory of morals or politics accepts, I trust, that its rules and institutions ought to be for the benefit of those subject to them. But how do we understand this? One general view of moral and political philosophy is to try to prescribe the proper personal goals for all, and then choose principles of morals that promote those particular goals. The claim will be that those are the intrinsically correct goals for people, whatever those people happen to think of them. Such is the general outlook that I shall call "conservatism"—though recognizing that it does not capture all the senses of that somewhat protean term. The *conservative*, then, is the theorist who thinks he can tell us what to do by telling us how to live. Perhaps he thinks there is no alternative to that. If so, he is wrong. The *liberal*, by contrast, holds that the selection of personal goals, of ways of life, is up to each person and may not be imposed on him by others.

In the liberal's view, then, the goal of social rules is to maximize benefit for each person in *that person's view* of what constitutes a benefit. Liberalism holds that the relevant inputs to moral and political theory consist entirely of what affects the well-being of individual persons, as seen by those persons themselves. The proper goal of politics and morals is, as Aquinas says, the *common good* of those to whom they issue their requirements and prohibitions—but that is not some "good" proclaimed by their leaders or by anyone else but themselves.

It is possible to tell people not to interfere with others' pursuits of their goals, whatever those goals may be, up to the point where those pursuits interfere with the pursuits of others. Disallowing any other ground of authoritative interference than invasion of liberty constitutes libertarianism. It is, in short, *pure* liberalism—ultra-liberalism.

That theory does not, on the other hand, imply or in any way require that our goals are independent of the causal structure of nature or of the influences of society or family. No view about the classic problem of the freedom of the will is presupposed. Doubtless, individual goals are at least heavily influenced if not altogether determined by one's nexus of interpersonal contacts plus one's biological makeup. If some individual fancies that he can escape the shackles of genes and social milieu, he is welcome to try, but neither that goal, if it makes any sense, nor any other is prescribed by the libertarian outlook. That outlook is, strictly, a *moral* doctrine, in the narrowest sense of the term: it is a doctrine about what sort of restrictions may reasonably be imposed on the conduct of individuals generally in relation to their fellows. And it invokes those restrictions *without* basing them on a vision of what particular goals people do or should have.

The "State of Nature"

The classic political philosophers of the modern era thought to derive the principles of politics from hypotheses about how things would be for people in a "state of nature," this being the situation where people interact in the absence of *any* authoritatively exercised general controls. They then hoped to justify proposals by demonstrating the superiority of the situations envisaged by them over the original condition. This raises two questions. First, can this be a useful conception, seeing that such states do not seem to occur in human affairs? Second, does the utility of contractarianism depend on the real possibility of such states? We briefly consider these central issues here.

First, let us note three distinctions. One is the familiar distinction between hypothetical and actual states of nature. Even if they are never actual, the idea may be useful. If (1) such a condition is at least possible, and if (2) from the point of view of any individual it would be terrible if it did occur, and if (3) certain behavior patterns in humans do head us toward such a condition unless certain social arrangements are made, then there need not ever actually be any such to show that we have reason to avoid those patterns.

The second distinction is between *political* and *moral* versions of the idea. A political state of nature is a social condition without political institutions. A moral state of nature is a social condition without morals: no one has any moral inhibitions about doing *anything*. The moral version is the more general and profound.

A third distinction is between *partial* and *complete* states of nature. A social condition is a partial state of nature if it has aspects of apoliticality or amorality, even though in other respects there are laws or moral inhibitions. A more abstract and useful characterization of the "state of nature" is that it displays certain game-theoretic structures, in particular what is called a prisoner's dilemma. State of nature is then identified with the default option. This again is relevant to our two questions: there are plenty of such dilemmas at hand; we needn't go to the ultimate one envisaged by Hobbes in order to make the argument for morality. (Or maybe the state? Note that I do *not* assume that the argument can work to justify a state, but do not pursue the question here.)

We can now make progress on the question before us. A state of nature that couldn't even approximately obtain under *any* circumstances is indeed pointless. But if the condition in question is clearly possible, and it can be established that we really would tend toward that condition unless we do x, while x produces a condition clearly superior to it, then we have an argument for doing x. So, for example, it is *logically* impossible that we should actually be behind Rawls' "veil of ignorance." But it is not obviously impossible at all to be in a situation where no body of people has effective political power—where there is a "breakdown of law and order." And we know cases of immoral behavior; generalizing from them doesn't seem impossible either. And so there is no problem about the reality of states of nature. At any given time, there are many matters that are not subject to specific controls of either the legal or the moral type, and where arguably all concerned would be better off if they were. That's all we need.

Starting Where We Are

The fundamental question in life is: what do I do *now*? Speculation on what we should have done yesterday might help answer that question, or it might not; the past is, after all, past. Speculation on what we should do if some or another condition should obtain is useful if the condition is probable. But deliberation about what to do right now isn't speculation—it's life. In my daily doings, I will encounter various people and innumerable features of my environment that are substantially different from what they would have been had previous human activity been different, and that are decidedly subject to change at the hands of further human activity in the foreseeable future. Having helpful dispositions at hand for dealing with various of these is likely to be useful. The contractarian proposal is that among these handy dispositions are recognizably moral ones, whose utility has a lot to do with the network of expectations we can or do generate by encountering and reflecting on the behavior of others with whom we interact. It is a useful idea if, and only if, features of our social situations answer to the contractarian descriptions and call for their sort of solutions.

The status quo itself may be taken as our point of departure for many purposes of theory, as it must for all purposes of practice. If my proposed action and your proposed response would produce alterations for the better from both our points of view, as compared with any obvious alternatives, and by reference to the status quo, then agreement between us about that particular interaction is, *prima facie*, rational. If a proposed rule would make for improvement over the current situation for all concerned, then we have a plausible argument for adopting such a rule. These are options that obviously can and often do obtain—thus showing that the contractarian idea is at least partially practical and cannot be rejected out of hand.

That the status quo itself may be affected by injustice, stupidity, or other defects is clearly possible. But we show this by looking at aspects of *preceding* states of affairs and showing how certain departures from those states were contrary to the contractual criterion. If we learn, for example, that the reason why A has $100 to offer and B has nothing is that A got it from B by threatening to beat him to a pulp if he didn't hand it over, that makes quite a difference. No *general* agreement could have led to that development. Of course the status quo is not sacred. But we detect defects by looking back as far as necessary to see where the alleged defects came from and whether those involved agreed or could have agreed to what produced them.

We may also propose a general rule of presuming innocence until guilt is proven. Assuming the opposite would bring social life to a standstill. It is impossible to prove innocence across the board; only specific charges can be refuted. To be required to refute all possible charges is to be required to devote one's life to assembling information, much of it unobtainable and almost all of it useless. We cannot proceed that way. We *can*, on the other hand, proceed by supposing that people are not routinely evil.

Veils of Ignorance

It has become popular in recent times to turn the contractarian idea into something quite different. Most prominent among them is the maneuver of Rawls, which calls for restricting the social contract to "people" who have no idea who they are. Others might hold that the parties to the contract must be something more than merely rational people concerned to pursue their interests. Such views have one fatal shortcoming. When it turns out that real people aren't like that, one's theory becomes unreal as well. We lose the very thing that it was the hallmark of contractarianism to claim: that morality is something that is in *everyone*'s interest to subscribe to.

To those who would load conditions into the specification of an "original position," then, we ask what they have to say to those who don't exemplify those conditions. Our procedure, by contrast, is to look at all profiles, whatever they may be, and see how and perhaps whether we could do business with such persons. No interests are ignored.

Nonunanimity?

Any contract view must address the question of what to do about those who will agree to nothing. My answer is Hobbes's: everyone else's behavior is, obviously, utterly unrestricted in relation to them. If in the process they end up on the gallows or in the tar-pit, that's tough for them—but it is not unjust. And the same for us, of course: if he does us in, that's too bad for us. All we can say is that in an all-out war, victory goes to the strong. However, our bet is that there are a great many more of us than of them—especially after they have finished doing each other in!

Nontuism

Contractarianism is often said to require an assumption of "nontuism"—that people take no interest in one another's interests. That they never actually are interested in others' interests is so obviously false that if it were literally required by contractarian theory, that theory would thereby stand convicted of absurdity. The only question is how it could ever have been supposed that such an assumption is indeed a requirement of the theory.

Almost everybody loves or hates at least a few other persons, and everyone prefers that some or all people have some interests rather than others. So much is obvious. But precisely whom do they hate or love, and just which interests of others do they prefer others to have or not, as such? Clearly, we can make no particular assumptions about that. Which if any tuistic attitudes any particular person has is a matter for empirical investigation, not abstract speculation. Our theory must cover all cases: it must tell us what to say about this, that, or the other tuistic profile. What it cannot do is to presuppose that all have the same profile. Morals must be derived from our interests, *whatever* those interests may be.

We must remember what we have all learned from Bishop Butler: that when person A takes an interest in person B's interests, it is still A's interest that A acts on. Whatever the objects of one's interests, it is the fact that they are one's interests that makes them relevant to one's practical life. If others' interests become relevant to us, it must be by attaching them to some interest of ours.

Sorting Interests

For purposes of morals, what matters about an interest in others is whether that interest is positive or negative: would its satisfaction be a pro or a con to those others? If positive, then we have, prima facie, a situation of harmony, and there should be no problem, nuances apart; but if satisfying A's interest in B requires dissatisfying B, we have problems. What would we do about public controls on the pursuit of interests of these types? No one will allow others routinely to block his pursuit of his own interests. Where interests conflict, agreement requires a rationale for allowing one to be subject to overturning at the hands of some other. This agreement is not going to be forthcoming from the one who loses out. It must be shown that there's something in it *for him*—that he stands to gain from the rule even if it is imposed on him by force. Inherently conflictual interests cannot be accommodated by a public charter. There simply is no basis for agreement to actions on interests that from their very nature can only be satisfied at the expense of someone else. These necessarily set people against each other.

We may now define a class of what we may call *liberal* interests. These are interests that do not take as their object the dissatisfaction of anyone else. There are no inherent obstacles to acceptance of interests that have no bearing on others' interests. They may be pursued unrestrictedly. On the other hand, interests that do affect the interest of others must be cleared with those others before we proceed.

To take an extremely important example, the pursuit of private wealth—contrary to the doctrines of socialists—is, if pursued by consensual means, inherently nonconflictual. One person's having more than he had before does not entail that any other persons have less than they had before. And if we make our way by exchange, then both of us must, barring accident or mistake, do better in each instance. This furthers the case for private property; such relations are inherently nonconflictual.

Of course, A's having more than B implies that B has less than A. But the interest in having more, or less, or the same as B has no status in the public charter. For example, egalitarianism, the passion for equality, has exactly the same inherently conflictual structure as any other relational motive. Society may not adopt as a goal that persons in class X have more, or less, *or the same*, as persons in class Y. By contrast, endeavoring to increase one's own wealth has no logical relation to other persons' levels of wealth. Each may do the best he or she can do; in principle, we can *all* win, improving our wealth with no adverse affects on any others. But we should also note that when we improve it by commerce—free exchange with others—then we benefit others even as we benefit ourselves. For this reason, it is plausible to propose that free exchange benefits the community maximally. Thus, the familiar policy of "soaking the rich" is absurd in all cases where the rich get rich by buying and selling. To have gotten rich by that means is to have improved the lot of many others. Reducing the incentive to acquire by such means reduces the real incomes of those other people, as well as of the immediate victim. Theft is counterproductive from the public point of view. It improves the lot of the thief (if it does) only by worsening the lot of someone else.

Charity, on the other hand, has a place of honor. The charitable person enjoys helping others; when they are helped, so is he. It should be noted, though, that charity has to be the exception, not the rule. If we *all* tried to live by charity, that would be the end of all wealth. Someone must actually produce in order for there to be anything to give away.

Utilitarianism

There is a tendency to say, at this point, that it matters how *much* the thief improves his own lot, compared with how little he worsens the lot of his victim. The poor thief has a greater marginal utility per unit of income than his victim; therefore, it might be thought, transferring wealth from the rich to the thief produces a net gain in social well-being. The argument, one may note, lacks appeal to the victims—yet they are among those we are asking to approve this practice! For the contractarian agreement is among *all*—not merely among the thieves and their friends.

By an understandably popular perversion, it has been widely argued that such transfers would nevertheless be approved by all, *if* the "all" first transported themselves behind a "veil of ignorance", concealing the erstwhile contractors' identities from themselves. If "I" assume that the probability of my actually being me is only the same as the probability of "my" being you, say .5 each, I will regard utilitarian transfers as prima facie desirable, since the recipient supposedly gains more than his victim loses, thus leaving "both" with an expected gain from the transaction.

That is an argument for philosophers in ivory towers, where differences among individuals are viewed *sub specie aeternitatis*. But in the real world, no one has merely a 50 percent chance of being himself rather than someone else: each of us merely is who he or she happens to be, and not someone else. They may love certain others, and do so to the point where they would gladly part with something of their own to benefit them. But such cases are clearly permitted in our private-property world anyway, along with all other consensual activity. However, in plenty of other cases the transfer would be anything but consensual, and those are the ones that the argument we are considering is primarily intended to cover.

The supposed interest of society in the utilitarian sense is, in fact, not the interest of *anybody*. Society is a whole lot of people, each with his own interests. Some of those interests are other-regarding, some are not. In the cases where they are, the promotion of A's interest may be benevolent, implying the promotion of some other person's well-being, or it may be malevolent, implying the opposite. Where they are not other-regarding, the promotion of A's interest has no necessary implication regarding B's. Society may be said to be better off if A gains and nobody loses; but this innocuous truth is about "society" only in a derivative sense: we may, if we like, define the idea of an interest of society in that fashion. But if we do so, then the utilitarian argument has no standing. In this new sense, society cannot be said to gain when person A gains by inflicting a loss on person B.

Utility

In some cases it may be that there is a good available to some set of people only in a way that makes it impossible to predict just who in particular will benefit or by how much. Suppose that n persons investing $m each can bring about a general gain of k, where k > n × m, for example by bringing it about that it rains in the neighborhood enough that on average, the investors prefer their situations with rain at the cost of $m to their situations without rain but retaining the $m. Each individual has an expected gain of $1/k, but precisely how much, if any, he in particular gains is not known in advance.

We can distinguish two versions of the arrangement. In one, a compensatory payment is made by each gainer to each investor who, as it happens, gets no rain after all; in the other, no such side payment is made—each takes his chances. Rational investors would always take an offer of the first type, other things being equal; but whether they took the second would depend on their aversion to risk and their perception of the probabilities involved. Yet someone who expected *no* gain for himself (or anyone he cared about) and who had no particular interest in the well-being of the others would not voluntarily agree to the scheme. The social contract, therefore, cannot impose it on all. Utilitarianism, in unqualified form, is not a live option, though what are known as public-goods projects certainly are.

Welfare?

Would contractarianism confirm the libertarian's refusal to allow coercively extracted support of the so-called safety net for the poor, public schooling, socialized medicine, and so on? I shall argue that it would indeed.

Nobody can deny that people enjoying a higher rather than a lower level of welfare is, generally speaking, a good thing. Even those who profess not to care about the well-being of their fellows will, in the first place, sign up for a general duty of nonaggression: they too will "seek peace and follow it," using violence only when necessary to counter the violence of aggressors.

It has to be pointed out that if this duty is perfectly general, it extends also to the case where the supposedly caring A steals from B in order to feed needy C. But it's not enough to point that out, as if it were a proof. What must be shown is that rational people will not modify or qualify the general duty of nonimposition, and opt instead for the idea that we do all owe each other something: for instance, a social minimum, funds for which we may extract from everyone, by force if need be. That is what most people we know do think. They think there is a difference between my putting a gun in your ribs and extracting a transfer of cash from you to me, on the one hand, and representatives of "the public" doing the same thing, with the difference that the transfer is only partly from you to them—some of the extracted cash really does end up in the pockets of the supposed poor, or provides schooling "free" to all who can benefit from it; or pays for the appendectomies of those who might not otherwise be able to afford them. Are they are right to make such a distinction? No—or so I will argue.

First, let's attend to what most defenders of the welfare state overlook. The world we live in has around five billion inhabitants at present, of whom perhaps one billion enjoy "first world" status. But if the alleged duty to provide a safety net for the poor had the status of a general duty to poor humans, no state welfare program would make any sense. All such programs would have to become universal-scope foreign aid programs. Yet virtually no supporter of the Welfare State accepts this obligation. Why not?

The short answer is that politics and the self-interest of some few play the major role in the equation, high principle having little to do with it. In fact, the supposed "high" principle is considered by most people to be *too* high. They do not believe that all well-off people have an enforceable duty to provide for all badly-off ones. Yet they don't actually have a *reason* for confining welfare programs to their own nations or their own communities.

The libertarian principle says that force is to be confined to dealing with aggression, and may not be used for any other end, however noble it may seem. That includes the welfare of others such as the poor. Why, it may be asked, should we insist on sticking only with the Scrooge-like principle advocated by us libertarians at the most fundamental level? There is a ready answer. If person A does not in fact care about person B, why would he accept an enforceable duty to help care for B? Perhaps A anticipates the possibility that one day he might be in bad shape and would like B to help him. This is solid reasoning. We should all be disposed to help those in need. But should we be so disposed to the point where we agree that if we don't help those people, we'll go to jail? Or the point where we allow others to garnishee our wages forever after? Surely not! The scope of the familiar idea of aid is much more restricted than that. If we can be very helpful without much cost to us, we should do so—yet we will not consent to being *forced* to do so.

On the other hand, there is good reason to consider arrangements whereby many people agree each to pay for the operations of the others, should need arise, for example, by paying a certain set sum each month.

That is precisely what insurance systems do, and they make perfect sense. But they in no way involve the involuntary duties considered in the foregoing. The fact of their availability in principle, however, makes a huge difference to arguments about welfare. It is not rational to sign up for an "insurance" pact from which you are certain to lose. Agreement to pay for operations by fellow "members" who didn't pay, didn't even have to join, and will never be any use to the ones who do pay makes no sense. Hardly fit material for a rational agreement!

Now consider the choice between (1) knowing that I will be forced to help others whom I wouldn't choose to help if I had my choice, with all others, in turn, being similarly forced to help me; and (2) knowing that our right to use our resources as we judge best, without interference by others, will always be respected, even though we also know that we won't *necessarily* be helped by others when the chips are down (i.e., nobody will *force* them to help). Is it obvious that everyone would take (1) rather than (2)? Certainly not. But that is not all. For to (2) let us add the knowledge that people are generally well-disposed toward their fellows and inclined to help when they can, and, of course, that no one may prevent them from helping when they are so inclined; add the fact that one has the right to refuse unwanted help, and you have a package that dominates the alternatives. Any supposed advantage that anyone might derive from being a beneficiary is utterly negated by his also being a forced contributor, whatever he might have preferred to do with his life.

How do we know, though, that this argument really holds? There are two points. First, it has to be noted that if most people were not at least disposed to be charitable, they also would not choose the welfare state in a social contract. But if there are enough votes to legislate the welfare state, then there must be so many charitable people out there that they can easily fulfill welfare needs without forcing their neighbors to help: most will help in any case.

Most have conceived the social contract as being concerned only with enforceable duties, that is, with strict justice. But that is a mistake. There are such things as public attitudes as well. In opting for the carrot rather than the stick in matters relating to welfare, what we are opting for is a public resolution that all will prefer that others be well-off to their being badly off, apart from any personal relation they may have to those others. That is to say, the way we should regard each other *qua* fellow persons, rather than in more local capacities such as fellow inhabitant of this part of town or fellow believer in the same religion, is not as indifferent pieces of furniture but as fellow humans trying to live good lives, and we are more likely to do so if people are well-disposed than if they are ill-disposed. This kind of disposition costs us little, after all. We do not take on a great burden when we agree that, all else being at least roughly equal, it is a better thing that Jones or Smith do well than badly, and to be disposed—but not conscripted—to lend an occasional hand or an occasional dollar if need be.

If by contrast we take the welfare-state option, it would mean that others over whom you have no control would be authorized to decide that a sizable fraction of your money will be spent on "the poor," whatever you may have wanted to do with it if you had your own way. Empirical considerations add to the case: Welfare expenditures tend to be counterproductive, discouraging or even effectively preventing the recipient from working, and thus from acquiring useful skills. And those who do not work when they might leave us as well as themselves with a lesser array of goods and services than we would otherwise enjoy.

Concluding Note

The position here advocated takes on, I suppose, the heaviest burden of proof in the field. On the one hand, it disavows any appeal to transcendental considerations in its defense of liberty—including a priori impositions on what the people who are party to the social contract may believe. On the other hand, it refuses to assume that we *must* sign some social contract or other. Everything needs to be supported, nothing simply assumed. Yet this is a burden of proof that can be borne. The appeal of social life for everyone is so enormous that our motivation to accept the terms proposed here greatly exceeds any interest in remaining outside. What we would sign for, I have argued, is, purely and simply, liberty—not, for instance, a package of handouts from our hapless fellows. Your private club or religion, and certainly your marriage or your job, may indeed involve much more. The advantage of liberty in that respect is precisely that it leaves the widest possible array of such further involvements open to all who, together with willing others, are ready to take them on. Precisely what makes that possible is the exclusion of arrangements that press unwilling participants into the act.

My argument, then, does not *presuppose* the libertarian scheme of rights. Instead it argues for those rights, by showing that that scheme of rights can be expected to work out better for every reasonable person, if applied uniformly to all, than any alternative scheme. That is why we should support strong rights of individual liberty rather than schemes imposing involuntary duties for the alleged benefit of the public, on shaky or confused grounds. The best politics, in short, is no politics.

Notes

1. Mill, *On Liberty*, Ch. IV, 3rd paragraph.
2. Hobbes, *Leviathan*, Ch. XIII.
3. The central source is David Gauthier, *Morals by Agreement* (New York: Oxford University Press, 1986).
4. Anthony De Jasay, *Social Contract, Free Ride* (New York: Oxford University Press, 1989) distinguishes three sorts of contract: the "spot" contract, where performance is essentially immediate for both parties, the "half-forward" contract where one acts significantly before the other, and the "fully forward" contract where both act in the medium to far future. Of these, only the second poses a major problem; it is my standard model, though he is right to point out that the others are at least as frequent. See 22–25 for starters.
5. See Jan Narveson, *The Libertarian Idea* (Philadelphia: Temple University Press, 1988).
6. Hobbes, *Leviathan*, Ch. XIV.
7. The author's unpublished study, "Property Rights, Original Acquisition, and Lockean Provisos," read at the meetings of the Canadian Philosophical Association, Calgary, Alberta, June 1994, goes into this at length. See also the exposition in *The Libertarian Idea*, Chs. 6–8.

Moral Individualism and Libertarian Theory

Eric Mack

> To every Individuall in nature, is given an individuall property by nature, not to be invaded or usurped by any: for every one as he is himselfe, so he hath a selfe propriety, else could he not be himselfe, and on this no second may presume to deprive any of, without manifest violation and affront to the very principles of nature, and of the Rules of equity and justice between man and man.
>
> Richard Overton, "An Arrow Against All Tyrants" (1646)

1. Introduction

The synoptic libertarian norm is that individual liberty must be respected and that coercive action, whether by individuals or political institutions, is legitimate only insofar as it protects people in their peaceful enjoyment or exercise of their liberties. The only morally permissible coercion is the counter-coercive suppression of coercion. There is much more to life than jealous regard for one's own liberties and fastidious respect for the liberties of others. But the teaching of libertarianism is that none of life's other concerns—whether they be social or aesthetic ideals, scientific or religious projects, or personal aspirations—justify the deployment of freelance or institutionalized force.

Liberty cannot, of course, *guarantee* that the particular aspirations of individuals will be fulfilled or that general societal conditions such as increased prosperity, cultural vibrancy, scientific progress, and environmental preservation will obtain. According to the libertarian, however, a social order that is respectful of liberty, viz., a regime of personal and economic freedom, of markets and other freely entered forms of association, of private initiative and virtue, will advance these diverse and sometimes competing ends as well as can be expected of any social order. In support of this contention, the libertarian asserts the efficiency and stability of social and economic structures that emerge from agents' noncoerced decisions and transactions and the inefficiency and irrationality of imposed, centrally planned structures. The libertarian maintains that moral virtues and economic values are fostered when individuals are held responsible for their own lives and decisions and are undermined when political policies penalize productive behavior and subsidize destructive conduct. The libertarian emphasizes the dangerously persistent human drive for coercive control over others, the distinctive allure of political power for the satisfaction of this drive, the limitless array of pretenses that have been offered in support of coercive power, and the need for eternal vigilance to constrain coercive institutions and to unmask power-serving pretenses. This essay, however, cannot address these crucial theoretical and empirical assertions. Its focus is confined to the core moral principles underlying the libertarian endorsement of liberty.

While many different philosophical accounts of this endorsement of liberty have been offered, the account I propose gives pride of place to the moral rights of individuals. An agent's liberty, correctly understood, consists in the nonviolation of her moral rights.[1] To delineate the liberties endorsed by libertarian theory, we must specify what rights individuals possess and explain why they possess them. To this end, I present the basic elements of a general moral theory, Moral Individualism (MI), whose fundamental theme is the ultimate and irreducible moral importance of each person's life. In section 2, I argue that any adequate moral theory must include two components, a theory of the good and a theory of the right, neither of which is reducible to the other. Within MI, these two components, each of which partially articulates MI's fundamental theme, are Value Individualism (VI) and Rights Individualism (RI). RI is the rights doctrine that best supports libertarian theory.[2] The next two sections are devoted to presenting these two mutually supportive strands of MI. Section 3 explicates the major features of VI, whose central claim is that, for each individual, that individual's well-being is the ultimate good. Section 4 explicates salient features of RI. This section focuses especially on the rationale for the right of self-ownership[3] but also attends briefly to justice in economic holdings and the right of property.

Other important moral elements of libertarian theory are, most unfortunately, beyond the confines of this essay. These include its fuller account of the generation of entitlements to extrapersonal resources, its attention to permissible procedures rather than mandated ends, its rejection of legal paternalism and the enforcement of morality, its vindications of self-defence and punishment, its conceptions of equality, legal neutrality among persons, and the rule of law, and its stance on what types of rights-enforcing institutions are legitimate.

2. The Two Primary Tasks of Ethical Theory

Ethical theory must discover both what ends are to be attained and what means may be employed in attaining those ends. Ethical theory needs to identify what is of ultimate value, what ends impart instrumental value to intermediary goals and to the actions that serve intermediary and final goals. In addition, ethical theory must identify what means—especially what forms of interaction among agents—are morally acceptable in the pursuit of valued goals.

Consequentialist moral theorists believe that the identification of ultimately valuable ends directly governs the determination of morally acceptable means. They believe that one ought to do precisely the action (or set of actions) that will most promote the ultimate value. Rightness of action, in the consequentialist view, consists in an action's propensity to yield valuable outcomes. So, if an action is more productive of the summum bonum than any other available action, that action cannot be wrong. Thus, according to consequentialism, the end—as long as it is correctly assessed as more valuable than any other available end—always justifies the means. The production of the best outcome always justifies the action necessary for that outcome.

This implication is the basis for a decisive objection to consequentialism. Consequentialism is incapable of recognizing norms of justice or rights that place principled limits on what may be done to people in the name of desirable consequences. Of course, according to most particular consequentialist theories, *on most occasions*, one ought not to kill, maim, deceitfully manipulate, or enslave other individuals. On most occasions, these actions will not have outcomes deemed to be most desirable. But this is simply to say that on most occasions, it does not pay to engage in killing, maiming, and so on. Nevertheless, whenever it *is* expedient that individual *I* be killed, maimed, or so on, that action ought to be performed and *I* can have no claim in justice or rights against it. Moreover, even when the killing, maiming, or so on of *I* is inexpedient and hence the consequentialist judges that the action against *I* is wrong, this action is condemned *for the wrong reason*.

It is merely condemned as inexpedient, as not sufficiently useful under the circumstances. *I* can never invoke any principle of justice or any right against the contemplated treatment. *I* is to be spared only because the killing, maiming, or so on would not serve the consequentialist's purposes; he is to be spared only because, on this occasion, it is not expeditious to sacrifice him to the summum bonum. These considerations show that the second task of ethical theory, viz., the determination of the means by which value may be attained, is *not* directly governed by an identification of what is of ultimate value. This second task requires the identification of an independent (albeit not utterly detached) dimension of morality—a dimension that delineates moral constraints on the acceptable means for attaining the good. What is needed is a theory of the right (i.e., of principles of justice or rights) that is independent of the theory of the good and, hence, is capable of issuing moral restrictions on what may be done in the pursuit of the good.

MI offers both a theory of the good and a nonsubordinate theory of the right that provide plausible and mutually coordinate and supportive answers to the primary questions of ethical theory. VI, MI's theory of the good, maintains that, for each individual person, well-being is the ultimate value, the ultimate end that merits his attainment. The well-being of each person is valuable-in-itself and not merely in virtue of some contribution that it may make to some transpersonal objective, such as the aggregate well-being. VI asserts that individuals are moral ends-in-themselves in the sense that each has, within his life and as the realization of his life, an end of ultimate value.

RI, MI's theory of the right, maintains that any being who has, for and within his life, rational ends of his own, is not among the means, the disposable resources, available for others' use in the advancement of their objectives. Each individual has sole moral authority over himself so that, while he may direct and utilize his person, e.g., his faculties, talents, and bodily parts, in the pursuit of his ends, no other agent (without the noncoerced consent of the individual) may direct or utilize that individual's life or person. RI asserts that individuals are moral ends-in-themselves in the (second) sense that each possesses a moral authority over himself that makes it impermissible for others to treat that individual as a means to their ends. It is this right of self-ownership that bars killing, maiming, deceitfully manipulating, or enslaving the individual independent of how effective these actions would be in the promotion of the goals of their perpetrators. RI also advances a doctrine of property rights to extrapersonal resources. These rights extend the domains within which individuals may freely pursue their chosen ends with moral immunity from subordination to others' purposes.

3. Value Individualism

According to VI, for each individual person, his own well-being is the ultimate value, the ultimate end for the measurement of his life. Individuals are not morally subservient to ends outside themselves; they do not have to justify their existence by service to some purportedly higher, impersonal purpose. The model of practical rationality offered by VI is that of the truly prudential agent who, not only in his choice of means and practical strategies, but even in his selection of life-defining ends, genuinely promotes his well-being. *I*'s having or adopting any formative end is, in the final analysis, desirable if and only if under the circumstances that confront him, *I*'s having, adopting, striving for, or attaining that end will make or will be apt to make his life more worth living. In commending to *I* any life-defining enterprise, the final reason one can offer is, "You'll be happier (or more apt to be happy), your life will be more enviable (or be more apt to be enviable) if you incorporate this enterprise into your plan of life." According to VI, no further ends-oriented reason is necessary or possible.

The conception of well-being employed by VI is inclusive. Rather than being composed of one type of state, e.g., one or another species of sensual pleasure, a persons' well-being is composed of a wide variety of different types of constitutive ends. These include various pleasant sensations and satisfying feelings, efficacy in challenging interactions with one's environment, knowledge, sustained allegiance to persons and causes, integrity, self-mastery, and the development of the character traits that support these achievements. Any given individual's well-being will be composed of a cohesive set of particular instantiations of these types of formative ends. Which instantiations of these human goods will compose *I*'s well-being will depend upon *I*'s natural propensities and capacities, his personal and cultural environment, and his own commitment to particular instantiations (this specific career ambition or that particular scientific project) as formative for his life. *I* ought to have or adopt a particular project or commitment or relationship as a formative end if and only if *I*'s having or acquiring that instantiated end enhances *I*'s prospects for his integrated attainment of the goods of human life.

Each agent has goal-oriented reasons to perform those actions that effectually advance or sustain his well-being. But this is *not* to say that the *only* reason *I* can have for or against his performance of some action is the tendency of that action to advance or inhibit his well-being. For VI does not assert that the only assessments of *I*'s actions are to be in terms of their promotion of valuable outcomes. VI at least leaves open the possibility that *I*'s actions may *also* be assessed in terms of independent principles of the right—in particular in terms of moral constraints upon *how* valued ends may be pursued.

The crucial structural feature of VI is its claim that the value of personal well-being and the actions and conditions conducive to it are agent-relative. Each individual I's well-being is the ultimate good *for that individual I*. It is not just that this *well-being* occurs within I's life, but also that the *value* of I's well-being arises within and obtains *in relationship to* I's life. The value is not generic, it is not value-at-large; it is essentially value-for-I. Whatever is genuinely valuable is valuable relative to this or that particular agent—either ultimately valuable as a constituent of this or that agent's well-being or instrumentally valuable as productive of his well-being.[4] VI differs radically from impersonal (or agent-neutral) theories of the good in that VI asserts the existence of many ultimate goods, many summa bona. All persons must acknowledge that I has reason to promote his well-being. But this does not imply that all persons themselves have reason to promote I's well-being. Affirming that everyone's well-being is of ultimate value in no way implies, pace John Stuart Mill, that everyone's well-being is part of a single, global, impersonal value to which everyone ought to be prepared to sacrifice anyone's well-being. Indeed, a crucial lesson for political theory of the agent-relativity of value is the radical undercutting of all putatively agent-neutral rankings of alternative social states that are supposed to provide everyone with reason to bear or to impose costs for the sake of the social state that is impersonally most highly ranked.

Let us understand a social state to consist in a set of pairings of an individual with a degree of attainment of well-being (or whatever is judged to be of ultimate value). For instance, one social state is represented by row I of the matrix below, where the numerals in the boxes represent the amounts of ultimate good attained by the designated individuals.[5] (An empty box signifies the nonexistence of that individual in the relevant social state.) Agent-neutral theories of the good each offer some formula for ranking such alternative states. For example, aggregative theories will give pride of place to II, while egalitarian theories will anoint III. In each case, the priority of the favored state is supposed to provide all agents with reason to contribute to the creation of that state rather than to any of the lower-ranked alternatives. Hence, the egalitarian will assert that, since state III is most valuable, I ought to be prepared to forego the additional five units of value he would enjoy under I, J ought to be prepared to forego the additional ten units of value she would enjoy under IV and L ought to be prepared to forego the ten units of value that would characterize her existence under IV.

VI denies that there is any such most highly ranked state. The values of alternative states are themselves always agent-relative. State I is the most

Social State	Agent *I*	Agent *J*	Agent *K*	Agent *L*
I	20	10	8	
II	18	12	10	
III	15	12	12	
IV	5	22		10

valuable state for *I*. Period. State III is the most valuable state for *K*. Period. State IV is the most valuable state for *J* and also for *L*. Period. The promotion of any one of these states will advance the good of some while inhibiting the good of others. That is all. There is no agent-neutral best end that all should endeavor to or be required to serve. There is no social goal on the altar of which the good of individuals may justifiably be sacrificed.[6] VI rejects the idea that it is part of the task of moral theory to provide any impersonal ordering of competing social states. Perhaps, in the course of diverse lives and their trials and tribulations, state I will emerge. Perhaps, instead, state II or III or IV will emerge. According to VI, moral theory ought not and cannot proclaim which of these states is ordained to exist.

The rejection of agent-neutral rankings rebuts all arguments that appeal to such rankings in order to justify coercive impositions on individuals. For example, it rebuts any attempt to justify subjecting *I* to a day of forced labor in order to move from state I to the purportedly more valuable state II. However, it is one thing to rebut a proposed justification for a coercive imposition. It is another thing to establish the wrongfulness of that imposition. It is one thing to show that a certain argument on behalf of subjecting *I* to forced labor fails. It is another thing to show that there is some interpersonally valid norm that *condemns* this subjugation. (Perhaps justice neither endorses nor condemns *I*'s subjugation.) Interpersonally valid norms that identify certain actions as wrongful—indeed, as violations of rights—have their primary location, not within MI's theory of the good, but within MI's theory of the right to which we now turn.

4. Rights Individualism

The advocate of MI maintains that a libertarian institutional framework that restrains political power, sustains the rule of law, and protects individuals in their legitimate private spheres and in their voluntary interactions—all in the service of individual rights—would be of great instrumental value, if not for everyone, then for nearly everyone.[7] To begin with, nearly everyone would have a direct, pragmatic, agent-relative stake in complying with and promoting others' compliance with such a framework of rules because of the degree to which that framework enhances peace and mutually advantageous coordination. Moreover, at least most individuals are naturally disposed to internalize allegiance to and abide by norms that are seen to facilitate peaceful cooperation and mutually beneficial interaction and that affirm each person's status as a moral end-in-himself. Such internalization adds moral structure to people's lives.[8] Furthermore, the effective and justifiable *enforcement* of these rules will provide to even more individuals—especially to those individuals who are not naturally disposed to internalize moral rules—additional agent-relative reasons to abide by these rules. And the greater the resulting overall compliance, the greater the likelihood that, for any given individual, the libertarian framework will serve him well and earn his support. These are important considerations that indicate the extent to which people blessed with a libertarian framework will be motivated to abide by and uphold its strictures.

These considerations in themselves, however, fall short of fully vindicating those institutions and the rights *for the sake of which* those institutions are championed. For these considerations presuppose and build upon, but do not in themselves provide, an independent delineation and justification of those libertarian rights. Once such rights are identified, justified, and made the object of moral allegiances and legal enforcement, the mutually advantageous libertarian framework will be at hand. But the benefits of the system arise as the product of our identification of and commitment to these individual moral rights. Thus, we need to discover a grounding for these rights that does not merely invoke the beneficial results of our identifying and committing ourselves to abide by them. More specifically, we need to inquire into what basis exists within MI for affirming rights that morally constrain others' pursuits of their valued ends.

I believe that there are two complementary bases within MI for affirming these rights and I propose to set out two arguments that articulate these grounds for rights: (A) the prerogative argument; and (B) the recognition argument. Each of these is an argument for the moral right of self-ownership.

(A) The prerogative argument.

As a component of MI, VI upholds the propriety of each person's articulation and promotion of his own well-being through his adoption and championing of formative projects and commitments. An adequate MI must articulate the moral condition of agents in a way that accords with their effectual pursuit of well-being. The central contention of the prerogative argument is that an agent's effectual pursuit of his well-being requires that he (at least tacitly) take himself to have a moral authority over himself that entitles him to decide toward what ends his personal resources will be directed. If this is true, then upholding the propriety of each person's articulation and promotion of his well-being requires an ascription to each person of a right of self-ownership.[9] The central contention of this argument rests on four subsidiary claims.

(1) A condition of an agent's effectual pursuit of his well-being is his wholehearted fidelity to the goals and commitments through which his well-being is articulated. In the absence of this tenacious allegiance, the agent will not merely lack motivation for attaining his well-being but may not even achieve a stable articulation of his well-being. Only resolute allegiance provides cohesive structure to one's life.

(2) For each agent, a condition of his wholehearted fidelity to his projects and commitments is that agent's (at least tacit) sense of being justified vis-à-vis *other agents* in his devotion of himself to these enterprises. Each agent must have a sense that morality authorizes his devotion of himself to these ends even in the face of challenges by others who propose that, instead, he devote himself to their ends or at least stand ready to abandon his ends for their sake. For each person to be vindicated vis-à-vis others in the devotion of his person to his favored plan of life, each person must possess the prerogative of determining by his choice the disposition of his own person—so that there is an asymmetry between *his* setting the bearing of his person and *others'* setting that bearing.

(3) This set of prerogatives cannot be accounted for by any appeal to agent-relative values or agent-neutral values. The agent-relativity of value allows each individual to rebut demands that he be prepared to forego his enterprises and the prospects for personal well-being that they provide in order to serve some pretended agent-neutral good. However, this rebuttal falls short of justifying the agent vis-à-vis other agents in his devotion to his own enterprises. For the judgment that it is reasonable for him to cherish his projects and commitments simply invites the response that it is also reasonable for others to press or even compel him to abandon those ends should that abandonment serve their purposes. The agent's citation of the value for him of self-determination as such provides no reason for others to honor or allow that self-determination. Nor can a vindication with interpersonal force derive from any agent-neutral value, for no agent-neutral value is available to vindicate anything. Moreover, for a theory of agent-neutral

value to account for each person's prerogative of self-determination, it would have to show how each person's enjoyment of this prerogative would yield more agent-neutral value than any compromise of that prerogative. It is most unlikely that this could be shown for any theory of agent-neutral value.

(4) What is needed to ground each person's prerogative of self-determination is the ascription to each of moral authority over himself. It is because people possess this moral authority that morality can be said to side with *each* individual's chosen disposition of his person as against any of the dispositions favored by others. It is each person's right of self-ownership that supplies him with this interpersonal vindication of his self-determination. This right supports *each* agent's sense that, of course, he is *entitled* to devote himself to the enterprises in which he seeks personal value—as others are entitled to devote themselves to their chosen plans of life—and that, therefore, it would be *outrageous* for others to impress him into the promotion of their ends even if this impressment were to have agent-relative value for them. Therefore, since an adequate MI must represent the moral condition of agents in a way that accords with their effectual pursuit of well-being, and since resolute fidelity to their respective goals and commitments is required for agents' effectual pursuit of their well-being, and since a prerogative of self-determination is required to support each agent's wholehearted fidelity to his goals and commitments, and since the right of self-ownership is required to ground this prerogative of self-determination, an adequate MI must ascribe to all agents this right of self-ownership.

Allegiance to VI's proclamation of the propriety of each agent's pursuit of his well-being requires, then, that one go beyond MI's theory of the good to a central tenet of RI, viz., the right of self-ownership. This right is included within MI for the sake of its role within individuals' pursuit of their good. Nevertheless, what is included to fulfill this role is a genuine right, i.e., a principled claim for each individual of discretionary authority over his own person and life.

(B) The recognition argument.

The advocate of MI subscribes to a radical version of value pluralism. He rejects all forms of normative monism—whether it be a monism that asserts the existence of one impersonal ultimate value or a monism that asserts the existence of one personal ultimate value. *Each* agent is affirmed as the possessor of rational ends of his own. *Each* is identified as a being who has reason to devote himself, i.e., his personal endowments, capacities, and energies, to the fullest feasible realization of value for himself. To acknowledge this pluralism is to attest to the propriety of each agent's dedication of his value-pursuing powers to the realization of value for this agent.

To this reiteration of MI's claim that each person has in his well-being an end that, within his life, is of ultimate value, the recognition argument adds two contentions. The first is that the existence of other persons as beings with rational ends of their own must itself have practical significance for one's own behavior. The normative reality of other persons as possessors of ultimate rational ends of their own itself makes rational demands upon one's own behavior. It is unreasonable for us to fail to adapt our behavior to the fact of others' existence as beings rationally directed to ends of their own. There is a failure of rationality in an individual who acknowledges that others are each separate beings with rational ends of their own but who, nevertheless, insists that this has no practical significance for him or no rational bearing on how he ought to behave. In failing to constrain one's behavior toward other persons, one manifests the cognitive fault of *failing to recognize* the existence of others as beings with rational ends of their own.

There are two finer delineations of this cognitive fault of failing. According to one delineation, agent J's failure of rationality consists in J's failure to constrain her behavior upon J's genuinely grasping the existence of others as beings with rational ends of their own. Here the cognitive fault is failure of restraint in light of certain beliefs. According to the other delineation, J's failure of rationality consists in J's failure genuinely to grasp the existence of others. On this delineation, J's failure to constrain her behavior is merely (!) especially compelling evidence of her failure genuinely to appreciate the existence of others. Whichever delineation is emphasized, failure to contour one's behavior to others' status as beings with ultimate ends of their own constitutes a failure of rationality.

Consider psychopathology. The psychopath seems to be a normative monist of the sort who (at most) grasps the existence of one personal ultimate value—his own. He seems to be a normative solipsist. While the psychopath may comply with certain constraints for strategic value-promoting reasons, he never genuinely recognizes the existence of others. This is to say either that the psychopath never genuinely grasps their existence as beings with ends of their own or that, while he does grasp their existence as beings with ends of their own, he never takes this to have any bearing on his conduct. Whichever more fine-tuned account of his psychopathology we opt for, the psychopath remains cognitively defective—perhaps irremediably so. Either with respect to his beliefs or his conduct, he does not get it—where the "it" is either the fact of the existence of others with ends of their own or the bearing of this fact on his conduct. How else could the cognitive defectiveness of the psychopath be explained?

Another way to get at the relevance of the fact of others' directedness to ultimate values of their own is to picture individual J's convictions being altered by the addition of a belief in this fact and see whether it is reasonable for this alteration in itself to make a difference in J's behavior. Suppose that J begins as a normative solipsist. As J sees it, the only real values in the universe are values-for-the-unique-J. Under these conditions, nothing could be more natural than that J perceive other persons as having no more independent moral standing than brute animals, vegetables, and minerals. J will perceive all of these things, other persons included, to be available to be exploited for her purposes. Each may be put to whatever use maximally promotes J's ends.

Of course, a prudent J will handle exploitable resources with care and foresight. While J disbelieves in the value of others' ends, she does not doubt that they will respond to threats and to opportunities much as J herself will. J will design her interactive strategies accordingly. It is, then, entirely consistent with J's *normative* solipsism that she have agent-relative reasons for constraining her behavior toward others in extensive and complex ways. Nevertheless, J accepts only one measure of her practical rationality, which is her cost-effective use of all available materials for the enhancement of agent-relative value.[10] In this single-minded focus on value promotion, J is like her fellow normative monist, who believes in the maximal promotion of agent-neutral value unconstrained by any independent principles of right.

Suppose, however, that J abandons her normative solipsism and replaces it with the normative pluralism associated with VI. This new acceptance of the reality of other persons as beings with ultimate values of their own involves a enormous shift in what J takes to be the furniture of the moral world. The world now is seen as populated by beings who are as strikingly different in rational directedness from, for example, plants and mineral deposits, as J previously took herself to be different from all other beings. It is incredible that this enormous transformation in J's view of the normative facts—the move from the solipsistic conviction that the only real values in the universe are the values of her unique self to the inclusion of other persons as beings comparably rationally oriented to final values of their own—should have no implications for how J, as a reasonable individual, ought to act. It is incredible that J should convert to this normative pluralism and still reasonably believe that she has a totally free hand in how she treats other persons—as long as she is effectively maximizing agent-relative value. Indeed, it seems that this conversion must introduce a new measure of practical rationality—a nonconsequentialist measure distinct from the gauge of cost-effective use of whatever is encountered in the world. For although this conversion radically revises J's view of the moral facts, it does not alter her view about what ends she ought to serve. J's acknowledgement that each other person has rational ends of his own does not imply that any of those ends are among J's rational ends. J's conversion to normative pluralism does not at all present her with goals that she now has reason to substitute for the goals she previously cherished.

Nor does J's new belief dictate any change in her goal-based assessment of actions and strategies. Prior to J's conversion, she has had the view that others act and react *as though* they have value-based reasons akin to hers. So she already has, to the best of her ability, factored these expectations about their actions and reactions into her assessment of which strategies would best promote her valued goals. And she has already been prepared to continue to factor these expectations into any subsequent, goal-oriented revisions of her strategies. J's adoption of normative pluralism does not as such make any difference in the goal-oriented, value-promoting reasons she has for or against any actions or strategies. Hence, if the conversion to pluralism does provide J with reasons she otherwise would not have—reasons that contravene value-based endorsements of actions or that supplement value-based endorsements of constraint—those reasons must not derive from any value that J is to seek. Rather, they must reflect limits upon *how* J may seek value. Those reasons, revealed in her conversion to pluralism, must correspond to moral constraints on what means J may employ in the pursuit of her ends. Only by constraining her conduct towards others can J give expression to her otherwise inchoate affirmation of their existence as beings with ultimately valuable ends of their own. Here we see the second contention within the recognition argument, the appropriate practical response to the existence of other persons as beings with ultimate ends of their own is restraint on the treatment of those persons as means to one's own ends—restraint that amounts to affirming each person's moral authority over himself.

Through her conversion from solipsism to pluralism, the bright line by which J divides objects in the world shifts. While previously it set her apart from all other beings, now it divides her and many other beings with ultimate ends of their own from all the remaining entities. If the adoption of normative pluralism has practical significance for J, then after conversion it must become reasonable for her to discriminate between her treatment of those beings now on her side of the bright line and those entities still on the other side. Since prior to conversion it was reasonable for J to view everything on the other side of the line as material available for her exploitation, the natural form of discrimination between the beings now on her side of the line and those entities still on the other side is that those now on her side are not to be viewed as exploitable material. Those beings now perceived by *J* as having ultimate moral purposes of their own are morally excluded as means available for *J*'s purposes.

Those beings are, of course, persons constituted by their bodily parts, faculties, talents, and forms of endeavor. While each person other than *I* is morally constrained from employing *I* as a resource for her purposes, *I* is not so constrained. *I* is morally free to direct his person as he chooses and this moral freedom combined with others' exclusion constitutes his moral authority over himself. *I* possesses an inviolability in his person and in his discretionary control of his person which is captured in the ascription to him of a right of self-ownership.

The conclusion of the recognition argument accords nicely with that of the prerogative argument, which focused on the need for a moral theory that endorses each agent's pursuit of personal value to support each agent's sense of being justified in dedicating himself to the enterprises through which his good is articulated. That argument maintains that there is a type of incoherence in perceiving *oneself* as a being with rational ends of one's own and not also perceiving oneself as having a right of self-ownership. The recognition argument maintains that there is a type of incoherence in perceiving *another* as a being with rational ends of his own and not perceiving that other person as having a right of self-ownership. Both arguments articulate the idea that because each agent is an end-in-himself in the sense of having (in his well-being) an ultimate end for and within his own life, each is also an end-in-himself in the sense of possessing a moral inviolability against being treated as a means to attainment of values external to himself.

It is important to appreciate that the right of self-ownership is a negative right. It merely requires that others abstain from trespass upon the right-holder. *I*'s right does not require that others serve him in any way, but merely that they not conscript him into service to them. The negativity of the right of self-ownership accords with its representing a moral side-constraint upon how individuals may pursue value, rather than a dictate that certain ends be pursued. The negativity of this right also insures its compossibility. That is, this right can always be accorded to everyone; no one's enjoyment of discretionary authority over himself requires that any other person undergo a loss of authority over himself. Thus, no conflicts among rights need arise for the resolution of which one might be tempted to seek out standards of impersonal value.[11]

Moreover, because of the negativity of this right, even though *I*'s right constrains *J*'s value-promoting behavior, it is misleading to say that *I*'s right requires that *J* sacrifice her well-being. First, it is *odd* to describe the requirement that *J* not violate others' negative rights as the imposition of a sacrifice upon *J*—since this requirement imposes no service upon *J* and provides nothing to others except immunity from *J*'s predation. Second, the requirement that *J* forego trespassing upon *I* leaves open the possibility of innumerable other strategies for the promotion of her well-being. Especially if *J* can anticipate the enforcement of these constraints, *J* is very likely to be able to develop talents, dispositions, formative ends, and suitable nontrespassing strategies that will be at least as apt to promote her well-being as any rights-violating strategy she might otherwise have pursued. Third, *J*'s constraint by *I*'s right is part of a general system of moral constraints that is very likely greatly to benefit *J*—directly by precluding others' trespassing upon *J* and indirectly by establishing a set of salient interpersonal rules from which peaceful coexistence and mutually beneficial cooperation within *J*'s social environment can emerge. Fourth, belief in the right of self-ownership fortifies *J* in her dedication to her formative ends and provides a (partial) map of a just (and profitable) social order, allegiance to which itself may serve *J* as a rewarding commitment. These last three considerations can be summarized as the claim that, for any given individual *J*, given her reasonable adaptation to a regime of these rights, the costs of her compliance are likely to be very low and the benefits from her own compliance and the compliance of others are likely to be very high.

Libertarian theory is, of course, notorious not merely for its assertion of individuals' rights over themselves, but also for its claims about individuals' rights over extrapersonal resources. Unfortunately, all that can be offered here is a quick survey of the most familiar features of libertarian property theory along with some supplementary claims that arise naturally out of the arguments of this essay, especially out of the recognition argument. Libertarian accounts of property almost always attempt to analyze property rights as extensions of a single fundamental right—typically, the right of self-ownership—which is not itself a right of (extrapersonal) property. Thus, it is often argued that, since *I* owns his talents or labor as aspects of himself, *I*'s rights of self-ownership will be violated if others seize objects within which he has (permissibly) invested his talents or labor. The process of purposive transformation of natural material generates an entitlement on behalf of the transforming agent to the now transformed object. Owned objects may also be transferred among agents by voluntary donation or exchange so that individuals can acquire entitlements to objects that they themselves have not produced. *I* will be entitled to whatever objects he has acquired either by transformation from (unowned) natural materials or by free donation or exchange from other individuals who themselves had title to those objects.

A distribution of holdings among individuals will be just insofar as the particular holdings of those individuals arise through these entitlement-generating procedures. If the distribution is just, it is so simply by virtue of the justice of its parts and not by virtue of any pattern that the distribution as a whole realizes, such as maximizing aggregate wealth or well-being or maximizing the wealth or well-being of the worst-off participants. There is no comprehensive pattern, no overall structural feature, like maximizing aggregate wealth or the wealth of the worst-off individuals, that the distribution of holdings ought to satisfy and that would have to be sustained by coercive political action.[12] The absence of any privileged pattern reflects the fact that there is no standard of impersonal value for ranking alternative distributions, for identifying one of them as morally mandated. (Recall VI's rejection of impersonal rankings of alternative social states.)[13] Instead of there being one mandated distribution, whichever set of holdings in fact arises through the actual entitlement-generating procedures that people have chosen is just in the sense that any forcible interference with those holdings will violate valid property rights. However, had individuals engaged in other entitlement-generating procedures, had I sowed rather than reaped and J hesitated rather than leaped, then the different set of holdings that would have emerged would be just.

The only weak link in this familiar chain of contentions is the presumption that the entitlement-generating capacities of procedures of initial acquisition and transfer can satisfactorily be traced to persons' rights of self-ownership (or to some equivalent right to liberty). I suggest instead that the entitlement-generating powers of these procedures be traced to a sui generis right of property. This fundamental right of property is not a right of individuals to any particular extrapersonal items or a right to any share or distributive pattern of extrapersonal holdings. Any such right for J would contravene I's self-ownership by obligating I (independent of any voluntary agreement) to supply the designated item or promote the ordained pattern. Rather, this right of property is a right to the practice of private property, i.e., a right to others' compliance with a system of rules under which individuals may peacefully acquire, transform, and otherwise exercise exclusive and discretionary control over extrapersonal objects.

The acknowledgement of this right of property is a second element both in the vindication of people's dedication to their distinctive, life-defining, ends and in the recognition of others as beings with ultimate ends of their own. This element, beyond self-ownership itself, is required because human beings live in and through a world of objects that extends beyond the space occupied by their respective bodies. It is in this extended world that people's lives are projected and enacted through their purposive employment of their capacities, talents, insights, and energies. In this process, particular extrapersonal objects enter into and help define the specific ambitions that comprise agents' lives. Since people live their lives in and through the extrapersonal domain, any recognition of them as moral ends-in-themselves who are owed immunity in their peaceful pursuit of values must extend to immunities regarding the extrapersonal objects through which they form and advance their lives. People must have moral immunity against the destruction, disruption, or seizure of extrapersonal objects incorporated into their ongoing projects that is comparable to the immunity they have against the destruction, disruption, or seizure of their persons. This means that people must be able to acquire, by appropriately defined procedures, entitlements over particular extrapersonal items—entitlements that provide individuals with the same sort of exclusive, discretionary, and stable control over extrapersonal items as they rightfully have over themselves. The rights of individuals to others' compliance with a system of rules under which individuals may peacefully acquire, transform, and exercise exclusive and discretionary control over extrapersonal objects is what gives the rules of such a practice their entitlement-conferring power.[14] Respect for the entitlements conferred by an appropriately articulated practice of private property enormously extends the realm of peaceful coexistence and the prospects for mutually beneficial cooperation. Even more to the point, respect for these entitlements is respect for individuals as beings with ultimate ends of their own, whose values and lives are defined and fulfilled through their engagement in the extrapersonal world.

Notes

1. A more precise statement is that individual *I*'s liberty consists in the absence of those interferences that violate his rights *or* would violate his rights had those rights not been waived or forfeited by *I*. The justly incarcerated *I* does suffer a loss of liberty even though no right of his is violated because he is subjected to interferences that would violate his rights had he not forfeited them.

2. For recent doctrines of rights that aim at libertarian conclusions see: Loren Lomasky, *Persons, Rights, and the Moral Community* (New York: Oxford University Press, 1987); Jan Narveson, *The Libertarian Idea* (Philadelphia: Temple University Press, 1988); Tibor Machan, *Individuals and Their Rights* (LaSalle, Illinois: Open Court, 1989); Douglas Rasmussen and Douglas Den Uyl, *Liberty and Nature* (La Salle, Illinois: Open Court, 1991); and Horatio Spector, *Autonomy and Rights* (Oxford: Clarendon Press, 1992).

3. Also see Eric Mack, "Agent-Relativity of Value, Deontic Restraints, and Self-Ownership," in *Value, Welfare, and Morality*, ed. R. Frey and C. Morris (Cambridge:

Cambridge University Press, 1993) and "Personal Integrity, Practical Recognition, and Rights," *The Monist* 76, no.1. (1993) 101–18.

4. The value of *I*'s well-being is *not* subjective either in the sense that *I* merely has certain favorable feelings about his well-being or in the sense that the value of *I*'s well-being is conferred upon it by *I*'s preference for or endorsement of it. Rather, *I*'s well-being objectively has value-for-*I*.

5. It is a fantasy to suppose that we can assign such commensurable well-being scores to the individuals who populate these social states. That this is a fantasy *strengthens* the agent-relativist's rejection of putatively neutral rankings of the states represented by the rows on this matrix.

6. A social state in which *each* individual would be better off than he or she would be in any other social state would be most valuable-for-*I*, most valuable-for-*J*, and so on. But even that would not add up to its being agent-neutrally best.

7. The claim is not that almost everyone who is a recipient of governmental largess that violates libertarian strictures would benefit from the elimination of that particular largess. Closer is the claim is that nearly everyone, including nearly all recipients of largess, would benefit from the general elimination of all policies contrary to libertarian strictures. Even this is more than the libertarian need or should assert. A tragic residue of some current policies may be that their recipients are disabled from benefiting from a transition to the libertarian framework. (This does raise difficult questions about second-best transitional policies.)

8. In the matrix of social states, this rights-based *recontouring* of agents' respective well-being is not factored in.

9. It is not just that MI endorses each agent's *belief* in self-proprietorship as having agent-relative value for that agent. Rather, the principle of self-ownership is revealed as part of the most adequate explication of the root thesis that each person's life is of ultimate and irreducible moral importance.

10. In order to give assurance to others and secure their cooperation, *J* may publicly *profess* a belief in abiding by these constraints for their own sake. She may even attempt to create in herself a firm (and *detectable*) disposition to abide by them. But *J*'s normative solipsism will undermine these stratagems.

11. Necessary self-defense against an aspiring trespasser is not a counterexample to this compossibility claim. The trespasser forfeits his rights not to be subject to the force that is necessary for his being repelled.

12. The contrast between procedural ("historical nonpatterned") principles and patterned principles is especially developed in Nozick's *Anarchy, State and Utopia*, (New York: Basic Books, 1974) 149–74.

13. Nor are any other attempts to establish some pattern of holdings as morally preordained successful, e.g., attempts to show that some pattern is *just* because it would be unanimously agreed to by agents who have no idea who they are or what they care about.

14. On property rights, see my "Self-Ownership and the Right of Property," *The Monist*, 73, no. 4 (1990) 519–43 and "The Self-Ownership Proviso: A New and Improved Lockean Proviso," *Social Philosophy and Policy*, 12, no. 1 (1995) 186–218.

"Rights" as MetaNormative Principles

Douglas J. Den Uyl and *Douglas B. Rasmussen*

> THOMAS MORE: The law is not a "light" for you or any man to see by; the law is not an instrument of any kind. The law is a causeway upon which, so long as he keeps to it, a citizen may walk safely.
>
> —Robert Bolt, A *Man For All Seasons*

If the free institutions fostered by the Enlightenment are to be maintained, if the liberal order is to overcome its current malaise, an adequate moral vision is absolutely necessary. Indeed, whatever else may sustain a political order on a day-to-day basis, it is the sense that the order is legitimate that will ultimately determine its fate. The moral vision that most eloquently characterizes our own sense of political legitimacy is the American Declaration of Independence. Its leading concept can be summed up in two words: individual rights.

Yet the doctrine of individual rights suffers from many difficulties and misinterpretations. Chief among these problems is explaining the exact relationship among rights, morality, and law or politics. This problem is primarily a result of a failure to grasp the moral function of individual rights. Indeed, this failure is found almost as often among defenders of individual rights as its opponents. In our book, *Liberty and Nature*,[1] we offered a theory of rights that was designed both to support individual rights and to be rooted in a solid moral framework. To construct this theory, we needed to do two things simultaneously. One was to explain the purpose or function of rights in such a way that the work they do is not reducible to the work done by some other moral concept. The other was to show how rights are grounded in the moral framework itself—in our case, a self-perfectionist moral framework.

In this essay we will lay out some of the structure of our argument in *Liberty and Nature*. Our purpose is to give a sense of that argument without all the detail that seemed necessary for a more complete account. We will begin by explaining just what kind of ethical concept "rights" constitute. Next, we will describe some of the central features of our account of virtue ethics necessary for presenting the summary of an argument for rights that follows. In the penultimate section, we will consider some objections to our argument, and in our concluding section we will consider how our view of rights, though based on a self-perfectionist virtue ethics, commits us not to a classical or communitarian political view but to a liberal one.

The Concept of "Rights"

"Rights" are an ethical concept, but they differ from other ethical concepts. They have a unique function. They are not directly concerned with either achieving the moral good or obtaining right conduct. Rather, rights are *metanormative* principles; that is to say, they are concerned with establishing a political context that protects the self-directedness or autonomy of individuals and thereby secures the liberty under which individuals can achieve their moral well-being.

Rights provide guidance in creating, interpreting, and evaluating political/legal systems so that individuals might be protected from being used by others for purposes to which they have not consented. Rights are used to determine *fundamentally* what ought to be a law. They provide the fundamental normative basis for a legal order; unlike the moral virtues, they do not provide individuals with any guidance regarding what choices to make in the pursuit of their own or anyone else's moral perfection.

The fundamental principles of a polity's legal system must have some normative basis if it is ultimately to have authority, and so the attempt to make law entirely independent from morality is a mistake. But it is also a mistake to reduce the moral concepts that underlie a polity's legal system to those moral concepts that provide individuals guidance in the conduct of their daily lives. What, then, is the fundamental difference between normative and metanormative principles, and how are they connected? An examination of the character of human moral well-being, as conceived by a certain account of virtue ethics, will provide answers to these questions.

Virtue Ethics

Human moral well-being—or as many virtue ethicists call it, "human flourishing"—is concerned with choices that necessarily involve the particular and the contingent. Knowledge of the moral virtues and true human goods may tell all of us what, abstractly speaking, we ought to do. But in the real world of individual human conduct, where all actions and goods are concrete and where human well-being takes a determinate form, what the moral virtues and human goods involve cannot be determined from the philosopher's armchair. A successful moral life is, by its very nature, something that is highly personal. For example, having a career, an education, a home, friends, and medical care are goods that, when considered from an abstract perspective, are beneficial or appropriate for all human beings. They ought to be created or achieved. Yet this claim is not too helpful in providing guidance to the individual in a concrete situation. None of these goods exists in an abstract or generic manner. How are they to be created or achieved? What kind of job, education, home, and medical care does one need? Who will be one's friends? To what extent and in what amount are these to be pursued? How is the achievement of one of these goods to be related to the achievement of other goods? What is the proper balance or mix?

These questions can only be answered by considering the unique needs and circumstances of the individual, and the insight of that same individual is crucial to determining the proper answer. Practical reason is needed in the achievement, maintenance, enjoyment, and coherent integration of these basic human goods. What moral virtue and goods call for in terms of concrete actions in specific circumstances can vary from person to person, and certain virtues can have larger roles in the lives of some persons than others. Determining the appropriate response for the situation faced is, therefore, what moral living is all about.

This view of human flourishing could correctly be described as entailing a "pluralistic realism" regarding human values. The human good is something real, *and* it is individualized and diverse. But there is something at the concrete level that really is common to all the various forms of flourishing and indeed must be. It is the essential core of practical reason itself, and this essential core has another name—self-direction. The act of exercising reason, of using one's intelligence, is not automatic. It is something that the individual human being needs to initiate and maintain. Thus, self-direction or autonomy pertains to the very essence of human flourishing—it is the formal essence—and thus is common to all forms of flourishing, regardless of how diverse.

Self-directedness is, therefore, both a necessary condition for self-perfection and a feature of all self-perfecting acts at whatever level of achievement or specificity. This is another way of saying that the phenomenon of a volitional consciousness[2] is both a necessary condition for, and an operating condition of, the pursuit and achievement of self-perfection. The absence of self-directedness implies the absence of self-perfection, although the absence of self-perfection does not imply the absence of self-directedness, nor does the presence of self-directedness imply the presence of self-perfection (but the presence of self-perfection does imply the presence of self-directedness).

None of this, of course, is to say that any choice one makes is as good as the next, but simply that the choice must be one's own and must involve considerations that are unique to the individual. One person's moral well-being cannot be exchanged with another's. The good-for-me is not, and cannot be, the good-for-you. Human moral well-being, then, is something objective, self-directed, and highly personal. It is not abstract, collectively determined, or impersonal.

This last point is crucial, because it allows us a way to determine the unique moral function of rights. According to our theory, rights are concerned with the protection of the condition under which self-perfection can occur. Obviously, securing the condition for the possibility of self-perfection is logically prior to and distinct from the pursuit of self-perfection. But securing the condition must be understood as essentially "negative," if we are correct that self-directedness does not imply or guarantee self-perfection and that one's self-perfection is not exchangeable with another's. In other words, we are *not* trying with our theory of rights *directly* and *positively* to secure self-perfection, but rather to protect, and thus prevent encroachments upon, the condition under which self-perfection can exist. Our aim is thus to protect the possibility of self-perfection, but only through seeking to protect the possibility of self-directedness.

The single most common and threatening encroachment upon self-directedness and consequently self-perfection is the initiation of physical force by one person (or group) against another. We therefore need a principle that will, to borrow a phrase from Robert Nozick, allow "moral space" to each person—a sphere of freedom whereby self-directed activities can be exercised without being trampled by others or vice versa.

The aim of our theory of rights is thus to secure politically and legally the possibility of self-direction. However, why is self-direction taken as *the* condition to be protected? Are there not many other conditions that are also necessary for the possibility of self-perfection? Why should not securing these conditions be a political and legal concern and not merely a matter of ethics? In other words, why do we need to consider rights as only fundamental political or legal principles? Should not rights be concerned with more than the protection of self-direction? Why should we consider them as only metanormative?

The Need for a MetaNormative Principle of Rights

The individualized character of human flourishing creates a need for another type of ethical principle, once we realize that human moral well-being is only achieved with and among others. We are social beings, not in the Hobbesian sense of merely needing others to get what we want because we are powerless on our own, but in the sense that our very maturation as human beings requires others. Indeed, a significant part of our potentialities is other-oriented. If this is true, however, there is a difficulty. If one person's particular form of well-being is different from another's and may even conflict with it, and if persons can prevent others from being self-directed, then certain interpersonal standards need to be adopted if individuals are to flourish in their diverse ways among others. An ethical principle is needed whose primary function is not guiding a person to well-being or right conduct, but providing a standard for interpersonal conduct that favors no particular form of human flourishing, while at the same time providing a context for diverse forms of human flourishing to be achieved. Such a principle provides such a context by protecting what is necessary to the possibility of each and every person's finding fulfillment, regardless of the determinate form virtues and human goods take in their lives. Thus, it is very important that there be such a thing as a metanormative principle.

Given what we have already said about our conception of human flourishing and the central, necessary role that self-directedness plays in this conception, self-directedness is that unique feature of human flourishing that everyone must first have protected in the concrete case if they are to flourish. Yet since this point is crucial to our theory of rights, the relation of self-directedness to practical reason, as well as to the virtues and goods of human flourishing, bears repeating: practical reason cannot be practical reason without self-direction; and no constituent virtue or good of human flourishing can be such a virtue or good without practical reason. Thus, self-directedness is both central and necessary to the very nature of human flourishing. It is the only feature of human flourishing common to all acts of self-perfection and peculiar to each. Thus, self-directedness is the only feature of human flourishing upon which to base a metanormative principle, because it is the only feature in which each and every person in the concrete situation has a necessary stake. Also, self-directedness is the only feature of human flourishing whose protection is consistent with the diverse forms of human flourishing.

We cannot have a metanormative principle that will structurally prejudice society more towards some forms of self-perfection than others. To do that would be, in effect, to act against the requirement that our theory support self-perfection. So, the principle we arrive at must be universal in the sense of being equally applicable to all individuals.

In addition, the universality requirement necessitates that we center our principle around that characteristic present in all forms of self-perfection (or its pursuit); otherwise, we will again prejudice the situation in favor of some forms of self-perfection over others. So-called "generic goods"—for example, food, clothing, shelter, knowledge, friendship, artistic appreciation, and love, or even central virtues like integrity, courage, and justice—will not suffice as our standard here. Even though they are universal in the sense of helping to define the meaning of self-perfection for all individuals, their particular form or application is given by the individual. This means that while, for example, artistic pursuit or appreciation may be necessary for anyone's self-perfection, the particular form it takes will differ widely. Our principle must apply to both the particular and general in the same way and in the same respect, or we will be back to an a priori slanting of the situation in favor of some forms of self-perfection over others. Now, of course, it becomes much more difficult to find a candidate for grounding our principle of rights—one that is retained across individuals and throughout the developmental process of achieving and maintaining individualized self-perfection. Nevertheless, a principle that provides for protection of self-directedness will not favor any particular form of flourishing, and yet will still allow the possibility that everyone can flourish. Such a principle is our metanormative conception of rights.

On the basis of what we have said so far, it is clear that the only type of rights we possess that are consistent with protecting the condition necessary for the pursuit of any form of self-perfection are *rights of equal liberty*, where no one is allowed to take an action towards another that threatens or destroys that other's self-directedness. The basic rights we possess are thus principles of mutual noninterference. This translates socially into a principle of maximum compossible and equal freedom for all. The freedom must be equal, in the sense that it must allow for the possibility of diverse modes of flourishing and, therefore, must not be structurally biased in favor of some forms of flourishing over others. The freedom must be compossible, in the sense that the exercise of self-directed activity by one person must not encroach upon that of another.

Because we are not directly concerned with the promotion of self-perfection itself, but only the condition for it, it is not the consequences per se that will determine encroachment. What is decisive is whether the action taken by one person towards another secures that other's consent or is otherwise in accord with that other's choices. One may violate another's rights and produce a chain of events that leads to consequences that could be said to be to that other's apparent or real benefit, or one may not violate another's rights and produce a chain of events that leads to one's apparent or real detriment. Yet since the purpose here is to structure a political principle that protects the condition for self-perfection rather than leading to self-perfection itself, the consequences of actions are of little importance (except insofar as they threaten the condition that rights were designed to protect in the first place). Our concern here is not with how acts will turn out, but rather with setting the appropriate foundation for the taking of any action in the first place.

Objections

The preceding outline of our theory is perhaps best clarified by answering some objections. The following four objections should be sufficient.[3]

1. The first objection runs as follows: a metanormative principle must be based on something in which each and every person, in the concrete situation, has a necessary stake. It must be something that is both common and peculiar to every act of self-perfection, as well as neutral to the various forms of flourishing. Self-direction certainly meets these criteria, but it is not the only thing to do so. Such constituent virtues as, for example, integrity, courage, and justice, are necessary to any form of flourishing. Everyone, if they are to flourish, must have integrity, courage, and justice. Though there might be different levels of involvement in artistic appreciation that are appropriate for different persons, there is no diversity when it comes to practicing virtues such as these. They are the same for everyone. If there is diversity or pluralism in practicing these virtues, then human flourishing is reduced to nothing more than a form of relativism—be it some form of conventionalism or simply subjectivism—and the claim to base rights on a self-perfectionist virtue ethics becomes a sham.

This objection is guilty of an ambiguity. Integrity, courage, and justice are the same for everyone only in the sense that these virtues must be applied by everyone to the task of self-perfection. What they are applied to, how they are applied, what specific actions they require, and how they are integrated with the other goods and virtues that make up human flourishing vary greatly from person to person. These virtues are the same for everyone only insofar as they are abstractly considered.

The assumption that such central virtues do not allow for diversity in the concrete comes from treating human flourishing in a Platonic manner. There is no such thing as "human flourishing," apart from individual human flourishing.[4] The human good does not exist apart from the choices and actions of individual human beings, nor does it exist independent of the particular mix of goods that individual human beings need to determine as being appropriate for their circumstances. Individuals do more than provide loci at which human flourishing becomes spatially individuated; human flourishing becomes real, achieves determinacy, only when the individual's unique talents, potentialities, and circumstances are jointly employed. The specifics of these individually distinctive features of human flourishing are neither implied by nor included in an abstract account of human flourishing.

The individualized character of human flourishing requires that the problem of balancing and prioritizing virtues not be solved in an a priori manner. An abstract consideration of human nature does not tell one what the proper relation should be of one virtue to the other virtues and goods. The proper mixture of the necessary elements of human flourishing cannot be read off human nature like one reads the Recommended Daily Allowances for vitamins and minerals off the back of a cereal box.[5] Rather, this is a task for practical reason, and practical reason occurs only through individuals' confronting the contingent and particular facts of their concrete situation and determining at the time of action what about that situation is truly good for them. This does not, however, mean either that one can with moral impunity ignore any of the necessary virtues or goods of human flourishing, or that one course of action in the concrete situation is as good as the next. We are not pushed to conventionalism or subjectivism. It simply means that ethical rationalism is false and that one must be very careful in trying to find something that is common at the concrete level to all forms of human flourishing. Certainly, such virtues as integrity, courage, and justice do not suffice as the basis for a metanormative principle.

2. Instead of thinking of some intrinsic feature of human flourishing as the base for a metanormative principle, why not consider something that is extrinsic but that also seems completely neutral with respect to forms of flourishing? Why not consider money? Does not money provide the power to attain one's ends, regardless of what those ends might be? Money is a medium of exchange and store of value. As such, it does not favor one form of flourishing over any other. All people need the ability to attain the ends their well-being requires, and money, by and large, will allow them to do

so. Thus, at least a minimal transfer of money to those who are not as well-off as others might fit the criteria for being a metanormative principle. This seems true, especially if done in the right amounts. Cannot money be taken from some without significantly altering their projects and given to others in such a way that, because of money's neutral character, they are able to flourish in their own individualized way?

This suggestion is, however, mistaken in a number of ways. First, money as a medium of exchange and store of value is indeed neutral to the various forms of flourishing, but the value of a person's money to that person is not so neutral. The value of Jane's money to Jane is, for example, found in the particular way it is used by Jane in fashioning a worthwhile life. Thus, to take people's money from them without their consent is not to take some neutral value but to take the particular values they achieve and maintain by the use of their money.[6] It is precisely because money has no intrinsic value that the coercive transfer of Jane's money to someone else is, regardless of the amount taken, not neutral with respect to her well-being. A metanormative principle must, however, be based on something that is in principle consistent with the flourishing of each and every member of the political community.

Second, it is not the case that transferring people's money to others without their consent affects simply a minor or nonessential part of their lives. There is no economic side of life that exists in splendid isolation, separate from and unrelated to the rest of a person's life. Although economic activities do not (and should not) exhaust human action, economic factors affect everything a person does. There can be no pursuit of human flourishing that does not involve the exercise of practical reason in the creation, maintenance, and use of wealth. So, to control how a person will use his money is, in the words of F. A. Hayek, "not merely control of a sector of human life; it is the control of the means for all our ends. And whoever has sole control of the means must also determine which ends are to be served, what values are to be rated higher and which lower—in short what men should believe and strive for."[7] It is, therefore, the height of presumption (not to mention paternalism) to suppose that the expropriation of certain sums of money will have no impact on a person's projects.

Third, it is, of course, possible that people will use their money in a way that is foolish and improper. Also, some people might be better off if they had less money, just as some might be better off if they had more money. We do not for a moment assume that an important moral critique cannot be made regarding how some people use their money, or that there are not some who simply need more money in order to have a morally worthwhile life. However, we should not let these issues distract us. Our concern here is with the basis for a metanormative principle and whether anything other than self-direction can meet the criteria that metanormativity requires. We have already argued for the necessity of an ethical concept whose concern is not with persons attaining self-perfection, but only with securing a political context in which self-perfecting lives, in all their various forms, might be achieved. Though the nature of their relationship will be discussed in greater detail later in this essay, it is important to realize that the ultimate principles of politics and ethics do not have the same function and should not be confused. Ethics is not social management, and politics is not a guide for virtuous living.

3. Why should the right to equal negative liberty be the only metanormative principle? Rights are concerned with the conditions for interpersonal living, but are there not other ethical concepts that also have this concern? Particularly, does not the concept of justice have to do with how human beings should treat each other? Is this not a notion one needs to consider when talking about interpersonal principles? In fact, is not justice the ethical concept that covers both normative and metanormative issues, and might it not be that justice requires the ultimate principles of politics to be concerned with more than just protecting self-directedness?

These questions are very important, for they allow us to discuss more precisely in what sense human beings are social in nature, and in what sense metanormative principles are concerned with the interpersonal. Further, these questions afford us the opportunity to distinguish two different senses of "justice" and thereby to address a confusion in political philosophy that is nearly as old as philosophy itself.

Human beings cannot achieve moral maturation in isolation. Their fulfillment demands a life with others. This need to live with others must be expressed in some form; but, considered abstractly, it can be expressed in any. The specific form in which human sociality is expressed can be termed an "exclusive relationship." Exclusive relationships cover a continuum of relations—everything from close friends and confidants to business and work relations to mere acquaintances—but they all involve a principle of selectivity on the part of the participants in the relationship. Some people are included and others excluded from the relationship on the basis of some value(s) the participants share. It is through exclusive relationships that various types of groups, communities, and even cultures are formed.

Since human flourishing is individualized, however, the way or manner in which the need for sociality is expressed is not limited to some select pool or group of humans. Though nearly everyone starts life within a family, a community, a society, and a culture, this does not mean that one must be confined to only those relationships that constitute one's family, community, society, or culture. The forms of human sociality are not necessarily limited or closed to any human being. Human sociality can involve the exploration of relationships with new and different people and varied ways of living, working, and thinking. This open-ended character of human sociality leads us to describe the relationships that might develop as being "nonexclusive." No principle of selectivity is involved, for we are noting that human sociality, prior to a person's choice and selection, imposes no limitation regarding with whom and under what circumstances one may have a relationship. Further, nonexclusive relationships often provide the wider context in which exclusive relationships are formed, because many, if not most, exclusive relationships come about only because there was first a nonexclusive relationship.[8] Thus, human beings are social animals in the sense that, though there must be some set of exclusive relations through which one expresses one's sociality, there is no a priori exclusion of anyone from participation in those relations.

Not acknowledging that human sociality allows for an openness to strangers or human beings in general is sometimes thought to be one of the central failings of a self-perfectionist virtue ethics. It is claimed[9] that, even though our self-perfection involves other-concern, this concern always involves some principle of selectivity based upon some value(s) of one's own; despite the fact that these relationships involve various degrees of commitment, they remain exclusive. Indeed, it is true that self-perfectionist virtue ethics have tended to emphasize exclusive relationships[10] with others, but this does not by itself preclude a self-perfectionist ethics from acknowledging that human sociality involves nonexclusive relationships as well. Nothing about a self-perfectionist ethics requires denying that human sociality is open to relationships with strangers, foreigners, or people with whom no common values are yet shared. In fact, it would seem that acknowledging the nonexclusive feature of human sociality is one of the things meant by claiming that human beings are by nature social animals.[11] To identify a need for sociality, regardless of the social or cultural form it takes, is to speak of relationships in a nonexclusive sense.

Yet the nonexclusive side of human sociality does require that two senses of "justice" be distinguished. Justice can be understood as a metanormative principle and as a normative one. As a metanormative principle, it does not assume a shared set of values or commitments. Hence, the context is as universal as possible. It is only concerned that possible relationships among humans, each of whom has a unique form of human flourishing, be ethically compossible. The type of moral requirement imposed for establishing this context must be something everyone's form of flourishing requires and something that everyone can in principle fulfill. Such a moral requirement is by necessity minimal in character. As we have explained, the right to equal negative liberty is such a requirement. Therefore, "justice" in the metanormative sense—that is, understood in terms of the basic right to liberty—is concerned only with the peaceful and orderly coordination of activities of any possible human being with any other in a social setting.

Justice understood as the normative principle of giving others their due is one of the central virtues of human flourishing. This virtue is not confined to merely some set of negative obligations. Positive obligations are often required.[12] However, the proper application of the virtue of justice, like that of every other normative virtue, requires practical reason. Not only does one have to know what action in the contingent and particular situation is just, one also has to integrate the actions required by this virtue with those required by the other virtues and goods that constitute one's flourishing. What is needed is knowledge of circumstance, the other person's character, and how a possible course of action integrates with the other actions that one's self-perfection requires. Knowing what the virtue of justice requires does not come in neat ethical recipes, and it requires more knowledge than that one is in the presence of a fellow human being. Therefore, depending on whether one is dealing with a personal friend, a business partner, a next-door neighbor, or a man on the street who asks for some extra change, the virtue of justice requires different courses of action. As a normative principle, justice is not something that is applied in an impersonal or uniform way. It requires discernment of differences of both persons and circumstances.

Justice as a metanormative principle and justice as a normative principle have been confused.[13] This confusion is due to the failure to see the difference between justice that is concerned with exclusive relationships and justice that is concerned with nonexclusive relationships. Justice is, by definition, concerned with the interpersonal or social.[14] But justice considered as a constituent virtue of human flourishing is concerned with others in a far more specific way than when it is considered as a basis for a political order, in which all we know is that there are other human beings involved. Certainly, justice as a virtue needs to involve more than just a respect for someone's negative rights. Interpersonal or social life in an exclusive sense needs more than this. This is the truth of the communitarian and classical ethical perspective. Yet when interpersonal or social life is understood in a nonexclusive sense—that is, when we are concerned with relationships with *any* human being, with relationships that are often the context for exclusive relationships—then negative rights are just the sort of principle that is needed, for only the protection of a person's self-direction can be sufficiently universal. To require anything more of justice in this sense would not only romanticize our commitment to other fellow human beings; it would ignore the real personal basis each of us has for respecting rights: the need for social or interpersonal life in both the exclusive and nonexclusive senses. This is the basis for the truth of the natural rights classical liberal political perspective.

4. Despite all our efforts to link our defense of liberty to a strong moral framework, it seems our theory still faces a fundamental dilemma. On the one hand, if liberty is to be anything determinate and identifiable, it must mean more than the absence of external impediment. Liberty cannot be merely the ability to do what one wants. If liberty occurs only when one is able to do what one wants, then whose liberty is to be protected? Which is to be preferred: Mary's liberty to do what she wants unconstrained by Fred, or Fred's liberty to do what he wants unconstrained by Mary? Given that people have conflicting wants, as is frequently the case, what does it mean to promote liberty? Liberty needs some normative basis for determining its scope and content. Otherwise, it provides neither guidance in adjudicating situations where there are conflicts of wants, nor understanding of what it would be to promote liberty. Liberalism becomes a meaningless political ideal.[15]

On the other hand, if we tie liberty to a normative standard—if we link liberty with reason, with morality, with law—then how can one ever have a moral right to do what is not morally proper? If we, in other words, agree with Lord Acton that liberty is "liberty to do what we ought to do," it would seem that we can offer nothing more than pragmatic arguments against philosopher or theologian kings who wish to legislate nearly every matter of morality. There would especially be no principled rights-based limit on what matters of morality should be enforced. This would undercut our attempt to show that people have a fundamental right to equal negative liberty, which overrides all other moral concerns in determining the fundamental character of polity's political and legal institutions. So, either liberty is tied to morality, or it is a meaningless political ideal. But if liberty is tied to morality, then people cannot claim that they have a right in any principled sense to do what is not morally proper.

There is, however, a deep ambiguity in this dilemma, and it is similar to that found when we were discussing different senses of justice. Is the "ought" in the maxim, "liberty to do what we ought to do," really a guide to the individual in the conduct of his life, or is this "ought" directed more toward the requirements of the basic principles of a polity's legal system? In other words, could not "liberty to do what we ought to do" mean that liberty is defined in terms of what a polity's legal system ought to protect and sanction? The law would, then, not be opposed to liberty but would provide the institutional context for its very existence. And could not the principles used to determine what a polity's legal system ought to protect and sanction be principles whose aim and function is providing a political context for interpersonal living—rather than those that lead persons to self-perfection, e.g., the virtues?

In other words, could not the conception of rights that we have put forth be the ethical notion that gives scope and determinacy to the concept of liberty? As we have made clear, such a concept of rights does not have the function of helping persons achieve self-perfection or performing right conduct. Rather, its primary ethical aim is providing guidance in creating and evaluating political contexts. Rights provide ethical guidance in the creation of a political context for social life in which any and every one—regardless of how diverse their manner of self-perfection—might have the possibility to choose for themselves how they should live. Such an approach would not guarantee that people would even choose, let alone choose as they should, but it would nevertheless provide a link between—though not an identification of—ethics and politics.[16]

A New Foundation for Natural Rights Classical Liberalism

It is fashionable today to proclaim the death of liberalism as the political expression of the failed Enlightenment project. The doctrine of universal natural or human rights, for example, is said to be an Enlightenment abstraction that undermines the importance of community by ignoring the specific forms of connectedness that constitute our actual social being. Indeed, the general abstractness of liberal ethical and political theories is said to contribute to the impersonal and atomistic quality of those theories. The crisis of liberalism has generated a wave of antiliberal polemics and their incumbent solutions. These range from repackaged forms of socialism to certain types of conservatism that never were very comfortable being linked to liberalism. They all share in positing society as the basic unit of analysis and the determinant of every important principle in ethics and politics.

How closely connected does liberalism as a political theory need to be to other doctrines propounded by Enlightenment thinkers? This itself is a large and arguable issue, but one that is of no concern to this essay. What does concern us is that the political theory outlined above is decidedly liberal, but its self-perfectionist neo-Aristotelian ethics is not traditionally connected to liberalism. To some, therefore, it may appear as though we are trying to square the circle. From our perspective, however, both the appeal and failures of traditional liberalism are the predictable result of a problem shared equally by its proponents and its critics—namely, the failure to distinguish the normative and metanormative.

Liberalism has a tendency towards ethical skepticism, reductionism, or minimalism. Theories that are richer in ethical content tend towards political paternalism, socialism, or authoritarianism. The tendencies in both directions are the result of treating all ethically normative propositions as being of the same type with perhaps varying degrees of importance. When this is applied to liberal politics, where the role of the state is limited to enforcing only matters of rights or justice, the ethically significant comes to be identified with justice or with one's rights. All else is moved to the category of the supererogatory. Modern liberals, in contrast to their classical counterparts, feeling uncomfortable that moral matters such as helping the less fortunate are minimized or left out entirely, want to expand the list of rights. They want, in other words, to turn what might otherwise be merely a matter of personal discretion (the supererogatory) into a matter of justice or respecting rights. Yet however much these modern liberals may dominate the academy today, their overwhelming numbers do not make liberalism any more amenable to this sort of expansion of rights; and, in the end, the efforts to make all moral matters a species of justice contribute to the skepticism that inevitably results when rights are devoid of limitations. Justice simply is not the whole of ethics. Since it is close to the whole of politics for the liberal, it would seem that liberal politics would have to give way, if ethics is to have anything beyond minimal content. To abandon this sort of politics is, obviously, to give away liberalism itself. Thus, to maintain liberal politics, we must either keep our obligations to a minimum or be skeptical about any well-developed ethical palate.

The alternative of abandoning liberalism for a content-rich ethical politics is no less fraught with problems. Apart from any arguments implied above about the pluralistic character of the good, the politics of ethical assertiveness is simply out of step with modern realities. Modern states are too expansive and diverse to impose ethical programs by political means in any but an inefficient, acrimonious, expensive, litigious, and, in the end, ineffective manner. Thus, while everything from aiding the poor to healthy living may qualify as worthy ethical goals, the benefits of defining their exact meaning politically and the subsequent enforcement by (necessarily) large bureaucratic states is a recipe for conflict and subservience. This erosion of liberty—that upon reflection no one seems to want, but that everyone daily has an incentive to clamor for—is the result of failing to see that the norms appropriate for politics are not necessarily of the same order as those suitable for ethical life, and vice versa.

It is our contention that the Aristotelian ethic provides a content-rich ethical matrix for living one's life. This seems beyond dispute, although some may perhaps find other frameworks more compelling or complete. We also contend that liberalism is a politics of allowing the individual maximum freedom with minimal coercible obligations towards others. This, too, seems undisputed, even if there is some variation on what those obligations might be. Although we endeavor to join these two undisputed perspectives, rather than to abandon either liberalism or ethics, we acknowledge that the combination will not work without a clear understanding of the normative/metanormative distinction. It has thus equally been our contention that to fail to make this distinction leaves vulnerable that liberty necessary for civilized life.[17]

Notes

1. Douglas B. Rasmussen and Douglas J. Den Uyl, *Liberty and Nature: An Aristotelian Defense of Liberal Order* (LaSalle, Illinois: Open Court, 1991).

2. Ibid., 34, 70–75, 92–96. Douglas B. Rasmussen and Douglas J. Den Uyl, "Reply to Critics," *Reason Papers* 18 (Fall 1983), 120–121. See also Douglas J. Den Uyl, *The Virtue of Prudence* (New York: Peter Lang, 1991), 181–186. The term "volitional consciousness" is taken from Ayn Rand, but the concept is as old as Aristotle. See *De Anima*, II, 5.

3. See "Reply to Critics," 115–132 for our response to different but related objections.

4. See *Liberty and Nature*, 63–64, 89–93.

5. *The Virtue of Prudence*, 187–223.

6. This is not to mention the time and effort used to obtain this money.

7. F. A. Hayek, *The Road to Serfdom* (Chicago: University of Chicago Press, 1944), 92.

8. Cf. *Liberty and Nature*, 173–219, and *The Virtue of Prudence*, 243–250.

9. Julia Annas, *The Morality of Happiness* (New York: Oxford University Press, 1993), 250–252.

10. See, for example, Aristotle's discussion of friendships.

11. It may be the case that the communitarian interpretation of self-perfectionist virtue ethics cannot support the idea that human sociality involves a nonexclusive dimension.

12. See Douglas J. Den Uyl, "The Right to Welfare and the Virtue of Charity," in this volume.

13. They were confused by Plato when justice in the state was used as a model for determining justice in the soul. This confusion was increased by Aristotle's use of the term "polis" to mean a complex system of human relationships—involving everything from households and associations of families to a state defined as an association of citizens in a constitution. As a result, the difference between justice

that is concerned with exclusive and with nonexclusive relationships was never clearly recognized by Aristotle. The confusion of these two senses of justice was not confined to classic philosophers, however. Modernity tended to view ethics as social management (e.g., Hobbes's claim that ethical obligations only arise as a result of trying to find a way by which humans might live together), and Kant adopted what could be called a jurisprudential view of ethics where individual differences, differences that could not be universalized, were regarded as irrelevant to ethics or morality.

14. Hence, there is a redundancy when the term "social justice" is used.

15. See Douglas B. Rasmussen, "Liberalism and Natural End Ethics," *American Philosophical Quarterly* 27 (April 1990): 153.

16. In *Liberty and Nature*, 131–171, we argue that this conception of rights is just in what the common good of the political community consists. This view of the common good might in the final analysis be closer to Aquinas's view than is generally thought. After all, Aquinas does differentiate between matters of justice that are morally binding and matters of justice that are morally *and* legally binding. Further, he notes that the common good of the political community does not require that all vices be prohibited, since human law is framed for any person, and only vices that threaten social life itself, such as homicide and theft, should be prohibited. Also, such a view of the common good might be much closer to Aristotle's view than is generally thought. See Fred D. Miller Jr., *Nature, Justice, and Rights in Aristotle's* Politics (Oxford: Clarendon Press, 1995), chapter 6.

17. This essay has benefited from the assistance of Roger Bissell.

The Anarchism Controversy

Aeon J. Skoble

Libertarians spend a good portion of their time explaining why government needs to be severely limited in its scope. This activity is frequently met with the rejoinder that the logical consequence of this view is anarchism. This is, of course, intended as a reductio ad absurdum. Most libertarians at this point explain that the government's only proper role is in protecting people from force and fraud, but nothing else, thus conceding the point that if the logical consequence *were* anarchism, then there would indeed be something wrong with the view. Some libertarians, however, deny the attempted reductio. They reply that the reasoning does lead to anarchism, but that there is nothing wrong with that. This proves that not all libertarians agree about everything. It is one thing to argue that the state should be strictly limited in the scope of its powers in order to preserve individual freedom; it is quite another to argue that the state is essentially incompatible with individual freedom and that, therefore, no state should be permitted.

Not all anarchists derive their views from a radical extension of the principles of libertarianism. If we look at the history of anarchist thought, we notice that the individualist anarchists represent but one of several types of anarchism. Others have attempted to derive the same conclusion—that no government is justified—from premises more typical of socialist theory. From the 1840s to the 1860s, anarchism was largely associated with the same social-revolutionary movements that produced Marxism. Hence, we find Pierre Proudhon asking in 1840 "what is property?" and answering with the word "theft"—not the answer one would hear from a libertarian. Yet Proudhon did think that social arrangements should be based on voluntary contractual agreement. The differences between individualist anarchists and collectivist anarchists are sometimes difficult to ascertain with any specificity. Mikhail Bakunin advocated public ownership of the means of production, yet split with Marx over the issues of authority and liberty. In the 1890s, Peter Kropotkin echoed Marx's slogan "from each according to his ability, to each according to his needs," but saw the state as an agent of moral corruption. Max Stirner, on the other hand, was a radical individualist. A contemporary of Marx and Bakunin, Stirner rejected the very notion of society, advocating a loose union of egoists.

The difference seems to be this: some see anarchism as the logical result of the social nature of man, freely joining into collective, yet decentralized, associations. Others see anarchism as the extension of the priority of individual liberty. Perhaps unsurprisingly, the American anarchists tended to be of the individualist variety. From Josiah Warren in the 1850s to Lysander Spooner and Benjamin Tucker in the 1870s and 80s to Albert Jay Nock in the 1930s, the development of anarchism in America has been an integral part of libertarian history. The individualist ideals of these early writers formed part of an intellectual landscape where the ideas of liberty could be developed free from any neo-Hegelian notions of History's Progress. In American libertarian thought, the problem has not been so much whether individualism or collectivism formed the basis for anarchism, but whether the priority of individual liberty could be reconciled with a minimal state, or required its absence.

Robert Nozick opens his 1974 book *Anarchy, State, and Utopia* by writing

> Our main conclusions about the state are that a minimal state, limited to the narrow functions of protection against force, theft, fraud, enforcement of contracts, and so on, is justified; that any more extensive state will violate persons' rights not to be forced to do certain things, and is unjustified; and that the minimal state is inspiring as well as right. Two noteworthy implications are that the state may not use its coercive apparatus for the purpose of getting some citizens to aid others, or in order to prohibit activities to people for their *own* good or protection . . . . it is only coercive routes toward these goals that are excluded. . . .[1]

This is a commonly accepted and explicit statement of the libertarian position, that is, the position of libertarians who do support the minimal state. Of the three "main conclusions" Nozick lists, the second two are accepted by anarchist libertarians as well; it is the first that is denied. Consider for contrast the anarchist libertarian position set out by Murray Rothbard in his 1978 essay, "Society Without a State":

> I define anarchist society as one where there is no legal possibility for coercive aggression against the person or property of any individual. Anarchists oppose the state because it has its very being in such aggression, namely, the expropri-

ation of private property through taxation, the coercive exclusion of other providers of defense service from its territory, and all of the other depredations and coercions that are built upon these twin foci of invasions of individual rights.[2]

On this view, competing (private) providers of conflict resolution and security would serve many of the same functions that government agencies currently do.

The contrast is plain: both assign top priority to individual liberty, both recognize that political authority poses a potential threat to individual liberty, yet Nozick argues that, *nevertheless*, some minimal level of state activity is justified, whereas Rothbard argues that, *therefore*, no state is justified.

A libertarian anarchist and a libertarian statist will agree about the basic reasoning here: human freedom is of the highest priority with regard to political values, and coercion is detrimental to human freedom, therefore, coercion is something to be avoided where possible. The last part, "where possible," is what will make the two camps part company.

Minimal-state theorists and anarchist theorists share a rejection of coercion as a legitimate political activity. Nozick tells us at the beginning of *Anarchy, State, and Utopia* that "Since I begin with a strong formulation of individual rights, I treat seriously the anarchist claim that . . . the state must violate individuals' rights and hence is intrinsically immoral."[3] Nozick's criticism of taxation as being "on a par with forced labor"[4] is only a criticism since he believes forced labor to be an objectionable thing. We would notice the same underlying assumption if we were to consider why the following is meant to be a criticism of patterned schemes of distributive justice: "[N]o end-state principle or distributional patterned principle of justice can be continuously realized without continuous interference with people's lives."[5] Tibor Machan puts it this way in his *Individuals and Their Rights*: "*chosen* conduct of the agent that attains his or her happiness, is a vital element of the human happiness that a good human community ought to facilitate for all."[6] In *The Libertarian Idea*, Jan Narveson says that the "central libertarian complaint" is that "you have no choice but to deal with . . . the Government; and this is not in the sense that your particular Government is the only one that happened to be around, but rather that it was the only one *allowed* to be around."[7] In each case, the denial of autonomy, the abrogation of individual freedom, and the reduction or removal of choice through the use of force or its threat, is presumed to be something to be avoided, or at the very least that needs to be justified in some way.

The distinction between society, i.e., the state of affairs consisting in people living together, and the state, i.e., a political entity with a particular role and various powers, will be a crucial one. As we shall see, it is only certain features of the state that are objected to by anarchists, particularly the state's reliance on coercion. One question to ask, then, is whether or not coercion may be seen as an intrinsic feature of the state, and indeed, examining the concept of the state will make the anarchist objection to it quite clear.

Rothbard defines the state as having two distinct, defining, features.

> (1) [I]t acquires its income by the physical coercion known as "taxation"; and
> (2) it asserts and usually obtains a coerced monopoly of the provision of defense service (police and courts) over a given territorial area.[8]

Must all states have these characteristics of monopoly control and the use of coercion, or is it possible to have a state that does not? One answer is that states have these features by definition, so anything that lacked them would fail automatically to be a state. The more interesting answer is that something that was said to be a state, but was in fact *not* a coercively maintained monopoly of power, would not be the sort of state (or not enough of a state) to generate the objections of the anarchist. In other words, any social association that did not have those features would not be the sort of thing that an anarchist would object to, and if it is to be called a state anyway, then the word "anarchist" would need a new definition. In any event, existing states *do* have these two features. In Machan's view,

> the justification and need of government arises from the objective value to all members of society of living with others without . . . the general insecurity that goes with lawlessness. Individuals who recognize the value of social life readily acknowledge the value of establishing an agency to provide them with the protection and preservation of their rights in the context of a system of objective law.[9]

Government activities could therefore, theoretically, be provided on a fee-for-service basis. Since the government, on this view, is only in the business of adjudicating conflicts, protecting rights, and securing contracts, and since one could choose not to employ the government's services for most of these, funding for these activities could occur noncoercively, by having users of a service bear its costs. This state would still, according to Machan, have to bar others from offering the services the government offers, e.g., an alternative provider of rights protection. The idea of a feasible system of alternative providers of rights protection is what will divide minimal-state libertarians from the anarchists. But assuming Machan's arguments about the "natural" monopoly of government on conflict resolution are valid, then the state he describes would be as noncoercive as possible. This is not by itself a successful dismissal of the anarchist position. The anarchist argument is that although society is a good thing, coercion is a bad thing, and states as we know them essentially involve coercion. A state that employed no coercion, or as little as possible for society to exist, would not be the same state that antistatists are against. Indeed, the whole point of contention turns out to be over this last qualifier, that since just a little coercion is required for society to exist, therefore the minimal state is justified.

The important point, however, is that minimal-state libertarians regard state power as a thing that needs to be justified *because* of its coercive features. This is a conception shared with anarchists. We have seen that both statist libertarians and anarchist libertarians view the state as a political entity that essentially involves coercion, coercion is seen as detrimental to human freedom, and freedom is to receive the highest priority among political values when developing a theory. The anarchist criticism, then, is that *given* this view of coercion and state power, such a justification cannot be provided coherently. No state could possibly be legitimate on this view. The minimal-state response seems to be based on an implicit Hobbesian concern about the unfeasibility of a system of alternative providers of rights protection. Even libertarians who are supporters of the notion of private sanitation companies and private road ownership remain skeptical about the idea of private courts. The anarchist must attempt to allay this skepticism not by showing how markets are more efficient providers of goods and services generally, but by demonstrating that rights enforcement is not an exception.

The intuitive appeal of the minimal-statist's concern rests on the common sense of the claim that society would be impossible if we were all attacking each other. One of the crucial assumptions here goes back to Hobbes himself, the claim that covenants cannot provide security in the absence of some sort of enforcement mechanism. It seems clear enough that a recognizably civil society, one that permitted people to develop and pursue their ends and so on, would be impossible given the total war of all against all. What is problematic is the claim that the *state* is necessary in order to avoid this situation. If cooperation enforcement *can* be provided in the absence of political authority, then this Hobbesian worry is mistaken: political authority is not a necessary condition of society.

The primary consideration in Nozick's account of the minimal state is efficiency. According to him, the services of protection and conflict resolution would be provided more efficiently with the minimal state than without it, and thus the state is inevitable. He defends the extension of the right to individual self-defense to one of collective self-defense in the sense that many might collectively engage the same means of exercising their right to self-protection, which means it would be morally legitimate to pay other people or companies to protect us. Then Nozick (famously) explains how, as a matter of economic efficiency, one of these protective agencies would come to dominate the others (at least in a particular geographic area) through a noncoercive process of mergers and acquisitions. This "dominant protective agency" would then fit the standard definitions of a state, as that agency provides protection for all and monopolizes this service, but would also satisfy the "moral objections of the individualist anarchist"[10] because it arose in a way that did not violate anyone's rights. Competing services are not ruled out a priori; rather Nozick thinks that stability and other market conditions will generate the dominant protective agency. Nozick argues that it would not be rights-violating for this "de facto monopoly" to coerce payment for the services. Presumably he arrives at this conclusion because each of the smaller protection agencies was voluntarily funded, so the new "parent company" is not violating rights to exact payment after the "merger." The question, then, is whether or not coercion is involved *after* the formation of the dominant protective agency. If someone who, despite having voluntarily subscribed to one of the smaller companies, disliked the operation of the new dominant protective agency wanted to opt out, would this be permitted by the agency? Would he be entitled to secure this service from someone else? If the dominant protective agency must use coercion to bar market entry of competing services and may force dissenters to continue paying them, then Nozick is in error in claiming that no rights are being violated. (And if one *can* opt out of what is simply the largest provider of the service, then Nozick's vision will be indistinguishable from Rothbard's conception of a society without a state.)

The only remaining justification would be a concern that "permitting" entry into this market would mean that everyone's rights would be made less secure by the competition between protective agencies, and that therefore it is not wrong to prohibit this. Nozick develops this idea by arguing that these companies would be inclined to find their interests best served by preemptive attack, and that the known proclivity towards striking first when this seems advantageous would, at the least, weaken everyone's ability to protect their rights, and at worst destroy society.

> A protective agency dominant in a territory does satisfy the two crucial necessary conditions for being a state. It is the only generally effective enforcer of a prohibition on others' using unreliable enforcement procedures [i.e., independent enforcement] . . . . And the agency protects those nonclients in its terri-

tory whom it prohibits from using self-help enforcement . . . even if such protection must be financed (in apparent redistributive fashion) by its clients. It is morally required to do this by the principle of compensation, which requires those who act in self-protection in order to increase their own security to compensate those they prohibit from doing risky acts which might have turned out to be harmless [i.e., seeking independent enforcement] for the disadvantages imposed on them.[11]

Of course, it makes sense to argue that *if* the dominant protective agency may prohibit private enforcement on the grounds that its members feel that private enforcement is risky and makes them less secure, *then* the agency must compensate those so prohibited. But why should the dominant protective agency prohibit? Because, Nozick says, private enforcement entails not chaos, but the risk of chaos. "An independent might be prohibited from privately exacting justice because his procedure is known to be too risky and dangerous . . . or because his procedure isn't known not to be risky."[12] "Our rationale for this prohibition rests on the ignorance, uncertainty, and lack of knowledge of people. . . . Disagreements about what is to be enforced . . . provide yet another reason (in addition to lack of factual knowledge) for the apparatus of the state. . . ."[13] This rationale is clearly based on a Hobbesian concern about the instability of a system of competing providers of rights protection.

Tibor Machan's arguments for the justification of state authority anticipate the aforementioned anarchist criticism, so they predominantly involve criticism of anarchist theories. In *Human Rights and Human Liberties*, Machan's argument for the legitimacy of the state specifically addresses Murray Rothbard's arguments for individualist anarchism. The key to Machan's criticism of Rothbard involves the idea that a "morally legitimate" state would satisfy the anarchist's objections. Rothbard and Machan agree on what "morally legitimate" entails here, that is, they both recognize the importance of individual liberty and the objections it poses to state coercion. "Governmental authority can be morally proper only when strictly limited to the protection and preservation of human rights."[14] Rothbard's point (this argument is also made by Randy Barnett) is that the services of conflict resolution and protection against violence can be provided more efficiently, and in greater concert with libertarian values, on an open market.

Rothbard has argued that there is no such thing as a morally legitimate state, since all states rely for their power on coercion.

[If] no one may morally initiate physical force against the person or property of another, then [even] limited government has built within it . . . impermissible aggression. . . . All governments, however limited they may be otherwise, commit . . . fundamental crimes against liberty and private property.[15]

Machan counters this by claiming that there is such a thing as a morally legitimate state, and that states of this sort are defensible on grounds that Rothbard should accept. "What I am saying against Rothbard is that it is in their interest and people are entitled to establish moral governments, ones that protect and preserve human rights (only)."[16]

Machan allows that, historically, states have contained the objectionable features Rothbard describes, although they ought not to be defined in this manner because they might conceivably be established without these features.

> [W]e must acknowledge that Rothbard is here making something other than a historical claim about what governments have done. His contention is more general: there *could* not be a government that is not compulsory . . . . His reason is that any government must serve some given geographical area, which already renders it compulsory because some property owners who would prefer service from some other agency would not then be allowed to obtain it. But is this true? Would a government *have* to disallow secession?[17]

Machan's answer to this question is that the valid self-defense needs mentioned above might contractually rule out secession during specifically enumerated time periods, but that the government as a legitimate hired agent of legitimate self-protection could be "fired" if it proved unsatisfactory. Thus, the government must exist to protect human rights, but need not be coercive in the manner Rothbard objects to. Although "there must . . . exist a court of last resort," Machan writes,

> [I]t follows from the principles of human rights that action ought to be taken to institute their systematic protection and defense. If "government" is the concept best suited to designate such agencies, then it is morally justified for people to establish (hire) a proper government. It may be that those administering the laws will do a bad job, in which case one is morally obligated to alter or abolish (fire) those involved, provided terms are met for such disassociation.[18]

Actually, Machan allows for the possible efficiency of market-generated protection and arbitration services and shows a considerable interest in the idea of noncoercive funding for government activities. If there were a free market in these services, and they were funded noncoercively, that would indeed satisfy both Machan's and Rothbard's conception of moral legitimacy, but it would fail to be a "state" by our (or indeed most people's) definition. Machan's claims about implicit consent to just government come so close to being anarchistic that the distinction is hard to ascertain. Machan says that the implicit consent to be governed need not imply consent to taxation, because the services traditionally provided by governments that make governments desirable in the first place can be provided noncoercively. But this is *precisely* Rothbard's point: that services traditionally provided by the state need not be (and that realizing this helps delegitimize the state).

Despite this development with regard to most services normally associated with the state, Machan's primary worry seems to be the service of conflict resolution, the only one he cannot imagine emerging on the market. "Unless something on the order of a court of *final* authority exists, this [conflict resolution] is impossible in some cases, e.g., [when competing courts arrive at contrary decisions in a given case]."[19] This claim is certainly true. It is precisely this challenge that motivates recent work in anarchist thought, such as that of Randy Barnett and Bruce Benson.

The anarchists suggest hypothetical scenarios of how nonmonopolistic and noncoercively financed legal systems would operate. Their claims about the feasibility of these systems depend on whether the state is *necessary* for social order. Is it possible for cooperative structures to emerge spontaneously, without political authority and coercion?

According to recent research in game theory, cooperation is the social strategy that produces the most favorable outcome in the long run, even if everyone is primarily concerned with self interest. Libertarian statists argue that the state, although undesirable in general, is necessary to ensure that the minimal social cooperation necessary for society's existence is present. Libertarian anarchists argue that schemes of conflict resolution and security provision could arise without coercion because the minimal level of social cooperation postulated by the minimal state theorists is the level that would arise spontaneously as a result of people pursuing their self-interest. What seems to be an insoluble hypothetical dispute about the necessity of the state for the provision of cooperation can be mediated, I think, by looking at what the game theory research suggests. If the statist libertarians all have at their base something like the Hobbesian worry about the results of a lack of political authority, and this concern can be allayed, then the anarchist libertarians will have a much stronger position.

Many interpret the familiar "prisoner's dilemma" situation, a staple of decision theory, as an illustration of the necessity of political authority to ensure minimal social cooperation. Here is a prisoner's dilemma:[20]

		B	
		cooperate	defect
A	cooperate	A = 3, B = 3	A = 0, B = 5
	defect	A = 5, B = 0	A = 1, B = 1

From A's point of view, if B is going to cooperate, A ought to choose defection, because this secures a higher payoff. On the other hand, if B is going to defect, A minimizes his (A's) penalty by choosing defection. In other words, it is rational for A to defect regardless of how B is expected to behave. However, B is in precisely the same situation relative to A. If both defect, the payoff to both is less than if both had cooperated. So both parties, acting quite rationally, end up in a worse situation than they might have, for mutual cooperation would result in a higher payoff for both. In a Hobbesian argument, the sovereign is necessary to foster cooperation; that is, to make sure that "players" (citizens) cooperate and therefore secure the more optimal "payoff" (mutual security). On this model, authorizing state coercion is in one's best interest, and this *is* the justification.

The question, then, is whether cooperation can evolve spontaneously, i.e., without being imposed by a coercive entity such as a state. In his 1984 book *The Evolution of Cooperation*, Robert Axelrod describes a computerized "tournament" to test the long-term success of different strategies for winning at the prisoner's dilemma (where "winning" is maximizing payoff not once, but over a long period).[21] The outcome of several repetitions of the tournament was a clear victory for a strategy he calls "tit-for-tat." Tit-for-tat attempts to foster cooperation while retaining a capacity to "punish" when other players refuse to cooperate. The method is deceptively simple: cooperate on the first round, and then on each subsequent round do whatever the other player did in the previous round. Thus, higher payoffs were secured overall. No other strategy did as well. For instance, purely selfish "players" who chose defection every round did not fare as well as "players" who attempted to foster cooperation.

Naturally, the winning strategy in a one-shot prisoner's dilemma is to defect. The point is that most of the life situations that are thought to resemble a prisoner's dilemma are iterated (repeated) versions of the game, in which case the "winning strategy" turns out to be to develop the sort of responsive cooperation that Axelrod describes.

Since Axelrod's influential work was first published, further experimentation has provided some interesting developments. Recently, Martin Nowak and Karl Sigmund have demonstrated greater success with a different strategy, one that outperforms tit-for-tat. It turns out that this new strategy, which they named Pavlov, also indicates that responsive cooperation of the sort described by Axelrod is indeed the most robust.

> The Prisoner's Dilemma is the leading metaphor for the evolution of cooperative behaviour in populations of selfish agents, especially since the well-known computer tournaments of Axelrod and their application to biological communities. In Axelrod's simulations, the simple strategy of tit-for-tat did outstandingly well and subsequently became the major paradigm for reciprocal altruism. . . . Pavlov's success is based on two important advantages over tit-for-tat: it can correct occasional mistakes and exploit unconditional cooperators.[22]

The Pavlov strategy is "smarter" than tit-for-tat in that simple tit-for-tat cannot correct a "misunderstanding" between players. Since tit-for-tat involves simply repeating the other player's previous move, tit-for-tat is reactive. It tries to foster cooperation by initiating it, but thereafter is stuck with responding. So if the other player is "dumb," that is, will not respond to tit-for-tat's attempt to cooperate, and defects, then tit-for-tat must defect. If both players are oriented towards tit-for-tat, but one makes a mistake, a cycle of mutual defection will result. Pavlov can adjust based on previous favorable or unfavorable outcomes by cooperating after securing higher payoffs and defecting after lower payoffs (Nowak and Sigmund call this "win-stay, lose-shift"). Thus errors are corrected quickly. Although Pavlov is more robust than tit-for-tat, Axelrod's main point is not challenged, but is in fact supported by these new findings, namely, that responsive cooperation is an effective strategy for maximizing self-interest. If this is so, it is less clear that political authority is necessary to bring about cooperation. The social cooperation that is deemed necessary by minimal-statism is the sort of cooperation that would have to develop naturally if it is the sort of cooperation that is represented by the iterated dilemma.

Another way to interpret the game-theoretic justification for political authority might lead one to question the accuracy of what it portrays. There are other historical counter-examples to what the argument claims would be the result of a lack of political authority. First of all, we might keep in mind the "international relations" objection to the claim. Upon reflection, one realizes that individual nation-states *are* in the Hobbesian state of nature relative to each other, there being no world government, and yet the world is not in a perpetual state of war of all against all. Countries work out tit-for-tat-like or Pavlov-like cooperative strategies (more often than not). Michael Taylor makes this point in his 1987 book *The Possibility of Cooperation*. Although Hobbes did not apply to the international "state of nature" the analysis he made of the domestic one, Taylor argues, "there is no reason in principle why such an application should not be made. . . . [So] the possibility of conditional cooperation amongst states in the absence of [a] supranational state has been taken more seriously in the last few years" regarding the possibility of cooperation generally.[23] Barnett also makes this observation: "The argument that we need court systems with geography-based jurisdictional monopolies does not stop at the border of a nation-state. Any such argument suggests the need for a single world court system . . . . After all, the logic of the argument against a competitive legal order applies with equal force to autonomous nations."[24]

We have seen that Nozick argues that the dominant protective agency can prohibit private enforcement of justice because allowing it entails risks that threaten the security of its clients. Since one has a right, on Nozick's account, to prevent others from engaging in risky behavior that could decrease one's security, one has a right to authorize another to do this on one's behalf. But does it follow from this that one has a right to forbid others from joining other protective associations? Nozick himself brings up this question in order to respond to it in advance. His answer seems to undermine his own argument, however.

> We have found a distinction, which appears to be theoretically significant, that distinguishes a protective agency's forbidding others from using unreliable or unfair procedures to exact justice on its clients from other prohibitions—such as forbidding others to form another protective agency—which might be thought to be allowable if the first is. . . . [But we] have rebutted the charge we imagined earlier that our argument fails because it "proves" too much, in that it provides a rationale not only for the permissible rise of a dominant protective association, but also for this association's forcing someone not to take his patronage elsewhere or for some person's forcing others not to join any association. *Our argument provides no rationale for the latter actions and cannot be used to defend them.*[25]

If the argument does not provide a justification for the dominant protective association forbidding individuals from opting out, then Nozick has no argument for the state other than that the minimal state *could* arise without violating anyone's rights. However, he views this development as more than simply logical possibility. He argues that the minimal state is actually justified as a matter of collective decision making. As we have seen, Nozick argues that the dominant protective agency is justified in prohibiting people from seeking other means of settling disputes on the grounds that it would be too risky to permit such actions. Although he describes the fair (i.e., non-rights-violating) procedures that would most likely be followed by the dominant protective agency, he must believe that no competitive set of such agencies could be fair and feasible. In fact, his dismissal of Rothbard's proposal for just such a system indicates this:

> Rothbard imagines that somehow, in a free society, "the decision of any two courts will be considered binding, i.e., will be the point at which the court will be able to take action against the party adjudged guilty." . . . Why is anyone who has not in advance agreed to such a two-court principle bound by it? Does Rothbard mean anything other than that he expects agencies won't act until two independent courts (the second being an appeals court) have agreed?[26]

In fact, it is precisely Rothbard's point that the sensible thing to expect is that the agencies would only act after the adjudicating was complete, and that a likely arrangement would be one in which the various courts of which one might be a "client" would have prearranged means for resolving *their* disputes. Do we have any reason to think the companies would seek this (cooperative) type of a solution, rather than resorting to violent conflict? According to Axelrod's research, we do have some reason for thinking this is plausible. Here we have a clear example of how the insights from game theory might support the position of an anarchist criticism of Nozick, specifically the one found in Randy Barnett's work.

Legal systems in our society involve monopolistic institutions, such as a court system and a police force. Unsurprisingly, these tend to be inefficient and susceptible to corruption, and, more to the point, they are coercive. Barnett thinks that a legal order need not involve any monopolistic institutions, and that doing without them better promotes justice, without sacrificing individual liberty. According to Barnett, Nozick's "invisible-hand" justification for the state does not match Nozick's own values as well as it could, because his conception of a legal system, that is, a system providing for redress of grievances and torts, does not need to be monopolistic or coercive.

In his 1970 book *Power and Market*, one of Rothbard's arguments against a state-based conception of property rights is that the principles operative in a free society in the first place are ones that provide a theory of property rights already, namely, self-ownership and ownership of resources transformed by one's labor. This is (obviously) Lockean, and Rothbard thinks that this Lockean conception means that the state is not necessary to define or allocate property rights. In any case, it means that statist libertarians should not be relying on the premise that the state is needed to define property rights.

Rothbard suggests that we reexamine the Hobbesian concern, present even in libertarians, with an irreverent attitude.

> Suppose, for example, that we were all suddenly dropped down on the earth *de novo* and that we were all then confronted with the question of what societal arrangements to adopt. And suppose then that someone suggested: "We are all bound to suffer from those of us who wish to aggress against their fellow men. Let us then solve this problem of crime by handing all of our weapons to the Jones family, over there, by giving all of our ultimate power to settle disputes to that family. In that way, with their monopoly of coercion and of ultimate decision making, the Jones family will be able to protect us from each other." I submit that this proposal would get very short shrift, except perhaps from the Jones family themselves. And yet this is precisely the common argument for the existence of the state.[27]

Reading "the sovereign" for "the Jones family," we see Rothbard's parody of Hobbes' argument here. But then the question remains of which societal arrangements to adopt. Rothbard suggests that we adopt not *a* system of conflict resolution, but several. We have already seen, for example in Machan, that any such suggestion will be challenged by the need to have a final arbiter of disputes if chaos is to be avoided. But Rothbard's response, that a spontaneously arising competitive legal system would be stable, is more plausible in light of Axelrod's conclusion that cooperation is the stronger social strategy, even for self-interested agents. This makes sense as long as there is sufficient social cooperation to allow the different enforcement agencies to develop strategies of coexistence that would not be chaotic. But according to Axelrod and the others, this condition can be met.

Barnett and Rothbard describe similar schemes whereby conflict resolution, conceived of as another service more efficiently provided on a market, is provided without a coercive authority, that is, by consent. The state, even when organized by majority rule, has free reign to violate the consent of the minority.

Barnett says that with regard to crime prevention, the problem of commons, i.e., the conception of parks and streets, etc., as being held in common, has an adverse effect on crime prevention for two main reasons: there is no right to exclude, since it "belongs to" everybody; and little incentive to commit resources to assist in crime prevention, since it is thought of as having already been paid for.[28] This is a necessary feature of statist society.

> When property rights are ill-defined, misallocations of resources will occur. If a particular resource is held in common . . . then no person has the right to exclude others from using the resource. Without the right to exclude, it is

unlikely that the benefits accruing to persons who privately invest in the care or improvement of a resource will exceed the costs of their efforts . . . . For this reason, commonly held resources are typically overused and undermaintained.[29]

Barnett sees law enforcement as, at least partly, a "commons" problem, creating adverse effects on the state's ability to prevent crime. A statist society that values freedom, for example, a libertarian state, has to deny government police agencies the rights to regulate public property that private property owners enjoy. "Yet steps taken to protect society from the government also serve to make citizens more vulnerable to criminally inclined persons by providing such persons with a greater opportunity for a safe haven on the public streets. . . ."[30] Barnett argues that the only way to resolve this dilemma while preserving freedom is to adopt a robust approach to property rights and to permit competing agencies to provide adjudication and enforcement services.

The protective agencies, Barnett argues (with Rothbard), have market-generated incentives to respect the "rights of the accused" that monopoly police agents do not have; and also that competing "conflict resolution specialists" (judges) have market incentives to be fair in their decision making that monopoly judges do not have. According to Barnett, this will mean that violations of (compossible) rights will have a venue for redress without a coercive state where such a venue would not in the process violate the rights of the innocent, particularly by not being coercively funded.

Bruce Benson makes a similar point when he argues that "The arguments for public provision of law and its enforcement are largely 'market failure' arguments, which imply that the private sector will not efficiently produce law and order. The implicit assumption underlying [this] . . . is that when the market fails, government can do better."[31] Free riding is possible, he says, but "we can expect that contractual arrangements will evolve that exclude free riders from the benefits of reciprocally organized protection arrangements, as they did in [e.g.] Anglo-Saxon England."[32]

This is a crucial observation by Benson: that arguments for the justification of the state based on an economist's conception of market failure to provide conflict resolution or rights protection (or any other service, for that matter) assume that governments will provide the service flawlessly and without corruption. Rothbard has assailed this pattern of argumentation: ". . . it is illegitimate to compare the merits of anarchism and statism by starting with the present system as the implicit given and then critically examining only the anarchist alternative."[33] Do governments in the real world provide services efficiently and uncorruptly, or are there moral and pragmatic difficulties with the manner in which governments operate? One cannot use the necessity of the state as a premise and as a conclusion.

So what actually are the "checks and balances" that Rothbard, Barnett, and Benson think will make a nonmonopolistic legal system work? Private courts would, on this model, depend for their success on a reputation for fairness and objectivity. What machinery ensures this? The normal operation of a system like this provides a finite number of scenarios. If Jones and Smith are in dispute, and both are clients of Adjudication Service A, or Court A, then both will have previously agreed to be bound by its decision. If Smith is a client of Court A, and Jones is a client of Court B, then there are more possibilities (although still finite). In this case, if both Court A and Court B agree that Smith's case (or Jones') is the more meritorious, then both parties will have previously agreed to respect the result. The troubling scenario is the one in which Court A finds for Smith and Court B finds for Jones (or the other way around, I suppose). But as long as Court A and Court B have a prior arrangement to have *their* disputes resolved by some third adjudication service, the situation might not be so troubling after all. In this case, the decision of two of the three adjudicators makes the decision. There is still room for trouble. Suppose Smith, upon the decision of Courts B and C that he is in the wrong, decides to violate his prior agreement to abide by such a decision. What mechanisms could exist to respond to this? One possibility is that Smith would be dropped from the protection service that is part of agreeing to all this. The fear of losing his protective service would operate as an incentive on Smith to "behave." Being dropped from a protective service in this manner would have the same effect on his ability to engage other protective services as failure to make car payments has on obtaining credit from other lenders. Cooperation in this respect at least can be accounted for by self-interest, as Axelrod suggests. Repeatedly reneging on agreements such as these would be like defecting in an iterated prisoner's dilemma: an unsuccessful strategy. Indeed, Barnett makes a passing reference to Axelrod in the following passage, in which he (Barnett) offers his answer to the fear that the competing systems would war with each other:

> Extended conflict between competing court systems is quite unlikely. It is simply not in the interest of repeat players (and most of their clients) to attempt to obtain short-run gains at the cost of long-run conflict. Where they have the opportunity to cooperate, in even the most intense conflicts—warfare, for example—participants tend to evolve a "live and let live" philosophy [Barnett's footnote here is to Axelrod]. . . . How much greater the incentive to cooperate would be if competing judicial services did not have access to a steady stream of coercively obtained revenue—that is, by taxation.[34]

This is Barnett's only mention of Axelrod, but clearly, the more one looks into Axelrod's work on cooperation, the more plausible Barnett's claims about cooperation become. When first reading Rothbard or Barnett on competing agencies of adjudication and enforcement, one's intuitions will either accept the claims as sensible or generate objections about whether such systems would break down. The game-theory material can help Barnett and Rothbard persuade readers of the latter disposition.

Nor is free riding a substantial worry, according to David Schmidtz:

> People would not be able to free ride on the general deterrent effect of other people's contributions for contract enforcement because the deterrent effect would be relevant only to those who have paid to become subject to it. If Jane's contract makes no arrangements for its own enforcement, the upshot is not that the level of enforcement suffers a light drop but rather that the *scope* of enforcement is not extended to protect Jane; Jane's contract is not enforced. . . . The paradigmatically emergent justification for [the use of force involved in enforcement of mutually agreeable contracts] is based on actual consent.[35]

While Rothbard and Barnett (merely) theorize that mechanisms like this would maintain social order, there is actually historical precedent for this sort of conflict resolution system. According to Terry Anderson and P. J. Hill,[36] during the settlement period in the American West, before federal power had extended into the territories, conflicts were resolved by exactly the sort of "private courts" that Rothbard and Barnett envision: "[A]rbitration came from a 'private court' consisting of 'three disinterested men,' one chosen by each side and a third chosen by the two. . . . Competition rather than coercion insured justice."[37] The wagon trains, mining camps, and frontier towns apparently maintained a considerable degree of social order and respect for persons and property prior to the arrival of federal power. Indeed, in each case Anderson and Hill cite, social order actually decreased after monopolistic justice arrived.

> [I]n five of the major cattle towns (Abilene, Ellsworth, Wichita, Dodge City, and Caldwell) for the years from 1870 to 1885, only 45 homicides were reported—an average of 1.5 per cattle-trading season. In Abilene, supposedly one of the wildest of the cow towns, "nobody was killed in 1869 or 1870." . . . Only two towns, Ellsworth in 1873 and Dodge City in 1876, ever had five killings in any one year.[38]

Surprising statistics like these suggest that the popular image of the "shoot-em-up" Wild West lifestyle is largely without basis in fact. In addition, the statistics are less surprising in light of what we learned from Axelrod about the stability of spontaneously evolved social cooperation when the disposition to respond reciprocally to "defection" is generally understood. Anderson and Hill's historical findings, like Benson's, fit Axelrod's theoretical framework neatly.

Anderson and Hill suggest that social order was maintained in "anarchistic" ways partially because of certain points of "commonality that exist . . . in the minds of the participants in some social situation."[39] Without making extravagant claims about human nature, it seems sensible that this sort of general agreement is what facilitates social cooperation in the absence of a political enforcement mechanism. "Thus when a miner argued that a placer claim was his because he 'was there first,' that claim carried more weight than if he claimed it simply because he was most powerful."[40]

This conception of points of general agreement would account for many examples of nonmonopolistic, consensual means of conflict resolution: the development of the English Common Law and Law Merchant prior to the consolidation of these by the crown, the Middle Eastern merchant associations, and the civil law in medieval Iceland and Ireland. The history of the development of law shows that socially emergent conceptions of legal principles—for example, that one is innocent until proven guilty—occur prior to their adoption by the political authority.

Benson explains why this is the case:

> The attributes of customary legal systems include an emphasis on individual rights because legal duty requires voluntary cooperation of individuals through reciprocal arrangements. Such laws and their accompanying enforcement facilitate cooperative interaction by creating strong incentives to avoid violent forms of dispute resolution. . . . Thus, the law provides for restitution to victims arrived at through clearly designed participatory adjudication procedures, in order to both provide incentives to pursue prosecution and to quell victims' desires for revenge. Strong incentives for both offenders and victims to submit to adjudication as a consequence of social ostracism or boycott sanctions, and legal change occurs through spontaneous evolution of customs and norms.[41]

Benson's hypothesis explains both why the customary law, developed from the "bottom up," is typically accepted by most people and why law imposed from the top down frequently is not. Benson arrives at this conclusion after noticing the extent to which Anglo-Saxon common law depended upon a conception of legal duty not rooted in imposed political power but in mutual benefit. Again, the insights we glean from Axelrod's findings make these arguments more plausible.

The conclusion one is directed towards by the theorizing of Rothbard and Barnett and the examples cited by Anderson and Hill and Benson is that law ought to be construed as a natural consequence of the people's attempts to live and work together, and that it is something that, although necessary for society, does not presuppose a coercive monopoly of power.

The fundamental dispute, then, appears to be centered around what form the final arbiter for conflict resolution takes, since all agree that some such mechanism is necessary, and what sorts of social institutions will adequately provide the mechanisms for such conflict resolution, since all concerned agree that this, if not centralized political authority, is a necessary condition of society. The divide between minimal-state libertarians and anarchist libertarians is not due to serious disagreements about values, but rather to an intuition gap concerning practical matters. It remains a live controversy.

Notes

1. Robert Nozick, *Anarchy, State, and Utopia* (New York: Basic Books, 1974), ix.
2. Murray Rothbard, "Society Without a State," *Nomos* 19, (1978): 191–92
3. Nozick, *Anarchy, State, and Utopia*, xi.
4. Nozick, *Anarchy, State and Utopia*, 169.
5. Nozick, *Anarchy, State, and Utopia*, 163.
6. Tibor Machan, *Individuals and Their Rights* (LaSalle, Illinois: Open Court, 1989), xiv.
7. Jan Narveson, *The Libertarian Idea* (Philadelphia: Temple University Press, 1988), 211.
8. Rothbard, "Society Without a State," 191.
9. Tibor Machan, "Dissolving the Problem of Public Goods," *The Libertarian Reader*, ed. Tibor Machan (Totowa, New Jersey: Rowman and Littlefield, 1982), 204.
10. Nozick, *Anarchy, State, and Utopia*, 114.
11. Nozick, *Anarchy, State, and Utopia*, 113–14.
12. Nozick, *Anarchy, State, and Utopia*, 88.
13. Nozick, *Anarchy, State, and Utopia*, 140–41.
14. Tibor Machan, *Human Rights and Human Liberties* (Chicago: Nelson-Hall, 1975), 146.
15. Murray Rothbard, "Will Free Market Justice Suffice—Yes," *Reason* (March 1972): 19.
16. Machan, *Human Rights and Human Liberties*, 152.
17. Machan, *Human Rights and Human Liberties*, 148.
18. Machan, *Human Rights and Human Liberties*, 151.
19. Tibor Machan, "Individualism and the Problem of Political Authority," *The Monist* 63 (October 1983): 523.

20. R. D. Luce and Howard Raiffa, *Games and Decisions* (New York: Wiley, 1957).

21. Robert Axelrod, *The Evolution of Cooperation* (New York: Basic Books, 1984).

22. Martin Nowak and Karl Sigmund, "A Strategy of Win-Stay, Lose-Shift that Outperforms Tit-for-Tat in the Prisoner's Dilemma Game," *Nature* 364 (1 July 1993): 56.

23. Michael Taylor, *The Possibility of Cooperation* (Cambridge, England: Cambridge University Press, 1987), 166.

24. Randy Barnett, "Pursuing Justice in a Free Society, Part II," *Criminal Justice Ethics* (Winter/Spring 1986): 42.

25. Nozick, *Anarchy, State, and Utopia*, 129, emphasis added.

26. Nozick, *Anarchy, State, and Utopia*, 343.

27. Rothbard, "Society Without a State," 195.

28. Barnett, "Pursuing Justice," 32.

29. Barnett, "Pursuing Justice," 31.

30. Barnett, "Pursuing Justice," 33.

31. Bruce Benson, *The Enterprise of Law* (San Francisco: Pacific Research Institute, 1990), 271.

32. Benson, *The Enterprise of Law*, 276.

33. Rothbard, "Society Without a State," 195.

34. Barnett, "Pursuing Justice," 41.

35. David Schmidtz, *The Limits of Government* (Boulder: Westview, 1991), 98–99.

36. Terry Anderson and P. J. Hill, "An American Experiment in Anarcho-capitalism," *Journal of Libertarian Studies* 3 (no. 1), 1979.

37. Anderson and Hill, "An American Experiment," 25.

38. Anderson and Hill, "An American Experiment," 14.

39. Anderson and Hill, "An American Experiment," 12.

40. Anderson and Hill, "An American Experiment," 12.

41. Benson, *The Enterprise of Law*, 36.

Part Two

Social Problems in a Free Society

Introduction

The aim of government for the libertarian is the protection of individual rights, and seeing to this goal both determines and limits what government should embark upon. Judicial, police, and military functions would be included as government responsibilities, but no room would be left for running the post office, maintaining "public" broadcasting, preserving national forests, establishing beaches, preserving historical buildings, setting up a social security system, or even providing disaster relief. What is classified within the realm of bona fide public affairs pertains only to what people face because they are in the community of other people, mostly unfamiliar, who may undertake hostile, aggressive actions. That is the correct scope of government, so it can do its proper job without violating the very principles this job is meant to uphold.

Since even the governments of the most libertarian bent have, to date, never quite confined themselves to such a minimal role in community affairs, since most people expect governments to do so much more than the libertarian considers proper, the question needs to be addressed of how a free society, as libertarians understand it, will deal with tasks often, albeit inappropriately, handled by governments. Schools, medical care, remedying unemployment, controlling environmental degradation, maintaining culture, rectifying social wrongs such as racism and sexism, etc., have all been deemed proper tasks of government by many who are far from champions of some kind of totalitarian or authoritarian system of state. How does the libertarian envision taking care of such matters in a free and decent society?

This is what the present section addresses. We have collected contributions to this section that exemplify the point that noncoercive approaches to essentially peaceful tasks in human communities are possible as well as proper. Obviously, not every such concern can be addressed—we have picked those that seem to us pressing and most challenging to libertarian theory. The general idea, however, is the same: in a free society, the government ought to function as the protector of individual rights, and every other task ought to be addressed by individuals and various companies of individuals without invoking any kind of coercion, not even taxation. This is not, as some claim, blind ideology or rationalist political thinking, but a principled approach to public affairs in terms of which significant matters of social and personal life are off-limits to coercive power. The libertarian sees the right to liberty of all individuals no less in need of principled protection than the feminist sees a woman's body as not subject to occasional aggressive intrusion, so now and then rape or other types of assault might be acceptable—as if one needed "to take such cases one at a time to see whether they might have merit." No, and neither is this the case with the other basic rights of individuals, including that to what they produce or what they make of their lives, be it good or bad.

Rights, Just War, and National Defense[1]

Eric Mack

> I believe that it is possible for modern war to be waged within the limits set by the laws of morality. [But if] anyone were to declare that modern war is necessarily total, and necessarily involves direct attack on the life of innocent civilians, . . . my reply would be: So much the worse for modern war. If it necessarily includes such means, it is necessarily immoral itself.
>
> —John C. Ford[2]

1. The Political Morality of the Free Society

Each individual is a moral end-in-himself and each individual's moral standing as an end-in-himself is manifest in his possession of moral rights over his life, his liberty, his labor, and his justly acquired property. These are rights that all other people and institutions are obligated to respect. To affirm these general natural rights (and the more specific rights that may arise through the exercise of general rights) is to recognize the moral sovereignty of each person. It is to recognize that each person is his own person. To deny these rights is to assert that, at least in some respects, individuals are to be viewed and treated as objects available for the use of others. To deny these rights is to assert that, at least to some degree, persons are natural servants or slaves of others.

These rights to life, liberty, one's own labor, and property, if coherently interpreted, are all negative rights. They only imply that others are obligated to leave the right-holders in peaceful enjoyment of their rights. Negative rights do not impose upon others positive obligations to provide the right-holders with any particular goods or services or any level of income or utility. Persons can and usually do *acquire* an array of specific positive rights, e.g., rights to this good from B or that service from B*. Thus, B may bestow a positive right upon A by freely promising to provide A with a particular good or by voluntarily placing A in a situation in which A will suffer grievous injury unless B provides A with certain assistance (as when B lowers nonconsenting A down a well or brings A*, a helpless newborn, into the world). In the absence of such special voluntary acts by B, A has no rights against B except her negative rights to her life, liberty, labor, and duly acquired property.[3]

A free society is one in which everyone's natural and acquired rights are respected. There are no "higher" ends beyond the individual and his rights, such as the aggregate happiness, the prestige of the presidency, or global order that can authorize the infringement of these rights. If political and legal institutions have any legitimate authority, they have the strictly limited authority to secure the rights of those individuals on whose behalf they claim to have authority. By securing these rights, political and legal institutions sustain a framework within which individuals, families, and other associations can pursue their respective ends either singly or in voluntary cooperation.

While the natural rights to life, liberty, and property are negative rights, which merely require that others forego trespass upon them, the right to *the protection of these rights by others* is itself a positive right. Such a positive right can come into existence only through voluntary actions performed by the individuals or agencies bound to satisfy it. Since there has been no general agreement among members of this society to bestow positive rights to protection upon individuals or groups in other societies, neither individuals at large within this society nor this society's government have any obligation to protect the rights of those foreign individuals or groups. Nor do we nor our government violate any rights in declining to expand the protection of rights to those foreign individuals or groups.[4] Thus, it cannot be part of the mandate of a duly limited government to protect the rights of other peoples, however worthy their protection is of our individual, freely chosen, support.

Since large-scale defensive activity requires resources, and resources come from people and do not (for the most part) grow on trees, and individuals are not naturally bound to supply others with these resources, we cannot avoid questions about how defensive systems may permissibly be staffed and funded. The general answer is that people may be called upon to contribute only what they have freely agreed to contribute, as in the staffing or funding of any other mutual endeavor. But have we agreed to (or otherwise voluntarily incurred) obligations to staff or fund our society's military structure? It seems not. Moreover, the tacit or hypothetical agreements that some philosophers appeal to are not worth the paper they are not written on. So one striking implication (or apparent implication) of our fundamental rights is the moral impermissiblity of coercing individuals, through taxation, to pay even for their common defense.

A fully free society would finance national-scale defense voluntarily, presumably in large part through the sale of this protection to individuals and associations who would remain legally free not to purchase this service. The special problem with such voluntary financing is that national-scale defense is, in the technical economic sense, a public good. It is a good the enjoyment of which cannot feasibly be withheld from anyone within a given area if it is produced at all. Since particular individuals do not face the likelihood of being denied national-scale defense should they decline to purchase it, the normal direct incentive to purchase the good is absent. This may lead to so few people offering to pay for the good that it will not be produced even though (nearly) all would be better off securing defense at some financial cost to themselves. The public goods problem is not that some will free-ride on the services financed by others, but that certain of commonly beneficial services will not be funded at all (or will be greatly underfunded). A complete vindication of the ideal of a free society must address this issue. It must indicate how, by noncoercive means, the incentives of individuals can be structured so as to generate sufficient voluntary support for public goods such as national-scale defense or must explain why, contrary to appearances, coercive taking to finance the good of defending rights does not truly contravene libertarian strictures.[5]

Fortunately, the problem of financing a defense system in a manner compatible with a free society can be set aside for the purposes of this essay. This is because we can distinguish between the justice of military policies and actions and the justice of their financing. No matter what our judgment about the funding of military forces, we must independently inquire about the justice of their deployment and use. Nevertheless, there is one implication of the libertarian understanding of people's rights that is so direct and manifest that it cannot be put aside. This is the impermissibility of conscription and all measures preparatory to conscription, such as mandatory registration. Conscription is a form of involuntary servitude. It can be acceptable only to those who deny that people are moral ends-in-themselves or who make a fantastic appeal to tacit or hypothetical consent or to some nonconsensual process by which individuals are supposed to have become indebted to society or to the state. It has often been argued, for example, that since the government has bestowed upon us the protection of our rights, all or at least some of us have become reciprocally bound to pay for this benefit in the form of service in the government's protective endeavors. But even if we allow that the government's military engagements have in the recent past actually effectively enhanced the security of our rights in morally permissible ways, the conclusion that those who have benefited may now be forced to serve the benefit-bestowing institution does not follow. Though each of us benefits enormously and in all sorts of ways from many activities and institutions in which we play no direct part, this does not make those who directly and freely participate for their own chosen purposes our victims with enforceable claims, in compensation, upon our lives or fortunes.[6] To those individuals who have defended our freedoms, we owe an unending gratitude. Yet it would be a sad irony for that past defense of freedom to be interpreted as a vindication for present involuntary servitude.

We turn, then, to the primary question of what people may do or have done for them in the way of forcibly defending their rights.

2. Theories of Justice in War

Moral theorizing about war usually focuses on two distinct questions. What ends, if anything, can justify war? What means may be employed in the pursuit of that justifying end? As it is often put, we are concerned both with justice *of* the war and with justice *in* the war. On the principles of a free society, the only end that vindicates a society's limited government in preparing for, supporting, and conducting war is the protection of the rights of its particular citizens. But the question remains how, if at all, do the rights of all those individuals who may be injured or killed in the course of defending rights constrain what may be done in defense of rights? This section surveys eight doctrines about justice *of* and justice *in* war. The first six doctrines accept the basic proposition that the end that vindicates defensive force, if any end does, is the protection of rights. These doctrines diverge on the question of what constraints, if any, there are on the pursuit of this justifying goal. The seventh and eighth doctrines are reminders of goals that often are invoked to justify war contrary to the principles of a free society. This survey provides the background for the defense of the just war doctrine that appears in section 3.

1. Principled pacifism. Defensive force is just as immoral as the violence against which it is directed. The former violates rights as surely as the offensive use of force.

According to principled pacifism, the prospect of suffering a rights violation does not absolve one from any of one's previously identified obligations not to use deadly or injurious force. These obligations stand and bind one to pacifist submission (or nonviolent evasion if that is possible). Moreover, it is better to suffer a wrong (to oneself) than to be the agent of necessarily wrongful violence (even against an aggressor).

2. *Strict defense. Defensive force may be used against guilty aggressors and only against guilty aggressors.*

Guilty aggressors are those who set out intentionally or recklessly to perform actions that violate the rights of some (non-aggressing) second party. Often the view that defensive force against guilty aggressors, but only against them, is permissible is associated with the view that the guilty aggressor, through his guilt, forfeits his right against harmful force.

3. *Broad defense. Defensive force may be used against innocent aggressors as well as guilty aggressors.*

Innocent aggressors (or "innocent threats") are those whose action or behavior threatens to infringe upon someone's rights, but who are not themselves responsible for their threatening action or behavior. Common examples of innocent threats are psychotic aggressors or children unaware of the dangerous character of their actions. Conscripts in an aggressor's army who themselves are acting under serious duress are also innocent threats. A doctrine of forfeiture of rights cannot be used in the vindication of broad defense, since forfeiture is, presumably, a function of blameworthiness.

4. *Just war defense. Defensive force may be used against guilty and innocent aggressors even if this force (also) inflicts losses on innocent bystanders.*

Innocent bystanders are those who themselves pose no threat to the party under attack but who will be harmed or killed by the use of defensive force against the attacker, e.g., the civilian refugees who happen to be living in the immediate vicinity of an aggressor's artillery. When an attacker consciously makes use of such bystanders in order to inhibit counterattack against his tools of aggression, e.g., by locating his weapons among them, those bystanders become innocent shields. (Those who are guilty of voluntarily supporting the aggression, such as civilian war planners, do not count as mere bystanders or shields.)

Just war defense requires that defensive force be directed only against guilty or innocent threats. It prohibits the direction of force at innocent bystanders. But it allows force directed at aggressors to proceed even if innocent bystanders will be killed as a "by-product" or "second effect." The just war doctrine would, for example, prohibit the World War II Allied (especially British Bomber Command) obliteration bombing of German cities, which was designed to undercut German war production by disrupting civilian life and morale through the destruction of the densely populated, blue-collar sections of German cities and the inhabitants there. The injury and death of these civilians, many of them not involved in war production, were not by-products of force directed against aggressors or even the machinery of aggression. Instead, these injuries and deaths were the specific intended means by which Bomber Command sought the further end of incapacitating genuine threats.

Just war defense replicates central features of traditional just war theory.[7] The key and controversial distinction within this theory is between untoward *intended* consequences of one's defensive actions and untoward *foreseen but unintended* consequences of one's defensive actions. If an injury or death suffered by bystanders is a foreseen but unintended result of one's defensive force, then one's moral responsibility for this injury or death is at least of a lesser order than if the same injury or death was intended. An agent's intention is *not* a matter of what particular images or feelings he manages to conjure up or banish from his mind at the moment of action. The bombardier on an obliteration mission cannot prevent the deaths of the bystanders from being his intended means by focusing his mind on something else as he releases his bombs e.g., the well-being of the people for whom he is fighting. The death of those bystanders is his intended means as long as their prospective death or injury plays an illuminating role in explaining why the bombardier is releasing those bombs at that place and time.

Advocates of just war theory usually also hold that the production of an evil effect will remain morally *impermissible* if the evil effect, even if unintended, is disproportionate to the good intended (or intended and accomplished) by the action. For example, it may be claimed that the evil involved in the death of 100 refugees in whose midst the aggressor's artillery has been placed is so disproportionate to the enhanced security that the counterattacking forces will enjoy if that artillery is destroyed by air attack that it would be morally impermissible for that air attack to proceed. Unfortunately, crucial as proposed principles of proportionality are to a full account of just war defense, their final role, if any, within a correct theory of defense cannot be explored here. Whatever that role, it is a maxim of just war defense that a defender must choose the prospectively successful defensive tactic that minimizes unintended bystander injury and death. (Just war defense prohibits tactics that will involve bystander causalities, or perhaps even innocent threat causalities, if those tactics offer no significant prospect of success.)

5. *Necessary force defense. Defensive force may be used in the protection of rights, and it is not worse to direct force against (innocent) bystanders than against (innocent) aggressors.*

Necessary force defense repudiates the proposition, central to just war defense, that the intentional killing of nonthreats is a special evil that may not be engaged in even in order to protect one's own rightful claims. To see how necessary force defense diverges from just war defense consider this complex example. There are only two ways to eliminate an aggressor's artillery battery. One way is the (counterforce) method of bombing the artillery, and this has the added consequence that an innocent refugee living in its vicinity is killed. The other way is the (countervalue) method of killing an innocent refugee who is safely distant from the artillery but who is so cherished by the artillery crew that his death will destroy their fighting morale. Doctrines (1), (2), and even (3) prohibit both defensive tactics. Just war defense sharply distinguishes between the two tactics. It allows the attack upon the artillery (which kills both the nearby refugee and the crew), but prohibits the attack on the more distant yet cherished refugee. In contrast, when only the two refugees are taken into account, necessary force defense is neutral between the two methods. But if any among the crew are innocent threats, necessary force will endorse the second, morale-destroying, method of defense.

6. *Limitless defense. While there may be some moral limits upon what may be done in self-defense of rights in small-scale or intrasocietal situations, no such moral limits make sense in the case of large-scale conflict.*

Limitless defense still requires that war be defensive, i.e., that it be fought to protect against the violation of rights. But it denies that there are any moral constraints on one's conduct within a just war. Advocates of limitless defense argue that once war comes the only value is winning; it is nonsense or moral hypocrisy to pretend that any gentlemanly moral rules remain in place. Or they may argue that in modern warfare all distinctions between threats and nonthreats, between combatants and noncombatants, and so on, break down. Everyone under the sway of the aggressor state must be treated as an enemy open to unconstrained attack. Collectivist thinking also contributes to limitless defense by encouraging us to perceive all individuals as functional parts of the (aggressor) state. We are not attacked by certain individuals, some of whom are guilty aggressors, others innocent aggressors, and so on. Rather, we are attacked by some holistic entity, the enemy state or nation in which all individuals are subsumed.

7. *National interest aggression. War is an expression of the interests of peoples. A rational war is one that advances the interest of the nation for whom and by whom it is fought.*

The shift from limitless defense to national interest aggression greatly expands the grounds for morally permissible warfare by substituting interests—indeed, the collective interest—for individual rights. We reach a point at which the use of the term "defensive" is clearly inappropriate. Interests are to be advanced by whatever effective means lie at hand. Nor are the occasions for justified war restricted by any merely bourgeois notion of individual interests. The state's or the people's or the class's interest may be served even though (or precisely because) people's individual interests are annihilated.

Both limitless defense and national interest aggression can be quickly rejected by proponents of individual rights and the free society. Limitless defense is to be rejected because it turns on the false and dangerous premise that the state and its agents need not abide by the same moral rules that constrain the actions of ordinary individuals and groups. National interest aggression is to be rejected because it abandons all concern for justice among individuals and states and at least radically discounts concern even for individual interests.

8. *Conflict management and humanitarian intervention. Among the legitimate purposes of a state's military is the suppression of local conflicts around the globe and the provision of humanitarian aid, especially in circumstances that require the forcible suppression of those who would endanger the provision of that aid.*

All individuals and voluntary associations should be free to offer military assistance to any of the many victims of aggression around the world. Moreover, all individuals and voluntary associations should be free to provide aid to people in distress wherever they may be. And those who are engaged in such humanitarian efforts have every right to secure for themselves the defense of their operations against local predators. But these propositions do not support conflict management and humanitarian intervention, which mistakenly assigns to the government of a free society tasks that are totally beyond its legitimate mandate.

3. Delineating Permissible Defense

The rejection of principles (6), (7), and (8) leaves us with the question of which position about permissible self-defense among doctrines (1) through (5) is most plausible. Unless a position at least as permissive as just war defense is adopted, all large-scale defensive measures, i.e., all wars, are sure to be morally impermissible no matter how just their ends. For any large-scale military measures, no matter how purely reactive to violations of rights, are certain to injure and kill innocent bystanders. In seeking to vindicate the forcible defense of rights, it is useful to begin with the case against principled pacifism. If pacifism is rejected, the next question will be: How far do the arguments associated with this rejection carry us toward necessary force defense, the doctrine that any use of necessary force in the protection of rights is morally acceptable? I contend that the most permissive acceptable principle for national-scale defense is the more stringent just war defense, which requires that all defensive force be targeted against aggressive force.

Against Pacifism.

In a forceful critique of pacifism, Jan Narveson focuses on the incoherence of ascribing rights to victims of violence while denying those victims rights to defend themselves against the violation of their rights.

> What could that right to their own security, which people have, possibly consist in, if not a right at least to defend themselves from whatever violence might be offered them?. . . . The prevention of infraction of that right is precisely what one has a right to when one has a right at all. A right just is a status justifying preventive action. To say that you have a right to X but that no one has any justification whatever for preventing people from depriving you of it, is self-contradictory. . . . In saying that violence is wrong, one is at the same time saying that people have a right to its prevention, by force if necessary.[8]

Rights are claims that people can insist others abide by. Such claims are to be contrasted with (mere) measures of moral stature that one person can apply to others, such as their degree of kindliness or integrity. One may judge, quite correctly, that others have acted wrongly on some occasion because they have not displayed kindness or integrity. But in employing such judgments, one does not invoke the rights that one has against these other individuals. Kindness or integrity is not something that one can require of them. Rights must have more interpersonal force than this. They are the bases for demands one can make upon others, and not merely for judgments one can offer about their lives. The sense in which rights allow the right-holder to require or insist that others act or refrain from action must be more robust than that involved in being licensed merely to pass critical judgment upon them. What could this more robust sense be except that right-holders can require others *in fact* to conform their activity to respect these rights? This can only mean that right-holders may prevent, by injurious force if necessary, infringements upon their rights. The right to resist violations of one's rights, to use injurious force if necessary to preserve one's rights, is then an implication of one's having a right against such violence and of this right's being a moral claim against others for which the right-holder may require respect.

How much force (against those subject to permissible defense) may be used in defense of rights? Narveson's own answer is "enough," by which he means just as much as is necessary. The major alternative answer is that no more force may be used than produces injury proportionate to the unjust injury being protected against. This is an alternative because the force that produces a proportionate injury may be less than necessary to accomplish the defense. The type of argument for permissible forcible defense given by Narveson and myself points to the former, more permissive, answer. Endangered individuals need not weigh the loss that threatens them against the loss to those subject to their permissible defensive activity. They may, instead, stand on their right not to submit to a violation of their rights.

Toward Permissible (Counterforce) Defense.

The argument against pacifism focuses on the right-holder who is being threatened and not on the party whose actions threaten those rights. It does not rely upon the guilt of the threatening party. Thus, the argument that shows the permissibility of using harmful force when necessary against guilty aggressors also shows its permissibility when necessary against nonguilty aggressors, i.e., against innocent threats. If one has a right to one's life, one cannot be obligated to allow another to be a causal agent in depriving one of that right. When necessary, such a deprivation may be resisted by means of harmful force. When under attack by a conscript, one may kill the conscript even though he is attacking only because were he not to do so his rulers would kill him or his family.

What about innocent bystanders? The argument against pacifism seems also to allow necessary defensive killing of them. It at least seems that the presence of an innocent bystander could not obligate one to submit to the violation of rights that will occur if an aggressor's behavior is not thwarted. Although it is the aggressor and not the bystander who is engaged in a process that will violate one's rights unless thwarted, one's right not to submit to a deprivation of life is a right one holds against everyone. No one can demand that one not resist such a deprivation. Nevertheless, one's right to resist violations of rights is not a sanction for engaging in aggressive behavior. And cannot the bystander, who would be killed by one's resistance to the aggressor, insist on one's abstaining from this action in the name of his right to life? The difficulty is that a particular course of action in this sort of situation is susceptible to the following two descriptions: (i) an exercise of one's rightful resistance to the violation of rights; and (ii) an aggression against the bystander's right to life. In virtue of description (i), the principle of self-defense applies, and one may proceed with the course of action. In virtue of description (ii), one's obligation not to aggress applies, and one may not proceed with the course of action. Just war theory's focus on the distinction between foreseen and intended effects is a basis for determining which description and associated principle (self-defense or nonaggression against rights) is the salient one for the purpose of establishing the permissibility of a given forcible act. That description is salient that explains the forcible action.

Recall the example discussed previously in comparing just war defense and necessary force defense involving the choice between the defensive counterattack against an artillery battery that foreseeably kills a nearby refugee and the demoralizing counterattack against the distant refugee cherished by the artillery crew. If one were to pursue the first alternative (with weapons designed for precision counterattack), the killing of a nearby refugee would in no way explain the course of one's action. One would have acted exactly in the same manner had the nearby refugee not existed at all. The refugee's death would not at all guide one's action. Thus, the salient description of the counterattack would be in terms of its responsiveness to a threat to rights, and it would be vindicated by the counterattacker's right to defend these rights. In contrast, if one were to pursue the second, antimorale, alternative, one's intermediate purpose would be the killing of the cherished refugee. One's chosen course of action would be contoured to, and explicable only by reference to, the presence of this refugee. Such a targeting of this bystander would give salience to the description of one's action as an aggression against this refugee. Given this salience and the bystander's right to life, this form of counterattack would be unjustified.

Just war defense incorporates into the overall theory of individual rights moral maxims that are naturally associated with an emphasis on individual autonomy and the separate and equal standing of each person's life and purposes. Specifically, it incorporates the idea that it is supremely wrong to employ others as means, against their will and to the detriment of their well-being or freedom, for the sake of one's own goals, no matter how natural or noble those goals may be. Although there is a broad sense in which any action that deprives a person of rightful possessions or conditions treats that person as a means, the use of people as means is most pronounced when the untoward result is not merely foreseen but intended. The direct intentional killing of a bystander as a distinct means to some further end violates this associated maxim about the wrongness of employing people as means, whereas the indirect, collateral killing of a bystander does not.

There is another line of consideration, indirectly connected with people not being obligated to forego resistance, which also suggests that the rejection of pacifism leads to just war defense, but no further. If pacifism is rejected, the person who escalates from verbal insistence that one surrender some rightful possession to seizing one's rightful possessions forcibly can still be resisted in kind. He does not, by his escalation to forcible seizure, gain a moral advantage. His increased wrongdoing does not confer upon him any immunity. But if either the intended killing of innocent threats or the unintended killing of innocent shields or bystanders is proscribed, a potential violator of rights will be able to acquire moral immunity in his aggressive pursuits by escalating his wrongdoing. If the defensive killing of innocent threats is proscribed, then guilty aggressors can gain immunity for their aggressions by organizing their attacks upon others with innocent conscripts. If the defensive killing of shields or bystanders is proscribed, guilty aggressors can gain immunity for their aggressions by forcing bystanders into the vicinity of their weapons or by locating their weapons in the midst of bystanders. If either the killing of innocent threats or the collateral killing of bystanders is prohibited, the more morally indiscriminate the aggressor, the more moral immunity he will enjoy. Since the rejection of pacifism itself involves a refusal to grant the evil aggressor a moral cloak, it is plausible that, having rejected pacifism, one also should reject other doctrines—viz., narrow defense and broad defense—that allow an aggressor, through evil means, to gain moral immunity for his aggression.

This conclusion about a person's right to use lethal force against innocent threats or in such a way as to endanger innocent bystanders does not imply that innocent threats or bystanders must submit to this permissible defensive force. Innocent threats or bystanders may have a right, under the circumstances, to defend themselves against the counterattacker's permissible action. There can be cases in which two innocent parties, thrust into conflict with each other, permissibly battle each other to death.

Despite its relative permissiveness, just war defense may require that we forego the most effective available defensive tactics. Hence, this restrictiveness may raise doubts about this doctrine. Imagine the sudden appearance of an assassin who will kill one's child unless one distracts him by killing his child. Just war defense requires that one forego this tactic. But to many it will seem that, horrendous as it would be to kill this child directly, one could not be obligated to resign oneself to the murder of one's own child. Whatever one's sense of this case, however, there are reasons why such a case should not be taken as a basis for adopting a more permissive doctrine of *national-scale* defense than just war defense. As this case is presented, the threat is sudden, immediate, and absolutely certain. There is neither time nor room for the formation of alternative defensive tactics. Furthermore, the threat is removed immediately and with absolute certainty upon killing the aggressor's child. The immediacy of the threat means that the use of this child seems less chosen than thrust upon one, and the immediacy of the relief from danger upon the killing of this child blurs the status of that killing as a separate intended consequence of one's action. These immediacies and certainties help explain why killing the assassin's child can be (perceived as) something less than thoroughly murderous. However, national-scale defense should not be modeled on such one-time emergencies. National-scale threats evolve over extended periods of time. We are not required, as in the child case, to react in a given moment to a situation the structure of which is simply presented to us. There are many long-term options. And because this is so, opting for one that involves the direct targeting of bystanders carries the burden of being a calculated choice of useful attacks upon these people. At the very least, a system of national defense whose operation would violate just war defense must be avoided if another system is available that accords with that doctrine and is likely to be comparably effective.

Just war defense requires more than that the weapons at hand at a given moment be directed, as best they can with the systems of delivery at hand, at the enemy's means of aggression. Justice in the conduct of war requires that one's weapons and methods of delivering them have been developed so as to strike as directly as possible against the means of aggression and with the minimum foreseeable collateral casualties. Only if the defending party has over time been committed to and constrained in its defensive preparations by allegiance to just war defense, and has been known to be so committed and constrained, will the *aggressor* bear full responsibility for the collateral casualties that ensue because of the aggressor's placement of its threatening forces in the vicinity of bystanders.

4. Policy Implications of Just War Defense

It is an enormously complex task to refine further the moral doctrine outlined here and to apply it, in the light of many difficult empirical questions, to the actual world. All that can be done here is to convey some further sense of just war defense by sketching its probable implications for certain broad categories of the defensive posture of United States, viz., strategic defense, military alliances, and local interventions.

Strategic Defense and Military Alliances.

By strategic defense, I mean defense involving major global engagement against other superpowers or aspiring superpowers of the sort that, since the 1950s, has involved the worldwide deployment of nuclear weapons with intracontinental and intercontinental delivery systems. I link the discussion of strategic defense with that of military alliances because, since the 1950s, military alliances have usually been sought either as a means to the worldwide deployment of nuclear weapons or as part of the geopolitical and conventional warfare dimension of that same global engagement. Of course, the mere existence of other globally significant military powers is not as such a threat to American lives, liberties, or property and does not as such justify any global engagement. Other powers may be benign (as U.S. military power is supposed to be) or, at least, sufficiently benign so that treaty constraints on armament and deployment can reliably and significantly defuse perceived threats and confrontation. But to engage in stupendous understatement, not all major military powers are benign or even relatively benign. Soviet power certainly was not benign and whatever efficacy U.S.-U.S.S.R. treaties had in defusing confrontation depended upon a background of American resolve and defensive capabilities.[9]

To say this is by no means to endorse, either in terms of justice or efficacy, the particular measures (including conscription!) that were employed in the name of defense against the Soviet threat. The strategy of massive retaliatory destruction of the Soviet population, which was the centerpiece of U.S. policy from the 1950s at least through the 1970s, was in violation of the crucial just war stricture that a just defensive posture must not encompass the injury or death of bystanders within its guiding intentions and that the just defender's weaponry, delivery systems, and war-making strategy must be entirely directed at the aggressor's means of aggression.[10] Only in the final five or ten years of our strategic confrontation with the Soviet Union did our nuclear weaponry and targeting policies begin to come into line with just war doctrine. Moreover, only during the last years of the Evil Empire did U.S. defensive policy appropriately attend to the primary end of legitimate governmental activity, viz., the actual protection of the lives, health, and property of that government's citizens. Indeed, a reliable *defensive shield* (of the sort envisioned by the Strategic Defense Initiative and derided as "Star Wars") should, *if* at all available, be the first priority of a morally upright defense policy. *If* such a shield is available, it renders unnecessary the defensive infliction of injury and death—most pointedly the infliction of injury and death upon innocent threats and on bystanders.

Furthermore, many of the alliances into which the United States entered during the confrontation with the Soviets either failed to enhance the security of the rights of Americans or brought the United States government into collusion with murderous and kleptocratic regimes or both. Arguably even the NATO alliance increased the likelihood of nuclear war between the United States and the Soviets over the fate of Western Europe beyond what that risk would have been had Western Europe itself been required to be more defensively self-reliant. More straightforwardly, U.S. alliances with Israel and South Korea increased the likelihood of a U.S.-Soviet nuclear engagement without providing any counterbalancing enhancement of American security. United States-Soviet competition for client states throughout the world led the U.S. government into often horribly costly support of brutal and plunderous "bulwarks of anticommunism" across Latin America, Africa, and Asia. In reality, support for these regimes served no justified end and embroiled the U.S. government in the violation of the rights of the many victims of those regimes.[11]

The world has changed with the burial of the U.S.S.R. These changes make it more difficult to identify justifying ends for strategic defensive policy and more difficult yet to justify alliances as effective and morally permissible means for advancing those justifying ends. Still, it is not clear how fundamentally and permanently the world has changed. (Does it ever fundamentally and permanently change?) It is still easily conceivable that resurgent Russian imperialism of either a nationalist or a socialist hue will again constitute an aggressive nuclear threat to American lives, liberties, and property. And other parties may achieve the status of significant nuclear threat, such as a radically anti-Western Iran, an increasingly phobic North Korea, or even a reradicalized China (not to mention the future course of Germany and Japan). Unfortunately, the more diffuse and nonsystematic the threat, the more difficult and less cost-effective any pure defensive shield will be. Aggressors with only a few nuclear devices are almost certain to deliver them by mini-van rather than intercontinental missile. Nevertheless, it seems reasonable to continue to devote resources to the development and possible deployment of flexible SDI-type defenses. (However, it also seems increasingly important to create and sustain intelligence operations capable of identifying and intercepting free-lance nuclear and non-nuclear terrorists and of retaliating effectively and precisely against individuals responsible for attacks on Americans.) It is clearly reasonable to maintain and refine distinctly counterforce weaponry as a means, consistent with just war doctrine, for deterring whichever strategic threats *against the people of the United States* emerge in an unstable world of nuclear proliferation. There is, however, no good reason for the United States to continue to bear responsibility for providing strategic defense against present or emerging threats to such regions as Western Europe and Japan. Similarly, there is no good reason for the United States to bear the responsibility and associated risk of garrisoning Western Europe, South Korea, and Japan.

Given the legitimate goal of maintaining a flexible strategic defense capability, some limited cooperative arrangements with other governments would probably be advantageous and morally permissible. These might include arrangements for the deployment of early warning devices and communications facilities and for the servicing of a wide-ranging fleet of submarines as a relatively invulnerable base for counterforce strategic weapons. Similarly, overseas sites may be crucial for the gathering of intelligence about potential large-scale aggressors or more free-lance terrorists. Treaties designed for these genuinely defensive purposes will be justified as long as they do not themselves generate risky commitments or blameworthy support of unjust regimes.

Local Interventions.

"Local interventions" are military excursions against less-than-major powers (indeed, perhaps, against quite puny military forces) that, therefore, involve no prospect for the justified use of nuclear weaponry. Indeed, because of the opponent's lack of military power, local interventions cannot be justified as thwarting a threat against the United States proper.[12] I also include under "local interventions" humanitarian expeditions where no or almost no hostile forces are present. If there exists no threat against the United States proper, what other justification could there be for the intervention of the U.S. military? One justification would be the provision of the protection promised to foreign individuals and agencies under treaties that themselves are warranted by their contribution to the defense of Americans against strategic and terrorist threats. I have suggested that the alliances that are currently warranted by their prospective contribution to the safety of Americans are quite limited in number and in scope. But when such limited alliances are undertaken, the provision of the protection promised to others is a justified end for U.S. military action—which action, of course, must conform to just war constraints.

One important justificatory possibility is the protection of American lives, liberties, and property outside of U.S. territory. In principle, this is an entirely legitimate goal of defensive force. The complication, however, is the disproportionate costs (in lives and material and economic resources) involved in defending the lives, liberties, and estates of those who have ventured into risky portions of the world. There is no good reason why the costs of intervening to come to the defense of vacationers who have chosen to go mountain climbing in Bosnia should be borne by those funding a system of common defense. Similarly, there is no good reason why contributors to the common defense should bear the extraordinary costs of protecting an international corporation's investment in some Third World country from the nationalizing impulses of that country's tyrant. The rough rule should be that protection should extend beyond U.S. territory only when the probable costs of that protection (in the form, e.g., of international coordination of police and courts) are comparable to the costs within U.S. territory. Those who choose to expose themselves to risks that are more costly to defend against are, of course, free to do so and free to reap the rewards of their extraordinary pleasures or profits. And, of course, they are free to devote their own resources to the justly conducted defense of their lives, liberties, and property.

Another putative justification for local intervention is American economic advantage. One of the arguments offered for the U.S.-dominated counterattack on Saddam Hussein's forces was that his seizure of the Kuwaiti oil fields along with his prospective seizure of the Saudi oil fields would have been very damaging to American economic interests (and even more damaging to the economic interests of many other nations who, therefore, were willing to fight to the last drop of American blood). But in itself economic advantage does not justify warfare, even if that warfare is carried on by justified means. And typically, when the economic advantage argument is advanced, the benefits to those who will actually have to bear the costs of the war (as opposed to those whose bacon will especially be saved) are systematically underestimated while the costs that will be borne if intervention is not undertaken are systematically overestimated. A complication in the Iraqi case is that Hussein would have been threatening denial of access to a resource *over which he had no just claim*. The oil fields were stolen goods—indeed, have in large part been stolen goods for some time. The most morally upright response from a libertarian perspective would have been a voluntarily organized, private military expedition, abiding by just war strictures, for the commercial liberation of those oil fields.

Another argument offered for intervention in the Iraqi case was the restoration of Kuwaiti rights—albeit this justification has less resonance when it is spelled out, not in terms of individual human rights, but rather in terms of national collective sovereignty or the rights of the Kuwaiti sheiks to tyrannize without outside interference. We have already noted, however, that even the protection of the correctly identified rights of victims of regional aggression is not within the mandate of a duly limited U.S. government, nor is military protection for humanitarian aid.[13] The members of a large and highly diverse free society will have radically divergent views about which victims of which aggressions or disasters should receive military or militarily-protected humanitarian support. There can be no justification consistent with libertarian principles for some members of such a society imposing, through coercive political means, the costs of their cherished military or humanitarian ventures on other members of that society.

Furthermore, to accept the principle of conflict management and humanitarian intervention is to encourage in practice the commitment of the society's military resources on the basis of contingencies of political influence. The U.S. military intervenes in Haiti, but not in Bosnia, in part because there is a powerful Black Caucus, but no Bosnian Muslim Caucus, within the party of a politically weak and desperate president. Such politically selective interventions typically lack the extent and depth of public support that they will need if they encounter any significant resistance. Thus, these interventions typically invite resistance (from local warlords who are tuned in to CNN) and when that resistance occurs, the only politically acceptable course is ignominious withdrawal—as in Lebanon in the 1980s and Somalia in the 1990s. And typically, these withdrawals generate a chorus of demands for new, and equally controversial, interventions to reestablish global credibility.

Belief in these further and divisive ends for U.S. defense policy has the overall effect of harmfully expanding governmental power and discretion and distracting attention from the special legitimate role for the governmental use of force, viz., the common defense of its citizens' rights.

Notes

1. An earlier version of this essay appeared as chapter 1 of *Defending A Free Society*, ed. Robert Poole Jr. (Lexington, Massachusetts: Lexington Books, 1984).

That version dealt much more extensively with the application of just war doctrine—especially its application to the world of 1984. Although the specifics of that discussion are "dated," they would still provide the interested reader with a more detailed guide to libertarian thinking about national-scale defense policy than is provided here in section 4.

2. John C. Ford, "The Morality of Obliteration Bombing," reprinted in *War and Morality*, ed. R. Wasserstrom (Belmont, California: Wadsworth, 1970), 15.

3. For one statement of libertarian rights theory, see my essay "Moral Individualism and Libertarian Theory" in this volume. For other statements, see the works cited in note 2 of that essay.

4. Foreigners will have rights to protection from our government only in the special cases in which treaties *that accord with the core mandate* of our government—viz., to secure *our* rights—bestow those rights to protection. The extent of such treaties is discussed briefly in section 4.

5. See David Friedman, *The Machinery of Freedom* (New Rochelle: Arlington House, 1978); Eric Mack, "The Ethics of Taxation: Rights versus Public Goods?" in *Taxation and the Deficit Economy*, ed. Dwight Lee (San Franciso: Pacific Research Institute, 1986); and David Schmidtz, *The Limits of Government* (Boulder: Westview Press, 1991).

6. The so-called Principle of Fairness on which this sort of argument turns is subject to a powerful critique in Robert Nozick, *Anarchy, State and Utopia* (New York: Basic Books, 1974) 93–95.

7. See James T. Johnson, *Just War Tradition and the Restraint of War* (Princeton: Princeton University Press, 1981).

8. Jan Narveson, "Pacifism: A Philosophical Analysis," in *War and Morality*, ed. R. Wasserstrom (Belmont, California: Wadsworth, 1970) 72. Also see Narveson, "Violence and War," in *Matters of Life and Death*, ed. Tom Regan (New York: Random House, 1980).

9. Especially during the years of the Cold War, some libertarians, being appropriately sensitive to the aggressive propensities of *all* states and being subject to the somewhat puzzling tendency to find most blame with one's own government, were eager to perceive the U.S. government as the *primary* instigator of this confrontation. In rejecting this analysis, I do not deny the injustice (and plain stupidity) of much of what was done in the name of resisting Soviet domination.

10. Or this vital stricture *would have been* violated were the threat of retaliatory destruction ever to have been carried out. The complicating issue is whether it is always impermissible *merely* to *threaten* to do what it would be morally impermissible to do. In any case, the strategy of mass retaliation was not *mere* bluff. Mechanisms were in place such that, had the United States been attacked by the Soviets, this retaliation against bystanders would very likely have been carried out.

11. For one study, see Jonathan Kwitny, *Endless Enemies* (New York: Cogdon and Weed, 1984).

12. Terrorist attacks originating abroad against American lives, liberty, and property within U.S. territory were dealt with briefly under Strategic Defense and Military Alliances.

13. I see no decisive reason why, in humanitarian emergencies, such as the flood of Rwandan refugees into Zaire, the U.S. military should not hire itself out *on very generous terms* to relief organizations as long as its activities will constitute good logistical practice and engagement in these activities will not cloud the recognition that the *raison d'etre* of the U.S. military is to protect the rights of Americans—through the use and threat of deadly force.

"Righting" Civil Wrongs: Toward a Libertarian Agenda

Steven Yates

1. Introduction

The civil rights movement is off-course. Affirmative action, understood here as government mandated preferential treatment for members of groups officially designated as American society's victims, has been one of the most conspicuous features of civil rights since the late 1960s. Its advocates defend it as making reparations to minorities and women for past discrimination (the "backward-looking argument"), or offering assistance that would help them catch up, supplying role models for black students, etc. (the "forward-looking argument"). A litany of objections, however, continues to haunt affirmative action. (1) Its benefits go disproportionately to those in targeted groups who are either already well-off or well-connected and, hence, in a position to benefit from the programs. (2) It has placed people in positions for which they are often marginally qualified or even unqualified, and, therefore, in danger of failing; colleges and universities offer a host of examples. (3) It further stigmatizes minorities and women by insinuating that they cannot succeed without government assistance; making them wards of the state helps reinforce, not reduce, racial stereotypes. (4) It has sabotaged language and introduced a world of Orwellian newspeak, with *equal opportunity* meaning preferential treatment and *discriminatory* meaning lacking officially approved race and gender balance. (5) It has created a climate of secrecy, dishonesty, and distrust, both to keep white male job seekers and the public as much in the dark as possible and to protect affirmative action from serious investigation, criticism, and legal challenge. (6) It manufactures "problems" out of whole cloth (e.g., the argument that there are almost no blacks in athletic front offices when they are earning multimillion dollar salaries down on the playing field). (7) It has expanded to include more and more groups claiming victimization, so that now almost *two-thirds* of the American public is in at least one protected group, with no end in sight.

(8) Worse yet, affirmative action has been a major contributor to the enormous build up in the power of unelected and unaccountable federal judges and bureaucrats to dictate the outcomes of hiring practices, university admissions, and other competitive processes, leading to an increasingly fascist, centrally controlled society. (9) It has set groups against one another instead of bringing them together. Tensions are at an all-time high. There are now countless "invisible victims" (white males who lack the connections to circumvent reverse discrimination). More generally, members of all groups are acutely worried that others are getting more government freebies; sometimes their fears are justified. Whites are not the only victims. Asians as well have become aware of "quota ceilings" on college admissions as a result of the influx of highly qualified Asian students into the school systems, particularly in California. Surely discrimination against Asians in the present is not a just or viable way of making reparations to blacks for discrimination against them in the past. (10) Finally, by lowering standards, affirmative action has nearly destroyed the educational system from the early grades on up, leading to today's graduates' well-documented inabilities to read effectively, construct intelligible paragraphs, or work elementary mathematics problems. Under the auspices of today's "multiculturalist" universities, they are learning little science, history, or geography. They often have to be trained from scratch by employers at a cost that is passed on to consumers. In sum, the New World Order of affirmative action and related policies is actually undermining American competitiveness in world markets.

Affirmative action is clearly at odds with libertarian principles. Its main instrument is coercion by government. It regards individuals' lives and careers as expendable in the service of an agenda many would not support voluntarily. It wantonly interferes with the right of individuals to hire and do business with individuals of their own choice instead of someone else's. In short, as government policy, it violates rights that government should be protecting.

Libertarians will point out that the civil rights movement was just one casualty of the progressive collectivization that began with the New Deal. We have seen the slow erosion of those values that alone lead to economic achievement and their replacement by an ethos of victimization, resentment, and dependency. The very idea of *rights* has been corrupted; its distinction from that of *entitlements*, blurred. As a result, every individual's sphere of autonomy is fast fading in the face of an ever-expanding web of forcibly imposed regulations, mandates, and requirements. The "politics of identity" has fueled distrust, suspicion, and calls for censorship instead of a positive climate of open discussion and multiracial tolerance.

The idea of *civil rights* is nevertheless essentially sound. Rights, after all, do not protect themselves. Hence, we need an institution whose sole business is protecting rights to life, liberty, justly-acquired property, and the pursuit of happiness. The Founding Fathers created a government based on these principles, but Americans failed to practice them consistently. It is true that blacks, other minorities, and to a lesser extent women, were mostly denied them. Slavery and forced segregation, after all, also contradict libertarian principles. Hence, the country needed a civil rights movement to insure that the American legal system protected the rights of *everyone* to life, liberty, justly-acquired property, and the pursuit of happiness.

Today's civil rights movement, though, is resolutely hostile to principles of individual rights to life, liberty, justly-acquired property, and the pursuit of happiness. Many advocates of affirmative action see such principles as protecting white male privileges and dishonestly wrapping them in moral language. Advocates of affirmative action have been trying to overturn rights-based principles and replace them with group-centered entitlements. The results are wreaking racial, economic, political, and educational havoc. Clearly the country needs a new agenda for civil rights, one that does not tie civil rights to affirmative action, entitlements, and identity-politics. Contemporary libertarian thought offers an excellent foundation for such a project.[1]

2. How the Civil Rights Movement Went Off Course.

The term *civil rights* is ambiguous. As just hinted, there have really been *two* movements laying claim to it, one guided by our country's founding principles and attempting to apply them consistently, the other working to subvert them. Civil rights attorney Clint Bolick has distinguished the *original civil rights vision* from the *revised civil rights agenda* (or *civil rights revisionism*).[2] The former defines *civil rights* as "natural rights—life, liberty, and property—enshrined in civil law."[3] The modern roots of this idea are in Thomas Paine, who wrote:

> Natural rights are those which always appertain to man in right of his existence. Of this kind are all the intellectual rights, or rights of the mind, and

also all those rights of acting as an individual for his own comfort and happiness, which are not injurious to the rights of others. Civil rights are those which appertain to man in right of his being a member of society. Every civil right has for its foundation some natural right pre-existing in the individual, but to which his individual power is not, in all cases, sufficiently competent. Of this kind are all those which relate to security and protection.[4]

Advocates of the original civil rights movement noted the lack of equal opportunities and equal protection under the law for blacks and women. The legal system originally prevented blacks and women from entering the labor market. Quite properly, the original civil rights vision aimed at freeing *them*, not empowering *government*.

The revised civil rights agenda places its trust in government. It is very questionable whether this trust is warranted. Bolick observes that the revised civil rights agenda (1) exchanged the ideal of equal treatment under the law for equality understood as predetermined statistical outcomes, (2) replaced the idea that rights reside in individuals with the view that they reside in groups; and (3) abandoned the idea of natural rights in favor of legally-based entitlements.[5] It assumes that injustices can only be rectified by large-scale planning. None of this is conceivable in the absence of expansionist government. Elsewhere, I have developed the view that civil rights tied to affirmative action, entitlements, discrimination as statistical imbalance, etc., expresses a *philosophy of social engineering*. Historical versions of this philosophy appear in Plato's *Republic*, More's *Utopia*, Hobbes's *Leviathan*, and Rousseau's *Du Contrat Social*. Though Marx was primarily concerned to diagnose what he took to be defects in capitalism and never offered a blueprint for communist utopia, recent forms of the philosophy of social engineering borrow freely from Marxism—often treating its dichotomies and the adversarial relations they posit as if they were as well-established as the law of gravity. Whenever social engineers, Marxist or otherwise, have gained full control over government apparatus, the results have been totalitarianism, economic decline, cultural decay, and ethnic cleansing. Nazi Germany, the former Soviet Union, and mainland China offer clear examples. In its more modest forms in the United States, social engineering is leading to more and more control over more and more aspects of human life by the federal government and unaccountable apparatchiks at all levels of social life.

The philosophy of social engineering as embodied in the revised civil rights agenda makes five fundamental assumptions: (1) collectivism, (2) determinism, (3) historical victimization, (4) elitism, and (5) economic egalitarianism. It constitutes an onslaught on liberty of historic proportions.

Free markets, says the social engineer, are too chaotic and individualistic. They give too much free reign to greed, indifference, and exploitation. They have left many groups behind and unable to catch up. Even free speech is dangerous, as it can be used to denigrate some groups. Only central economic planning and social control will do.

Let's review these assumptions. *Collectivism* as a social metaphysic holds that *groups* are primary units. Society consists of groups divided along lines of race, ethnicity, gender, class, sexual preference, special circumstances such as physical limitation, or some combination of these. Individual identity derives from group membership. As a component of the broader philosophy of social engineering, collectivism encourages, in F. A. Hayek's words, "the deliberate organization of the labors of society for a definite social goal."[6] Collectivists conceive of societies, races, ethnic groups, etc., as if they were organisms with autonomous life cycles, goals and aspirations of their own, capable of acting in history. They can harm or benefit other groups, or be harmed by them. The "genuine" interests of individuals ultimately harmonize with those of the group; individuals who reject their "genuine" interests may be ostracized or blacklisted (in societies that are still somewhat free) or imprisoned or even killed (in totalitarian ones).

Collectivism explains the popularity of the argument holding that the "dominant culture" (white males) can make reparations to blacks, other minorities, and women, for offenses decades and even centuries old. Blacks as a group, this argument holds, were harmed first by slavery and then by systematic segregation and discrimination; women, too, were excluded from the dominant culture and their contributions ignored. All are behind because of harm done to them as groups, harm for which white males bear collective responsibility. Today, white males are obligated to make amends, allowing government to tilt the scales to favor harmed groups. The main problem is white males who refuse to acknowledge their collective guilt and take their medicine—who refuse to do what is in the interests of all. In short, collectivism is one of the chief foundations of the revised civil rights agenda.

Determinism, the second element in the philosophy of social engineering, is more a thesis about the nature of the universe and our place in it. It holds that efficient causation is sufficient to explain every event in reality. Determinism generalizes the Newtonian conception of physical nature, collapsing the distinction Newton and his contemporaries would have drawn between physical phenomena and human social reality. Hobbes was the first English-speaking philosopher to infer a complete *reductive materialism* with regard to human beings; De la Mettrie soon followed on continental Europe. Determinism has important consequences. It leads to the view that human behavior results from internal causes and/or external stimuli, not autonomous decisions. Determinists disagree over which is more prevalent, internal causes or external stimuli, but agree that "free will" is a prescientific myth.

After Comte founded positivism and tried to relegate metaphysics to the intellectual scrapheap, determinism became a central tenet of social science, sufficiently entrenched that not even Mises or Hayek challenged it. To the social engineer, it suggests that if enough can be learned about the determinants on social behavior and *their* causes, both can be changed. By changing social determinants on a large enough scale, one could produce a new kind of human being. This has long been the dream of scientific utopianism. Marxists still hold that the end of capitalism will usher in this result.

"Multiculturalist" ideology combines collectivism with determinism. It holds that experience and cognition themselves are products of group identity, a "social construction" of the dominant group. No individual can really escape the constraints imposed by race, ethnicity, gender, class, and history.[7] The combination is a natural one, for determinism asserts that all social groups and socioeconomic strata are products of impersonal historical forces that have left minorities *historically victimized*. Thus, the philosophy of social engineering encourages a *psychology of victimization*. Neither victimized group nor victimizer can escape their plight without help from outside. The victimizer, or oppressor, sees himself as superior and behaves accordingly. His victim is immersed in an ambience of helplessness and self-loathing that comes from being hated, oppressed, and regarded as inferior.

Nicholas Capaldi gave a clear statement of this view and its consequences for both immediate and long-term public policy, especially educational policy, before the term *multiculturalism* gained currency:

> The heart of doctrinaire liberalism is the belief that man is the victim of circumstances greater than himself—social, political, psychological. The masses cannot comprehend these great impersonal forces that guide their destiny. Understanding is necessarily limited to a vanguard of enlightened men and women who can free mankind by obtaining control of the state machinery and using their new-found power for the purpose of breaking the chains that have always fettered mankind. If government intervention, regulation, and control of all existing institutions is necessary in order to liberate the oppressed, then surely the university will be no exception. Indeed, the university is one of the keys to the success of the program. It is but a short step from this to preferential hiring and curriculum control.[8]

In other words, according to the philosophy of social engineering, there is an *elite* capable of redressing historical victimization. A select few have the knowledge and insight necessary to liberate history's victims and lead the way to a new order. They alone can be trusted with state machinery. In practice, this elite has come to consist of a labyrinth of academicians and administrators, politicians and lobbyists, bureaucrats, federal judges, affirmative action officers and other "diversity" managers—what Capaldi calls the *academic-bureaucratic complex* (echoing that nemesis of an earlier generation, the military-industrial complex).

Behind the philosophy of social engineering is the conviction that all people ought to be economically equal (or as equal as possible), and, thus, entitled to economic equality and proportional representation everywhere: *progressive economic egalitarianism*. All have contributed equally to Western culture, so it is said. All have equal contributions to make now. From this, egalitarians infer that something is amiss when one group can be seen as dominant. This can only be due to exploitation, discriminatory exclusion, and sometimes outright cultural theft.[9] The elite must act—through the educational system, whenever possible, and through the courts where necessary. It must restore as much as possible the economic equality that would exist had there been no domination, exploitation, or theft. Naturally, this involves the gradual restructuring or transformation of nearly every American institution from the ground floor up.

This, I submit, best explains the revised civil rights agenda. However contrary to our country's founding principles, it has proven enormously powerful and resilient. Efforts to reverse it and return the country to the original civil rights vision, particularly by the U.S. Supreme Court in the late 1980s, were stymied by the 1991 Civil Rights Act. It has moved steadily forward with the passage of the Americans With Disabilities Act (1992) and with increasingly successful efforts to bring homosexuals and bisexuals under affirmative action protections despite the opposition of large numbers of the American public.[10] Defenders of civil rights revisionism routinely argue that reverse discrimination, black racism, reverse sexism by feminists, etc., are all bogus concepts—dishonest inventions of those who fear loss of their privileges. They hold that discrimination, racism, sexism, etc., are all exclusionary practices and beliefs, and groups other than the dominant one (white heterosexual males) are not in a position to exclude.

Such clearly collectivist reasoning continues to stifle criticism. That it carries the weight it does testifies dramatically that in the real centers of power, supporters of the various aspects of the philosophy of social engineering are basically in control. This may seem an extreme, even paranoid claim. The country's intellectual "center," however, has collapsed amidst a guilt stemming from the moral confusion of its leaders, many of whom not only lack firm convictions but celebrate this state of affairs as a virtue. Thus, social engineers can write of a "dominant culture" of white, heterosexual, males, and masquerade as beleaguered outsiders despite their enormous influence, particularly in colleges and universities where their views and the dogmatic, authoritarian ways they are maintained are commonly known as political correctness. There is evidence that they will attempt to destroy people they perceive as a serious enough threat.[11]

3. Against the Philosophy of Social Engineering

In this light, it might seem futile to think the philosophy of social engineering can be overturned by reason alone. After all, its advocates seem only to understand force; in fact, its academic representatives advocate a world view steeped in antirealism, irrationality, and neomysticism. No doubt, a long and possibly furious struggle for control of the educational and legal systems is ahead. But be that as it may, more and more people, some of them women and minorities, are aware that something bad has happened to the civil rights movement and appendages such as the women's movement.[12] Blacks in particular know that something is wrong when despite decades of government effort and expenditure, so many of their number are failing to advance economically. Their neighborhoods are crime-ridden; their lives are often decimated by violence, broken families, teenage pregnancies, chemical dependencies, and hopelessness. If affirmative action and welfare-state measures worked, surely there would be some evidence of their benefits, and this evidence would be obvious to everyone. Instead, large segments of the black community have slipped backward during the affirmative action era. On the other hand, another segment of the black community has advanced steadily through the efforts of its own members. Many of these advances took place during the 1980s, supposedly a decade of hostility toward minority interests. Could it be that these people know or have discovered something that has eluded the academic-bureaucratic elite? Could it be that the latter's premises are simply false?

Many doubts about the premises of the philosophy of social engineering should emerge merely by looking at their effects. Many of these have been expressed succinctly by women and minorities themselves. My criticisms will be more direct. I believe we can reject the philosophy of social engineering not because it has this or that negative consequence but because it *is* false. It is in fact a fabric of mutually inconsistent and sometimes self-contradictory claims. Its falsehood ought to help explain its social failure.

Collectivism has come under fire from several quarters. Ayn Rand attacked it as immoral and antirational. Mises and Hayek offered instrumental arguments against it. Both sets of insights are important. Crucial differences between individuals and groups show collectivism to be impossible. An individual has an unimaginably complex brain and central nervous system that receives and integrates enormous amounts of information. Since no two individuals' experiences are identical—nor, for genetic reasons, are their brains and senses exact copies of one another—while different individuals should arrive at many of the same concepts, they may arrive at them by different routes and make use of them in different ways. Hence, differences exist even between siblings raised in virtually identical environments, as do similarities between individuals from different environments. Rand asserted that, "there is no such thing as a collective brain."[13] She was right. There is nothing in any collective entity that approaches a cognitive process or even a genuinely organic existence. While corporations do have internal structures and are treated as persons for certain legal purposes, they are composed of individuals each of whom has a separate life, quite unlike a cell or organ in an organic body. All "corporate action," moreover, reduces to structured aggregates of actions taken by those in the corporation; to say of a corporation that it "acts," as if there were some supervening, ghostlike entity standing above the individuals making it up, is quite clearly a category mistake. In the case of race and gender, collectivism becomes vastly more problematic. Races and ethnic groups are dispersed across the globe, as are men and women. There can be no structured leadership for an entire race, or for women. This makes it difficult to make sense of, much less maintain, the view that a dominant group can do harm. No single group has that kind of influence. "Multiculturalist" efforts to create "solidarity" among "persons of color" notwithstanding, there is simply no basis for positing supervening collective agencies or claiming that individuality reduces to some combination of group identities.

Collectivism, thus, corresponds with nothing real. Actual groups and organizations are simply too complex. While individuals may share, for example, a racial trait with other individuals, they will differ in countless other ways that are essential to their identities as people. A complete description of these differences would be impossible. There are too many, some are known only to the individuals themselves, and they are always changing unpredictably. This explains the allocation problem that Austrian economists observe at the heart of every attempt to practice socialism, this century's most prevalent form of collectivism. It also explains, in part, the failure of civil rights revisionism. Civil rights revisionism does not see people as individuals, but almost exclusively as group members. It parcels out jobs, college admissions, and the like, accordingly. Its inability to take account of the myriad differences among individuals and identify their real needs is at the root of its more visible inability to cope with the problems of minority communities.

Turn now to *determinism*. A vast literature exists on the problem of determinism and free will, much of it technical and very high in quality. The problem is difficult, and enormous effort has been necessary just to clarify it. Yet it appears that a consistent determinist must endorse the idea that in principle every human action, down to the finest detail (including details of human cognition) can be assigned efficient causes. According to determinism, metaphysical freedom does not exist. True, sometimes we are free in the sense of being free to do what we want to do. Our wants, however, are as describable in terms of efficient causation as anything else; we are not free to "want what we want." Determinists profess to find metaphysical freedom unintelligible, as seeming to introduce an inexplicable *something* into our account of human beings that science cannot describe and conceptual analysis cannot pin down.[14]

Historically, the most persistent objection to determinism has come from its own internal logic. Determinism being a thesis about human beings, it incorporates a thesis about human cognition. Since determinism itself results from human cognition, if true, its own formulation and defense are as subject to deterministic strictures as any other natural process. Hence, the determinist, like everyone else, could not have reached any conclusion other than the one he did in fact reach. All reasoning, whether about determinism or anything else, is automatic and its conclusions foregone! Thus if determinism is assumed true then the determinist himself had no control over his own cognitive processes and, hence, over the content of his thoughts. There can, therefore, be no compelling basis for accepting his conclusions.[15] Many determinists respond that this begs the question; the concept designated by *control* as just used assumes metaphysical freedom. But, in practice we distinguish *causes* of beliefs from *reasons* for them. To say that someone believes *p* because he was caused to do so has a pejorative connotation; such a ploy might be used to expose one's belief in *p* as irrational or unfounded. The *rationality* of a belief, at the very least, implies or presupposes the possibility of reflective judgment and deliberation outside efficient causation. To be sure, this does not answer every question or address every subtlety. More attention is needed to causality itself and its various forms, as well as to the connection between rationality and cognitive independence. These go outside our topic. But surely, regarding determinism, there is sufficient reasonable doubt that the social engineer cannot simply assume it.

Indeed, the consequences of determinism for other parts of the philosophy of social engineering make matters worse. If determinism is true, elitism is almost certainly impossible, and economic egalitarianism very likely unintelligible. For if determinism is true, elites are no less affected by causal determinants than anyone else. These might be different from those that condition the behaviors of the masses. But they are, nevertheless, outside the scope of what can be controlled; to suggest otherwise is to suggest that the elites can control the determinants on their own behavior, which is self-contradictory. In this case, determinism vitiates the possibility of universal social engineering. At best, it suggests a kind of technocracy that, if determinism is in fact false, would lead to a totalitarianism of the *Brave New World* variety. Turning to determinism versus economic egalitarianism, we find more incompatability. Again, determinism suggests that contemporary culture could not be other than it is. It is merely the result of historical forces whose effects could not be other than what they are. If history has produced a nonegalitarian state of affairs, then it simply makes no sense to condemn this state of affairs on moral or any other grounds. This would presuppose that matters could be otherwise, and this is just what determinism precludes. Probably as much effort has been spent on clarifying the three-way relationship between determinism, free will, and moral responsibility as on the determinism-freedom question itself. "Soft" determinists believe that determinism and moral responsibility are compatible; hence, their preferred term *compatibilism*. But the upshot of their position is that only a weak, instrumental sense of morality is really compatible with determinism. One can easily argue that moral language and beliefs are among the causal factors that produce certain kinds of behavior. Those who desire to produce a given behavior may adopt an appropriate moral vocabulary; what they cannot give their vocabulary is rational, cognitive force. Thus, given determinism, the claim that egalitarianism is in some sense the morally proper state of affairs is mere propaganda at best, and at worst simply unintelligible. Egalitarianism is further contradicted by the very idea of elitism, which affirms the existence of a class of people who know more, have better moral insight, and can make better contributions to social improvements than anyone else. It is, in fact, hard to imagine a more inegalitarian notion than elitism in the sense social engineering presupposes. Finally, if the cognitive determinism of multiculturalism is true, then again it applies to the multiculturalists themselves, and we should wonder how they have transcended the determinants of race, ethnicity, gender and class in order to achieve the multiculturalist perspective.

With collectivism gone and huge question marks hanging over determinism, the whole basis for a psychology of victimization is in doubt, if only because we can no longer make sense of its premises. The psychology of victimization presents us with the specter of entire groups having victimized other groups, so that victimization is a global and not merely local phenomenon so far as a given group is concerned. A small but growing literature has begun to document the damaging effects of the psychology of victimization on the black community.[16] Yet again, allegations about historical victimization itself are only as good as their premises. It is dubious that genuine victimization can ever happen to more than a fraction of the members of a group. It is hardly clear, that is, that blacks today can be said to have been directly victimized by slavery. Far better evidence documents the victimizing effects of the last 30 years of welfare-statism; prior to the 1960s there was much more discrimination and segregation, but black neighborhoods tended to be safe and black families tended to stay together. Evidence to support the psychology of victimization as the result of a global phenomenon is simply not there.

4. Toward a Libertarian Agenda for Civil Rights

Today's arguments for large-scale affirmative-action reparations for blacks because of historical victimization (slavery, segregation) therefore fail. No one alive today was a slave or even born to a slave; nor are there any former slave-owners alive today. Indeed, when slavery was practiced only a small percentage of whites owned slaves. Yet with all that said, one may reply that *some* blacks were harmed greatly by laws and practices aimed at them by *some* whites; the same can be said for women and other minority groups (American Indians come to mind). Racism, though fading in the face of near-universal disapproval, still exists; *some* whites would still use the legal system to lock blacks out of markets if they could. Thus arises the need for a civil rights agenda of *some* sort.

Libertarianism has the most powerful starting point available for an appropriate civil rights agenda that offers protections to everyone: the concept of self-ownership, coupled with the denial that anyone owns the life or the fruits of the labors of others. This constitutes the most forceful objection to slavery possible. According to libertarian principles, the sole purpose of government is to protect individuals' rights to life, liberty, and justly-acquired property. Slavery presupposes that some individuals may own other individuals as property and dispose of their lives as they see fit. This clearly violates the latter's rights to life and liberty, at the very least! Doing away with slavery was in fact a libertarian move, if a mostly unconscious one. How can we develop further an explicit libertarian agenda for civil rights?

Elsewhere, I have developed what I call the *philosophy of social spontaneity*,[17] inspired in part by Bolick's definition of *civil rights*: natural rights embodied in civil law—the rights to life, liberty, and property. The philosophy of social spontaneity includes propositions such as the following:

(1) Individualism: individuals, not groups, are the most basic units in society.

(2) Metaphysical freedom or "free will": individuals are capable of acting freely in the world. Hence, they are economic actors and moral agents, not historically or culturally conditioned automata. Indeed, reality—the physical and biological space we inhabit—is such that intelligent beings must take specific courses of action in order first to survive and then to prosper. Individual, natural rights to life (self-ownership), liberty (to take action) and property (the fruits of one's actions or transactions made with others) follow from the conditions required by life itself.[18]

(3) Personal responsibility: the need to take specific courses of action requires that individuals identify their options and act in ways that will bring them genuine benefit, not harm. One can repudiate the psychology of victimization.

(4) Limited government: the primary purpose of government is to protect rights to life, liberty, and property; it should not be in the business of granting group-entitlements (forcibly expropriating the fruits of the labors of some and distributing them to others).

(5) Voluntarism: all transactions should be voluntary and not coerced. Government can, therefore, tell no one whom he or she must hire or in what proportions. Government, in this view, should not interfere with workaday business transactions at all, provided the transactions are voluntary. This would violate property rights.

(6) Reliance on the independent sector: a variety of private associations and institutions—neighborhood organizations, clubs, churches, philanthropic societies, etc.—within which individuals may pool their resources to improve their lives and those of their less fortunate fellows without calling on government.

Let's expand on these remarks, with an eye to how their adoption can help minority-group members.

(1) At first glance, that the interests of minorities are better served by individualism than collectivism sounds counterintuitive. Some collectivists make the argument that individualism automatically serves the interests of the dominant group. Says one such writer, a university administrator, "This is a RED FLAG phrase today, which is considered by many to be RACIST. Arguments that champion the individual over the group ultimately privi-

leges [sic] the 'individuals' belonging to the largest or dominant group."[19] However, *racism is a form of collectivism*. The genuine racist hates, is bigoted toward, believes in the inferiority of, etc., a person of another race exclusively on the basis of race, i.e., *group identity*. Given that racism presupposes collectivism, *a genuine individualist cannot be a racist*. The two ways of viewing human beings are incompatible. This is one of the strongest arguments a libertarian can make.

Another powerful argument lies with the realization that individualism, as a social metaphysic like collectivism, purports to name a basic fact of human reality, one that, if true, individuals ignore at their peril. What we know is that individuals in any given group share many traits but also differ widely in personal experiences, levels of ability, motivation, and innumerable other respects. These differences matter for affirmative action purposes, since obviously it is a person, not a group, appointed to a position or admitted to a university. While someone can design an affirmative action program under the assumption that a black person had to work harder than a white person to achieve equal qualifications, the logistics of testing this assumption on a proper case-by-case basis are impossible, and not even attempted. All a committee can readily determine is the degree of fit between a person and a job description from the person's credentials, references, and an interview. Personal effort may well be greater for some than others, and for a variety of reasons of which race is only one. But personal effort is not quantifiable or publicly observable; from the hiring or admitting committee's point of view, concrete results are what is visible. Simply to assume that a black person had to make more effort to reach a given level of competence than a white person and hire on that basis is just to lapse back into hiring by race.

In the final analysis, individualism often fails to appeal because it is easily confused with similar ideas of less merit—confusions collectivists are all too willing to exploit. Individualism asserts that human beings are *individuals*, not parts of larger collective entities. While this may entail some form of normative ethical egoism, it surely does not lead automatically to *social atomism*, the idea that individuals are psychologically, epistemologically and ethically isolated atoms unable to identify *any* common interests, in which there is only competition for limited quantities of goods in a Hobbesian "war of all against all." This seriously misconstrues individualism. If anything, it combines individualism with determinism by insinuating that no one is free to choose cooperation over competition for mutual, long-term benefit. Genuine individualism, however, does not deny that we can act in the interests of others if we choose. The contention that an individualist must be an *irrationally* selfish, vaguely bloodthirsty fellow, in eternal competition with and invariably at odds with others, is, therefore, a strawman and not a serious criticism of individualism.

(2) The idea that people are free agents is the idea that they are capable of acting either in one specific way or in some other way, all other things being equal, and in so doing initiating sequences of causes and effects that would not exist otherwise (and for which they are responsible). Rights are rights to take specific actions. A libertarian civil rights agenda may then proceed by adopting metaphysical freedom, a strong interpretation of the Austrian economist's basic axiom: human beings act.[20] They affect their environment to make it more to their liking. The importance of action as a means both to survival and self-improvement cannot be stressed enough. Many philosophers have held that metaphysical freedom is a necessary condition for a moral view of the world. Again, some clarification is called for. To affirm the reality of metaphysical freedom is not to affirm that all are equally free, or that one can choose to act in any way one sees fit without restraints of various sorts. Obviously, we are bound by physical and biological laws governing our nature. We are not free to violate the laws of physics or of our own nature by, say, flapping our arms and flying. Metaphysical freedom, therefore, asserts that in any given situation where a decision must be made there is a range of finite options. In this context an *option* is a possibility for successful action. Ignorance may narrow one's actual options, which are obviously limited to what one knows. Honesty demands the admission that some people have fewer actual options than others. No one, though, has *zero* options (unless, of course, one is catatonic or in a coma). There is no one in such bad shape as to be incapable of learning that (for example) smoking crack is harmful, or that having a baby while still a teenager severely limits one's options. One can learn that formal education will open many doors, and finish school. Individuals *can learn to take action* to improve their situations. Should the inner-city teenager smoke crack or have a baby anyway, then her problem is her own bad choices, which have automatically worked against her own long term best interests. Should she drop out of school, her actions close doors rather than open them.

(3) This suggests a *third* and absolutely critical aspect of a libertarian civil rights agenda: *personal responsibility*. Some of one's options will further one's best long-term interests, others will harm them; the rational individual is the person who makes a concerted effort to identify one's best long-term interests and take the appropriate actions, while avoiding actions which lead to long-term harm (this will usually include taking actions which benefit others as a matter of course). The psychology of victimization creates disincentives for taking beneficial actions by suggesting that action is either impossible or futile, building on the deterministic view that personal

responsibility is an illusion. It nurtures the idea that blacks are helpless automata because of slavery and discrimination. Moreover, it encourages the very sort of resentment that leads to attacks on others rather than actions taken to improve oneself. But no one can never *not act* (even sitting in one's room and doing nothing all day qualifies as *action* in a broad sense that it has consequences). The crime of the psychology of victimization, therefore, is that it encourages individuals to act in ways that are harmful to themselves. Of course, in a free society one has the right to act in self-destructive ways so long as one is not destroying others in the process. But if one attaches *personal responsibility* to individual rights, one will normally not be motivated to act in such ways. In fact, defending rights without responsibilities is itself irresponsible. A society firmly grounded in principles of *laissez-faire* economics and individual freedoms will deteriorate just as fast as a socialist society if enough of its individuals are pursuing irresponsible, self- and socially destructive patterns of action.

A libertarian civil rights agenda, in this case, should affirm a psychology of personal responsibility, which involves realizing that actions (like ideas) have consequences, and then taking actions that have beneficial consequences for one's life. In practice, this means acquiring an education including basic literary skills, marketable skills, and enough information to participate in the workings of a free society by electing responsible leaders. It means avoiding harmful actions (e.g., being violent, or abusing drugs and alcohol).[21] Without a psychology of personal responsibility to replace the psychology of victimization, even the best intentioned civil rights agenda with the best premises will not succeed.

(4) Another cornerstone of a libertarian civil rights agenda is the need to limit government. Basic libertarian principles hold that individuals are the basic units in society, that they must sustain and improve their lives through specific courses of action. Their rights to do so do not protect themselves and must be defended—there will always be a few who interfere with the rights of others. Therefore, government must exist to protect individuals' rights to life, liberty, and justly-acquired property; and to punish those who infringe on the rights of others according to a specific, publicly available code of laws. But government must be limited to these functions, and otherwise pursue a policy of noninterference with the private, noncoercive actions of citizens. It should not be in the business of granting *entitlements*. A libertarian civil rights agenda will stress that when government grants entitlements it only harms those it sets out to help: it creates dependency by creating disincentives to take those courses of action that lead to self-improvement. There is a hard and fast difference between rights and entitlements: rights can be acted upon without interference with others;

entitlements can only be fulfilled through such interference.[22] Government, therefore, must be limited to protecting rights.

(5) A libertarian civil rights agenda will uphold the *voluntary* nature of all legitimate transactions. In practice, this will mean that *in principle* individuals who own businesses will be free to hire and promote individuals on any basis they see fit; they will also be free to do business or refuse to do business with individuals on any basis they see fit. In principle, they will be free to hire exclusively whites or exclusively blacks; exclusively men or exclusively women; they may adopt affirmative action initiatives or even overt quotas; or they may hire exclusively on perceived merit independently of race and gender considerations.[23] The *in principle* is important, for *in practice*, if a business owner is to act responsibly, he will adopt procedures that will increase his prosperity and avoid practices that are damaging (personal responsibility again). This means hiring the best employees available and maximizing the number of satisfied customers. A business owner who refuses to hire or do business with blacks because of racism may find himself passing over good employees who go to work for a nonracist competitor; his customer base and, hence, his profits will also erode, because blacks will purchase from the competition, and so will whites who find racism sufficiently objectionable. In this way, a free market actually discourages racism as unprofitable and irresponsible, in addition to whatever moral arguments can be mustered against it.

Libertarians cannot stress enough that distrust of voluntarism has harmed minorities more than it has ever helped them. Think of the minimum wage. One cannot overlook how minimum-wage laws have priced thousands of members of minority groups out of the labor force. In this way, government prevents blacks from working at jobs they can obtain for wages that match their skills on an open market, thus preventing them from obtaining skills that would eventually improve their earning power. The poorest are harmed the worst. This has the effect of a more subtle form of segregation.[24] Or think of licensure laws. Licensure laws (1) place control over entry into a given occupation in the hands of a group of overseers with noneconomic—perhaps racial—incentives to permit entry to some while excluding others, (2) raise the cost of admission by stipulating a specific form of education, often requiring heavy fees, that may permanently bar entry into the field for many would-be minority entrepreneurs or employees; therefore (3), they arbitrarily narrow the number of practitioners in a given occupation, while (4) raising the price of services to consumers. The taxicab industry offers a good example of a heavily licensed occupation.[25] Licensure laws impact negatively on blacks and other minorities because they impact negatively on all vulnerable persons, including blacks. They protect the established from new and unwanted competition. In all these ways, a government that persists in interfering with individual liberties and property rights actually brings more harm than genuine assistance to those it would assist.

(6) Yet many members of minority groups are behind whites economically. If they cannot obtain government assistance, or if, as we have argued, government assistance actually does harm, then how do they get started? Surely such notions as independence and a psychology of personal responsibility are not self-evident. Or even if they were, surely one does not simply wake up one day and start a business if one does not have the capital resources. Where can minorities turn in order to get on the ladder to a better life? This is a good question, and a legitimate civil rights agenda ought to address it. In my judgment, libertarians can answer it; moreover, the institutions to which the libertarian answer appeals do not have to be built from scratch. They exist now. All that needs to be done is to harness their energy.

Richard Cornuelle has discussed the *independent sector* in detail.[26] The independent sector is a loose and unstructured array of institutions, from philanthropic foundations and societies to churches, private clubs, and neighborhood and professional organizations. In the past, such associations spontaneously arose to meet human needs that government could not meet and were left mostly untouched by profit-motivated enterprises. They allow individuals from disadvantaged groups to pool their resources; others *not* disadvantaged are also encouraged to pool *their* resources to help out those who are, or who have suffered setbacks of one form or another. Those who are attempting to start up new enterprises ranging from neighborhood schools to small businesses may then draw on these resources. The superiority of such organizations to governmental ones should be obvious. The focus of the independent sector is grass-roots. Those taking action are in direct contact with the problems, and have a direct stake in the outcome. This is not the case with government, whose focus is at the center and whose procedures tend to be rigid and bureaucratic rather than flexible, entrepreneurial, and aimed at problem-solving. Bureaucracies tend to perpetuate rather than solve the problems, since if they solved the problems their *raison d'etre* would disappear. Bureaucrats rarely have close association with the specifics of a problem situation, which may differ from neighborhood to neighborhood, and thus have little stake in the outcome of their actions. The independent sector thus automatically encourages actions leading to prosperity, while bureaucracy tends to discourage them. In the past, numerous philanthropic organizations existed; they helped the country survive the Great Depression and made numerous other contributions to American culture. Today, the independent sector has receded in the face of expansionist government. A version of it exists, however, in Asian communities. Koreans, for example, have often succeeded because of their commitment to a strong extended family unit, which can pool its resources with other such units. Many Korean businesses have started this way. Blacks, on the other hand, have fallen consistently behind. The reason lies with their leadership, which today looks to government. Through a willingness to rely on government programs, their communities have faltered. For this to continue would be truly unfortunate, since the black community contains many organizations that could provide the nucleus of a flourishing independent sector. Black churches are powerful sources of unity. The NAACP and the National Urban League are two more long-established institutions that could do much to inspire black economic self-empowerment if they ceased looking to government for answers. Finally, organizations such as the Nation of Islam, despite their presently dubious reputations, have enormous potential should their leaders shed their hostility towards whites and Jews and concentrate exclusively on improving the lives of blacks. All must consciously renounce the civil rights revisionism implicit in their assumption that federal legislation has the capacity to help those in their targeted groups.

5. Conclusion

Prevailing approaches to civil rights are not working. They are harming not only white males but those in their targeted groups. I have tried to explain why and outline an alternative.

It was a mistake for civil rights leaders to place their trust in government and in large-scale social planning as an instrument of progress for minorities. Government, after all, was the institution responsible for most of their problems. Slavery, segregation, and discrimination all originally had the full support of government power (even though opponents of all three existed in government). The collectivism that more and more permeates American society today is only increasing problems for everyone. Academics and bureaucrats who seek the "root causes" of the problems of minority communities in deterministic terms, see minorities and women as helpless victims, and advocate more government hiring mandates, government money, and, ultimately, government control, are doing no one any favors. Civil rights revisionism has accomplished little other than to trade one form of coercion for another and create a host of new problems and dilemmas.

The traditional civil rights vision emphasized individual economic empowerment for minorities: freedom to offer one's labor on a market, buy and sell property, etc. A sound libertarian civil rights strategy is really just a call for the rediscovery of these roots. Individuals can begin to realize their potential only when they are free of the heavy hand of government. If the civil rights movement can adopt ideas such as the philosophy of social spontaneity, it can rediscover its true purpose. Admittedly, this is only a start. I have said little about strategies for convincing an entire generation of individuals accustomed to looking to government as its only support. I have also said nothing about how to instill a psychology of personal responsibility into those who have either lost their moral compass or never had it to begin with. Individualist ideas, finally, continue to meet with hostility (or more usually, complete indifference) within academe, government, and the minority communities who ultimately must be convinced. Purveyors of expanded government continue to dominate much of public discourse (aside, perhaps, from talk radio, which tends to be conservative rather than libertarian). All this means that if *we as individuals*, black or white, male or female, want to live in a free society, we have our work cut out for us.

Notes

1. A more complete statement of the argument of the following sections of this paper can be found in my book *Civil Wrongs: What Went Wrong With Affirmative Action* (San Francisco: ICS Press, 1994), esp. chs. 4 and 6.

2. Clint Bolick, *Unfinished Business: A Civil Rights Strategy for America's Third Century* (San Francisco: Pacific Research Institute, 1990). Though I lack space to develop the point, I believe Christina Hoff Sommers has documented the very same ambiguity in recent feminism. She distinguishes between *equity* feminism and *gender* feminism. The former is consistent with the extension of basic individual rights to women; the latter is resolutely hostile to the very idea of individual rights and other founding principles of this country (e.g., free speech). See her *Who Stole Feminism? How Women Have Betrayed Women* (New York: Simon and Schuster, 1994).

3. Bolick, *Unfinished Business*, 15.

4. Thomas Paine, *The Rights of Man* (Buffalo, New York: Prometheus Books, 1987, 43; orig. pub. 1787).

5. Bolick, *Unfinished Business*, 32–33.

6. Friedrich A. Hayek, *The Road to Serfdom* (Chicago: University of Chicago Press, 1944), 56.

7. For a discussion and critique of this position see my "Multiculturalism and Epistemology," *Public Affairs Quarterly* 6 (1992): 435–56.

8. Nicholas Capaldi, *Out of Order: Affirmative Action and the Crisis of Doctrinaire Liberalism* (Buffalo, New York: Prometheus Books, 1985), 2.

9. For two examples of this latter claim see George G. M. James, *Stolen Legacy* (Trenton, New Jersey: Africa World Press, 1992; orig. pub. 1954) and Martin Bernal, *Black Athena* (New Brunswick, New Jersey: Rutgers University Press, 1991).

10. For some discussion of this point see my "Civil Wrongs and Religious Liberty," *Journal of Interdisciplinary Studies* 6 (1994): 67–87.

11. The events surrounding the nomination of Clarence Thomas to the Supreme Court in September of 1991 confirm this. Anita Hill not only had no evidence in support of her accusation that Thomas had sexually harassed her, but it was widely felt—by radical feminists, at least—that "evidence" was not required!

12. See Joseph G. Conti and Brad Stetson, *Challenging the Civil Rights Establishment: Profiles of a New Black Vanguard* (Westport, Connecticut: Praeger Publishers, 1993). For the women's movement, see Christina Hoff Sommers, *Who Stole Feminism?*

13. Ayn Rand, "What is Capitalism?" in *Capitalism: The Unknown Ideal* (New York: Mentor Books, 1967), 16.

14. For recent accounts see Daniel Dennett, *Elbow Room: The Varieties of Free Will Worth Wanting* (Cambridge: MIT Press, 1984) and Ted Honderich, *A Theory of Determinism: A Theory of Mind, Neuroscience, and Life-Hopes* (Oxford: Clarendon Press, 1988). But cf. Peter von Inwagen, *An Essay on Free Will* (Oxford: Clarendon Press, 1983) for a technical defense of metaphysical freedom.

15. This argument is very controversial. Various versions of it exist and have been formulated from within various philosophical perspectives. See C. S. Lewis, *Miracles* (New York: Doubleday, 1947), 23–31; Nathaniel Branden, "The Contradiction in Determinism," *The Objectivist Newsletter* 2 (May 1963): 17, 19–20; Warner Wick, "Truth's Debt to Freedom," *Mind* 73 (1964): 527–37; James N. Jordan, "Determinism's Dilemma," *Review of Metaphysics* 23 (1969): 48–66; J. R. Lucas, *The Freedom of the Will* (Oxford: Oxford University Press, 1970), 114–72; Noam Chomsky, "The Case Against B. F. Skinner," *New York Review of Books*, (December 30, 1971), 20–26; A. Aaron Snyder, "The Paradox of Determinism," *American Philosophical Quarterly* 9 (1972): 353–56; William Hasker, "The Transcendental Refutation of Determinism," *Southern Journal of Philosophy* 11 (1973): 175–83; J. M. Boyle, G. Grisez, and O. Tollefsen, *Free Choice: A Self-Referential Argument* (Notre Dame: University of Notre Dame Press, 1976); Leonard Peikoff, *Objectivism: The Philosophy of Ayn Rand* (New York: Dutton, 1991), 203–05.

16. See Shelby Steele, *The Content of Our Character* (New York: St. Martin's Press, 1989) and Anne Wortham, "Black Victimhood," *The World & I* 11 (1993): 369–83.

17. See my *Civil Wrongs*, ch. 6.

18. See Ayn Rand, "The Objectivist Ethics," in *The Virtue of Selfishness* (New York: Signet Books, 1961), 13–35; Douglas Rasmussen, "Essentialism, Values and Rights," in *The Libertarian Reader*, ed. Tibor R. Machan (Totowa: Rowman and Allenheld, 1982), 37–52; Tibor R. Machan, *Individuals and Their Rights* (LaSalle, Illinois: Open Court, 1989), ch. 2, for full-length versions of this argument.

19. Quoted in Alan Charles Kors, "It's Speech, Not Sex, the Dean Bans Now," *The Wall Street Journal*, 12 October 1989. Original emphasis.

20. See Ludwig Von Mises, *Human Action* (New Haven: Yale University Press, 1949; 2nd. ed. New Haven: Yale University Press, 1963; 3rd ed. Chicago: Contemporary Books, 1966), for the definitive statement of the Austrian position.

21. Libertarians have spent a great deal of energy defending the idea that drugs should be legal. Strictly speaking, they are of course correct. But if people adopt the psychology of personal responsibility advocated here, the issue will be cut down to size, if not rendered largely moot, because responsible people do not take mind-altering drugs.

22. See my "Rights Versus Entitlements," *The Freeman* 44 (1994): 478–79.

23. Tibor Machan qualifies this in a way that is worth a brief look. A business that hires or a restaurant that serves only whites or only blacks ought to say so up front, Machan believes; otherwise a kind of fraud is being perpetuated on the potential employee or the potential customer. In other words, businesses should adopt a policy of *full disclosure*. See his "Liberty and Racial Justice: An Alternative to Coercive Affirmative Action," *The Journal of Private Enterprise* 9 (1993), 32–38.

24. The definitive account here is that of Walter Williams, *The State Against Blacks* (New York: McGraw-Hill, 1982). Cf. my "Interventionism: The Misean Critique and Its Implications," *Public Affairs Quarterly* 9 (1995): in press.

25. See Williams, *The State Against Blacks*, ch. 3; *Civil Wrongs*, ch. 6; for some general reflections on the effects of occupational licensure on professions, see David M. Young, *The Rule of Experts* (Washington, D.C.: The Cato Institute, 1987).

26. Richard Cornuelle, *Reclaiming the American Dream: The Role of Private Individuals and Voluntary Associations* (New York: Random House, 1965; 2nd ed. New Brunswick, New Jersey: Transaction Publishers, 1993).

Business Ethics in a Free Society

Tibor R. Machan

A most serious controversy about capitalism is whether people who manage commerce and business (the professional arm of commerce) may be trusted to use their own judgment concerning how to conduct themselves. One need only look for the topic under the label, "the social responsibility of corporations," even though this label begs the question by assuming that businesses have basic, binding responsibilities to society and the communities in which they live and conduct their professional tasks, whether they have made any commitment to fulfill such responsibilities. While not entirely unreasonable, the idea shouldn't simply be assumed to be correct. Is there a social responsibility for artists, the press, athletes, or writers? Certainly no subdisciplines in ethics developed throughout universities, colleges, and professional schools focus on such issues. Juilliard does not teach such a course, nor do other institutions of higher learning where the various arts are taught. Some would argue, plausibly, that spelling out such standards for (not to mention imposing them on) artists is an infringement on artistic creativity. The same may be said about writers and dancers. (There are no courses in the ethics of scholarship, either, let alone in how to teach professional ethics.)

Graduate schools preparing students for teaching positions at universities have no such courses. It is assumed, apparently, that when the students arrive at their jobs, they themselves will make sure that they behave ethically in their classrooms, and as they carry out their scholarly work. Or perhaps it is assumed that students who embark on degrees in art, philosophy, or literature are already sufficiently moral and require no special courses on ethics. But this assumption is unfounded. Why, then, should we impose ethics courses on those who are obtaining education in the field of business?

Whatever we conclude about the teaching of applied ethics in art, science, and the professions, let us assume for the moment that we need some help in how we think of our ethical responsibilities in various fields of work. Accordingly, we can ask the question, "What are the moral responsibilities of those who embark upon a career in business?" It is this topic that I will explore here by way of considering the views of Milton Friedman, someone who is closely identified with the free market and whose writing on precisely this topic has been widely discussed and criticized.

In the field of business ethics, Friedman's account of the social responsibility of corporations stands out as work that is under extensive scrutiny if not relentless criticism. His basic view—that corporations have the obligation to make a profit within the framework of the legal system, nothing more—is discussed by nearly everyone who writes in this field, and Friedman's own piece is reprinted in virtually all collections of business ethics essays.[1]

The main complaint about his view is, first of all, that it is basically intolerant of government intervention in economic affairs. But criticism begins with the lament that Friedman's moral outlook is too thin. The belief that executives in business enterprises are *morally* obligated, primarily if not exclusively, to make a profit is just too incredible, isn't it? There surely must be something more to what such executives ought to do in their professional capacity. This scepticism about Friedman's view shows the impact of neo-Kantian moral theory, exhibited in most works in contemporary moral philosophy, including some that deal explicitly with business ethics.[2] According to this theory, nothing can be morally praiseworthy or even significant that enhances only personal or even public objectives, that is directed to the satisfaction of some private or vested interest or inclination.

Despite some recent analytical, as distinct from strictly critical, work on Friedman's ideas, the question can and should be raised as to whether the libertarian economic philosophy Friedman himself embraces might not be compatible with a different, let us say richer, conception of the moral responsibility of corporations. This essay will argue that it is. In particular, a position called "classical individualism" will be spelled out here, and it will be shown that this position can address the issue of the social responsibility of corporations better than the one that Friedman defends. Yet classical individualism will remain fully compatible with the position that everyone, including people in business, have a basic right to negative liberty. It will not yield to the contention that the freedom of action of corporations should be limited by government in the effort to advance responsible corporate conduct.[3]

Classical Individualism

Classical individualism (or egoism) is the view that all ought to benefit themselves, first of all (though not exclusively) and that an objective view of human nature provides standards of guidelines on what benefits a person. Furthermore, it is by reference to such standards that private, professional, and political conduct ought to be carried out. According to this form of individualism, contrary to Marx's claim that "the human essence is the true collectivity of man,"[4] the human essence is the true individuality of every human being,[5] without the implication, however, that the human individual is self-sufficient, capable of living a full life cut off from others.

Classical individualism is an ethics of self-development, self-perfection, only with a greater role for individuality than found in similar views, mainly because of the discovery of the fundamental individuality of human nature. Accordingly, whereas it is often argued that a communitarian theory of politics could be inferred from an Aristotelian virtue ethics, classical individualism rejects this and holds that the politics that is justified is libertarian. The reason for this view is that in classical individualism the task of self-perfection must be chosen by the individual. There is here a greater emphasis on individual choice and responsibility, following the Kantian stress that "ought" implies "can." If a person or group of people ought to act in certain ways, this is of moral significance only if the option of not so acting is actual and not foreclosed, even by the punitive measures of the law. Morally significant conduct cannot be regimented or imposed by force.[6] This is how classical individualism gives support to the libertarian polity. Yet it is also important that classical individualism provides such a libertarian polity with its distinctive rationale, not with the standard classical liberal or *homo economicus* support that stresses the greater efficiency of free action for purposes of securing public prosperity.

Classical Individualism and Corporate Responsibility

Because the central features of the free market system may be defended on the basis of this more robust individualism, Friedman's position on the social responsibility of corporations could now be amended without entailing any compromise of his libertarianism—that is, his laissez-faire economics. Nevertheless, as will be evident presently, corporations have a broader range of responsibilities than Friedman ascribes to them.

The essential task of businesses—firms, partnerships, companies, enterprises, and other establishments—needs to be defensible by reference to the general tenets of whatever turns out to be the ethical theory that is most successful, most suited to the task of guiding us most consistently, coherently, and completely in our conduct. Needless to say, it would be difficult to demonstrate here that classical individualism is this ethical theory. What can be achieved here, I think, is to show that classical individualism is a richer ethical framework from which to identify the ingredients of a system of general and professional ethics than that presupposed in Friedman's often-discussed theory of the social responsibility of corporations.

Let me define "professional ethics" as a code of conduct pertaining to a specialized field of activity—law, medicine, education, diplomacy, or business—justified in terms of a sound ethics.[7] Professional ethics, to have any binding persuasive force, must rest on a sound general ethical system, lest it amount to nothing more than a conventional framework that some people prefer and wish to impose on others.

By "business," I have in mind an organized human endeavor that has as its dominant end economic enhancement or prosperity, or wealth. That is, businesses are profit making institutions[8]. Whereas physicians heal, attorneys make cases before the law, educators develop and impart knowledge, business professionals have as their central task increasing wealth.[9] Business ethics, then, is a branch of professional ethics. It is concerned with how people engaged in commerce and working in the field of business ought to conduct themselves.

Is Business Morally Legitimate?

Any profession, whether very generally conceived, e.g., as medicine, or highly specialized, such as a branch of it, for example plastic surgery, can be subjected to ethical scrutiny. Those who embrace the morality of pacifism argue that the military profession is morally misguided, if not outright vicious. Those convinced that Christian Science preaches the moral truth argue that physicians do wrong. Most Roman Catholics argue that abortionists are morally corrupt. Those opposed to euthanasia claim that physicians who assist people in their efforts to commit suicide are violating their professional ethics, based on the Hippocratic oath. Some utilitarians, in turn, condemn the use of animals for purposes that support our pleasures and medical needs because doing so diminishes total welfare.

Whether we judge from a narrow or broad moral perspective, we often hold professions up to such critical scrutiny. From a rather common-sense moral perspective, some professions seem to be on the verge of immorality. Espionage comes to mind here; that aspect of the profession is exploited to full measure by John LeCarre in his numerous novels, most notably *The Spy Who Came In From The Cold*.

In common-sense morality or the ethics that tends to guide most people within a given culture and that requires philosophical assistance only when dilemmas arise, the profession of business may be viewed as based, ultimately, on the virtue of prudence. Prudence has been identified as the first of the cardinal virtues, and it requires that we take conscientious care of ourselves. It is a virtue to do so, whereas slothfulness, recklessness, carelessness, inattentiveness, etc., are all deemed moral failings.[10]

The fact that prudence is a virtue does not settle the matter of the moral basis of commerce. Two questions need to be addressed so as to be sure that prudence does indeed give commerce moral support. First, what exactly is the nature of the self of which we must take care? An idealist and even dualist idea of the self will lead us to understand prudence as less focused upon prosperity here in life than would a naturalist conception. If human beings are essentially divided into two parts, one tied to this world, the other reaching for a superior, supernatural dimension, prudence will in this view have different implications from one that conceives of the self as part of the natural world alone.

The second question is whether we can rank the familiar moral virtues when they seem to be in conflict from the viewpoint of common sense.[11] Here we need an ethical theory that places our common-sense ideals and ethics in a coherent framework. Hard cases in ethics aren't decidable without a systematic moral viewpoint. Classical individualism is a candidate for serving this purpose. One point in its favor would be if it managed the hard cases well and could be applied readily within the fields of professional ethics, such as business.

Classical Individualism and Business Ethics

Assuming for now that classical individualism—otherwise referred to as classical egoism, the ethics of individual flourishing, and the ethics of self-perfection—is sound, what are its implications for professional ethics and for business ethics in particular?

A significant part of what a person ought to do in life is to secure economic values: objectives that enable one to obtain worldly goods, pleasures, joys, delights, etc. We may regard this as implied by the virtue of prudence. But unlike the individualism of many textbooks on ethics,[12] in classical individualism one aims to make oneself a good human being as the individual one is, and *that involves many capacities to be realized outside economic ones*.

While it is vital to serve one's economic or, more broadly, prudential goals, even these can extend far beyond the mere satisfaction of one's desires. Thus, given the classical individualist outlook, one's desires should be shaped by the vision one creates of oneself as the human being one can and would ideally or optimally become.

Professional versus Social Responsibilities

There are—to focus on the distinction between this and Friedman's thesis concerning the social responsibility of corporations—vital community and political dimensions of one's self that may require enhancement even in the course of conducting one's professional tasks. In the case of corporate business, for example, one may be morally responsible not only for reaching one's economic objectives—which are moral in their own right—but also various objectives associated with being a member of one's community.

Professional ethics involves determining the responsibilities and restraints one needs to observe in relationship to the profession one has chosen to pursue. Of course, there are preprofessional ethics that guide one in determining what one's profession will be, so it is assumed that the choice of profession is itself capable of being morally justified. Once so justified, the question then left is what that choice implies—mostly conscientiousness in one's professional conduct—and what else ought to be attended to in connection with one's chosen profession.

Friedman's thesis was that no moral claim may be made on those in corporate business other than to fulfill their implied promise to their clients, namely, to secure for them the greatest possible economic benefits "while conforming to the basic rules of the society, both those embodied in law and in ethical custom."[13] This view is consistent with the radical individualist conception of the human being; beyond the mere imperative of keeping a promise made in the service of one's self-interested goals, there is nothing one ought to do in one's capacity as a business professional.

Critics view this as an impoverished conception of what a human being ought to do in a professional role. Often, they go to the other extreme and argue that business should nearly be sacrificed for whatever alternative need is evident in the community. Furthermore, business is to be tamed so that it is not pursued with the kind of rapaciousness that one associates with an innately selfish drive for profiteering.

The classical individualist position understands professional ethics to require that one's *dominant* yet not *exclusive* objective is the conscientious performance of one's professional tasks, to fulfill one's job description, as it were, to carry out what one has embarked upon in one's capacity as a professional. In business, this amounts, indeed, to what Friedman believes is the exclusive or sole task of business: the pursuit of profit. To the contrary, one's professional responsibilities are not all one is responsible for carrying out. They are fully consistent with paying heed to other goals, including, fulfilling parental duties, being a good friend, enhancing the quality of one's community, improving the environment, and developing and maintaining sound political institutions. First, one has obligations to achieve goals other than those one takes up professionally, and some of these take priority over one's job. Second, even in the course of fulfilling one's professional responsibilities one might have to pay attention to goals that do not directly bear on profit maximization. Thus, the totality of one's moral tasks, combined with those arising from the fulfillment of professional tasks within the physical and political setting of one's place of work, oblige one who is in the world of business to go beyond what Friedman claims he ought to pay exclusively heed to.[14]

Ethics and Choice

One dimension to classical individualism recalls a certain feature of deontological ethics. This is the importance of moral sovereignty, the role of the choices of the moral agent in the determination of conduct. This is where fundamental individuality or selfhood enters the moral situation, by recognizing that it is the person who chooses morally significant conduct for himself, not others for him. Instead of atomistic individualism, this view embraces moral individualism, which is the view that the individuality of human beings is central and emerges through everyone's moral agency, in being the initiator of morally significant conduct.

Accordingly, the scope of legally enforceable moral responsibility within classical individualist ethics is respect for others' moral agency, nothing more. This framework does not identify individuals as being naturally *connected* to society, in the fashion in which a team member is tied to the team or a business partner is tied to the partnership. Social ties in adulthood, even if they are essential and proper, must in classical individualism be left to choice, not imposed by law. And law enters only when citizens' sovereignty is intentionally or negligently infringed upon.

Hence, while the moral demands of classical individualism on those in various professions, including business, are greater than those advanced in Friedman's position, the political framework of business conduct implicit in this ethics is close to that advocated by Friedman. For example, although businesses ought to support neighborhoods to improve their quality, they may not be coerced to do so.[15]

Business Ethics: Some Issues in Focus

Now that we have explored the ethical foundations of business and the main tenets of business ethics, we can now take a brief look at some of the implications of this viewpoint for certain frequently raised concerns within business ethics. Although many of those concerned are actually focused upon public policy—i.e., what governments ought to or ought not to do about business—there are others that are indeed *bona fide* ethical concerns. Among these, we find such issues as: Is racial discrimination in conducting trade, employment, and promotion morally wrong? What should advertisers do or not do in their endeavors to attract buyers to their products or services? Ought those in the financial professions engage in insider trading? How should one deal with laws and customs when doing business abroad? Should employees be treated as subordinates in a firm? Is it morally wrong to hire non-union employees when one's employees have gone on strike? Is nepotism always morally objectionable? Is there moral merit to any type of affirmative action? And, finally, is it always a form of morally objectionable bigotry to hire or fire on the basis of the prospective employee's beliefs?

We will look at these matters briefly here, merely to suggest the implications of classical individualism for these and other concerns that arise in business ethics proper. We will not concern ourselves here explicitly with broader issues of public policy and law. Let us take some of these issues under consideration:

Is racial discrimination in conducting trade, employment, and promotion morally wrong?

It is nearly always wrong, unless race has a direct bearing on advancing the business. Thus, a casting agency for movies would have a concern with employing people who can indeed be cast in parts that the motion picture industry needs in its films, and paying attention to race in such a business would be morally legitimate. Otherwise, it would be wrong because (a) race is no indicator of any kind of talent or skill and (b) paying attention to race distracts from the responsibility of those engaged in business, namely, to generate profit, that is, to prosper. Generally, racial discrimination is unjust and unproductive.

Despite this, no general prohibition of racial or any other type of discrimination can be justified. What can be legally actionable, in the systems of laws of a free society, is the failure to disclose racial or similar irrelevant criteria for engaging in trade, when the reasonable assumption is that no such criteria are invoked (as when one walks into a restaurant designated only as "restaurant," whereas, in fact, it is a restricted place of business).

What should advertisers do or not do in their endeavors to attract buyers to their products or services?

Advertising involves, in essence, calling attention to one's products and services, not mainly conveying information. Thus, advertising is necessarily a partisan, promotional activity, wherein only some of the truth about products or services is of relevance. (One does not have to promote possible liabilities—e.g., the high cost of one's wares relative to competitors, just as a resume needn't contain unfavorable information.) Advertising ought to involve gimmicks, if these achieve the goal of gaining customers' attention—celebrities, jingles, and humor. Where, however, information is being utilized for advertising purposes, honesty is required, mainly because honesty is generally required in human relationships and also because dishonesty distorts one's business processes and undermines the prospects of business success. Advertising is not a creator of desires, but a means of turning those who already desire something to one's products and services in hope of having these achieve the satisfaction of those desires. Of course, potential customers may learn from advertising—but that is true of anything regardless of whether teaching is its central purpose (entertainment, adventure). Advertisers do need not to concern themselves about the vulnerability of adult consumers—that is the responsibility of the consumer, except in some cases where advertisers know that a significant segment of their target group has special deficiencies that may distinguish it.

Ought those in the financial professions engage in insider trading?

Unless a fiduciary duty is violated or information is illegally obtained, insider trading is sound business practice. Getting a jump on others is part of doing good business. One would not demand that people forgo important opportunities solely to benefit total strangers. Insider trading is merely prudent and entrepreneurial trading, and it is to the credit of traders to embark on it.[16]

How should one deal with laws and customs when doing business abroad?

Doing business is not mainly proselytizing or advancing causes, but promoting one's economic well-being. If the basic individual human rights of potential trading partners are respected, and if one's own integrity need not be compromised, one ought to do business wherever profitable. But contributing to the torture of innocent people so as to make money is morally wrong, as is the facilitation of slavery or other types of oppression. Yet things may not be what they appear—doing business in a country with oppressive practices could help ease those practices, depending on the business policies employed. However, sending a black to head a division in a country that practices apartheid would be bad business and not required by justice, as long as it is understood that, aside from business objectives, it is morally decent to promote racial justice as well. Sending a woman to head a division in a country in which sexual discrimination against women is the rule would have to be considered imprudent. But when one tolerates morally objectionable practices, one does not necessarily condone them. One is not guilty of any moral wrongdoing.

Should employees be treated as subordinates or partners within a firm?

Employees are not owners. They are trading partners who join a business on certain mutually agreed-to terms. If those terms require subordinating one's judgment to that of others, that is what the employee will be asked to do. A manager should manage those who are hired with the understanding that this is what will be going on. But subordination has its proper scope—it may not be extended to areas that do not fall under the purview of the enterprise. Thus, managers or other leaders and "bosses" would act immorally in utilizing their job-specific position of superiority for irrelevant purposes. (This is where sexual and other exploitation would be morally wrong.) It may be a controversial issue of public policy, yet, employees have no special rights outside those everyone has and ones that have been created through honest negotiation.

Is it morally wrong to hire nonunion employees when one's employees have gone on strike?

This depends on the employee agreement. But if people walk away from a job, to hire others to work is sound business policy, and morally unobjectionable. "Scabs" are competing employees who demand less from the employer than others. It may well be their best chance at employment. In a free society, no one can be made to work for others, and this applies also to employers—they may not be forced to work for the employees.

Is nepotism always morally objectionable?

Nepotism, favoring kin in hiring, promotion, and trade in general, is usually morally objectionable because it tends to undermine the purposes of business and to deceive others to whom it has been indicated that the employment relationship depends on merit, not blood. But there are many exceptions—when some family members are in dire need, and business objectives might have to give way to more important ones, or when the business itself would improve by way of family cooperation, (in which case nepotism is merely apparent).

Is there moral merit to any type of affirmative action?

Affirmative action, when not a public mandate and thus an intervention in freedom of trade, is often morally unobjectionable. People from some ethnic, racial, religious or national group may have succeeded to the point where they are in a position to help those who are just starting, and if the policy does not undermine business, following it can be generous and charitable.

Is it always a form of morally objectionable bigotry to hire or fire on the basis of the prospective employee's beliefs, etc.?

Sometimes what people believe and would act on is so repulsive morally that even if they are best qualified for a job, they should not be hired. A very skilled engineer or manager who happens also to be a Nazi should not be hired, since the business objective that might be enhanced by employing the person would not outweigh the betrayal of one's values. A private firm owned by a Roman Catholic cannot reasonably be expected to give economic support to someone who despises Roman Catholicism. Freedom of association is well-founded on the need to trust people's judgments, especially when it comes to something that is a matter of choice, namely, what people believe and use for guidance in their lives.

Conclusion

The purview of professional ethics, as any area of applied ethics—indeed, of ethics itself—is in constant flux. While some very broad principles can be identified—and this is what gives the field of ethics its standing and constant relevance—it is not possible to tell just what the results of ethical judgment will be in the constantly developing world around us. This is what makes writing codes of ethics so difficult—no sooner does one spell out how people ought to act, for example, in the computer industry or telecommunications, than the variables change and adjustments are needed.

It is, thus, always important to keep in mind that professional ethics depends mainly on constant vigilance, on sustained discretion and prudence, and on wisdom, rather than on certain set rules. It is true here as elsewhere that character is destiny.

Notes

1. Milton Friedman, "The Social Responsibility of Business Is to Increase Its Profits," *New York Magazine*, 13 September, 1970, 33. See, also Milton Friedman, *Capitalism and Freedom* (Chicago: University of Chicago Press, 1961), 133–36. Friedman's essay is widely reprinted and also discussed in numerous collections of business ethics textbooks and journal articles. For some of the nuances of Friedman's position, see Thomas Carson, "Friedman's Theory of Corporate Social Responsibility," *Business and Professional Ethics Journal*, 12 (Spring 1993): 3–32. It is notable that Friedman is usually represented as holding the more radical view that business ought to aim solely at profit rather than the milder version in which the ethics of society ought also be followed in the course of doing business. This is understandable, though, especially in light of the apparent cultural relativism implicit in Friedman's position. In an international and intercultural world of commerce, however, the prescription to strive for profit is far more direct and practicable than that requiring one to follow "law [and] ethical custom." In short, the only genuine ethical position Friedman addresses is that profit ought to be pursued, although he agrees that allowances need to be made to circumstances.

2. See, most prominently, Kurt Baier, *The Moral Point of View* (Ithaca, New York: Cornell University Press, 1958) and Amitai Etzioni, *The Moral Dimension* (New York: The Free Press, 1988).

3. John Kenneth Galbraith, *The Affluent Society*, 3rd edition (New York: Houghton Mifflin, 1982), and Ralph Nader, M. Green and J. Seligman, *Taming the Giant Corporation* (New York: W. W. Norton, 1976). For a different view, see Robert Hessen, *In Defense of the Corporation* (Stanford, California: Hoover Institution Press, 1979).

4. Karl Marx, *Selected Writings*, David McClellan, ed. (Oxford: Oxford University Press, 1977), 126.

5. The most developed version of this type of individualism is found in David L. Norton, *Personal Destinies: A Philosophy of Ethical Individualism* (Princeton, New Jersey: Princeton University Press, 1976). Earlier, Ayn Rand sketched a similar position in *The Virtue of Selfishness: A New Concept of Egoism* (New York: Signet Books, 1961).

6. This point raises the perennial issue of freedom of the will. The classical individualist position can draw on the work of, e.g., Nobel Laureate Roger W.

Sperry, *Science and Moral Priority* (New York: Columbia University Press, 1983), who defends free will based on his scientific research and analysis. See also Sperry's technical paper, "Changing Concepts of Consciousness and Free Will," *Perspectives in Biology and Medicine*, 9 (autumn 1976): 9–19. See also Tibor R. Machan, *The Pseudo-Science of B. F. Skinner* (New Rochelle, New York: Arlington House, 1974).

7. I elaborate this in "Ethics and its Uses," in Tibor R. Machan, ed.,*Commerce and Morality* (Totowa, NJ: Rowman & Littlefield, 1988).

8. By "profit" I do not have in mind the technical term defined in tax law or even economics in general, but the familiar idea of prospering in one's ability to obtain goods and services for purchase in the market place.

9. This is not the place to work out a full ethical system in which wealth pursuit can be seen as morally proper. Nevertheless, it should be hinted that such a system is person-relative about the nature of the good and sees living economically, successfully, or prosperously as a goal that constitutes a significant aspect of the good life for any human moral agent. See Douglas J. Den Uyl, "Teleology and Agent-Centeredness," *The Monist*, 75 (January 1992): 14–33.

There is an ontological feature of a moral perspective that would be applicable to evaluating the various professions people embark upon, namely, that there is no basis for precluding the possibility of free will in human living. Indeed, there is both philosophical and special scientific justification, beyond a reasonable doubt, to believe that human beings are facilitated to activate their mental functions, as it were, to initiate their own conduct and, thus, to govern themselves. Instead of the reductionist approach found in much of economics, a pluralistic ontology with different kinds and types of entities in nature would be more sensible. Within such a perspective, the moral dimension of reality arises in connection with living entities that have the faculty of choice and thus can govern their own conduct. This brings into nature the problem of how they ought to act and how their living as the kind of beings they are ought to be carried out. For more, see Tibor R. Machan, "Applied Ethics and Free Will: Some Untoward Results of Independence," *The Journal of Applied Philosophy*, Vol. 10 (1993): 59–72

10. See, Douglas J. Den Uyl, *The Virtue of Prudence* (New York: Peter Lang, 1991).

11. This is akin to our not understanding the structure of the physical world from simply experiencing it by way of the normal use of our senses.

12. For a survey of these, see Tibor R. Machan, "Recent Work in Ethical Egoism," in *Recent Work in Philosophy*, eds., Kenneth J. Lucey and Tibor R. Machan (Totowa, New Jersey: Rowman and Allanheld, 1982), 185–202.

13. Friedman, "Social Responsibility," 33.

14. This point is advanced by Fred D. Miller Jr. and John Ahrens, "The Social Responsibility of Corporations," in Machan, *Commerce and Morality*, 140–160.

It's worth noting that Carson, *op. cit.*, faults Friedman for not including as a requirement of the social or ethical responsibility of business to "warn the public about all serious hazards or dangers created by the firms which they represent." (p. 20) One might think that the current position also falls prey to this flaw. Yet arguably neither Friedman nor I can be so faulted.

Friedman is, after all, a defender of an individual—including private property—rights based free-market economy, including privatization in all possible realms of production, trade, transportation, etc. In such a system, exposing customers to known hazards and dangers that pose risks (beyond what is reasonable, i.e., significantly above the normal prevailing hazards and dangers of their lives) without informing them about these constitutes legally actionable misrepresentation or deception. Product and service liability law suits are entirely consistent with, indeed, native to, a *bona fide* free-market system. A socialist system, for example, cannot make theoretical room for such an individual rights based legal action. It is even doubtful that a government regulated legal system can escape the force of the charge that, in view of such regulation of business, liability action might have to be significantly circumscribed. Responsibility for hazards and dangers would, in such a system, be shared between the business and the regulatory agent (the public!) ultimately complicit in the hazardous or dangerous behavior. For more on this, see Tibor R. Machan, "Bhopal, Mexican Disasters: What a Difference Capitalism Can Make," in *Liberty and Culture* (Buffalo: Prometheus Books, 1989), 180–181, and "Corporate Commerce vs. Government Regulation: the State and Occupational Safety and Health," *Notre Dame Journal of Law, Ethics, and Public Policy*, 2 (1987): 791–823. See also Tibor R. Machan, *Private Rights and Public Illusions* (New Brunswick, New Jersey: Transaction Books, 1995).

15. In *Individuals and Their Rights* I explain in detail why the moral dimension of human nature requires the classical liberal political framework. Incidentally, for a treatment of negative externalities such as air or water pollution, see my "Pollution, Collectivism and Capitalism," *Journal des Economists et des Etudes Humaines*, 2 (March, 1991): 83–102. For more on our relationship to animals, see "Do Animals Have Rights?" *Public Affairs Quarterly*, 5 (April 1991): 163–173. For an application of this framework to government regulation of business, see Tibor R. Machan, *op cit.*, "Corporate Commerce," and "Should Business Be Regulated?", in *Just Business: New Introductory Essays in Business Ethics* ed., Tom Regan (New York: Random House, 1983), 202–234. For more on environmental ethics in general, see Tibor R. Machan, "Pollution and Political Theory," in *Earthbound: New Introductory Essays in Environmental Ethics*, ed., Tom Regan (New York: Random House, 1984), 74–106, and "Environmentalism Humanized," *Public Affairs Quarterly*, 7 (April 1993): 131–147. For a discussion of parental responsibilities, see Tibor R. Machan, "Between Parents and Children," *The Journal of Social Philosophy*, 23 (winter 1992): 16–22. I discuss some of the issues of this paper bearing on the philosophy of the social sciences and the moral foundation of the free market system in Tibor R. Machan, *Capitalism and Individualism* (New York: St. Martin's Press, 1990).

16. See, for more on this, Tibor R. Machan, "What is Morally Right About Insider Trading?" *Public Affairs Quarterly* (forthcoming).

Environmentalism Humanized

Mike Gemmell

To many observers, the resolution of environmental issues with the libertarian principles of private property, personal liberty, and limited government appears a hopeless goal. If we are overheating the planet with CO_2 emissions, destroying the ozone layer, overpopulating the earth, and destroying species, how can such a limited perspective cope with these problems? Moreover, how can it be that the Western perspective of continuing improvement in our standard of living, which we have come to expect since the advent of the Industrial Revolution, has in the space of thirty years become a cruel delusion?

In the case of virtually all environmental problems, perception does not equal reality. The reality is that since the revival of the environmental movement thirty years ago, environmental policy has been based on the perception that humans are destroying the planet. Historically, science has been an enterprise based on the premise that the knowledge gained by understanding nature's laws can be used to better human life. Modern environmental science has been based on a very different philosophic perspective that can be summarized as follows:

- Nature has intrinsic value independent of human well-being.
- Nature is a collective entity of which man is only a part, with no higher status than any other entity in nature.
- Since man's status is no higher than that of other plants and animals, conscious modification of the environment is destructive and morally wrong.

The purpose of this essay is to identify how this philosophic foundation underlies each major area of environmental science, and how its existence has led to destructive environmental policies. In addition, a replacement philosophy, one with a prohuman standard of value, will be used as a basis for recommending fundamental reforms in environmental policy. The remainder of this essay will uncover how the environmental philosophic and scientific status quo has affected policy in the major branches of environmental concern, including natural-resource use, waste disposal issues, risk from industrial chemicals, global-climate issues, and biodiversity/ecosystem/endangered-species issues.

We all want a clean, safe environment in which to live, one in which we can enjoy natural beauty while still enjoying the material gifts available from a technologically advanced civilization. We can have both if we use a prohuman standard to guide our actions in environmental policy.

Resource Use

The last quarter century has seen dozens of pronouncements about how exploding population growth and excessive consumption of natural resources are leading the world to the brink of destruction. In 1972, a MIT study entitled "The Limits to Growth" concluded that the human race had perhaps only 100 years to live unless it immediately ended economic growth. This study was in turn largely based on Paul Ehrlich's *The Population Bomb: Population Control or Race to Oblivion?* In 1980 the *Global 2000 Report to the President* was submitted to President Jimmy Carter. That document dominates the thinking behind much of environmental policy to this day. The letter of transmittal of *Global 2000* states: "Our conclusions summarized in the pages that follow, [sic] are disturbing. They indicate the potential for global problems of alarming proportions by the year 2000. Environmental, resource, and population stresses are intensifying and will increasingly determine the quality of human life on our planet. The trends reflected in the Global 2000 suggest strongly a progressive degradation and impoverishment of the earth's resource base."[1]

Fortunately, *Global 2000*'s conclusions have been thoroughly dissected and disproved by scientists like Julian Simon. Simon points out that *Global 2000* projects a five percent yearly increase in the rate of consumption of nonfuel minerals to the year 2000, while another portion of the report notes "the real price of most mineral commodities has been constant or declining for many years." In addition, *Global 2000* shows an upward trend for energy consumption, which it uses to predict future shortages, but fails to mention that the price of energy has fallen during the period of increasing energy consumption.

To dramatize his opposition to the conclusions of *Global 2000*, Julian Simon in 1980 bet Paul Ehrlich on the long-term price trends of five metals of Ehrlich's choice. Ehrlich contended that the price of a unit amount of the metals (chrome, copper, nickel, tin, and tungsten) worth $1000 in 1980 would increase in price while Simon contended it would fall. The time period for the bet was ten years. In 1990 Ehrlich sent a check to Simon for $576.07, the amount the metals had fallen in price.

Industrialists do face genuine problems with resources from time to time. The timber industry, for example, has had to upgrade its forest management practices to prevent the depletion of timber resources in the United States. In the late nineteenth and early twentieth centuries, due to an abundance of land and low-priced timber, replanting of tree seedlings was not practiced. But as the population increased, resulting in increased pressure on land use, the planting of tree seedlings became necessary. In 1934, Weyerhauser began tree planting and introduced the concept of sustained yield. Through constant research the company has been able to have an initial yield rate of seventy-five percent and improve it to ninety-five percent. Because of this research, annual growth in privately owned forests has exceeded harvest every year since 1952.[2]

The rationale for the environmentalists' views on resource economics can be discerned in the following statements by economist Paul Ekins:

- "Much of the planet's accumulated wealth, its fossil fuels has [sic] now been spent."
- "Energy once spent is dissipated forever."
- "Renewable energy sources must be developed to replace fossil fuels."[3]

These views reveal several fallacies. First of all, viewing natural resources as "accumulated wealth" is incorrect, as they do not become wealth until someone learns how to transform them into a useful commodity. Secondly, if energy is "dissipated forever," it cannot be renewable.

These contradictions are the result of the environmental philosophic perspective that conscious modification of the environment destroys it. Modification, according to this perspective, destroys the flow of energy through nature. Because of nature's impenetrable secrets, i.e., its intrinsic value, the knowledge to efficiently transfer energy or resources cannot be obtained. However, if we use energy sources that require no modification of nature, such as renewable energy, we are acting as the other creatures in nature's garden. Unfortunately, this form of energy doesn't allow us to progress economically beyond the status of a medieval village.

Countering this flawed rationale demands adherence to objective standards in natural resource affairs, not appeals to nature's intrinsic value. We live in a natural, knowable world, one that consists of discrete entities. These entities possess specific characteristics. The evidence does not indicate we are part of a collective organism. To transfer energy from one place to another requires a tracing of cause-and-effect relationships. In resource and energy issues, our best matchmaker for nurturing these relationships is the science of thermodynamics.

The first, second, and third laws of thermodynamics have to do with energy states and the transfer of energy. The first law states that energy is conserved in any system. It may be transferred from state to state and place to place, but it can not be destroyed. The second law of thermodynamics has to do with randomness or entropy. It states that systems insulated from external influences tend to go to maximum randomness. The third law of thermodynamics unites the first two laws and allows predictions of the direction and rate of reaction based on its energy and entropy values.

These laws of nature are constantly acting on all natural and biological systems at all times. For instance, a living organism does not have the stability of an inanimate object such as a rock. It takes energy to maintain its life functions; the more complex the organism, the more energy is needed. A continuous expenditure of energy is necessary for a living organism to maintain itself and to hold off the forces of entropy that tend to break it down.

Sciences such as thermodynamics, together with property rights, are what made it possible for Weyerhauser to increase its seedling yields and for Julian Simon to win his bet with Paul Ehrlich. Once we identify what we value, we can take the time and effort to discover how to best direct nature's energy to protect that value. By establishing boundaries, via property rights, around aspects of nature we most value, we can develop standards to measure whether we are efficiently using natural resources. Energy and resources are values that must be defined by using a prohuman standard. Appeals to nature's intrinsic value or its fragility lack scientific rigor and should be rejected. Man does have a nature—a thinking nature—that allows him to modify and transform nature to sustain human life. We should celebrate this.

Industrial Chemicals and Risk

The first textbook on toxicology was written by the maverick physician Paracelsus, and published, posthumously, in 1567. Paracelsus was the first person to relate dose to toxicity, noting that, all things are poison and nothing is without poison. It is the dose only that makes a thing not a poison.

Paracelsus knew that standards for evaluating the risks of chemicals must be defined within a rational context. When an appropriate context is defined, exposures from industrial chemicals can be compared with those from natural ones and decisions concerning their use made in a rational fashion.

The 1972 banning of the pesticide DDT, was a classic case of not comparing risks from industrial activities to nature's activities. DDT was known for decades to be cheap, effective, and of low toxicity. By the early 1950s, because of its effectiveness and low cost, it had become the overwhelming pesticide of choice. At the same time, it was considered a "miracle chemical" in preventing an estimated two million deaths each year from malaria. A large part of its effectiveness was its exceptional stability in the environment, up to two weeks under optimum conditions before it would start to break down.

The fact that DDT could accumulate in the biosphere was alarming to environmentalists who viewed any man-made chemical suspiciously and one that did not break down quickly even more so. The leading environmental organization fighting to ban DDT was the Environmental Defense Fund. Their chief scientist, Charles Wurster, revealed his antihuman bias when asked whether banning DDT might require other even more toxic chemicals to achieve the same benefits: "So what? People are the cause of all the problems; we have too many of them; we need to get rid of some of them; and this is as good a way as any."[4]

Environmental Protection Agency Director William Ruckleshaus stated in 1970: "DDT is not endangering the public health and has an amazing and exemplary record of safe use."[5] However, in 1972, Ruckleshaus overruled the recommendation of his own hearing examiner, Edmund Sweeney, and banned DDT without attending a single day of the seven-month proceedings and without reading any of the transcripts. After leaving the EPA, Ruckleshaus entered an agreement with the Environmental Defense Fund to sign membership solicitation letters.[6]

The following facts add a needed perspective when considering the evaluation of risk from industrial or natural chemicals:

- Five to ten percent of any plant's weight is from natural pesticides.
- These pesticides are as toxic or nontoxic (depending on your perspective) as industrial pesticides.
- Ninety-nine percent of toxic chemicals are natural, not man-made.

A standard that evaluates risks must compare man-made hazards to natural ones to have any basis in reality. The Human Exposure Rodent Potency (HERP) index, developed by Bruce Ames and his colleagues at the University of California, makes such comparisons.[7] The HERP index compares theoretical values from animal testing (dose needed to cause tumors in fifty percent of tested animals, known as TD 50) with typical concentrations found in the environment. This value applied to a cup of coffee (catechol), and trichloroethylene (TCE) at 267 micrograms/liter[8] yields values of .002 and .0006, respectively. In other words, by this standard, drinking a cup of coffee entails a risk factor that is approximately three times higher than the risk factor associated with the consumption of a liter of water containing 267 micrograms of TCE. This does not mean it is time to abandon everyone's favorite source of caffeine. It does mean, however, that the use of any chemical or substance entails some risk. The risk may be trivial, but it does exist.

The greatest risk to human life is to do nothing. By taking this course of inaction, we have the option of dying from starvation or exposure, to name two possibilities. To live, we must act to direct nature's energy and resources to serve human life, while at the same time reducing risk as we gain greater understanding and control of nature's resources. Our best friend in performing this function is technology. The higher the level of technology, the greater the efficiency of the process of transferring energy and, consequently, the smaller the amount of waste produced.

The issue of waste disposal is closely related to risk. The misperception concerning municipal solid waste disposal is the result of environmentalists' ignoring what technology does and how it reduces waste and risk. This ignorance is unfortunately echoed by Vice President Albert Gore in his book *Earth in the Balance*: "The volume of garbage is now so high that we are running out of places to put it." Apparently Mr. Gore neglected to talk with Clark Wiseman of Gonzaga University who calculated in a study sponsored by the organization Resources for the Future that all municipal solid waste in the United States for the next five hundred years could be contained in a landfill three hundred feet deep with sides twenty miles long.[9] A big landfill, to be sure, but still one that would take up less than 0.01 percent of the continental United States. Even so, other innovations could easily reduce solid-waste volumes even further. One approach would be to go from passive to active landfilling. Rather than simply burying the wastes, as is currently done, we could actively ferment them to reduce their volume and toxicity.[10]

There will always be waste from any natural or man-made process. Some wastes such as municipal solid waste are relatively easy to isolate. Other waste products, such as air pollutants, are more difficult to isolate. This is where a standard that compares risk between nature and human influences can help develop a more objective evaluation of pollution controls. Unfortunately, this sort of comparative standard has been missing from air pollution standards for constituents such as Volatile Organic Carbon (VOC)/oxidant, sulfur dioxide (SO_2), and total suspended particles (TSP), among others. Each of these constituents showed declining levels prior to implementation of air pollution controls.[11] The possibility of nature as a polluter of the air was not considered. However, a check on the VOC levels has indicated that it is. From 1974 to 1988, VOC levels were reduced by more than 40 percent in American urban areas. Ozone levels, however, commonly assumed by environmental regulators to be related to VOC levels, increased slightly during that time.[12]

A better approach to air pollution control would be to use the HERP index or its equivalent for TSP, VOCs, or any other constituent of concern. A more objective evaluation of risk, such as the HERP index provides, would greatly decrease the enormously expensive air pollution controls in use today. This, in turn, would lead to greater economic health and a correspondingly higher level of technological development, and therefore to progressively smaller volumes of waste and lower levels of risk to human health.

Developing a comparative standard for natural versus industrial chemicals is the fundamental requirement for an objective approach to risk assessment and waste management. A comparative standard provides the means to objectively evaluate the effects of man's versus nature's actions.

Global Issues

Global climate issues have always been among the core issues of environmentalism. Today the focus is on global warming and ozone depletion, in particular. Twenty years ago, it was on the coming of the next ice age. A lack of objectivity is evident in Stephen Schneider who, in the 1970s, was a proponent of the theory of an incipient man-made ice age: "to [reduce the risk of global warming] we need to get some broad-based support, to capture the public imagination. We need to offer up scary scenarios, . . . Each of us has to develop what the right balance is between being effective and being honest."[13]

One way to be effective and honest is to consider some pertinent facts:

- CO_2 has been increasing in the atmosphere. The CO_2 content in the mid-nineteenth century was between 260 to 280 parts per million (ppm), compared with approximately 340 ppm today.
- Global temperature rose approximately one degree Celsius from 1900

to 1940; fell approximately one degree Celsius from 1940 to 1965; and showed no net increase during the 1980s.
- Most of the temperature rise in the early twentieth century occurred before the rise in CO_2 concentrations occurred.
- Termites contribute ten times more CO_2 to the atmosphere than industry.[14]

Scientists with an environmentalist philosophical perspective have ignored both nature's direct contributions, as in the case of termites, and its feedback mechanisms. James Hansen of NASA, for example, stirred up a media frenzy in 1988 with his statement that based on his model projections he was ninety-nine percent sure that 1988 would be the warmest year on record and that global warming had arrived. Hansen, however, failed to consider the effect of the oceans as a factor in global climate. Unfortunately for Hansen, nature cooled down later that year, severely damaging his credibility. In addition to the oceans, which act as heat sinks, major feedback mechanisms include cloud reflectivity (albedo) and the release of cloud-condensing aerosols by phytoplankton.

Those promoting concern over ozone (O_3) depletion also suffer from the misperception that man's contributions overshadow those of nature. Ozone has been a prominent issue since 1984, when an "ozone hole" was found over Antarctica. In April 1991, the EPA announced that ozone concentrations over the United States had thinned by four to five percent. It then alleged that 200,000 deaths from skin cancer could occur over the next fifty years due to increased ultraviolet light intensity at the earth's surface.

As with global warming, a look at some facts concerning ozone depletion is instructive:

- There is a five percent natural decrease in ozone content as one travels south from Los Angeles to San Diego, and a seasonal variation of up to twenty-five percent over Denver.
- Ultraviolet light measurements taken at eight measuring points from 1974 to 1988 showed a decrease rather than an increase at the earth's surface.
- Ozone concentrations decreased by 0.47 percent per year from 1978 to 1985 and increased 0.28 percent per year from 1985 to 1990.[15]

The ozone alarmists also neglected to check on nature's feedback mechanisms. Under changing conditions, reactions can be pushed (temporarily) in one direction or another. This occurs with the Antarctic seasonal "ozone hole." During the Antarctic night, due to a lack of sunlight and drop in temperature (-80° C), the ozone layer thins by approximately fifty percent. But when the seasons change and the ozone layer receives light, the reactions shift and the hole repairs itself. The three equations below are typical of the feedback mechanisms that operate to moderate the change in ozone concentrations:

O_2 + ultraviolet (<242 nanometers) = (primarily) 2 O above 20 kilometers
$O + O = O_2$, $O + O_2 = O_3$ and
O_3 + ultraviolet (<320 nanometers) = $O + O_2$[16]

Scientists who are biased by the environmentalist philosophical perspective fail to compare nature's contributions to that of man. This bias causes them to jump from one data fragment to another, without establishing the proper context for scientific evaluation. Since their science is flawed, they are forced to substitute scare tactics for scientific rigor.

The world viewed through the eyes of reason is knowable. The law of identity and its corollary, the law of causality (cause and effect), have been known explicitly since Aristotle, and have worked for Aristotle and every other human who has taken heed of them, since the first day of human existence. Since no entity or system operates in a vacuum, the expression of these laws in the scientific realm gives rise to feedback mechanisms. All natural systems (physical, biological, and chemical) have feedback mechanisms that tend to stabilize their functioning within certain ranges. The global systems have the ability to moderate much larger forces, than what man can produce. Even when some men went on an orgy of destruction, torching Kuwait's oil fields during the Persian Gulf War, the global climate systems showed nary a blip of change.

Man's pursuit of a progressively improved existence will inevitably lead to a greater understanding of nature's laws. This knowledge will be used to achieve greater control over nature via the development of successively higher levels of technology. Higher technology equals greater control over the aspects of nature we actively use, which in turn means less waste. For instance, a 1000-megawatt coal-fired power plant produces seven million tons of CO_2 per year, while the equivalent nuclear power plant produces none.[17]

A rational policy on global-climate issues does not require any sort of global cooperation to control CO_2, chlorofluorocarbons, or any other constituent. In fact, it does not require any governmental action at all, except perhaps a roll back of the many laws and regulations that restrict the development of energy and advanced levels of technology.

A philosophical perspective that treats human action as natural is the key to clearing away the needless confusion regarding nature's feedback mechanisms. Nature has many wonders in its possession, but its greatest creation is the human mind. We may be able to destroy ourselves by abusing that gift, but we cannot destroy the planet.

Ecosystem Preservation, Biodiversity, and Endangered Species

Biodiversity and ecosystem preservation is the issue that represents the "vision" of what environmentalists believe our society should strive to be. An early piece of legislation developed to implement this viewpoint was the Endangered Species Act, passed in 1973. Biodiversity and ecosystem preservation have become, in recent years, the framework for EPA policy. The EPA's August 1993 National Performance Review on Ecosystem Protection states, "The EPA must make ecosystem protection a primary goal of the agency, on a par with human health . . . The United States should develop human population policies that are consistent with sustainable economies and ecosystems." As of this writing, eight hundred fifty-three species of plants and animals are listed as endangered or threatened, and eighty seven million acres of public and private land have been placed under the jurisdiction of the U.S. Fish and Wildlife Service.[18]

For a country founded on the idea that the individual's right to dispose of his property reigns supreme to become one where the importance of ecosystem preservation allegedly justifies the confiscation of eighty seven million acres, requires a fundamental change in philosophical outlook. That change in outlook is made explicit by David Graber in his review of Bill McKibben's book, *The End of Nature*:

> This ["man's remaking the earth by degrees"] makes what is happening no less tragic for those of us who value wildness for its own sake, not for what value it confers upon mankind. I, for one, cannot wish upon either my children or the rest of Earth's biota a tame planet, be it monstrous or—however unlikely—benign. McKibben is a biocentrist, and so am I. We are not interested in the utility of a particular species or free-flowing river, or ecosystem, to mankind. They have intrinsic value, more value—to me—than another human body, or a billion of them.[19]

The view of nature as having intrinsic value is actually a negation of the concept of value. For something to be a value, it must be a value to some living thing. Values are the objects of goal-directed behavior, which can only be engaged in by living organisms. Food may be a value in the case of animals, while human beings adopt more sophisticated ones. The worth of any value is dependent on the valuer's identity and context. An industrialist may see an open field as a place for a factory, whereas a farmer may see it as a location for an apple orchard.

The acceptance of nature as having intrinsic value opens the door to other arbitrarily constructed ideas that form environmentalism's philosophical foundation. Another portion of its foundation is the idea of "Gaia" or "mother nature" as being a literal megaorganism. John Muir illustrates the idea: "The world we are told, was made especially for man—a presumption not supported by all the facts. . . . Why should man value himself as more than a small part of the one great unit of creation?"[20]

Muir's view subordinates living organisms, those we can directly perceive, to a megaorganism we cannot directly perceive. He substitutes an arbitrarily conceived megaorganism for the interactions of different organisms acting within the framework of natural scientific law. The unit of value should be the individual living organism, not an arbitrary construct. And man being the most highly evolved organism in nature should value himself over other entities.

The third component that comprises the foundation of environmental philosophy is ethics. Since man is part of creation it follows that he should act as the other members do, adapting to, rather than consciously modifying, the environment. To consciously modify nature is morally wrong, says John Muir: "How narrow we selfish, conceited creatures are in our sympathies! How blind to the rights of all the rest of creation!"[21] The implication is that man has to be reduced to the level of an animal to achieve moral stature.

Considering that this philosophical triumvirate is the foundation of environmentalism, it becomes understandable how environmental science has degenerated in the area of endangered-species studies. Philosophical objectivity necessarily precedes scientific objectivity. Without it, science inevitably degenerates.

The science underlying the Endangered Species Act is a perfect example of what happens to science when it is based on a faulty philosophical foundation. This science is flawed in three crucial areas: 1) inadequate definition of species, with an associated lack of standards to evaluate whether they are endangered; 2) inadequate baselines on endangered populations; 3) a general lack of documentation for allegedly endangered species.

As some have observed, among them Montana State biologist David Cameron, as regards the difficulty of defining species: evolution teaches that life adapts constantly and in many cases it is difficult to determine exactly where the dividing line is between species. The issue of inadequate base lines has caused the U.S Fish and Wildlife Service to adopt a case-by-case basis for defining endangered species. The lack of adequate information is evident in many recovery plans:

- Desert Slender Salamander: "No information is available on the historical distribution of the desert slender salamander . . ."
- Flat-Spired Three-Toothed Snail: "We do not consider surveys to be extensive enough to provide reliable population estimates."
- Louisiana Pearlshell Mussel: ". . . practically no information on the life history, population levels, and habitat requirements for this species . . ."
- Noonday Snail: "Essentially nothing is known about the snail's biology. . . . No estimates of population size have been made since the exact range has never been determined."[22]

When pressed about this lack of scientific rigor Edward Wilson, editor of *Biodiversity*, states: "The masses of species on the verge of extinction is [sic] absolutely undeniable. There are literally hundreds of anecdotal reports."[23] The question of why anecdotal reports are relied on rather than rigorous research, Wilson leaves unanswered.

A review of the geologic record reveals again environmentalism's flawed perspective. Mass extinctions appear repeatedly in the geological record with the two most spectacular examples being at the end of the Paleozoic era (225 million years ago) and the end of the Mesozoic era (65 million years ago). By the conclusion of those eras, approximately ninety percent and seventy-five percent, respectively, of the species on the planet had become extinct.

To stop the destructive policies concerning ecosystems and biodiversity, environmentalism's foundation must be replaced with one that allows humans the right to thrive on the planet. Living organisms select values for the purpose of sustaining life. In the case of nonhuman life, the selection occurs at the perceptual level, meaning adaptation to the environment. We humans, with our conceptual capacity, can choose to consciously modify the environment to sustain life. With a prohuman standard, ecosystems, endangered species, and biodiversity issues can be addressed in a rational fashion. A pro-human environmental philosophy is one that recognizes that the initiation of force is anathema to human life. Decisions concerning what aspects of nature to use or preserve need to occur within the context of the free market. The free market provides a framework for people to objectively evaluate what their hierarchy of values really is.

Clearly, preservation of nature in a relatively untouched state is a value to many people. The desire to get away from it all drives thousands of people to America's national parks every year. Full privatization of the park system would create a large marketplace for evaluating nature's value. Until that step is taken, an approximation of the free market could be achieved by charging user fees that cover the full cost of maintaining national parks. This would prevent the deterioration that has occurred in many parks and allow for multiple uses of the parks for activities such as logging.

Private nature reserves are a fully prohuman method for evaluating nature's value. In Zimbabwe, for example, a market-based program has been used to maintain wildlife populations. The Nyaminyami District Council each year sells permits that govern hunting of selected species. These permits generated $120,000 in 1989, so the council has every incentive to not sell an excess of permits and thereby deplete the species. Another example is the permits sold by White Mountain Apache Reservation in the United States. By managing the wildlife for profit the managers of the preserve are able to sell approximately fifty permits per year for bull elk. The permits are sold for $15,000 each.[24]

Nowhere is the driving principle of environmentalism, nature's intrinsic value, more prominent than in the quest for biodiversity/ecosystem preservation through endangered species protection. It is the ultimate vision of environmentalism. But the attempt to implement this vision has led to the trampling of individual rights and increased human misery. It is time to end the decades of destructive environmentalism by implementing policies that are consistent with the celebration of human life.

Summary

In every area of environmental policy, actions based on environmentalism's philosophical foundation have led to political and economic destruction. Environmentalism came to be a significant force in modern-day American culture as a result of a philosophical and moral vacuum present at the time that Rachel Carson's book *Silent Spring* generated a renewed interest in environmental issues. This vacuum was created by the culmination of philosophical developments occurring over a number of centuries. To understand fully how to counter the appeal and effects of environmentalism, we need to examine the historical context in which it evolved.

Ideas concerning man's place in nature are ancient. A key figure in the modern rise of environmentalism and ecology was the eighteenth-century French philosopher Jean-Jacques Rousseau (1712–1778). His philosophical perspective is strikingly similar to the modern-day environmentalists: "The more we depart from the state of nature, the more we lose our natural tastes ... All is good coming from the hand of the Author of all things; all degenerates in the hands of man."[25]

Rousseau's ideas influenced Marx, Hegel, and other European intellectuals, including Ernst Haeckel. In 1866, Haeckel coined the term ecology, which he defined as the science of the relationships between organisms and the environment. Haeckel and his followers were a major influence in incorporating the ecologic ideal into German culture. Their influence grew until, by the 1930s, the ecologists' influence had reached its peak in Germany. In the political sphere, the German ecologists lobbied successfully for antivivisection laws, creation of nature reserves, implementation of organic (biodynamic) farming, and the redistribution of large land holdings to the German peasants in the back-to-the-land movement.[26]

Haeckel preached self-sacrifice for nature and advocated a totalitarian state. His followers saw this hope come to fruition with the rise of Nazi Germany. The "Blood and Soil" ethic developed by the ecologists was an integral part of the Nazi ideology.

A large dose of German and European philosophy was imported to America in the period following the American Civil War, when many American intellectuals studied abroad. Another came following World War II. Although the European ecology movement collapsed in Germany with the end of World War II, the Soil Association was founded in 1945 in England. The association published the journal *Mother Earth* to promote its concerns about soil erosion, soil fertility, pollution, and chemical-based agriculture. This group kept ecological issues alive during the 1940s and 1950s and influenced American biologists such as Rachel Carson and Barry Commoner.[27] The publication of *Silent Spring* by Rachel Carson in 1962 marked the rise of environmentalism as a cultural force in the United States and around the world.

As interest in environmental issues was growing among American intellectuals, ideas it shared in common with collectivist ideologies were spreading within American culture at large. Collectivism in America took the form of the welfare state, initiated by the administration of Franklin Roosevelt. Roosevelt and his braintrust showed their disdain for individuals: "We are turning away from the entrusting of crucial decisions ... to individuals who are motivated by private interests."[28]

By the 1960s, American culture had deteriorated badly, as these ideas became public policy. Ideas that would be used as the basis for environmentalism's philosophical triumvirate were widespread within the culture. In addition to the anti-individualist ethics described above, an undercutting of philosophy's epistemological foundation was evident: "In epistemology and natural science it's been pretty well proven that there's no such thing as objectivity. There are only different patterns of subjectivity. . . ."[29] And in the area dealing with man's relationship to the external world (metaphysics), a change from the perspective of the America's Founding Fathers was evident: "Whether we like it or not, modern life has become so highly integrated, so inextricably socialized, so definitely organic, that the very concept of the individual is becoming obsolete."[30]

With the widespread acceptance of these ideas into America, people such as student radical Tom Hayden were starting to act on them by the 1960s: "First we will make the revolution and then we will find out what for."[31] Most of the openly irrational movements of the 1960s died out quickly as their true nature became evident. But ecology and environmentalism were different. They were not just against something, such as technology and industrial civilization: "The road we have long been traveling . . . a smooth superhighway on which we progress with great speed, but at its end lies disaster."[32] They championed the preservation of benevolent nature: "the other fork . . . offers our last, only chance to reach a destination that assures the preservation of our earth."[33]

One final catalyst was needed to spread the acceptance of environmentalism widely within the culture of the United States. It needed the sanction of a respected institution to give it widespread legitimacy. It received it from the scientific community, or rather those people such as Rachel Carson, Paul Ehrlich, and authors of the "Limits to Growth" study who claimed to represent the scientific community. With this sanction, environmentalism was catapulted onto the national and international stage virtually overnight.

Now, thirty years later, people are beginning to see that environmentalism is inherently destructive. As a result a backlash is building. In June 1994, the Supreme Court placed new limits on the ability of governments to require developers to set aside part of their property for environmental uses. In the legislative arena, several bills in Congress, known by environmentalists as "The Unholy Trinity" are gathering steam. The first issue concerns "takings" legislation. Property-rights advocates are proposing that any government action that lowers the value of private property requires compensation and that the rules for such compensation be set by Congress. The second issue is cost-benefit analysis and comparative risk assessment. Advocates are arguing that all government laws and regulations be subjected to cost-benefit analysis and comparative-risk assessment. The third issue is unfunded mandates. The principle behind unfunded mandates would prevent the federal government from forcing mandates on the states unless money is attached to enforce them. As of this writing, legislation concerning unfunded mandates passed in early 1995. Property takings and cost-benefit legislation is pending.

These bills get to the heart of the environmentalists' political agenda. The Sierra Club, National Audubon Society, Greenpeace and a number of other prominent environmental organizations have issued a citizen's action guide with arguments to use against this legislation. The Sierra Club pamphlet, "How to Defend Our Environmental Laws," is accompanied by a letter that concludes with genuine alarm: "Two decades of environmental progress are in danger of being rolled back. Now is the time for action."

Beneath the environmental vision is the deep antihuman bias that drives the environmental movement. The greens have a deep fear of modern civilization. They fear cheap energy, technology, and the free enterprise system in general. They fear it because of the constant change its dynamic nature requires of us.

What is needed to combat the destructive nature of environmentalism is a replacement philosophy that recognizes that human beings are different from any other form of life. We have a need to find meaning and purpose in life because we possess a conceptual faculty. We can not live at the perceptual level, as animals do. We must not only be allowed to modify our environment, we must celebrate the fact that we can do so consciously. By the intelligent use of our conceptual faculty, we do not destroy the value of the environment, but create value, as measured by the standard of enhancing human life.

To replace the destructive image of man brought to life by Rachel Carson and others, we need to use the principles mentioned above to further develop a "man-the-creator" image. There are many real-life examples that illustrate this image, but the story of the men behind the minimills of Nucor Steel is one of the best.

The story of Nucor Steel begins with a man named Ken Iverson who imagined revolutionizing the sheet metal rolling process. Iverson dreamed of replacing the two-step process of casting and rolling sheet-metal with a single step process, a dream that had eluded metallurgists for over one hundred years. Richard Preston chronicled that dream and the technology used to make it come to life:

> A machine as long as four football fields that can swallow melted automobiles and spit out sheets of glistening steel, a daring device that turns garbage into gold. Their army? A diverse collection of hot metal men who live to create the fiery blasts and white light that happens when everything works just right to produce steel. Their dreams? To not only beat Big Steel at its own game but bring America's steel industry back from Japan and maybe even begin to restore some of the 300,000 jobs lost in that industry over the past decade.[34]

Ken Iverson and Nucor Steel probably did not have the conservation of nature's resources foremost in their minds. Yet the process they created allowed for a six-fold increase in the efficiency of resource and energy utilization in the production of steel. The process not only uses less raw material, but is being used to recycle the large volumes of existing steel in the American Midwest.

There are no contradictions in reality. The economic well-being created by industrial civilization and the wise use of nature's resources are inherently compatible. But neither well-being nor wise use happens automatically. We must choose appropriate values and standards. We need to single out the pursuit of human happiness as the all-encompassing value, and the systematic upgrading of human life as the standard for achieving it. When we do this, we will finally have humanized environmentalism.

Notes

1. Julian Simon, "The Global 2000 Report to the President of the United States," in *The Resourceful Earth* (New York: Basil Blackwell, 1984), 45. References by Simon are to *Global 2000 Report to the President, Vols. 1,2 and 3* (Washington, D.C.: US Government Printing Office, 1980).

2. Joseph L. Bast, Peter J. Hill, and Richard C. Rue, *Eco-sanity: A Common-sense Guide to Environmentalism* (Lanham, Maryland: The Heartland Institute, 1994), 45. Also, Michael Crouse, *Loggers World* (Chehalis, Washington: Michael Crouse Publishers, 1991).

3. Paul Ekins, *The Gaia Atlas of Green Economics* (New York: Doubleday Dell, 1992), 28, 52, 90.

4. Quoted in Richard Sanford, "Environmentalism and the Assault on Reason," *Rational Readings on Environmental Concerns*, ed., Jay Lehr (New York: Van Nostrand Reinhold, 1992), 20.

5. Quoted in Elizabeth Whelan, *Toxic Terror* (Ottawa, Illinois: Jameson Books, 1985), 59–85.

6. Wheland, *Toxic Terror*, 59–85.

7. Lois Swirsky Gold, et al., "Rodent Carcinogens: Setting Priorities," *Science* 258 (1992): 261-265.

8. As a point of comparison, a concentration of 5 micrograms per liter for TCE is commonly used as a standard in groundwater cleanups.

9. Bast, Hill, and Rue, *Eco-sanity*, 27.

10. Lee and Jones, "An Alternative to Municipal Solid Waste Landfills," *Biocycle* 31(5): 78–83.

11. Hugh Ellsaesser, "Trends in Air Pollution in the United States" (Guest Scientist Lawrence Livermore Laboratories, California, unpublished paper, 1992), personal communication.

12. Warren Brookes, "Will Senate Declare War on Family Autos?" *Human Events* (February 1990).

13. Quoted in George Reisman, "The Toxicity of Environmentalism," in *Rational Readings on Environmental Concerns*, ed. Jay Lehr (New York: Van Nostrand Reinhold, 1992), 826.

14. Dixy Lee Ray, *Trashing the Planet: How Science Can Help Us Deal With Acid Rain, Depletion of the Ozone, and Nuclear Waste (Among Other Things)* (Washington, D.C.: Regnery Gateway, 1990), 206.

15. Petr Beckmann, *Access to Energy*, 15, no. 11 (1988) and 19, no. 4 (1991).

16. Hugh Ellsaesser, interview with author and via personal correspondence.

17. Ray, *Trashing the Planet*, 133.

18. Robert Gordon, *Costs of the Endangered Species Act as Revealed in Endangered Species Recovery Plans* (Washington, D.C., National Wilderness Institute, 1994), 60.

19. Reismann, *Rational Readings*, 819.

20. Quoted in Roderick Frazier Nash, *The Rights of Nature* (Madison, Wisconsin: University of Wisconsin Press, 1989), 33.

21. Nash, *Rights of Nature*, 3.

22. Gordon, *Costs*, 18.

23. Quoted in Charles Oliver, "All Creatures Great and Small: Species Preservation Out of Control," *Reason*: 11 (1992): 25.

24. Terry Anderson, "Zimbabwe Makes Living With Wildlife Pay," *Wall Street Journal*, 25 October 1991.

25. Ray, *Trashing the Planet*, 80.

26. Anna Bramwell, *Ecology in the 20th Century: A History* (New Haven: Yale University Press, 1989), 292.

27. Bramwell, *Ecology*, 195–236.

28. Quoted in Leonard Peikoff, *The Ominous Parallels* (New York: Stein and Day, 1982), 279.

29. Peikoff, *Ominous Parallels*, 307.

30. Peikoff, *Ominous Parallels*, 290.

31. Peikoff, *Ominous Parallels*, 306.

32. Rachel Carson, *Silent Spring* (Greenwich, Connecticut: Fawcett Crest, 1962), 277.

33. Carson, *Silent Spring*, 277.

34. Robert Preston, *American Steel* (New York: Prentice Hall, 1991), 278.

Education in a Free Society

James E. Chesher

Whether one conceives of society as existing for the sake of its individual members, or the members existing for the greater good, the efficient functioning and continued existence of a society, as well as the happiness of its individual members, will depend significantly upon the quality and extent of education among the citizenry. Who shall provide that education, in what manner, with what content, to whom, and at whose expense are certainly among the most important questions one could ask. Over the centuries, the greatest thinkers in Western history, from Plato and Aristotle to Augustine and Aquinas, through Mill, Adam Smith, and Whitehead, have offered diverse answers. The nature, purpose, and proper methods of education are among the perennial questions of philosophy. The more limited purpose of this essay is to inquire whether the education of citizens is possible in a free society. That is, assuming that citizens must be educated not only for their own sake but for the cohesion and functioning of society, can a free society provide such an education? This question arises because, in a free society, education would neither be required nor provided by the state.

Consider the challenges to education in a free society:

Universal Education:

If education is not compulsory, will children be educated at all? How are children of the poor to be educated? Does the state have a responsibility to educate those who would not otherwise be educated? In short, without compulsory education, won't vastly fewer people be educated?

Standards:

Children, like adults, are a diverse lot: what counts as an education when students are so different in talents, potentialities, tastes, desires, and temperaments? Wouldn't education in a free society, a system of private education, result in something of a hodgepodge, where citizens would have little in the way of shared values and beliefs? Wouldn't this be harmful for a society and its members?

Outcomes:

Can private schools do as good a job at providing students with motivation, career training, and general education as public schools are doing?

Citizenship:

If certain virtues/values are essential to good citizenship, ought these not be required? But if education were not state-mandated and provided, what guarantee is there that these virtues and values would be adequately promoted?

These questions are among the most frequently raised by those who support public education, in their effort to undermine the libertarian alternative. Put in declarative form, the objection to private education is this: If education were neither compulsory nor provided by the state and, given that private education would respond to the diverse demands of the population, large numbers of citizens would go uneducated, get an unacceptably poor-quality education, or lack sufficient agreement on the virtues and values essential to good citizenship necessary for the functioning of our society. It follows from this, the argument goes, that however free society ought to be otherwise, no society can afford to be free of public education.

Universal Education

Supporters of public education have argued that large numbers of children will go uneducated if education is not compulsory and if the state does not provide education. Many parents, especially the poor, will be unable to afford to send their children to private school, and so the children will remain uneducated. The consequences of this for the lives of those children, as well as for society generally, are unacceptable and unnecessary, given the public education alternative.[1] This argument assumes, first, that the present system of compulsory, state-supplied education is working, is in fact educating our children, and doing so for considerably greater numbers (and presumably with the same or better quality) than a purely private system would. This is a highly doubtful assumption.[2] Let's take the matter of compulsory education first: there is no reason whatever to believe that, were education not compulsory, parents would not see to the education of their children. It is presumption of the highest order for the state to act as if parents were so irresponsible that they must be forced to do what they ought to do; compulsory education is aimed at parents, not children. It is the epitomy of paternalism.

One could argue that the education requirement is something of a deterrent to those parents who might in fact be irresponsible and serves as a safeguard to protect children of such parents. There is, however, a presumption of guilt here, as well as the implication that the possible abuse by the few justifies limiting the freedom of the many. Furthermore, how is freedom limited if the many would educate their children without the compulsion? The answer is that, with compulsion comes all manner of corollary requirements by the state, including the number of days in school, the subjects taught, and who is allowed to teach, all of which add up to a considerable restriction on freedom. In other words, the state cannot require "education" in the abstract and leave it at that; it must specify what is to count as an education. Specificity means restriction. If parents are truly free to educate their children, they must be allowed to exercise that freedom as they deem fit. Compulsory education necessarily precludes this.

But isn't it the responsibility of the state to educate at least those who would not otherwise be educated? After all, these children are also citizens, and to deprive them of an education is in effect to deprive them of an opportunity at happiness. Thus, even if universal education were not state mandated, at the very least the state should see to the education of those who are without. First, it should be observed that the primary responsibility for children is with the parents. If parents are seriously irresponsible in this regard, there are sufficient laws protecting children that can be appealed to without compromising the freedom of those who do act responsibly. If some parents are seriously negligent, there is legal recourse that can be aimed directly and specifically at them, and the matter can be settled in a court of law, if necessary. In cases where parents cannot afford to educate their children, there could be recourse to private-school scholarships for charitable assistance, just as there are private remedies for other hardships due to poverty. It is not necessarily the case that, were there no public schools, the poor would go uneducated, anymore than that the poor would go hungry were there no food stamp program. Consider that, in the absence of public schools, the number of private schools would increase to meet demand and, given that the cost of educating a child in private schools is, on average, less than that of educating them publicly, there would be sufficient resources to support the poor. Private schools could be given incentives—for example, tax breaks or free advertising—for offering a certain percentage of scholarship admissions; private corporations might fund a variety of scholarships for the poor, as a civic gesture. Money for scholarships could also be raised through state and local lotteries.

Additionally, as we approach the twenty-first century, the unprecedented growth of technology, particularly in telecommunications, will profoundly transform our methods of education. Though the likely effects of this new technology are still a matter of speculation and are the subject of great discussion and debate, it seems almost certain that people will be receiving more and more of their education through a variety of interactive computer programs, either at home or in learning centers much smaller, less centralized, and ultimately less expensive than the present system of public schools. The very idea of a school, where large numbers of people gather in one place to receive instruction, is undergoing radical change. In the future, a "school" may be a particular curriculum, method, or program that one selects; it may even be personally designed and self-paced. These possibilities are much more conducive to private, rather than to public systems of organization, management, and delivery. For one thing, the variety of programs and schools available will be greater than can be accommodated efficiently by a large, bureaucratized, and centralized institution. For another, "learning centers" will be experimenting with a variety of schools or programs, which will call for a degree of flexibility more typical of private systems than of public. This raises the question of standards.

Standards

It could be objected that private schools, whether traditional classroom schools or futuristic interactive learning centers, are not accountable in the way public schools are. Indeed, private systems tend to favor certain types of students over others; private systems vary widely in their methods, goals, materials, and assessment methods. Given the great diversity in human beings, and the tendency of private systems to cater to diversity, won't the final product be something less than ideal, something not amenable to evaluation? The greater the diversity, the likelier the end result will be a hodgepodge. Surely there should be some uniformity of content, methods, standards, and evaluation? But the only way to guarantee such uniformity is through a public system, where the standards are mandated. If we let each private school or system determine its own methods, content, standards, and evaluation procedures, then education will fall victim to a form of relativism, which is the death of standards. Neither society nor individuals seeking happiness can afford this.

At least two things are at issue here: are standards possible in a private system? And second, do standards require homogeneity rather than heterogeneity? In both the arts and in science, there are recognized standards of excellence totally independent of the state. Indeed, there is good reason to be concerned about state support of the arts and sciences precisely because the standards that make for excellence are likelier to be compromised as government becomes the source of funding. Suffice it to say that standards are inherent in activities themselves, given by the goals that define the activity. For example, the standards of good medical practice are inherent in the goal of medicine, which is health; the standards of good farming are inherent in the goal of agriculture, which is abundant crops; of a good mechanic, which is an efficiently running machine and so on for every human activity. The standards are not external, imposed on the activity by some group, agency, or institution; they emerge from the nature of the activity itself and the human purposes that the activity serves. Thus, with education the standards by which to assess educational programs and methods are implied in the goal of education: to produce individuals who are independent, productive, and self-sustaining. To the extent that a program or method can be shown to enhance student independence and growth, just to that extent is the method or program properly said to be good, to have met the standard.

Now certainly there can be debate about the aims of education, and that debate comprises, essentially, the area of study called the philosophy of education. The point here is that once the goals of an activity are identified or agreed upon, the standards according to which practices within that activity are to be evaluated will be implicit. That there may be debate about the goals of education is itself an argument against public schooling, in as much as a public system will necessarily rest upon some common conception of education. Whatever the conception, there is room for intelligent debate, but a public system must take a position in order to be practicable. That will be the official position against which educational practice is evaluated. Suppose that position is in error?[3] With a private system, there will be no official view; varying ideas, methods, and programs will compete, and outcomes can be assessed. It is likely that features of one system will prove more effective than the features of another, while certain features of yet another system may prove worthy, thus suggesting a revision or new method. In the free market of products and services, competition tends to bring the best forward to force desirable accommodations. The consumer benefits from this, as would students benefit were education open to market forces. Rather than private systems blurring standards, it would make quite apparent which methods of educating are effective.

Furthermore, given that human beings are a diverse lot, it is reasonable to assume that we do not all learn effectively in the same way, under the same conditions, at the same rate, or by the same methods. The very diversity of human beings suggests that education ought also to be diverse, accomodating as much as possible the relevant differences in individuals. A system that allows for diversity would more likely realize the goals of education than one that requires uniformity, as a public system inherently does.

The issue of diversity becomes pronounced when one considers that ours is a pluralistic society, with a growing "multicultural" perspective. It is politically correct and generally reasonable to speak about respect for various cultures and to promote and encourage diversity among people. However, in the name of "equality," a public school system would have to pay considerable attention and devote considerable energy to avoiding ideological, cultural, or religious bias. A public school could not, for example, promote "Chicano Studies" more vigorously than "Black Studies" or "Asian Studies" without inviting charges of discrimination. The more that a public school teaches or recognizes diversity, the greater the risk of discrimination complaints. No doubt, one way around this would be to adjust the curriculum of a school to the demographics of the student population, and to introduce a form of "affirmative action" to the selection of courses, textbooks, teachers, and administrators. This of course would be bureaucratically complex and expensive and would be open to constant revision. There is thus an inherent incentive for public schools to avoid promoting plurality. But the more public education does this in a truly pluralistic society, the less effectively it will educate students to function in such a society.

Private education, on the other hand, does not have to pass the litmus test of equality and may therefore proceed in whatever fashion, with whatever emphasis it deems pedagogically appropriate (within, of course, the limits of the law). Though a private school may have to consider the effect of its program on enrollments (unhappy parents have the option of pulling their child out of the school), it does not suffer the added threat of—and thus burden and expense of prevention and preparation for—a lawsuit from a citizen claiming civil-rights violations or abridgment of due process. Public institutions are subject to considerably more regulatory and legal restrictions than are private institutions.

Outcomes

It would seem to follow from everything discussed so far that an open market in education would be more likely to produce better educated people than would a compulsory system. For the same reasons and with essentially the same mechanisms or market forces that make evident which products and services are the most efficient, economical, and satisfactory, a private system of education would make evident which techniques, programs, instruments of assessment, and methods of instruction are the most efficient, economical, and satisfactory. And just as in the world of commerce it emerges that not every product or service is suitable for every consumer, so too is it the case in education that not every teaching method, style, or curriculum is suitable for all students. With a private system of education, the demand for the varying needs of diverse segments of the population would create a response. A private system, less burdened by bureaucratic inertia and political pressures than a public system, would respond more efficiently and quickly to the perceived needs. Parents would take the initiative and assume the responsibility for selecting the school or program that in their judgment or on the advice of an education counselor would best suit the needs and abilities of the child. Thus, rather than the student having to conform to the system, which is essentially the case with public education, the system, in effect, would conform to the student.[4]

Apart from these practical considerations, there is a moral issue at stake: parents have both the right and the obligation to see to the needs of their children. If this were not so, one wonders how the state could conceivably assume that right and obligation. But parents can be said to enjoy that right only if they have a choice in how to exercise it. Compulsory public education denies that right in particular to those parents who cannot afford to both pay taxes and pay for private schooling.

Citizenship

It can hardly be denied that the larger and more complex a society, the greater the need for its citizens to be educated to function in such a society. At stake is social cohesion. This is even clearer for democratic societies, where citizens are called upon to participate in the political process. A free society would, perforce, be a democratic society. Opponents of an open market in education are concerned that the values and virtues necessary for a democratic society will not be taught in private schools. Putting it another way, they contend that only by state mandate can it be guaranteed that the values, skills, attitudes, and general knowledge required for good citizenship will be taught. If true, this alone would suffice to make an open market in education impossible, for the state would always have the power and opportunity to dictate a great deal of the content, methodology, and assessment procedures of private education.

First, the opponent is surely not saying that only public education can provide education for citizenship, since this would be false on its face: a good many exemplary citizens, including presidents of the United States, have had exclusively private education. So the claim must be either that public education can provide it better or that only public education can do it universally, for all of the citizens. If the claim is that public education can produce better citizens (i.e., people better educated for citizenship), there is little evidence of this. Indeed, the voter turnout rate of elections would suggest that public schools are doing a poor job of instilling the virtues, values, attitudes, motivation, and skills of citizenship. Even if other factors (poor weather, media influence, or government corruption) are associated with poor voter participation, one could argue that a properly educated citizen would rise above these influences to exercise her political right/obligation.

Nor is there reason to believe that public education could teach citizenship any more effectively than a private system could. Indeed, using success in mathematics, English, history, or any other of the disciplines as a standard, it can hardly be argued that public education has done an admirable job in these areas. Apart from this, if education for citizenship were not required and guaranteed by the state, would such education be provided to all citizens? Basically, the question here is whether parents and private schools would recognize the importance of teaching children how to be effective citizens. The answer is, clearly, yes. Proponents of the public system could argue that a private system would in no way insure that the values and principles necessary for citizenship would be taught; the only way to insure that would be to mandate it. Again, this presupposes that the public system is in fact promoting those ideals—a questionable assumption, given the consistently poor voter turnout at elections. Furthermore, consider the virtues, values, and principles of citizenship that are involved: such matters as an understanding of due process, the rights and duties of citizens of a democracy, an understanding of the mechanisms of political action, the importance of representative government and rule of law—in short, the content of so-called "civics" courses in the traditional curriculum. There is simply no reason to believe that a private school, simply because it is private, will be less inclined to include such matters in its curriculum, or less effective in its teaching of citizenship. After all, it is in the best interest of all individuals and institutions in a democracy that its citizens be politically educated. Indeed, a private system would have more reason to promote these matters since at the heart of democracy is the love of freedom, including freedom to choose an education of one's choice. The more responsible and responsive the citizens of a democracy, the freer such a society can and will be.

Will parents and private schools all agree on what counts as good citizenship and what the limits and obligations of citizenship are? Certainly not. But rather than threatening society, such diversity of opinion is healthy—citizens will enter into discussion and debate about government and citizenship. Democracy thrives, rather than diminishes, in such a climate, with such citizens. Surely, there is room for debate about exactly which values, principles, etc. are central to citizenship or what their relative significance is, or how citizenship ought to be taught. But, precisely because there is room for debate, there ought to be room for diversity in practice. Through the practical application of competing theories, their actual merits and liabilities can be determined. A private system, a free market, in education is much likelier to do this than is a public system.

There is a major, untenable assumption underlying the citizenship objection to private education: the state is in the best position to determine what is necessary for good citizenship, and so the state ought to determine how citizenship is taught. On what grounds is the state in the best position here? Why is someone who got elected to public office, or some person (or group) otherwise employed by a public institution, better positioned to understand and answer the philosophical and pedagogical questions of citizenship than are private individuals? Isn't the very point of democracy that such questions ought to be asked and answered by (private) citizens themselves, individually, and ought not the education of a citizen consist in putting these questions and all possible answers before the student's mind, so that he can decide for himself? Anything less would be conditioning, conformism, and could not properly be called education. Or so it can be reasonably argued, which in itself suggests that such questions ought not be left to the state.

Let me conclude by approaching this issue from two radically different perspectives: education within a communist framework, and education in a free society. In communist states education is necessarily public, a function of the state. A government remains in power either through force or through the consent of the governed. Since communist ideology is intolerant of dissent, it will quash it with force or attempt to prevent it with indoctrination. Communist ideology champions collectivity over individuality, homogeneity over heterogeneity, and equality over liberty. Education in a communist state will then promote these ideals, with the ultimate goal of producing a citizenry that is at one with the state. A striking feature of this view is its admission of the enormous power and value of education, and of the realization that education is essentially formative, not informative: communist education is a deliberate attempt to mold people in a particular way, to form certain kinds of characters by instilling certain beliefs, values, attitudes, and habits of behavior. Given this view of the function of education (to produce citizens who value collectivity, homogeneity, and equality), the search for truth and knowledge is subordinate to the goal of indoctrination. And so it must be for any totalitarian state. Thus, if necessary, history will be revised or interpreted along acceptable ideological lines; the truth, if necessary, will be stretched or shrunk accordingly. In short, the greatest casualties of such a system of education are truth and knowledge. This is a feature of any ideologically grounded society—a theocratic, communitarian, egalitarian, or fascist state would, to varying degrees and in a variety of ways, manipulate education to perpetuate itself. The tendency is thus inherent in ideologies.

But doesn't this hold for free societies as well, except that the values are different? In democratic societies such as ours, where liberty, individuality, and heterogeneity are valued, there is recognition of the danger of a particular ideology becoming dominant: liberty is not just another political value peculiar to a particular ideology. Rather, liberty is recognized as a precondition of human flourishing, the recognition that human beings realize their highest aspirations best under conditions of freedom, not restraint. In other words, political liberty is proper to human beings as human beings, and ought to be acknowledged by all human institutions as much as is possible. Individuality and heterogeneity are simply the natural and logical derivatives of a society that recognizes that liberty is the most important, because it is the most fundamental, political value. Liberty is the most fundamental value because if the individual does not have the liberty/right to decide matters that affect her welfare, no one else (and certainly no institution) could possibly have that right.

Given the danger of ideological dominance and of the injustice of a public system that would tax all for the sake of a special ideology, there is a built-in resistance in our system of public education toward using the classroom to champion one ideology over another, one system of values, one opinion, over another. Freedom of and from religion, combined with the principle of equal treatment under the law, puts pressure on public institutions to avoid ideological bias. While this suspicion that ideologies may be inappropriately promoted has merit, it has the unfortunate tendency in public education to produce a classroom atmosphere that is less lively and engaging than genuine education requires: there develops an inclination toward emphasizing "facts" and "information" that are "objective" and "value-free" and thus less likely to offend any particular taxpaying group that might protest. The net result is a system of education that is suspicious and fearful of ideological control as well as susceptible to it and so deprives itself of the very thing that education requires: a direct and lively examination of the nature, value, and meaning of human activities, purposes, and institutions. A publicly funded system of education in a free and pluralistic society such as ours tends to appeal to the lowest common denominator so as not to offend the interests of any particular group. The irony is that a free society cannot long remain free unless it is willing to run the risk of offending, a risk inherent in the search for truth and knowledge. A strict policy of avoiding that risk becomes itself an ideology, seeking justification in the name of equality, and unwittingly moving toward the very kind of system that we have recently witnessed the collapse of in Eastern Europe. When equality becomes the guiding criterion of public policy, rather than being one of a number of significant criteria, then liberty and its derivative benefits are soon compromised. Under such conditions, a society cannot remain democratic in the true sense, nor are its people free.

Public education in totalitarian states tends to sacrifice truth in order to mould students ideologically; public education in democratic societies tends to sacrifice intellectual and character formation for the sake of remaining ideologically independent. The result is that, given the dangers of ideology, public education is inherently limited. In its best sense, the term "liberal education" is free of political meaning, suggesting instead a condition of intellectual freedom: the person so educated has an active mind, an inquiring mind, a mind admirably free of prejudice and preconceived notions, a mind capable of being objective, impartial, and open to alternative ways of viewing issues. Such a mind is prepared to grapple with the problems of life and of society without being bewildered by change and complexity. Such a mind is made possible by a system of education that encourages inquiry, that is itself free of prejudice and preconceived notions, that is itself objective, impartial, and open to alternative ways of viewing the world. Clearly, a system that produces such minds is inconsistent with particular ideologies whatever their names; it is also inconsistent with the view that education ought not to tread where it might give offense. It follows from this that a free society would have, along with a free market in commerce, a free market in education in the marketplace of ideas.

Notes

1. The logic here parallels the logic of those arguing for universal national health care: the private system is not providing for everyone, so let's nationalize health

care. In other words, by spreading out the costs, medical care will be available to everyone. In fact, our private system of health care has made possible the highest quality of health care in the world. Much of the great cost of health care in this country is due to the simple fact that medical technology, research, and skill are very expensive to provide. Notwithstanding this, few citizens, especially children, go without necessary medical care and the crisis in health care is in spiraling costs, not in underavailability. Much of this cost is due to a system that is "overbuilt, overused, and overpriced." (Robert J. Samuelson, "Rethinking Health Care," *Newsweek*, 6 June 1994: 50) Were education privatized, there is reason to believe that, through the forces of competition, the quality of education would improve, while the cost would decrease, relative to the present system. And just as with our present system of heath care, we could provide the poor with some minimal public assistance, in the form of scholarships for their education. But wouldn't the poor get poorer education than those who could afford the better schools? Perhaps, but no more than in the present system, in which inner-city children do not enjoy the same quality education as children who live in more affluent areas. Suppose that education were not compulsory, wouldn't children then go uneducated? The assumption here is that parents would not take the initiative to see to the education of their children, which is an insult at best. Parents have a responsibility to educate their children.

2. Consider the vast number of parents who, for a variety of reasons and despite availability of free public education, choose to send their children to private schools, at additional expense and often inconvenience. Would this be the case if public education were superior to private? Equally telling is the number of public school teachers who send their own children to private schools.

3. One rather serious example of this concerns the California Assessment Program: English Language/Arts Assessment, a program of reading and writing assessment for K–12. According to Richard W. Paul, in *Critical Thinking* (Santa Rosa, California: The Foundation For Critical Thinking, 1994), the official criteria for the State of California are themselves not only inadequate but critically barren: the criteria do not offer standards for assessing the critical merits of argumentative writing, with the result that critically poor and logically deficient writing may be given the highest possible assessment!

4. This fact of human diversity becomes increasingly significant as we approach the end of this century. The two major features of life facing young people as they enter the new millennium are the accelerating rate of change and intensifying complexity in nearly all human institutions. The best way for people to prepare for a life of change and complexity is to develop flexible, critical, skilled minds. This is a major function of education—but, in as much as there is diversity in individual minds, which vary widely in potential, interest, discipline, originality, and creativity, a system that accommodates those differences is much more likely to succeed than one that does not.

The Repeal of Prohibitionism

Mark Thornton

> "It seems certain, therefore, that the Eighteenth Amendment cannot be repealed, in whole or in part."
>
> —Irving Fisher, 1928

Introduction

Prohibition represents the repeal of the first and foremost freedom, our right to make consumption decisions.[1] Furthermore, prohibition undermines all other rights. It sets a legal precedent that corrupts the foundations of liberty, while the enforcement of prohibition places our remaining freedoms on the cost-benefit chopping block of despotism.[2]

The certainty in the permanence of alcohol prohibition that Irving Fisher spoke of applied equally during the first seventy-five years of narcotics prohibition. Only recently have the concepts of repeal and legalization been reintroduced into the debate over public policy. Despite growing public support for repeal and debate over legalization, prohibition is institutionally stronger within government than ever before. In fact, the most pronounced and visible trend in sumptuary policy is the extension of prohibition to alcohol and tobacco.

The repeal of drug prohibition is a radical proposal in the sense that it goes to the root of the problem. Prohibition fails to address the problems of drug abuse and creates many negative unintended consequences, such as political corruption. Repeal is not radical in the sense that it has never been tried, would have unusual content or results, or would represent some form of communism. In addition to the 21st amendment to the Constitution, many state and local prohibitions of alcohol and tobacco have been repealed, as have similar prohibitions in other countries. In fact, the interesting and important question is not whether prohibition repeals are feasible, but what will replace them.

A number of alternative policies have been proposed to replace prohibition. Most of these suggestions are *decriminalization* proposals that would repeal prohibition but retain some amount of government control. If, for example, the prohibitions on drugs were repealed, then these drugs would likely be placed under the jurisdiction of existing interventionist regimes. Narcotics would be available by prescription only and marijuana would be regulated and taxed like alcohol and tobacco. Such an alternative would rank high in terms of political feasibility, while *legalization*, the complete removal of government intervention, would rank low.

As W.H. Hutt warned, *political viability* should be the last consideration of the policy analyst, if he is to consider it at all. Despite its political feasibility and advantages over prohibition, decriminalization suffers from two important defects. First, government intervention is unable to correct true problems in society and tends to create new problems and exacerbate old ones. Second, government intervention is politically feasible but is also politically unstable. The failure of decriminalization to cure problems and its propensity to create new ones in turn create a general tendency for more severe interventionism, often culminating in the return of prohibition. The only way in which policy might be moved towards decreased intervention over time is if the case for legalization had already been made and accepted. As Hutt clearly explained, the intellectual and ideological battle must be won with its strongest arguments, not with watered-down and sugar-coated proposals.

The Failure of Prohibition

The pragmatic case for legalization rests on a knowledge of how the market works and how government interventions affect the market. The market-as-a-process approach of the Austrian school of economics provides the most comprehensive and holistic understanding of the economy and the impact of government intervention. This approach begins with a conception of a market completely unhampered by government intervention. The economy is driven by consumer demands and by competition among entrepreneurs for both customers and production inputs. Such an economy permits individuals to raise their standard of living and entrepreneurs to discover new ways of improving the standard of living in society. The *discovery process* of the market is the insatiable search for new ways in which our stock of resources can be rearranged to improve consumer satisfaction.

Interventionism is therefore the result of a lack of understanding of how the unhampered economy acts to employ resources in such a way as to correct for social problems. This myopic view of the economy is called the *undiscovered discovery process*. Policymakers adopt prohibition policies in part because of their (and their constituents') failure to recognize the market's ability to correct for existing imperfections and emerging problems. The market, of course, does not make such corrections instantaneously or ideally (as insinuated by the Neoclassical model of perfect competition), but it does address such problems in an unbiased and efficient manner. In the case of prohibition, temperance advocates became impatient for wider influence after their initial successes and resorted to political-based solutions, such as prohibition.[3]

When the undiscovered discovery process results in interventionism and government control, the *unsimulated discovery process* is introduced into the economy. This unsimulated discovery process refers to the inability of bureaucracy (established by government intervention) to act as a substitute for the market process. The bureaucratic nature of government is incompatible with experimentation, innovation, and entrepreneurial discovery. Bureaucracy has no clear and objective mechanism for recognizing efficient solutions.[4] Innovation and evaluation are further hampered in bureaucracy by the need to institute system-wide policies and rules rather than those appropriate to local conditions. Bureaucracy, therefore, is unable to achieve the desired results.

In addition to its own failure, bureaucracy also hampers the market's ability to produce desired solutions. The *stifled discovery process* that bureaucracy imposes on the market is illustrated by Sam Peltzman, who found that regulation stifled the discovery of new drugs in the pharmaceutical industry.[5] Withdrawl of resources from the economy to fund bureaucracy also hinders the market's discovery process. The stifling of discovery is more severe under prohibition than under regulatory interventions, because prohibition completely eliminates the market, while regulation merely hampers and distorts it. Prohibition's stifling of the discovery process extends to other areas, such as product quality, the availability of complements and substitutes, and product information.

Information is distorted by prohibition in many ways. In the infamous case of the 19th-century patent drugs, state prohibition laws and exemptions for patent medicines containing opiates resulted in the widespread addiction of unsuspecting consumers. Individuals seeking relief from addiction or attempting to avoid addiction were duped by the coexistence of state prohibition laws and the availability of legal narcotic preparations.[6]

While such bureaucratic miscalculation might be treated as ignorance or the result of rent-seeking behavior, it must nonetheless be seen as a normal and predictable result of interventionist policies. A more recent example is the case of cigarette warning-label requirements, which had the unintended effect of increasing teenagers' consumption of alternative tobacco products, such as chewing and snuffing tobacco, for which warning labels were not required.

Interventionism and bureaucracy not only suppress the market, they create a whole new process of discovery. The *wholly superfluous discovery process* is the result of new incentives established when government intervenes in the market. In black markets, the incentives of suppliers tend to be completely dominated by the effects of prohibition.

The issue of drug potency and product quality demonstrates that new opportunities in the black market not only make prohibition more difficult to enforce, they produce results that run counter to the goals of prohibition and thus have important implications for the possibility of effective prohibition. As more resources are devoted to the enforcement of prohibition (or penalties are increased), suppliers resort to increasing potency, higher potency drug-types, reductions in product quality (such as safety and information), and elimination of complimentary goods (such as needles, filters, and antidotes) in order to reduce the risks of arrest. Most importantly, changes in potency and product quality subvert the prohibitionist argument that reducing the quantity consumed *partially* achieves the goal of prohibition.

The issues of crime and corruption also have important implications for the possibility of prohibition. Prohibition is based on the *association* of drug use and crime. However, most drug-related crime is actually *caused* by prohibition, not drug use or abuse per se. Black-market prices lead some consumers to commit property crime to finance their purchases and lead some suppliers to bribe public officials in order to reduce the risks of doing business. Prohibition also causes crime because suppliers and demanders have no access to the legal process and therefore commit crimes in order to enforce contracts and defend sales territories. By destroying job opportunities in the legal economy, prohibition also increases the relative return on criminal behavior and therefore the criminal population.[7] In response to prohibition-induced prison overcrowding, early release programs reduce the cost of crime and thereby increase the crime rate.[8] Increases in crime and corruption due to prohibition act as a counterbalance to prohibition enforcement, hindering the attainment of *effective prohibition*, while making the underlying social problems worse rather than better.

Is Effective Prohibition Possible?

The debate about prohibition has traditionally centered on its costs and benefits.[9] This has led to a stalemate, because each side can claim victory in a scientifically valid way simply by valuing costs or benefits higher or lower depending on their subjective evaluations of those costs and benefits. The costs and benefits of prohibition must be viewed by economists as just as subjective as the value of lollipops or the *Mona Lisa*. The prohibitionists could validly claim, for example, that the prevention of one drug addiction is worth $1 million or $1 billion dollars to them. The case against prohibition presented here does not rest on the cost of prohibition's outweighing the benefits, but rather on the absence of benefits. Based on the economic (i.e, subjective) theory of value, we cannot claim that the benefits of prohibition are not worth the cost, but we can possibly challenge all of the alleged benefits and thereby force the prohibitionists to demonstrate the existence of such benefits.

The neglect of this more fundamental level of analysis of prohibition is grounded in the notion that prohibition reduces the quantity consumed, and that the benefits of prohibition are a function of the quantity consumed. In general, if prohibition reduces market supply and increases price, then, *all other things being equal*, there will be a smaller quantity consumed and therefore benefits from prohibition. For example, if wife beaters, child molesters, and street brawlers commit their sins while intoxicated, then a reduced supply and less intoxication would be expected to result in fewer sins being committed. It is the assumption, *all other things being equal*, on which the case *for* prohibition is demolished. If anything is true of prohibition it is that under it *virtually nothing remains the same*.

While prohibition certainly does increase price, it is not guaranteed that it will also decrease the quantity consumed. Prohibition can also increase the *demand* for a product and thereby offset or even outweigh the decrease in *supply*. Prohibition might increase the demand for a good due to the additional attention and information available about the good. For example, restricting the sale of glue to prevent people from using it as an intoxicant could inadvertently increase the demand for glue if there had been limited information about the intoxicating effects of glue prior to the prohibition. There is also the often talked about "forbidden fruit" syndrome, where alienated and risk-loving individuals (often male teenagers) will demand anything that they are prohibited from consuming. As Michel de Montaigne wrote in 1580, "To forbid us anything is to make us have a mind for it."[10] Of course, the increase in demand would have to more than offset the decrease in supply in order to increase total consumption.[11]

Even with no increase in demand, consumers might be worse off, because prohibition also leads to an increase in potency and a decrease in overall product quality, both of which make drugs much more dangerous to consume. As a result, prohibition would produce no benefits, because higher potency and lower quality are associated with increased rates of addiction, violent and volatile behavior, and negative health consequences, including death by overdose.

Consumption patterns do, however, change as a result of prohibition. Some people will cease their demand for the product altogether. Unfortunately for the prohibitionist case, this almost never involves the people and social problems that prohibitionists seek to address.[12] To the extent that it does reduce consumption of the good among problem groups, prohibition simply shifts "abuse" to substitute goods.[13] Prohibition also affects the time and social patterns of consumption, but again to no positive result. Due to the risks of consumption, consumers are more likely to conceal their activities rather than expose them to the monitoring of social groups. The risks of capture also imply that consumers are more apt to binge rather than to moderate or spread their consumption over time.

It might be argued that prohibition could provide some benefit, however dubious, if it decreased expenditures on the prohibited product. However, prohibition can only reduce expenditures under the most extreme, restrictive, and temporary conditions, i.e., where demand is elastic, and does not result in the substitution of other intoxicants. Most estimates of expenditures show that total expenditures during National Alcohol Prohibition (1920–1933) remained the same or increased from what would have been spent in the absence of prohibition. The first year of National Alcohol Prohibition appears to be the only documented case of reduced expenditures.[14] As Warburton noted, "we must conclude that the adoption of national prohibition has failed to reduce the use of alcoholic beverages and has increased the sum spent on them."[15] No one argues that prohibition has reduced total expenditures on heroin, cocaine, or marijuana. In fact, it is well-recognized that the national expenditure on products such as cocaine and marijuana are significantly higher with prohibition.

Prohibition does not eliminate access to the product and does not discourage the very type of consumption it was designed to discourage. Therefore, the argument that increased price reduces quantity consumed and therefore produces benefits is yet to be established either in theory or in fact. The quantity of drugs captured by law enforcement is not a benefit of prohibition; it is merely a cost of doing business in the black market.

Prohibition neither decreases demand nor prevents increases in demand.[16] Government statistics indicate that the consumption of marijuana has decreased or leveled off in recent years. However, it would be a mistake to declare this a benefit of prohibition and increased enforcement. First, the statistics themselves are in some doubt. Marijuana production shifted to small plots and indoor gardens, making information on production difficult to obtain. The potency of marijuana has also increased dramatically in recent years. Despite government claims to the contrary, the evidence supports the case that potency-adjusted consumption of marijuana may have increased.[17]

Even if a decrease in consumption has occurred, it would not be a benefit of prohibition—quite the contrary. Government estimates have shown that as the street price of marijuana has increased, the price of cocaine has decreased, and the consumption of cocaine has increased. This is clearly consistent with a shift in demand from marijuana to cocaine and this shift in demand between substitute products is a predictable result of increased enforcement.

This economic analysis has demonstrated the *possibility* of the impossibility of prohibition. The stronger case—that prohibition *is* impossible (that is, without any benefit)—has also been established. In fact, this inquiry finds that prohibition only exacerbates the problems that prohibitionists seek to address, and that more law enforcement and higher penalties only further aggravate these social problems. The ball is now in the prohibitionists' court, and I eagerly await their attempted return. Their response should be an attempt to scientifically demonstrate the existence of *any* public-spirited benefits that can be derived from prohibition.

Alternatives to Prohibition?

The policy debate over prohibition is generally concerned with how much to spend, how to enforce, where to allocate resources, and how to punish consumers, producers, retailers, and wholesalers (i.e., "kingpins"). Substantive policy alternatives such as nationalization (government drug stores), licensing requirements, price controls, regulation, maintenance and rehabilitation programs, and sin taxes involve some measure of decriminalization. These alternatives would be improvements over prohibition and would provide evidence of the benefits and corrective potential of comprehensive legalization.

Decriminalization, however, is a double-edged policy reform. These policies can reduce some of the worst consequences of prohibition, but they have negative consequences similar to prohibition and have a limited capacity to address underlying problems. The disadvantages and limited effectiveness of decriminalization combine to undermine the political stability of such policies and to eventually result in increased government intervention. Full legalization (the complete elimination of government intervention) is the only rational alternative to prohibitionism. Its only problem is political feasibility.

Clague examined several strategies for dealing with heroin addiction, including prohibition, strict and permissive methadone maintenance programs, heroin maintenance, and quarantine. These schemes were then evaluated against seven criteria: amount of crime, number and well-being of addicts, police corruption and violation of civil liberties, legal deprivation of traditional liberties, and respect for law (in general). Based on his analysis, Clague ranks each scheme's performance on the seven criteria on a five-point scale. The fact that prohibition ranks last and heroin maintenance ranks first is indirect evidence of the potential benefits of legalization.[18]

While he found that heroin maintenance was best among the policies studied, Clague admits that for a variety of reasons, it is not "an ideal solution to the heroin problem."[19] In addition to maintaining addiction and posing several practical problems, government-sponsored maintenance programs involve taxpayer subsidies to addicts. This option creates resentment on the part of antidrug taxpayers and therefore leads to political instability.[20] Kaplan also examined a variety of policy options for heroin. He also found that heroin maintenance and other options faced operational drawbacks and political obstacles.[21]

Moore suggested that a policy of heroin maintenance for addicts, combined with prohibition, would achieve price discrimination in the heroin market. Maintenance would reduce the costs of addiction to the addict and society, while prohibition would impose a greatly increased price on illegal heroin (over general prohibition) and therefore discourage experimentation with heroin. Moore's "highly speculative discussion" was not meant to demonstrate which policy is most desirable, but rather to investigate the determinants of effective price and, by extension, demand for heroin.[22]

Fines have been suggested as an efficient substitute for imprisonment. If prohibition can be viewed as a form of price control, then fines could be substituted as a deterrent that would save prison resources. Lott and Roberts have examined this question and found that a price-control approach for victimless crimes lacks the necessary incentives for effective enforcement. The one-sided enforcement that works in the case of rent controls and minimum-wage laws does not work in the case of prohibitions.[23]

The sin tax is an often-suggested alternative to prohibition. Frequently, it is seen as a viable alternative in the cases of alcohol, marijuana, and tobacco, but not in the cases of cocaine and opiates.[24] The presumed benefits of sin taxes include a reduction in crime and the deterrent effect of taxation. However, the actual benefit of this policy option is political. Sin taxes allow voters and their representatives to tax their fellow citizens to pay for the general expenses of government. Therefore, while this option has much to recommend it, many of its beneficial aspects would be reduced or eliminated as the tax rate increased.[25] High rates of taxation would maintain the black market, smuggling, crime, and corruption, would have little positive impact on drug use, and therefore would create the preconditions for the reintroduction of prohibition.[26]

The repeal of Prohibition in 1933 set the stage for extensive policy experimentation.[27] Some states remained dry, while others resorted to licensing requirements or state monopoly. The federal government employed taxes, tariffs, regulations, and license requirements. Some state governments imposed taxes, allowed certain forms of alcohol sale, such as by-the-drink, or beer and wine sales only. Regulations were placed on the potency of the product. For example, the potency of beer was limited to 3.2 percent in some states, although these regulations were primarily for taxation purposes. Additional interventions included age restrictions, advertising restrictions, local option, restrictions on the hours of sale, and price controls.[28] Although decriminalization offers many improvements over prohibition, interventionism continues to produce mediocre results at best.[29]

In summary, policy analysts have considered a variety of control policies. They have generally found that decriminalization policies are superior to punitive and prohibitionist measures. Extensive evidence, however, supports the notion that decriminalization does indeed produce mixed or mediocre results. Ironically, many of these same analysts either ignore or dismiss the potential of legalization. In their perspective, legalization is the source of "sinful" behavior or at least does not provide a method by which society can control such behavior. This is an obvious case of the undiscovered discovery process.

Hugging the middle ground between prohibition and legalization, the pragmatic stance of decriminalizationists masks the unscientific nature of their position. Dating back to the Puritans, this results-oriented view has been transformed from theocratic to technocratic. Indeed, the latest contribution from this perspective emanates from a location not far from the original Puritan colony.[30]

The Free-Market Solution

Prohibition has been found to be effectively impossible in the economic sense. Alternative policies such as government-sponsored maintenance programs also exhibit problems, but represent an improvement over prohibition. The free-market solution differs from these alternative policies in that it involves no government intervention.

The free market has traditionally been viewed as the cause rather than a cure for the problems of drug abuse. The historical and theoretical investigations undertaken here suggest otherwise. The free-market solution involves voluntary choices of individuals within an environment of free entry, property rights, and the rule of law. Entrepreneurs hire labor and purchase resources to produce, promote, and sell products to consumers. Consumers choose among diversified products in an attempt to maximize utility. Exchange provides gains to both parties and an efficient allocation of resources. Social institutions, firms, charitable organizations, and self-help groups form to solve problems.

Prohibitionists would, of course, scoff at such a description as it applies to the market for drugs.[31] Indeed, the market as it has been described here is not perfect, especially in the neoclassical economics sense. It is characterized by risk, uncertainty, and decentralized information, as it must necessarily be in the real world. Mistakes, such as overdoses, and individual problems, such as addiction, will no doubt occur in any system. However, competition and the discovery process of a market promote solutions to the problems of drug abuse.

The benefits of the free-market solution would include the following.

1. Competitive prices would free up resources for the consumption of goods such as food, clothing, shelter, and medical care.
2. The profit motive would stimulate producers to discover and introduce goods with characteristics that enhance consumer satisfaction. Deadly products that were created by prohibition would be eliminated. Producers would compete by improving their products to meet the desires of consumers. The market for a particular drug, such as alcohol, marijuana, or aspirin would be characterized by diversified products.
3. As with any dangerous product, suppliers would prefer regular customers who are familiar with the product, thereby reducing expenditures on marketing and exposure to liability law. Suppliers would no longer enlist the services of minors to retail their products.
4. Information about product availability, price, and product quality would be available. Advertising would convey information about the unique features of a particular brand.
5. Producers would engage in product standardization and brand-name

labeling and supply directions for use, product-safety information, and so on.
6. Crime and corruption that result from prohibition, taxation, regulations, and other policy options would be eliminated.
7. Government expenditures on law enforcement, prisons, and courts could be reduced. Courts would not be as backlogged, prisons would be less crowded, and the police could concentrate resources on traditional crimes such as murder, rape, and robbery. These changes would promote respect for law and order.
8. Individuals would be self-responsible for their actions with respect to drugs. More resources and public attention could be devoted to education, treatment, maintenance, and rehabilitation.
9. Consumers would have access to the legal system to protect them against fraud and negligence on the part of the producer. Producers would no longer have to resort to violence to enforce contracts and ensure payments. Sales territories could only be defended by voluntary agreement, rather than by violence.
10. Many of the products that have been prohibited have legitimate uses and were important products in the development of modern civilization. Legalization would allow for their use in these and other areas, and would promote general economic development.

This list covers many of the major benefits of the free-market solution. These benefits can be summarized as freeing up valuable resources, providing incentives for improvements, eliminating the costs (both direct and unintended) of prohibition, and providing new opportunities for people to pursue.

The Extended Free-Market Solution

The free-market solution as applied to one drug or all drugs will not achieve ideal or utopian results. Short-run adjustments to free-market conditions involve substantial costs. Discovering techniques to avoid and cure addiction and to develop new institutions and safer products will all take time. In fact, in the case of addictive products, achieving solutions may take years.

Extending the free-market solution to areas other than the immediate market for drugs will help in the development of such solutions. Circumstances such as war, poverty, discrimination, and a loss of economic opportunity are associated with drug abuse and addiction. Applying the market solution economy-wide, or to specific markets such as insurance, medicine, and labor, also provides opportunity for improvement. Some of the possible benefits of the extended free-market solution are that:

1. A free-market economy would produce the most efficient use of resources and the highest standards of living. Market economies are characterized by capital accumulation and lower time preferences.
2. Removal of barriers to entry into the medical profession would reduce the costs of health care and treatment for addiction. Removal of government-subsidized medical care would place the entire cost of drug abuse on the abuser, rather than providing a subsidy for abuse.
3. Insurance companies and employers could control and discriminate against persons who abuse drugs, placing a direct and visible cost on drug users and abusers.
4. Economists have found discrimination and exploitation in nationalized and regulated industries. Removal of these barriers would create economic opportunities for the disenfranchised.
5. War has been found to play an important role in creating and stimulating the problems of drug abuse (and prohibitions). The absence of war would greatly enhance the success of legalization.

The extended free-market solution is a complement to the free-market alternative to prohibition and an important component of the ultimate solution to the problems of drug abuse. In summary, the reasons legalization will work are that:

1. Legalization eliminates prohibition, government intervention, and the plethora of problems these policies cause.
2. Legalization discriminates between use and abuse, while other policies do not. Use is normalized while abuse is identified and stigmatized. These are important intermediate goals of public policy.
3. This alternative removes or diminishes many of the sources of abuse, such as war, poverty, ignorance, and irresponsibility.
4. This alternative also frees up resources to help curtail the negative impact of abuse and produces incentives for self-responsibility and longer time horizons.
5. Legalization enhances the role of social institutions such as drug education, drug treatment, drug maintenance, self-help organizations, church, family, friends, doctors, help lines, and civic organizations. It also magnifies the role of private prohibitions that protect us against the worst consequences of drug abuse.

The Moral Case for Legalization

Many opponents of legalization recognize the failures of prohibition but are ideologically attached to sumptuary legislation. They may acknowledge the economic weaknesses of prohibition but maintain a moral case against legalization. Upon reflection, this stance is based on a myopic view of the market and on "heretical" moral views that do not pass the test of logical consistency.

Prohibitionists make the claim that the use of certain goods, such as alcohol, create the potential for the user to commit "sinful" or socially damaging acts. For the Puritans, alcohol was the devil's brew, while for the modern technocrats, addiction to other drugs plays the role. In both scenarios, the individual has been eliminated in terms of choice and, to a lesser extent, responsibility for the act. In this objective view of "sin," the object causes the sin, while in traditional moral and religious teachings, sin is the result of individual choice.

Although most drinkers, smokers, and drug users are not social deviants, prohibitionists push for comprehensive polices that vilify everyone in these groups. This is in keeping with their objective view of sin: certain objects such as alcohol, tobacco, and playing cards are inherently evil no matter how they are used. This leads to further contradiction when the cases of the industrial use of alcohol, the medicinal use of tobacco, or the recreational use of playing cards are raised.

The prohibitionist approach eliminates the distinction between legal and moral activity and thereby undermines both morality and the rule of law. Reliance on individual initiative and responsibility is no sin. It is not only the key to success in the battle against drug abuse, it is also a reaffirmation of traditional American values. How can one make a moral choice when one is in fact forced into a particular course by the threat of government coercion? How is society strengthened when guns and prisons enforce a mode of behavior rather than allowing behavior to be determined by individual responsibility? When society allows individuals to choose and then punishes them for actual transgressions, it discourages criminal behavior, promotes self-responsibility, and champions the rule of law. However, when society tries to prevent sin by removing temptation, it increases crime, discourages the development of moral behavior, and undermines the rule of law in society.

As classical liberals from John Stuart Mill to Ludwig von Mises have exclaimed, the repeal of prohibition is of the highest importance. This analysis, they would no doubt agree, finds that relegalization is the only alternative for a free and virtuous society.[32]

Notes

1. It seems historically logical that John Stuart Mill wrote his famous *On Liberty* in part as a response to the Maine Law movement in America. Mill's preliminary essay appears during the height of the Maine law movement (1851–1855) and the first edition of the book appears belatedly in 1859. He refers to the Maine laws and liquor control measures often and seems to have rendered the major new thrust of his argument against prohibitionism. While Mill attacks prohibition and sin taxes, he does indicate that "dealers" have some legal obligations concerning the sale of their products.

2. Mises (1949, pp. 733–734) stressed the important political consequences of direct interference with consumption as it relates to the prohibition of drugs:

> Opium and morphine are certainly dangerous, habit-forming drugs. But once the principle is admitted that it is the duty of government to protect the individual against his own foolishness, no serious objections can be advanced against further encroachments. A good case could be made out in favor of the prohibition of alcohol and nicotine. And why limit the government's benevolent providence to the protection of the individual's body only? Is not the harm a man can inflict on his mind and soul even more disastrous than any bodily evils? Why not prevent him from reading bad books and seeing bad plays, from looking at bad paintings and statues and from hearing bad music? The mischief done by bad ideologies, surely, is much more pernicious, both for the individual and for the whole society, than that done by narcotic drugs.
>
> These fears are not merely imaginary specters terrifying secluded doctrinaires. It is a fact that no paternal government, whether ancient or modern, ever shrank from regimenting its subjects' minds, beliefs, and opinions. If one abolishes man's freedom to determine his own consumption, one takes all freedoms away. The naive advocates of government interference with consumption delude themselves when they neglect what they disdainfully call the philosophical aspect of the problem. They unwittingly support the case of censorship, inquisition, religious intolerance, and the persecution of dissenters. (1949, pp. 733–734)

Therefore, the consequences of prohibition include its direct effects, its unintended consequences, and the tendency for intervention to influence the philosophy, size, and scope of government.

3. One can suffer from the *undiscovered discovery process* if, like the temperance advocate, one views the market as unable to deal with certain problems at all, or as in the case of neoclassical economics, one expects solutions to be forthcoming and, when they fail to emerge, *market failure* is declared and intervention is resorted to. For a description of the 19th century temperance movement see Dow (1898), Krout (1925), and Furnas (1965).

4. Conversely, the market has several mechanisms, most notably the system of profits and losses, that weeds out inefficient firms and redirects resources to their most highly valued uses. See Mises (1944).

5. Peltzman, 1974.
6. See Thornton (1991), especially 56–69.
7. Beil and Thornton (1994).
8. Benson et al. have shown that asset forfeiture policies provide enforcement agencies with an incentive to direct their resources at prohibition and away from personal and property crimes, thereby reducing the cost of crime and increasing criminality.
9. It is possible to enact prohibitions under virtually any form of government, and in fact, prohibitions have been enacted by virtually every existing national and supranational government, including the United Nations. It is also now generally agreed that complete prohibition is impossible, except in the most limited sense (where there is little or no existing demand for the product or where there exist near-perfect legal substitutes). The political possibility and the effective impossibility of complete prohibition are therefore not at issue here.
10. Mencken, 979.
11. Also see Brecher (1972) who argues that prohibition can create an increase in demand.
12. For example, alcohol prohibition might discourage some teetotalers, but will certainly not discourage the alcoholic. Addicts and heavy users do eventually end their use of addictive or harmful drugs, but this has mainly been attributed to aging or maturing, rather than higher prices or imprisonment. Similarly, the purpose of gun control is to reduce crime and death, but it only prevents some law-abiding citizens from owning guns without stopping criminals from obtaining and using armaments.
13. Prohibition of certain drugs will increase the sales of legal intoxicants such as alcohol. However, it would not be legitimate to compare the harmful or potentially harmful effects of drugs produced in the market to drugs produced in the black market. Therefore this substitution cannot be considered socially beneficial.
14. While expenditures supposedly fell in 1921, there is ample reason to expect that consumption did not fall or did not fall to the same extent as expenditures because of the inventory building that took place after the enactment of prohibition, but prior to its implementation.
15. Warburton, 170–171.
16. Here we make a distinction between demand, which prohibition cannot effect and quantity demanded, on which prohibition may have some effect.
17. See Thornton (1991, chapter 4) and Kleiman (1989).
18. Clague (1973) freely admits that his ranking is highly subjective and that in two instances he is unable to assign an ordinal ranking. His rankings are based on the long-term effects of the policies and do not consider short-run adjustments or the relative weight of each criterion. He found that the quarantine scheme ranked high in several criteria. However, he found that serious problems in law, the Constitution, notions of justice, and increases in "resentment and alienation in many quarters" result in very low ranking in "legal deprivation of traditional liberties" and "respect for law." Therefore, one would have to place little or negative importance

on matters of justice, liberty, and respect for the law in order to rank quarantine above heroin maintenance.

19. Clague, 263.

20. Providing subsidies to drug addicts can be seen as just as abhorrent to certain taxpayers as providing taxpayer-subsidized abortions. Musto (1987, 64 and elsewhere) showed that the early narcotic-maintenance programs were "unwieldy and unpopular" and were quickly closed. In addition to creating resentment and costs to taxpayers, this policy tends to condone heroin use and reduces the perceived and real costs of addiction to the addict.

21. Kaplan, 1983. It should be noted that the difficulties associated with "free availability" were based on a "greatly increased addiction rate" and the public health and personal aspects associated with an increased addiction rate. This catastrophic view of legalization has no basis in experience.

22. Moore, 1973.

23. Lott and Roberts (1989) note that victimless crimes are difficult to monitor; the goods are highly mobile, a social stigma is attached to these goods, and the queuing or surpluses that result from price controls present special social problems.

24. Kaplan, 150–151.

25. High tax rates would lead to smuggling, tax avoidance, home production, increased crime, and corruption. See Smith (1976) on government's tendency to maximize net revenues and its impact on the alcohol industry.

26. Even an ad potere sin tax, which would increase the tax rate on higher potency and more dangerous drug products, has drawbacks, such as sending signals to potential consumers that low-potency or nontaxed products are safe to consume. For a complete analysis of the causal relationships between sin taxes and prohibition, both historically and theoretically, see Thornton (1994).

27. For a history of the repeal movement see Kyvig (1979). For an unsympathetic view on the repeal movement see Dobyns (1940).

28. For a history of the plethora of policies enacted after repeal, see Harrison and Laine (1936).

29. See Sylbing (1985) and Sylbing and Persoon (1985). One benefit of legalization is the development of social institutions that deal directly or indirectly with the problems of addiction and drug abuse, such as the formation of Alcoholics Anonymous (mid-1930s), which today claims over one million members. A great deal of this organization's success can be attributed to the anonymous status of its members. Noteworthy is that the organization *does not* advocate prohibition or severe restrictionism on the part of the government to decrease the problems of alcohol abuse.

30. Mark Kleiman (1992). See my "The Harvard Plan for Drugs: A Review of *Against Excess: Drug Policy for Results*" (1994) for a complete criticism.

31. Some critics of the market view it as "too practical," focusing only on consumers' or producers' direct interests, rather than on political (i.e., the majority's) interests. Other critics claim that the market solution is too "impractical," that it does not address the problems of consumers and producers, or that such a substitution is "politically impossible."

32. For further elaboration of the case for repealing drug prohibitions, see Machan and Thornton, 1991.

References

Beil, Richard O. and Mark Thornton, "The Economics of Prohibition and Crime: An Experimental Approach," Working Paper, Auburn University, 1994.
Benson, Bruce L., David W. Rasmussen, and David L. Sollars, "Police Bureaucracies, Their Incentives, and the War on Drugs," *Public Choice*, forthcoming.
Brecher, Edward M. *Licit and Illicit Drugs*, Boston: Little, Brown and Company, 1972.
Clague, Christopher, "Legal Strategies for Dealing with Heroin Addiction," *American Economic Review*, May 1973, 63, 270–77.
Dobyns, Fletcher, *The Amazing Story of Repeal: An Expose of the Power of Propaganda*, Chicago: Willett, Clark & Company, 1940.
Dow, Neal, *The Reminiscences of Neal Dow, Recollection of Eighty Years*, Portland, Maine: The Evening Express Publishing Company, 1898.
Fisher, Irving, *Prohibition Still at its Worst*, New York: Alcohol Information Committee, 1928.
Furnas, J.C., *The Life and Times of Late Demon Rum*, New York: Capricorn Books, 1965.
Harrison, Leonard V., and Elizabeth Laine, *After Repeal: A Study of Liquor Control Administration*, New York: Harper and Brothers, 1936.
Hutt, W.H., *Politically Impossible. . . ?*, London: Institute of Economic Affairs, 1971.
Jenkins, Philip, "The Puritanism That Dare Note Speak Its Name," *Chronicles*, Vol. 18 No. 7 (July 1994), 20–23.
Kaplan, John, *The Hardest Drug: Heroin and Public Policy*, University of Chicago Press, 1983.
Kleiman, Mark A. R., *Marijuana: Costs of Abuse, Costs of Control*, Westport, CT: Greenwood Press, 1989.
———, *Against Excess: Drug Policy for Results*, New York: Basic Books, 1992.
Krout, John Allen, *The Origins of Prohibition*, New York: Alfred Knopf, 1925.
Kyvig, David E., *Repealing National Prohibition*, University of Chicago Press, 1979.
Lott, John R, and Russel D. Roberts, "Why Comply: One-Sided Enforcement of Price Controls and Victimless Crime Laws," *Journal of Legal Studies*, June 1989, 18, 403–14.
Machan, Tibor R., and Mark Thornton, "The Re-legalization of Drugs," *The Freeman*, April 1991, 41, 153–55.
Mencken, H.L. edited, [1942] *A New Dictionary of Quotations On Historical Principles from Ancient and Modern Sources*, New York: Alfred A. Knopf, 1991.
Mises, Ludwig von, [1944] *Bureaucracy*, New Rochelle, NY: Arlington House, 1969.
Moore, Mark, H., "Policies to Achieve Discrimination on the Effective Price of Heroin," *American Economic Review*, May 1973, 63, 270–77.

Musto, David F., *The American Disease: Origins of Narcotic Control*, Oxford University Press, 1987.
Peltzman, Sam, *Regulation of Pharmaceutical Innovation: The 1962 Amendments* (Washington, D.C.: American Enterprise Institute, 1974).
Smith, Rodney, T., "The Legal and Illegal Markets for Taxed Goods: Pure Theory and an Application to State Government Taxation of Distilled Spirits," *Journal of Law and Economics*, August 1976, 19, 393–430.
Sylbing, G. *The Use of Drugs, Alcohol and Tobacco. Results of a Survey Among Young People in the Netherlands Aged 15–24 Years*, Amsterdam: Foundation for the Scientific Study of Alcohol and Drug Use, 1985.
Sylbing, G. and Persoon, J.M.G. "Cannabis Use Among Youth in the Netherlands," *Bulletin On Narcotics*, October/December 1985, 37, 51–60.
Thornton, Mark, *The Economics of Prohibition*, Salt Lake City: University of Utah Press, 1991.
———, "Prohibition: The Ultimate in Sin," Working Paper, Auburn University, 1994.
Warburton, Clark, *The Economic Results of Prohibition*, New York: Columbia University Press, 1932.

Part Three

Answering Critics and Responding to Other Views

Introduction

Libertarianism simply isn't widely embraced among intellectuals, including political philosophers. We do not wish to speculate here just why this is so—that is another kind of discussion. We will only suggest that the polity of individual liberty is radical beyond any other system. It uproots centuries of varieties of tribalism, whereby some more or less sizable collectivity of human beings is deemed to be the primary beneficiary of public policy. In contrast, libertarianism takes the human individual—not some atomistic entity, however, contrary to how critics often choose to characterize it—as being of primary political value. Because of this focus, it is individual liberty that needs to be given the greatest attention, since as far as their political identity is concerned, everyone is equally valuable and equally deserving of having his or her sovereignty respected and protected. (Yet this is not to say that morally, individuals might not differ significantly in their worth and excellence.)

This libertarian political vision has been challenged not only by contemporary liberalism in the United States, but by streams of political thought that owe their inspiration to insights of thinkers from pre- and postmodern times. Sometimes this opposition is best described by the label "conservatism" and at other times by the label "communitarianism." Regardless of the description, libertarianism is challenged by some of the same forces that object to contemporary American liberalism. Further, there are those who continue to mount their opposition to the libertarian political vision from a reconstruction of a more or less Marxian perspective.

This section contains essays that answer criticism brought against the libertarian or natural-rights classical liberal political perspective. Some essays also respond critically to the views of opposing political perspectives. Together, these essays make it clear that libertarianism is a political view of much greater sophistication and power than its critics and even some of its defenders fully realize.

As a result of the essays in this volume, we hope that the range of coverage and depth of examination of libertarianism will extend beyond that which has been generally found to date in standard textbooks and anthologies. We look forward to a richer political dialogue regarding libertarianism. Possibly, as we approach a new century, libertarianism will be better understood and come to be seen by more and more as a political view that is worthy of very serious consideration.

The Nonexistence of Basic Welfare Rights

Tibor R. Machan

James Sterba and others maintain that we all have the right to "receive the goods and resources necessary for preserving" ourselves. This is not what I have argued human beings have a right to. They have the right, rather, not to be killed, attacked, and deprived of their property—by persons in or outside of government. As Abraham Lincoln put it, "no man is good enough to govern another man, without that other's consent."[1]

Sterba claims that various political outlooks would have to endorse these "rights." He sets out to show, in particular, that welfare rights follow from libertarian theory itself.[2] Sterba wishes to show that *if* Lockean libertarianism is correct, then we all have rights to welfare and equal (economic) opportunity. What I wish to show is that since Lockean libertarianism—as developed in this work—is true, and since the rights to welfare and equal opportunity require their violation, no one has these latter rights. The reason some people, including Sterba, believe otherwise is that they have found some very rare instances in which some citizens could find themselves in circumstances that would require disregarding rights altogether. This would be in situations that cannot be characterized to be "where peace is possible."[3] And every major libertarian thinker from Locke to the present has treated these kinds of cases.[4]

Let us be clear about what Sterba sets out to show. It is that libertarians are philosophically unable to escape the welfare-statist implications of their commitment to negative liberty. This means that despite their belief that they are only supporting the enforceable right of every person not to be coerced by other persons, libertarians must accept, by the logic of their own position, that individuals also possess basic enforceable rights to being provided with various services from others. He holds, then, that basic negative rights imply basic positive rights.

To Lockean libertarians the ideal of liberty means that we all, individually, have the right not to be constrained against our consent within our realm of authority—ourselves and our belongings. Sterba states that for such libertarians "Liberty is being unconstrained by persons from doing what one has a right to do."[5] Sterba adds, somewhat misleadingly, that for Lockean libertarians "a right to life [is] a right not to be killed unjustly and a right to property [is] a right to acquire goods and resources either by initial acquisition or voluntary agreement."[6] Sterba does realize that these rights do not entitle one to receive from others the goods and resources necessary for preserving one's life.

A problem with this foundation of the Lockean libertarian view is that political justice—not the justice of Plato, which is best designated in our time as "perfect virtue"—for natural-rights theorists presupposes individual rights. One cannot then explain rights in terms of justice but must explain justice in terms of rights.

For a Lockean libertarian, to possess any basic right to receive the goods and resources necessary for preserving one's life conflicts with possessing the right not to be killed, assaulted, or stolen from. The latter are rights Lockean libertarians consider to be held by all individual human beings. Regularly to protect and maintain—that is, enforce—the former right would often require the violation of the latter. A's right to the food she has is incompatible with B's right to take this same food. Both the rights could not be fundamental in an integrated legal system. The situation of one's having rights to welfare, and so forth, and another's having rights to life, liberty, and property is thus theoretically intolerable and practically unfeasible. The point of a system of rights is the securing of mutually peaceful and consistent moral conduct on the part of human beings. As Rand observes,

> "Rights" are . . . the link between the moral code of a man and the legal code of a society, between ethics and politics. *Individual rights are the means of subordinating society to moral law.*[7]

Sterba asks us—in another discussion of his views—to consider what he calls "a *typical* conflict situation between the rich and the poor." He says that in his situation "the rich, of course, have more than enough resources to satisfy their basic needs. By contrast, the poor lack the resources to meet their most basic needs even though *they have tried all the means available to them that libertarians regard as legitimate for acquiring such resources*"[8] (my emphasis).

The goal of a theory of rights would be defeated if rights were typically in conflict. Some bureaucratic group would have to keep applying its moral intuitions on numerous occasions when rights claims would *typically* conflict. A constitution is workable if it helps remove at least the largest proportion of such decisions from the realm of arbitrary (intuitive) choice and avail a society of men and women of objective guidelines that are reasonably integrated, not in relentless discord.

Most critics of libertarianism assume some doctrine of basic needs that they invoke to show that whenever basic needs are not satisfied for some people, while others have "resources" that are not basic needs for them, the former have just claims against the latter. (The language of resources of course loads the argument in the critic's favor since it suggests that these goods simply come into being and happen to be in the possession of some people, quite without rhyme or reason, arbitrarily [as John Rawls claims].)[9]

This doctrine is full of difficulties. It lacks any foundation for why the needs of some persons must be claims upon the lives of others. And why are there such needs anyway—to what end are they needs, and whose ends are these and why are not the persons whose needs they are held responsible for supplying the needs? (Needs, as I have already observed, lack any force in moral argument without the prior justification of the purposes they serve, or the goals they help to fulfill. A thief has a basic need of skills and powers that are clearly not justified if theft is morally unjustified. If, however, the justification of basic needs, such as food and other resources, presupposes the value of human life, and if the value of human life justifies, as I have argued earlier, the principle of the natural rights to life, liberty and property, then the attainment or fulfillment of the basic need for food may not involve the violation of these rights.)

Sterba claims that without guaranteeing welfare and equal-opportunity rights, Lockean libertarianism violates the most basic tenets of any morality, namely, that "ought" implies "can." The thrust of " 'ought' implies 'can' " is that one ought to do that which one is free to do, that one is morally responsible only for those acts that one had the power either to choose to engage in or not to engage in. (There is debate on just how this point must be phrased—in terms of the will being free or the person being free to will something. For our purposes, however, all that counts is that the person must have [had] a genuine option to do X or not to do X before it can be true that he or she ought to do X or ought to have done X.) If an innocent person is forced by the actions of another to forgo significant moral choices, then that innocent person is not free to act morally and thus his or her human dignity is violated.

This is not so different from the commonsense legal precept that if one is not sound of mind one cannot be criminally culpable. Only free agents, capable of choosing between right and wrong, are open to moral evaluation. This indeed is the reason that many so-called moral theories fail to be anything more than value theories. They omit from consideration the issue of self-determination. If either hard or soft determinism is true, morality is impossible, although values need not disappear.[10]

If Sterba were correct about Lockean libertarianism typically contradicting " 'ought' implies 'can,' " his argument would be decisive. (There are few arguments against this principle that I know of and they have not convinced me. They trade on rare circumstances when persons feel guilt for taking actions that had bad consequences even though they could not have avoided them.)[11] It is because Karl Marx's and Herbert Spencer's systems typically, normally, indeed in every case, violate this principle that they are not bona fide moral systems. And quite a few others may be open to a similar charge.[12]

Sterba offers his strongest argument when he observes that " 'ought' implies 'can' " is violated "when the rich prevent the poor from taking what they require to satisfy their basic needs even though they have tried all the means available to them that libertarians regard as legitimate for acquiring such resources."[13]

Is Sterba right that such are—indeed, must be—typical conflict cases in a libertarian society? Are the rich and poor, even admitting that there is some simple division of people into such economic groups, in such hopeless conflict all the time? Even in the case of homeless people, many find help without having to resort to theft. The political factors contributing to the presence of helpless people in the United States and other Western liberal democracies are a hotly debated issue, even among utilitarians and welfare-state supporters. Sterba cannot make his argument for the typicality of such cases by reference to history alone. (Arguably, there are fewer helpless poor in near-libertarian, capitalist systems than anywhere else—why else would virtually everyone wish to live in these societies rather than those where welfare is guaranteed, indeed enforced? Not, at least originally, for their welfare-statist features. Arguably, too, the disturbing numbers of such people in these societies could be due, in part, to the lack of consistent protection of all the libertarian natural rights.)

Nonetheless, in a system that legally protects and preserves property rights there will be cases where a rich person prevents a poor person from taking what belongs to her (the rich person)—for example, a chicken that the poor person might use to feed herself. Since after such prevention the poor person might starve, Sterba asks the rhetorical question, "Have the rich, then, in contributing to this result, killed the poor, or simply let them die; and if they have killed the poor, have they done so unjustly?"[14] His answer is that they have. Sterba holds that a system that accords with the Lockean libertarian's idea that the rich person's preventive action is just "imposes an unreasonable sacrifice upon" the poor, one "that we could not blame them for trying to evade." Not permitting the poor to act to satisfy their basic needs is to undermine the precept that " 'ought' implies 'can,' " since, as Sterba claims, that precept means, for the poor, that they ought to satisfy their basic needs. This they must have the option to do if they ought to do it.

When people defend their property, what are they doing? They are protecting themselves against the intrusive acts of some other person, acts that would normally deprive them of something to which they have a right, and the other has no right. As such, these acts of protectiveness make it possible for men and women in society to retain their own sphere of jurisdiction intact, protect their own "moral space."[15] They refuse to have their human dignity violated. They want to be sovereigns and govern their own lives, including their own productive decisions and actions. Those who mount the attack, in turn, fail or refuse to refrain from encroaching upon the moral space of their victims. They are treating the victim's life and its productive results as though these were unowned resources for them to do with as they choose.

Now the argument that cuts against the above account is that on some occasions there can be people who, with no responsibility for their situation, are highly unlikely to survive without disregarding the rights of others and taking from them what they need. This is indeed possible. It is no less possible that there be cases in which someone is highly unlikely to survive without obtaining the services of a doctor who is at that moment spending time healing someone else, or in which there is a person who is highly unlikely to survive without obtaining one of the lungs of another person, who wants to keep both lungs so as to be able to run the New York City marathon effectively. And such cases could be multiplied indefinitely.

But are such cases typical? The argument that starts with this assumption about a society is already not comparable to the libertarianism that has emerged in the footsteps of Lockean natural-rights doctrine, including the version advanced in this book. That system is developed for a human community in which "peace is possible." Libertarian individual rights, which guide men and women in such an adequately hospitable environment to act without thwarting the flourishing of others, are thus suitable bases for the legal foundations of a human society. It is possible for people in the world to pursue their proper goals without thwarting a similar pursuit by others.

The underlying notion of society in such a theory rejects the description of human communities implicit in Sterba's picture. Sterba sees conflict as typically arising from some people producing and owning goods, while others having no alternative but to take these goods from the former in order to survive. But these are not the typical conflict situations even in what we today consider reasonably free human communities—most thieves and robbers are not destitute, nor are they incapable of doing something aside from taking other people's property in order to obtain their livelihood.

The typical conflict situation in society involves people who wish to take shortcuts to earning their living (and a lot more) by attacking others, not those who lack any other alternative to attacking others so as to reach that same goal. This may not be evident from all societies that team with human conflict—in the Middle East, or Central and South America, for example. But it must be remembered that these societies are far from being even near-libertarian. Even if the typical conflicts there involved the kind Sterba describes, that would not suffice to make his point. Only if it were true that in comparatively free countries the typical conflict involved the utterly destitute and helpless arrayed against the well-to-do, could his argument carry any conviction.

The Lockean libertarian has confidence in the willingness and capacity of *virtually all persons* to make headway in life in a free society. The very small minority of exceptional cases must be taken care of by voluntary social institutions, not by the government, which guards self-consistent individual rights.

The integrity of law would be seriously endangered if the government entered areas that required it to make very particular judgments and depart from serving the interest of the public as such. We have already noted that the idea of "satisfying basic needs" can involve the difficulty of distinguishing those whose actions are properly to be so characterized. Rich persons are indeed satisfying their basic needs as they protect and preserve their property rights. . . . Private property rights are necessary for a morally decent society.

The Lockean libertarian argues that private property rights are morally justified in part because they are the concrete requirement for delineating the sphere of jurisdiction of each person's moral authority, where her own judgment is decisive.[16] This is a crucial basis for the right to property. And so is the contention that we live in a metaphysically hospitable universe wherein people normally need not suffer innocent misery and deprivation—so that such a condition is usually the result of negligence or the violation of Lockean rights, a violation that has made self-development and commerce impossible. If exceptional emergencies set the agenda for the law, the law itself will disintegrate. (A just legal system makes provision for coping with emergencies that are brought to the attention of the authorities, for example, by way of judicial discretion, without allowing such cases to determine the direction of the system. If legislators and judges don't uphold the integrity of the system, disintegration ensues. This can itself encourage the emergence of strong leaders, demagogues, who promise to do what the law has not been permitted to do, namely, satisfy people's sense of justice. Experience with them bodes ill for such a prospect.)

Normally persons do not "lack the opportunities and resources to satisfy their own basic needs." Even if we grant that some helpless, crippled, retarded, or destitute persons could offer nothing to anyone that would merit wages enabling them to carry on with their lives and perhaps even flourish, there is still the other possibility for most actual, known hard cases, namely seeking help. I am not speaking here of the cases we know: people who drop out of school, get an unskilled job, marry and have kids, only to find that their personal choice of inadequate preparation for life leaves them relatively poorly off. " 'Ought' implies 'can' " must not be treated ahistorically—some people's lack of current options results from their failure to exercise previous options prudently. I refer here to the "truly needy," to use a shop-worn but still useful phrase—those who have never been able to help themselves and are not now helpless from their own neglect. Are such people being treated *unjustly*, rather than at most uncharitably, ungenerously, indecently, pitilessly, or in some other respect immorally—by those who, knowing of the plight of such persons, resist forcible efforts to take from them enough to provide the ill-fated with what they truly need? Actually, if we tried to pry the needed goods or money from the well-to-do, we would not even learn if they would act generously. Charity, generosity, kindness, and acts of compassion presuppose that those well enough off are not coerced to provide help. These virtues cannot flourish, nor can the corresponding vices, of course, without a clearly identified and well-protected right to private property for all.

If we consider the situation as we are more likely to find it, namely, that desperate cases not caused by previous injustices (in the libertarian sense) are rare, then, contrary to what Sterba suggests, there is much that unfortunate persons can and should do in those plausible, non-emergency situations that can be considered typical. They need not resort to violating the private-property rights of those who are better off. The destitute can appeal for assistance both from the rich and from the many voluntary social service agencies that emerge from the widespread compassion of people who know about the mishaps that can at times strike perfectly decent people.

Consider, as a prototype of this situation on which we might model what concerns Sterba, that if one's car breaks down on a remote road, it would be unreasonable to expect one not to seek a phone or some other way of escaping one's unfortunate situation. So one ought to at least try to obtain the use of a phone.

But should one break into the home of a perfect stranger living nearby? Or ought one instead to request the use of the phone as a favor? " 'Ought' implies 'can' " is surely fully satisfied here. Actual practice makes this quite evident. When someone is suffering from misfortune and there are plenty of others who are not, and the unfortunate person has no other avenue for obtaining help than to obtain it from others, it would not be unreasonable to expect, morally, that the poor seek such help as surely might be forthcoming. We have no justification for assuming that the rich are all callous, though this caricature is regularly painted by communists and in folklore. Supporting and gaining advantage from the institution of private property by no means implies that one lacks the virtue of generosity. The rich are no more immune to virtue than the poor are to vice. The contrary view is probably a legacy of the idea that only those concerned with spiritual or intellectual matters can be trusted to know virtue—those concerned with seeking material prosperity are too base.

The destitute typically have options other than to violate the rights of the well-off. " 'Ought' implies 'can' " is satisfiable by the moral imperative that the poor ought to seek help, not loot. There is then no injustice in the rich preventing the poor from seeking such loot by violating the right to private property. " 'Ought' implies 'can' " is fully satisfied if the poor can take the kind of action that could gain them the satisfaction of their basic needs, and this action could well be asking for help.

All along here I have been considering only the helplessly poor, who through no fault of their own, nor again through any rights violation by others, are destitute. I am taking the hard cases seriously, where violation of " 'ought' implies 'can' " would appear to be most probable. But such cases are by no means typical. They are extremely rare. And even rarer are those cases in which all avenues regarded as legitimate from the libertarian point of view have been exhausted, including appealing for help.

The bulk of poverty in the world is not the result of natural disaster or disease. Rather it is political oppression, whereby people throughout many of the world's countries are not legally permitted to look out for themselves in production and trade. The famines in Africa and India, the poverty in the same countries and in Central and Latin America, as well as in China, the Soviet Union, Poland, Rumania, and so forth, are not the result of lack of charity but of oppression. It is the kind that those who have the protection of even a seriously compromised document and system protecting individual negative human rights, such as the U.S. Constitution, do not experience. The first requirement for men and women to ameliorate their hardship is to be free of other people's oppression, not to be free to take other people's belongings.

Of course, it would be immoral if people failed to help out when this was clearly no sacrifice for them. But charity or generosity is not a categorical imperative, even for the rich. There are more basic moral principles that might require the rich to refuse to be charitable—for example, if they are using most of their wealth for the protection of freedom or a just society. Courage can be more important than charity or benevolence or compassion. But a discussion of the ranking of moral virtues would take us far afield. One reason that many critics of libertarianism find their own cases persuasive is that they think the libertarian can only subscribe to *political* principles or values. But this is mistaken.[17]

There can be emergency cases in which there is no alternative available to disregarding the rights of others. But these are extremely rare, and not at all the sort invoked by critics such as Sterba. I have in mind the desert-island case found in ethics books where instantaneous action, with only one violent alternative, faces persons—the sort we know from the law books in which the issue is one of immediate life and death. These are not cases, to repeat the phrase quoted from Locke by H. L. A. Hart, "where peace is possible." They are discussed in the libertarian literature and considerable progress has been made in integrating them with the concerns of law and politics. Since we are here discussing law and politics, which are general systematic approaches to how we normally ought to live with one another in human communities, these emergency situations do not help us except as limiting cases. And not surprisingly many famous court cases illustrate just this point as they now and then confront these kinds of instances after they have come to light within the framework of civilized society.

Since the time of the original publication of the above discussion—as part of my book *Individuals and Their Rights*—James Sterba has made several attempts to counter the arguments advanced here. The central claim on which he attempts to rest the argument that within a libertarian system many people would have no chance for self-directed flourishing goes as follows:

> [W]ho could deny that most of 1.2 billion people who are currently living in conditions of absolute poverty "lack the opportunities and necessities to satisfy their basic needs"? And even within our country [USA], it is estimated that

some 32 million Americans live below the official poverty index [$14,000 per annum for a family, $7,000 per annum for an individual], and that one fifth of American children are growing up in poverty. Surely, it is impossible to deny that many of these Americans also "lack the opportunities and resources to satisfy their basic needs."[18]

There is little discussion in Sterba's work of why people are poor or otherwise experience circumstances that afford them little or no opportunity for flourishing. Among libertarians, however, there is considerable agreement on the position that many who face such circumstances make significant contribution to their own plight. Many others suffer such circumstances because their negative rights to liberty (to produce and to keep what they produce) are violated.

Certainly, libertarians draw a sharp distinction between those who are in dire straits because they are unfortunate, through no fault of their own, and those who fail to act in ways that would probably extricate them from their adverse living conditions. In the philosophical literature that draws on the legacy of Marx, Engels, and their followers, this distinction is not easy to make, since in this tradition human behavior is taken to be determined by a person's economic circumstances, so one is bound by one's situation and cannot make choices that would overcome them. More generally, in modern political philosophy there has been a strong tendency to view human beings as passive, unable to initiate their own conduct and moved by innate drives or environmental stimuli. Thus, those who are well-off could not have achieved this through their own initiative, nor could those who are badly off have failed in significant ways. Accordingly, all of the poor or badly off, be they victims of others' oppression, casualties of misfortune, or products of their own misconduct are regarded alike. It is not clear how much Sterba's reasoning may be influenced by these considerations. In the absence of significant discussion of the matter, it is understandable why Sterba appears to view life as largely a zero sum game.[19]

Sterba claims, then, that poverty is typical, including, we must assume, of libertarian societies. Without that assumption, the story about poverty would have no bearing on libertarian politics. Sterba, therefore, needs to argue, as he does, that in a fully libertarian system, which respects and protects only negative individual rights (to life, liberty, and property), massive poverty would ensue—it would be the typical situation for there to be great masses of poor people.

Libertarians, as suggested above, seriously dispute this point. Indeed, they are not pure deontologists regarding negative individual liberty or the right to it, for they believe that respect for and protection of it would produce a better life for most people, in all relevant respects (moral, economic, intellectual, psychological, and cultural), provided they make an effort to improve themselves. They argue, in the main, that the most prosperous and otherwise beneficial societies are also those that give greatest respect and protection to negative individual rights. In turn, they hold, that where poverty is widespread, negative individual liberty is, in the main, left unrespected and unprotected.

This part of their argument is, for most libertarians, a fairly reasonable analytical and historical stance. They would argue, analytically, that it is the protection of negative individual liberty—the right to free association, freedom of trade, freedom of wealth accumulation, freedom of contract, freedom of entrepreneurship, freedom of speech, freedom of thought—that provides the most hospitable social climate for the creation of wealth. While no libertarian claims that this guarantees that no one will be destitute, those who are poor would either have failed of their own accord or would have been the few unfortunate people who are innocently incapacitated and do not enjoy the benefit of others' generosity, charity, compassion, and similar support. According to libertarians, there is no reason to think that there would be many such persons, at least compared to the numbers one can expect in societies lacking respect and protection for negative individual rights. Thus, even the most well known opponent of capitalism (the economic system of libertarianism), Karl Marx, was aware that unless human nature itself changes and the "new man" develops, socialism can do no more than to socialize poverty, i.e., make everyone poor.

As to the historical evidence, it is hard to argue that other than substantially capitalist economic systems, which tend in the direction of libertarianism (at least as far as the legal respect for and protection of private property or the right to it are concerned) have fared much better in reducing poverty than have others, without also causing massive political and other social failures (such as abolition of civil liberties, institution for forced labor and involuntary servitude, regimentation of the bulk of social relations, arresting scientific and technological progress, or censorship of the arts and other intellectual endeavors). Thus, America is still the freest of societies, with many of its legal principles giving expression to classical liberal, near-libertarian ideas, and it is, at the same time, the most generally productive (creative and culturally rich) of all societies, with its wealth aiding in the support of hundreds of other societies across the globe. Barring the impossible-to-conduct controlled sociopolitical-economic experiment, such historical evidence is all we can adduce to examine which political economic system produces more poverty. No one can seriously dispute that the near-libertarian systems have fared much better than those going in the opposite direction, including the welfare state. Even though some people wish for more in the way of empirical backing, it is difficult to know what they could wish for apart from the relatively plain fact of history that societies in which negative liberty flourishes produce far more (tangible) wealth than do ones in which such freedom is systematically denied. It is no secret that the Western liberal nations in general and the United States of America in particular contribute the most to the rescue of casualties of famines and other natural disasters across the globe. The US supports the United Nation's treasury far more than do other nations. While factors other than the political-economic conditions of a country contribute to these circumstances, baring some kind of controlled experiment in which those factors can be isolated, this will have to do for present purposes.

There is another point to be stressed, though, that Sterba has not taken into consideration. This is that there can be people in a libertarian society—indeed, in any society—for whom a lack of wealth, even extreme poverty relative to the mean, may not be a great liability. Not everyone wants to, or even ought to, live prosperously. For some individuals a life of ostensible poverty could be of substantial benefit. Contenders would be monks, hobos, starving artists, and the like who, despite the protection of their negative liberty or the right to it, do not elect to seek economic prosperity, at least in preference to other important objectives. Among the citizens of a libertarian society, then, we could find some who are poor but who are not, therefore, worse off than the rich, provided we do not confine ourselves to counting economic prosperity as the prime source of well-being.

At one point, Sterba suggests that libertarians, because they do not see the need to affirm as a principle of justice the right to welfare, may not care sufficiently for the poor. As he puts it:

> Machan seems reluctant to take the steps required to secure the basic needs of the poor. Why then does he balk at taking any further steps? Could it be that he does not see the oppression of the poor as truly oppressive after all?[20]

There is perhaps something to this, although not in the way Sterba's rhetorical question suggests, namely, that libertarians are callous or uncaring where the cultivation of care is warranted. But it is true enough that just being poor does not necessarily warrant being cared for, just as simply being sick does not place upon another the obligation to help, if the sickness is the result of self-abuse or gross negligence, or affects a thoroughly evil person.

Furthermore, some artists who are poor are happier than some merchants who are rich. There is no justification for feeling compassion for such artists, despite their poverty. In short, being poor in and of itself does not justify special consideration.[21] Being in need of what it takes to attain one's well-being warrants, if the need is a matter of natural misfortune or injury from others, feelings and conduct amounting to care, generosity, and charity. Poverty does not always constitute such neediness.

Nevertheless, Sterba may also underestimate what Marxists might call the objective generosity or charity of libertarians. One must consider just how much greater the long range prospects for economic well-being are for everyone within a libertarian political economy, and how benevolent it is for people not to be cuddled and treated as if they were inept in attaining prosperity; this system fosters institutional conditions within which they will probably be much better off than they would be in any welfare state (which seems clearly to encourage long-range economic ineptitude and dependence) the libertarian could well be regarded as the political theory with the greatest concern for the poor.[22]

It seems, therefore, that Sterba hasn't supported his main contention: that libertarianism implies the welfare state. The reason is that he has failed to appreciate the analytical and historical context within which libertarianism is argued. But there is more.

Sterba has also failed to appreciate that, although in some cases a person might not be required to respect the negative individual rights all citizens have—e.g., in some rare case of helpless destitution—nothing follows from this regarding the rights that everyone in society has by virtue of being a human individual living in a community of other human individuals. As Rasmussen and Den Uyl so carefully argue, the system of negative individual rights is a metanormative system or, in other words, a political framework within which human beings normally would and should pursue their highly varied flourishing. Focusing on exceptional, rare cases, wherein "peace is not possible" and, thus, it is justified to disregard consideration of basic (political) rights, does not justify the abrogation of the system of justice based on such rights that does, in fact, best befit human beings in their communities. On rare occasions, for particular persons, exceptions might be made, just as courts in extraordinary circumstances make such exceptions in the criminal law by pardoning someone who has violated a law but could not be expected to abide by it; these pardons do not abolish the law in question.

The point is, one ought not to abandon political principles to accommodate what can only be deemed extraordinary circumstances, Sterba's advice to the contrary notwithstanding.

Notes

1. Quoted in Harry V. Jaffa, *How to Think About the American Revolution* (Durham, NC: Carolina Academic Press, 1978), p. 41 (from *The Collected Works of Abraham Lincoln* [R. Basler (ed.), 1953], 108–15).

2. See, in particular, James Sterba, "A Libertarian Justification for a Welfare State," *Social Theory and Practice*, 11 (Fall 1985), 285–306. I will be referring to this essay as well as a more developed version, titled "The U.S. Constitution: A Fundamentally Flawed Document" in *Philosophical Reflections on the United States Constitution*, edited by Christopher Gray (1989).

3. H. L. A. Hart, "Are There Any Natural Rights?" *Philosophical Review* 64 (1955), 175.

4. See, for my own discussions, Tibor R. Machan, *Human Rights and Human Liberties* (Chicago: Nelson-Hall, 1975), 213–22; "Prima Facie versus Natural (Human) Rights," *Journal of Value Inquiry* 10 (1976), 119–31; 'Human Rights: Some Points of Clarification', *Journal of Critical Analysis* 5 (1973), 30–39.

5. Sterba, op. cit, "A Libertarian Justification", 295.

6. Ibid.

7. Ayn Rand, "Value and Rights", in J. Hospers, (ed.), *Readings in Introductory Philosophical Analysis* (Englewood Cliffs, NJ: Prentice-Hall, 1968), 382.

8. Sterba, "The U.S. Constitution: A Fundamentally Flawed Document."

9. John Rawls, *A Theory of Justice* (Cambridge, MA: Harvard University Press, 1971), 101–02. For a discussion of the complexities in the differential attainments of members of various ethnic groups—often invoked as evidence for the injustice of a capitalist system, see Thomas Sowell, *Ethnic America: A History* (New York: Basic Books, 1981). There is pervasive prejudice in welfare-state proponents' writings against crediting people with the ability to extricate themselves from poverty without special political assistance. The idea behind the right to negative liberty is to set people free from others so as to pursue their progressive goals. This is the ultimate teleological justification of Lockean libertarian natural rights. See Tibor R. Machan, *Human Rights and Human Liberties: A Radical Reconsideration of the American Political Tradition* (Chicago: Nelson-Hall, 1975). Consider also this thought from Herbert Spencer:

> The feeling which vents itself in "poor fellow!" on seeing one in agony, excludes the thought of "bad fellow," which might at another time arise. Naturally, then, if the wretched are unknown or but vaguely known, all the demerits they may have are ignored: and thus it happens that when the miseries of the poor are dilated upon, they are thought of as the miseries of the deserving poor, instead of being thought of as the miseries of undeserving poor, which in large measure they should be. Those whose hardships are set forth in pamphlets and proclaimed in sermons and speeches which echo throughout society, are assumed to be all worthy souls, grievously wronged; and none of them are thought of as bearing the penalties of their own misdeeds.

(*Man versus the State* [Caldwell, ID: Caxton Printers, 1940], 22)

10. Tibor R. Machan, "Ethics vs. Coercion: Morality of Just Values?" in L. H.

Rockwell, Jr. et al., (ed.), *Man, Economy and Liberty: Essays in Honor of Murray N. Rothbard* (Auburn, AL: Ludwig von Mises Institute, 1988), 236–46.

11. John Kekes, "'Ought Implies Can' and Two Kinds of Morality," *The Philosophical Quarterly* 34 (1984), 459–67.

12. Tibor R. Machan, "Ethics vs. Coercion." In a vegetable garden or even in a forest, there can be good things and bad, but no morally good things and morally evil things (apart from people who might be there).

13. Sterba, "The U.S. Constitution: A Fundamentally Flawed Document."

14. Sterba, "A Libertarian Justification," 295–96.

15. Robert Nozick, *Anarchy, State, and Utopia* (New York: Basic Books, 1974), 57. See, also, Tibor R. Machan, "Conditions for Rights, Sphere of Authority," *Journal of Human Relations* 19 (1971), 184–87, where I argue that "within the context of a legal system where the *sphere of authority* of individuals and groups of individuals cannot be delineated independently of the sphere of authority of the public as a whole, there is an inescapable conflict of rights specified by the same legal system." (186) See, also, Tibor R. Machan, "The Virtue of Freedom in Capitalism," *Journal of Applied Philosophy* 3 (1986), 49–58, and Douglas J. Den Uyl, "Freedom and Virtue," in Tibor R. Machan (ed.), *The Main Debate: Communism versus Capitalism* (New York: Random House, 1987), 200–16. This last essay is especially pertinent to the understanding of the ethical or moral merits of coercion and coerced conduct. Thus it is argued here that "coercive charity" amounts to an oxymoron.

16. See, Machan, op. cit., "The Virtue of Freedom in Capitalism" and "Private Property and the Decent Society" in J. K. Roth and R. C. Whittemore (eds.), *Ideology and American Experience* (Washington, DC: Washington Institute Press, 1986).

17. E.g., James Fishkin, *Tyranny and Legitimacy* (Baltimore, MD: Johns Hopkins University Press, 1979). Cf., Tibor R. Machan, "Fishkin on Nozick's Absolute Rights," *Journal of Libertarian Studies* 6 (1982), 317–20.

Sterba has gone on to raise further objections, for example, in his "From Liberty to Welfare," *Ethics* 105 (October 1994), 64–98. All these rest on Sterba's refusal to examine the ethical foundations of natural rights. Thus Sterba can claim that "Machan seems reluctant to take the steps required to secure the basic needs of the poor." This, simply because I will not sanction theft as a means to "secure" those needs. What about generosity, charity, philanthropy, kindness, compassion, help, assistance, etc.? All these appear not to interest Sterba, since they do not involve the force of law or coercion, whereby Machan and others can be compelled, one may assume by Sterba & Co., "to secure the basic needs of the poor." But there is more to coping with life's problems than foisting political "solutions" on people.

If history is any indication, what the oppressed poor need is not giving them permission to steal but a polity of liberty where they can put their own initiative to productive use, where what they create or obtain by trade may be kept by them, invested and built into nest eggs or substantial wealth. The poor, as the saying goes, need to become rich, not be placed into a polity wherein no one is allowed to get too rich and all those who have unsatisfied basic needs can legally raid the wealth of others.

18. James P. Sterba, *Morality and Social Justice* (Lanham, MD: Rowman & Littlefield, 1995), 15.

19. In so far as Sterba is a reasonably close follower of John Rawls' thinking in politics, and since Rawls denies the efficacy of individual initiative in the formation of personal assets such as one's character, it is quite possible that Sterba follows suit. (See John Rawls, A *Theory of Justice* [Cambridge: Harvard University Press, 1971], 104.) Since, however, Sterba also endorses the Kantian notion of "ought implies can" and advances numerous claims as to what people ought to do, there is evidence that he is also committed to a theory of free will. Which view dominates is unclear since there is no explicit discussion of this matter in Sterba's work with which I am familiar.

In contrast, most libertarians would invoke views drawn from philosophies of human nature, action theory, or motivational psychology, and embrace the position that when human beings are not kept in subjugation, they will tend or have good reasons to work toward their improvement, regardless of where they are on the continuum between destitution and abundance. Libertarians differ on the details, of course, with some subscribing to a neo-Hobbesian idea about what leads people to act and others to an agency view drawing from Ayn Rand and others. Some embrace the Hayekian notion of natural evolution. None accept what seems to underlie many statist positions, namely, that most people are congenitally passive, even when they are not actively kept in subjugation. On this view, of course, neither the poor (and some among them who are lazy) nor the rich (and some among them who are greedy) are personally responsible for their economic position in life. Nor, of course, can those who resist Sterba's analysis be blamed for possible moral blindness (a charge implicit in some of what Sterba has said about libertarians), since they, too, presumably are the way they are because of circumstances beyond their control.

It is notable that the statistics Sterba cites are drawn from societies, including the United States of America, which are far from libertarian in their legal construction and are far closer to the welfare state, if not to outright socialism. It is surprising why Sterba does not consider that perhaps what accounts for those statistics is the absence of libertarianism, given that there is ample historical evidence for the impact of socialism on the economic conditions of the members of various societies around the globe. Seeing, then, that socialism does not improve the general welfare and the welfare state leaves a great many people badly off, a not unreasonable alternative would be that greater stress on the protection of negative individual liberty would promise the results Sterba desires. In contrast to Sterba's empirical assertions about poverty *vis-a-vis* capitalism (the economic system of libertarianism), see Nathan Rosenberg, *How the West Grew Rich: The economic transformation of the industrial world* (New York: Basic Books, 1986), and Nathan Rosenberg, Ralph Landau, and David C. Mowery, *Technology and the Wealth of Nations* (Stanford, CA: Stanford University Press, 1992). Both works go a long way toward demonstrating the superior wealth-creating record of economies that rest, more so than alternative systems, on the principles of the right to private property, free competition and the pursuit of private profit.

20. James P. Sterba, "Liberty and Welfare," note 34. In this paper Sterba repeats the claims about the alleged connection between libertarianism and significantly widespread poverty, with no attempt to establish them except by reference to unanalyzed statistics. (An attempt by the present author to challenge his analysis was rejected by the editors on grounds that the challenge was based on no more than "confident empirical speculations." See note 19, above, however, for references to works containing historical evidence supportive of the claim against Sterba's unanalyzed statistics.)

21. This may account, in part, for the indignation felt by some poor when they are offered help. Their dignity has been offended, for they know that their poverty follows from their conscious or implicit choices, ones they find and which may indeed be fully justified. For a general argument against the enforceable duty to serve others, see Lester H. Hunt, "An Argument Against a Legal Duty to Rescue," *Journal of Social Philosophy* 36 (1994), 22.

22. Let me spend a few paragraphs on the difference between meaning and doing good, for Sterba's implied charge gains its moral force from what seems to me a misunderstanding of morality along certain Kantian lines. (See, for a comment along lines similar to what follows, Shelby Steele, "How Liberals Lost Their Virtue Over Race," *Newsweek*, January 1995, 41-42.)

There is, among many moral theorists as well as politicians and pundits, much concern with who is mean spirited, who lacks compassion, who is kinder and gentler among those vying to be political leaders. For too many people what appears to count most for having moral character is the quality of the feelings that motivate one's conduct. If you *mean or intend* well, if what you feel in your heart is good, decent, caring and such, what follows is supposed to be morally upstanding, commendable. It doesn't even matter much what actually results from the conduct motivated by such good feelings. "It's the thought that counts," as the saying goes.

Yet there is clearly something wrong with this idea. People may feel good for having done one thing or another from certain generous, charitable, kind or compassionate sensibilities or motives but it doesn't follow at all that this assures that the consequences are actually going to produce much benefit. Indeed, it is often quite likely that by focusing on how one feels about what one does, one loses sight of whether the action actually achieves any good at all. Furthermore, by focusing on these elevating feelings, one can run the very real risk of trying to please others instead of actually helping them.

Very often, indeed, helpful conduct does not square with conduct that pleases. One knows this well enough in personal relations: some friends or relatives want us to do for them things that are definitely not very helpful. Such conduct more often simply satisfies some desire, never mind whether it is actually worthy of being satisfied. Consider young friends who want to have, say, cigarettes or alcohol purchased for them, never mind what these actually produce. Consider the deadbeat who would so much like another loan, or the lazy person who would like to escape all hardship and just sit around. Or consider the moments when you, too, are tempted to plead merely to be satisfied, hoping that no one will critically examine the merits of your desires. Those who comply with such calls for unwise generosity may often fool themselves and feel moral righteousness about what they do. And they are certainly often liked for this by the people whom they have "helped."

In contrast, bona fide help is much more risky. And it is demanding. One needs to learn what actually is good for the person who seeks it. One needs to do some research. And one often upsets those whom one helps, just as doctors often displease patients with treatments or prescriptions that are unpleasant, as coaches do with the training they demand from athletes.

The more remote one is from those in need of help, the less likely it is going to be that such research is going to be undertaken. Instead some standard formulas will be invoked and the gauge to success will be how much gratitude is forthcoming, never mind whether such gratitude means serious thanks for useful help or mere pleasure in response to compliance.

In the current political climate there is a lot of talk about how some people are mean-spirited, who lack compassion, versus others who care and feel for those in need. It will pay handsomely, especially for those who are to be benefited from various public policies, to take a very close look at what actually is at issue. Are those derided for callousness perhaps thinking harder than their critics about what will be most helpful to the targeted beneficiaries? Are their proposals perhaps more fruitful in the long run, than those motivated by kinder and gentler feelings, regarding the actual task of securing for people a better life? And are these so called mean spirited policy architects perhaps the ones who ought to obtain real moral credit for generosity and compassion, rather than those who are flooded with feelings of compassion and kindness and thus are filled with moral pride and righteousness?

If one considers, also, that the generosity and compassion of those full of good feelings for others tend to come at other people's expense, the answer might be quite easy to discover.

Capitalism, Socialism, and Equity Ownership*

N. Scott Arnold

What does one have to believe to be a socialist? Typically, socialists speak of various ideals and values they would like to see realized. These ideals and values include polar opposites of the defects and social ills that socialists have claimed to find in capitalist society. A commitment to socialism, however, involves more than a commitment to certain ideals and values. It also involves a commitment to certain institutional means, in particular to a certain type of economic system, as essential to realizing those ideals and values. But what type of economic system? With the collapse of communism and the worldwide repudiation of central planning, the answer these days is no longer obvious. There seems to be an emerging consensus that only some form of a market economy is economically viable; this means that if socialists are to be taken seriously, they must favor some sort of market economy. But what sort? Although various models or proposals of a market economy have been discussed by people who call themselves socialists, it is fair to ask what makes these systems socialist and whether or not they can realize widely shared socialist ideals and values. These questions are important, since their answers determine whether political and intellectual history have turned the page on the capitalism/socialism dispute or whether socialism, at least as a system of ideas, endures as a standing challenge to capitalism in all its manifestations. My purpose in this paper is to address these questions and to argue that market socialist economic systems that could avoid some of the chief evils that socialists have attributed to capitalism are systematically exploitative in ways that capitalist systems are not. If, as seems reasonable, exploitation is a form of injustice, this is a serious charge.

Although socialists have substantial disagreements on a wide range of issues, it is fair to say that they all agree that the capitalist economic system is bad in the sense that it is responsible for a range of important social ills. These include alienation, significant inequality in wealth and income, and the macroeconomic problems of recessions and depressions and their associated social ills.[1] Since the essence of the capitalist economic system is private ownership of the means of production, this socialist view entails that any capitalist system, actual or (empirically) possible, has or would have these problems or defects. This in turn implies that the problems cannot be corrected without abolishing private ownership of the means of production.[2] Let us consider in detail the nature of private ownership of the means of production and how and why socialists have blamed it for these problems of modern society.

Since the rise of modern capitalism, the manner in which private ownership of the means of production has been manifested is in the predominance of one or two distinctive types of organizations, the classical capitalist firm and the modern corporation. In the classical capitalist firm, the same individual occupies three economically significant roles: provider of capital, ultimate decision-making authority, and residual claimant. Although the classical capitalist occasionally borrows funds or even capital goods from others, he is typically the primary provider of the firm's capital, and in that capacity he receives the returns to capital (sometimes called "interest income"). As the ultimate decision-making authority, he has final say in how the firm's assets are to be deployed. This means that he manages the firm himself or hires those who do. Finally, as the residual claimant, he is entitled to whatever pure profits the firm earns, i.e., profits over or under the going rate of return on capital; such profits are due to exceptionally good or bad entrepreneurship (or luck) exercised by the capitalist or those in his employ. Let us define the equity owner of the firm as anyone who occupies these three roles. One implication of equity ownership in a capitalist system is that the equity owner has the right to sell any or all of these rights to whomever he chooses. Whether the classical capitalist manages the firm himself or hires the manager, the distinctive feature of the classical capitalist firm is that there is one and only one equity owner. Thus, such firms include not only small mom-and-pop operations, but also somewhat larger firms that employ dozens or even a few hundred employees.

It used to be fashionable to pronounce the classical capitalist firm dead or dying; modern capitalism was alleged to be completely dominated by very large corporations. But the contemporary record simply does not bear out this claim. The 1980s witnessed explosive growth in small to medium-sized classical capitalist firms; that some of them grew into corporate giants highlighted the fact that this is where many large corporations come from. It is also now clear that certain niches in the economic environment are best filled by these smaller organizations.

There is no denying, however, that large corporations are important economic actors. This organizational form also has equity owners, i.e., individuals who are the primary providers of capital, ultimate decision-making authorities, and residual claimants. They provide the capital by purchasing shares of stock in the company. In their capacity as capital providers, they receive the returns to capital, and as residual claimants, they are entitled to any positive or negative residuals the firm earns. They are ultimate decision-making authorities because they have a proportional vote on the membership of the highest governing body of the corporation, the board of directors. Management is hired by and answerable to the board, which in turn is answerable to the stockholders. In this sense, the corporation is said to be run in the interests of its equity owners, just as a classical capitalist firm is run in the interests of its equity owner.[3] Finally, just as in the classical capitalist firm, the equity owners of the modern corporation can sell their ownership shares in the firm.

The classical capitalist firm and the modern corporation are the most common and important forms of economic organization in existing capitalist systems, though they are not the only ones. There are closely held corporations, in which a few individuals own most of the stock, and one of them is the manager. There are also partnerships, in which some but not all of those who work for the firm have a role in managing it and are its equity owners. These other forms of organization, while not predominant, are at least common in existing capitalist systems. (Actually, partnerships were more common in 18th- and 19th-century capitalism than they are today.)

What these organizational forms have in common is that they all have equity owners. According to many socialists, this is the root of many of the evils of the capitalist economic system. For example, equity ownership is blamed for alienation in the workplace, because either the managers do not answer to the workers but instead to the equity owners, or the managers are the equity owners. The main interest of the equity owners is profits, which means that management has little interest in giving workers control over their productive lives. More meaningful work, worker control over the methods and pace of production, and, more generally, democracy in the workplace are generally perceived as inimical to maximizing profits. By contrast, speed-ups, extreme fragmentation of task, and harsh discipline are often conducive to maximizing profits and thus in the interests of the equity owners.

A second problem with equity ownership is that since the equity owners (and not the workers or society at large) receive all of the returns to capital plus the residuals, dramatic inequalities of wealth and income are endemic to capitalist societies. Some individuals own outright large classical capitalist firms or many shares of large corporations; others own very small businesses or a small number of shares of corporations. And of course, many individuals in capitalist systems (mostly workers) are not equity owners at all. While not all income inequalities are traceable to equity ownership (some workers earn very high salaries), equity ownership is a major factor in explaining income inequalities in capitalist society.

A third problem with capitalist systems, according to its socialist critics, is that it is inherently unstable at the macroeconomic level. This is explained, at least in part, by the fact that private individuals, acting in their own self-interest, make all decisions about how social wealth is to be invested. Typically, Keynesian arguments are then invoked to explain economic downturns and their associated evils (e.g., unemployment) as a result of this essentially anarchical method of controlling new investment.

This brief account of some of the evils of equity ownership from a socialist perspective is intended to identify and explain some of the sources of socialists' dissatisfaction with private property in the means of production and the organizational forms in which it is embodied. In a market socialist system, equity ownership in the forms identified above would be outlawed. However, the above considerations do not show that a market socialist must oppose all forms of equity ownership. It might be argued that a system in which the workers are the equity owners of their own firms or a system in which the state is the equity owner of all firms are forms of social ownership. The case of equity ownership by the workers might fulfill the Marxist conception of social ownership as worker control of the means of production. State ownership, if the state fosters a high degree of participatory democracy, might also be thought to be a form of social ownership on the grounds that the state represents society as a whole. However, in point of fact, few socialists favor either type of system, and from a socialist perspective, there are good reasons why they do not.

Let us consider first a system in which the workers are the equity owners. If the workers were the equity owners of their firms, this would clearly have some benefits from a socialist perspective. First, as the ultimate decision-making authorities, they would either manage the firms themselves, or they would elect (i.e., hire) and vote out (i.e., fire) the managers. In theory, this would bode well for eliminating or ameliorating various forms of alienation in the workplace, since the workers' interests would be paramount. Furthermore, the workers' status as residual claimants would encourage them both to work hard and to exercise their ultimate decision-making authority responsibly, since they would receive any positive or negative profits the firm earns. Equity ownership by the workers would also spread the returns to capital and the returns to entrepreneurship (i.e., the residuals) much more widely throughout society than in capitalist systems.

There are, however, a number of problems with equity ownership by the workers. One is that such a system is likely to be unstable and prone to degenerate into a capitalist system. To see why, notice that if the workers were the equity owners of their firms in the same sense as stockholders are the equity owners of their firms, they would be able to sell shares to anyone, including outsiders. Indeed, this is likely to happen for two reasons. One is what has been called "the portfolio problem." It has been widely remarked that a system in which the workers have equity shares only in their own firms presents them with risks that could be avoided by portfolio diversification.[4] To put it another way, if workers have all of their nonlabor assets tied up in their own firm, they are taking risks that could be avoided by owning equity shares in a diverse portfolio of companies.[5] Since it would be rational for them to diversify their risks by selling some of their own stock and buying stock in other companies, it is reasonable to suppose that they would do just that. It is easy to see how a process of diversification could reproduce a capitalist system over time.

David Ellerman has called attention to another reason why these firms are likely to degenerate into capitalist organizations.[6] At some point, workers in successful firms would want to realize at least some of the capital gains on their equity accounts. The easiest way to do this, of course, is to sell some of their shares on the open market. This means that outside investors could buy equity shares. As time goes on, these outsiders would acquire a controlling interest in the firm, and the firm would no longer be a worker-owned cooperative. Indeed, the more profitable and better managed the firm is, the more quickly this would happen.

This problem might be dealt with by stipulating that shares could only be sold to other members of the firm or possibly not sold at all. However, each alternative faces difficulties. Restricting ownership shares to members of the firm would create at least two problems. First, it is likely that workers would not be able to realize the full value of their shares in the firm when they quit or retired, since the pool of potential purchasers would be so restricted. Indeed, in the absence of a fully functioning stock market, it is not clear how anyone could estimate the value of shares in the firm. If the firm commits itself to buying back any shares that cannot be sold at an agreed-upon price to other workers, there is no guarantee it would have the cash to do so. (Suppose, for example, a large percentage of the current workforce is scheduled to retire over a period of a few years.) Second, it is likely that over time, workers who are improvident or who have had to bear unusual financial burdens would find themselves without any equity shares and thus would revert to the status of proletarians within the firm; correspondingly, those who are ambitious or who are especially astute traders would acquire disproportionate power, money, and influence within the firm. For all these reasons, equity ownership by the workers has little to recommend it from a socialist perspective.

Suppose now that there is a ban on all sales of equity shares. All and only workers in the firm would be equity owners, and to preserve relative equality of income within the firm, intrafirm sales of ownership shares would be prohibited; voting might be in accordance with a principle of one man, one vote, and the distribution of the net income of the firm might be fairly egalitarian (e.g., shares might be equally distributed among the workers). Incomes within the firm need not be exactly equal, however, since pay differentials could and probably would continue to exist to attract and keep those with scarce talents and abilities. However, the huge pay differentials characteristic of capitalist firms, especially between management and ordinary workers, would likely disappear if people with dirty fingernails sat on the compensation committee of the workers' council.

Despite the attractions of this scheme, it has a number of problems from a socialist perspective. First, if new investment is left up to individual firms (which is implied by full equity ownership), there is no guarantee that the business cycle and its attendant evils would be suppressed. Perhaps more significantly, there is no guarantee that large income inequalities would be eliminated. The reason for this can be explained as follows: As a technical matter, firms differ widely in their capital-to-labor ratios. Oil refineries, for example, are very capital-intensive, whereas truck farming is very labor-intensive. If workers received the returns to capital, as this proposal implies, workers in highly capital-intensive industries would have much higher incomes than those in less capital-intensive industries. Thus, the refinery workers would have much higher incomes than the vegetable growers, and both would be paupers in comparison to the members of some large financial cooperatives. It is a fair generalization to say that, at least among 20th-century socialists, these large inequalities in income must be judged intolerable.

It might be responded that the state could adopt a steeply progressive income tax to equalize incomes, or at least reduce the range of income inequality. These taxes could be levied on the firms or on the workers individually. This proposal has two problems. The first is that it is unlikely to succeed for roughly the same reason it has not succeeded in existing democratic societies with a capitalist economic system: One of the things that people in a democracy do when their wealth or income is threatened by the state is to invest resources in the political process to abate that threat. The oil refinery workers and the workers in similarly situated cooperatives would undoubtedly form political action committees or something similar to help elect those who believe that the tax code should insure that gross and net income are relatively close together. As recent decades have made clear, the tax code is indefinitely manipulable by special interests in a democracy. A second difficulty is that if taxes are too steeply progressive, the workers' incentive to produce efficiently is impaired. Part of the motivation for making the workers the equity owners is to give them a good incentive to produce efficiently. One cannot maintain the form of equity ownership while eviscerating its reality with steeply progressive income taxes.

Let us turn now to the other form of equity ownership that might be possible in a socialist system: equity ownership by the state. State ownership of the means of production is a form of social ownership because the state represents society as a whole. The thought is that, just as private ownership serves private interests, public ownership serves the public interest. However, this also has little to recommend it from a socialist perspective, but for different reasons. If the state is the ultimate decision-making authority, the firms are not self-managed; management is answerable to the state, not the workers. Consequently, the amelioration of alienation is no longer assured. There is no guarantee that the interests of the workers in the firm and the interests of society at large would coincide on matters affecting the terms and conditions of labor. By contrast, in self-managed firms or in firms where management answers to the workers, workers would have a say in matters such as plant layout, work schedules, task design, and even trade-offs between more income and more intrinsically satisfying work.

A second problem with equity ownership by the state has to do with the incentive effects of this form of ownership. What are the incentives to produce efficiently in this system? In part, this is a question of whom the managers answer to. In this model, managers are appointed by the state, which means that managers are answerable directly or indirectly to political authorities, who in turn are answerable to society at large, or at least to the electorate. Abundant evidence from the public sector in capitalist societies demonstrates that political authorities and those they represent lack either the interest, knowledge, or means to monitor effectively either the (managers of) organizations that produce goods and services for the public or the politicians who are supposed to monitor them. In other words, the ownership structure of cooperatives in this model is really the same as public bureaucracies such as the post office or passenger railroads (e.g., Amtrak).

Organizations like this have a remarkably consistent record of paying only negative residuals to their residual claimants: society at large, or more exactly, the taxpayers. As a practical matter, socialists probably would face an insurmountable challenge in trying to convince the public of the wisdom of this form of ownership.

But perhaps the most compelling reason to be deeply suspicious of complete state ownership of the means of production is that it unites in the state both political and economic power. It is plausible to maintain that one of the most important lessons of the 20th century is that this arrangement is inherently totalitarian. Indeed, few socialists in the last third of the twentieth century have advocated full state ownership of the means of production. Experience with totalitarian state socialism is—or at any rate should be—part of the reason for this.

What, then, is left for market socialism? In two books, David Schweickart has argued in favor of a form of nonequity ownership of business enterprises that has considerable attractions from a socialist perspective.[7] The three roles that constitute equity ownership—ultimate decisionmaking authority, residual claimancy, and the provision of capital—are divided between the workers and the state, with the workers assuming the first two roles and the state assuming the third. In this system, all and only the workers are the ultimate decisionmaking authorities in the firms in which they work. Smaller firms would probably be self-managed, and in larger firms, the workers—or a democratically elected workers' council—would decide who would be the managers. As in the case of equity ownership by the workers, the main motivation for making the workers the ultimate decision-making authorities is to eliminate or ameliorate the various forms of alienation associated with capitalism. The motivation for making all and only the workers in the firm its residual claimants is that they are thereby entitled to whatever pure profits the firm earns; this gives them an incentive to produce efficiently.

However, in Schweickart's model the workers are not the providers of capital. The state is. Although the state does not have operational control of the cooperative's assets, the state is the owner of those assets in the following respects: First, the cooperatives have to pay a capital-usage fee to the state. This represents the returns to capital; it is analogous to a rental fee that a capitalist firm would pay if it rented some capital good (e.g., a backhoe or a compressor) from another firm. The size of that fee would be collectively determined through the political process. Second, the cooperative would be required to maintain the value of the assets it controls by following proper maintenance procedures and by paying into a depreciation fund, which would be used to replace capital goods as they are used up.

Third, the cooperative would not be permitted to sell off the capital that the firm controls and pocket the proceeds. Finally, the firm's assets would revert to the state if the cooperative were to go out of business. Though the workers have operational control of the means of production, the state in effect owns all the capital and rents it to the cooperatives. In this way, both the workers in the firm and society as a whole have an ownership stake in society's means of production. This gives expression to the idea of social ownership. However, neither the state nor the workers are the equity owners of the firm or its assets; although the workers are the ultimate decision-making authorities and residual claimants, the state and not the workers is the provider of capital. In this system, there are no equity owners.

The state would control most new investment by formulating an investment plan for the economy and by lending funds to existing cooperatives for expansion or to groups of workers who wish to start a new cooperative. The funds for this would come from the capital-usage fee. The plan could be implemented in a variety of ways. For example, the proceeds from the capital-usage fee could be funneled through state-owned banks, which would be given a list of investment priorities (so much for biotechnology projects, so much for tourism, etc.), or they could charge different interest rates for different projects. It would then be up to the banks to choose which new investment projects to fund, so long as they stayed within the guidelines for new investment determined through the political process.

One motivation for this method of determining new investment is that it makes possible the collective control of the rate and direction of economic growth and development. In theory, this is supposed to prevent the ups and downs of the business cycle and their attendant problems. This system is also designed to reduce significantly income inequalities. Within the firm, this is insured by the workers' status as the ultimate decision-making authorities. This means that they have the authority to decide how to divide up the income of the firm, net of nonlabor expenses. As in a system in which the workers are the equity owners, some workers would probably earn more than others because of their scarce talents and abilities, but income differentials would likely not be as great as those found in capitalist firms. Interfirm variations in income would also exist, since some firms would do better than others in meeting their customers' needs; indeed, the efficiency of the system depends on this. However, those differentials represent only the pure profits, positive or negative, that come from exceptionally good or bad entrepreneurship (or good or bad luck). Assuming markets function tolerably well, those profits are small, ephemeral, or both. On the other hand—and this is vitally important—the returns to capital do not go to the workers in the cooperatives. The returns to capital are represented by the capital-usage fee, and they go to the state, which uses them to finance new investment. Because of this, interfirm variations in income are substantially reduced, and this occurs more or less automatically and not through the tax code. For all these reasons, in theory this type of system could avoid some of the perceived problems of capitalism and realize a number of important socialist goals.

Despite the attractions of this type of system from a socialist perspective, in point of fact it would be responsible for a systemic problem no socialist could easily accept: widespread and systematic exploitation. The exploiters would be the cooperatives and their members; the exploited party would be the state, and through it, society at large.[8] The basis for this problem is to be found in the conjunction of three facts: First, the workers would not own the cooperative's assets, and yet they would have full control over those assets in virtue of their status as the ultimate decision-making authorities. Second, the workers collectively would be entitled to any residuals the firm generates. Third, the workers would occupy these two roles only for so long as they work in the cooperative.

To see how these three facts combine to create opportunities for exploitation, a comparison with capitalist firms is helpful. Although capitalist firms often rent capital goods, e.g., backhoes, computers, or printing presses, it is instructive to note that these rentals are typically short-term and for a particular job. Long-term rentals that cover the entire useful life of a capital good are quite rare; such assets are usually owned outright by the firms that use them. This is because for most capital goods, it is difficult to write complete, easily enforced, long-term rental contracts governing every contingency. In a long-term contract, acceptable maintenance becomes harder to define, and the depreciation of assets becomes more speculative and problematic. For these reasons, it is usually more efficient for capitalist firms to own outright most of the capital goods they employ. It is precisely here that capitalism, with its system of equity ownership, possesses advantages over Schweickart's version of market socialism. For although the state would require the market socialist cooperative to maintain its assets properly and to pay into a depreciation fund, both of these features of the system create opportunities for workers in the cooperatives to exploit society as a whole—opportunities that do not exist in a capitalist system of equity ownership.

Let us consider maintenance first. As was indicated, defining what counts as proper maintenance becomes increasingly problematic over the life of an asset. The state would have to set standards and incur other monitoring costs to try to insure that capital goods are properly maintained by the cooperatives. The interests of the cooperative's members are likely to lie elsewhere, however. Because they receive income from the firm only for so long as they are members of it, they have a limited time horizon. Once workers leave the cooperative, they receive no income from it, and while they may wish it well, they do not have the financial interest in its well-being that they have while they are members. Unlike equity ownership shares of capitalist firms, rights to the net income of the market socialist cooperative are neither portable nor alienable. Because of their limited time horizon, it would be in the workers' interests to defer or skimp on maintenance as a way of increasing net revenues in the near term; the costs of weak or poor maintenance would be borne by future workers and the owners of the firm's capital, i.e., the state and, ultimately, society at large. For example, if a machine has a twenty-year life and the average member of the firm believes she will not be there more than seven years, there is an obvious incentive for the cooperative to forego costly maintenance procedures whose benefits will only be realized after most of the current membership has left. Of course, the state will try to prevent this, but given that monitoring is both costly and imperfect, there would be obvious opportunities for the current membership of the cooperative to exploit the owners of the cooperative's capital, the state, and through it, society at large.

This form of market socialism will also encounter difficulties in guarding against a too-rapid depreciation of capital goods. All (tangible) capital goods wear out eventually, even if they are well-maintained. How can the state ensure that the cooperatives do not use up society's capital without replacing it? As was suggested above, each firm would be required to pay into a depreciation fund. But how much should they pay? If an asset's value declines sharply for previously unanticipated reasons (e.g., technological developments render it obsolete), it should be written down correspondingly faster. This is something that the cooperative would be reluctant to do, since that would cut more deeply into net revenues than if the firm followed the standard straight-line depreciation rule. Indeed, the value of an asset to a firm at a given time may be dramatically different from its original cost or its replacement cost. Economic conditions are always in a state of flux, which means that the value of assets is similarly variable and difficult to ascertain. What does it mean to set aside enough funds to maintain the value of a firm's mainframe computer when both computer technology and the firm's computing needs are rapidly changing? Business judgment has to be exercised, and it is management's call. Management, of course, is answerable to the workers, and the workers have a limited time horizon.

Ultimately, what has to be preserved is the value of the firm itself, and yet the value of the firm is more than the sum of the values of its physical assets. Accountants call this difference "good will," but the term is misleading since this value represents not merely name recognition and customer trust; it also includes complementarities among the firm's assets and the value of the specialized knowledge and skills of those who work those assets.[9] The problem is that there is no way to ascertain the value of the firm itself in this system because there are no equity markets (i.e., stock markets and markets for firms). The value exists, yet no one knows even approximately what it is. And yet the workers, in their capacity as ultimate-decisionmakers and residual claimants, have access to it. It is obvious that there is a significant potential for exploitation in this situation.

There is empirical evidence from what used to be Yugoslavia that lends some support to these speculations about what would happen in Schweickart's version of market socialism. In the Yugoslav system, the state owned the capital, but the workers were entitled to the residuals. According to Jan Vanek,

> the danger often referred to in the Yugoslav experience of the work collectivities 'eating up their factories' can therefore be seen not merely in its crude form of lack of maintenance . . . but also in the more subtle form of greater or lesser depreciation of all assets in real terms through improper or inadequate operation of the enterprise.[10]

It is important to understand that the manipulation of maintenance and depreciation does not create comparable opportunities for exploitation in capitalist firms because those who get the residuals are also the providers of capital and the ultimate decision-making authorities to whom management answers. And they can sell their shares at any time on the equity markets. For these reasons, the equity owners suffer the full financial consequences of any decisions about maintenance and depreciation, and management is answerable to them for those decisions. They even suffer the consequences that take place in the distant future because those consequences are capitalized into the value of the firm. If, for example, a classical capitalist gradually degrades the good name and reputation of his firm by selling lesser-quality goods at premium prices, the decreased value of the firm will be reflected in the price he gets for the business when he sells the firm. Or, if he leaves it to his heirs, the value of his bequest will be similarly reduced. In contrast, Schweickart's market socialist firm separates ownership of capital from residual claimancy and ultimate decisionmaking authority and prohibits the workers from selling their stake in the firm; this makes it possible for the residual claimants who control the firm's assets (i.e., the workers in the cooperative) to exploit the capital providers (i.e., society at large).

One source of the problem is that the notion of a residual is something of an accounting fiction.[11] Residuals are not automatically extruded by the firm at regular intervals. Instead, the payment of residuals represents a decision by management to turn over some of the firm's financial assets to the residual claimants. Even when the firm is in trouble, the ultimate decisionmakers in the cooperative can continue to make payments to the residual claimants (i.e., to themselves), and they can get the money by siphoning value from the capital the firm controls or from the value of the firm itself. Some of the general ways they could do this are indicated above, but if they are having trouble devising ways to do this, consulting firms, staffed by exceptionally clever and rapacious lawyers, would undoubtedly spring up to show them the way. Clearly, in an ownership arrangement like this, the ultimate decisionmakers/residual claimants can exploit those who provide the capital.

It might be thought that this potential for exploitation could be eliminated by putting representatives of the state on the governing body of the firm. The problem with this suggestion is that it assumes that a board of directors composed in this manner would represent a kind of blending of the various interests that board members represent (i.e., the workers and the state), whereas, in point of fact, the board is likely to represent the interests of the dominant group. This has sometimes been called the "law of one majority."[12] So if the workers are the predominant ultimate decisionmaking authorities, their interests will decisively determine the policies and procedures of the firms, and the opportunities for exploitation will continue to exist. On the other hand, if state representatives are the ultimate decisionmaking authorities, then their interests will be determinative and the benefits of self-management will no longer be assured.

A full-scale evaluation of the potential for exploitation in this version of market socialism, especially in comparison to what takes place in a capitalist system, requires a more elaborate comparative analysis of the structure of capitalist and market socialist organizations than can be accomplished here. It also requires a thorough analysis of state control of new investment (a fertile source of opportunities for exploitation).[13] However, the above considerations make it clear that there would be significant opportunities for exploitation in this version of market socialism—opportunities that are foreclosed by equity ownership in a capitalist system.

Schweickart's model is not the only model of market socialism,[14] but it exemplifies the essence of market socialism in the following sense: A market socialist system must, as Schweickart's system does, join ultimate decisionmaking authority and residual claimancy on the one hand, and on the other hand, it must separate these two roles from the role of capital provider, if it is to have a chance of achieving three important socialist objectives, viz, the elimination of alienation, tolerably efficient production, and dramatically reduced inequality in wealth and income. The workers in the firm must be the ultimate decisionmakers if the various forms of alienation associated with capitalism are to be eliminated. They must also be its residual claimants, if they are to have an incentive to produce efficiently. However, they cannot be the capital providers. If for no other reason, because of widely varying capital-to-labor ratios among firms, the workers cannot get the returns to their firm's capital, if income inequality is to be kept within tolerable bounds. The returns to capital must be socialized. The most natural way to do this is Schweickart's, which sends the returns to capital to the state in the form of a capital-usage fee. The state then uses those monies to fund new investment, which in turn permits the realization of other socialist goals (at least in theory), such as controlling the business cycle and its associated evils. The state is supposed to represent society as a whole, and although some may doubt that states can do this, there seems to be no other institution to which socialists can turn to fulfill this function.

The problem is that the decomposition of equity ownership in this way creates opportunities for exploitation that do not exist in a capitalist system. The basic difficulty is that if the returns to capital are socialized, then the workers in the cooperatives, who are the ultimate decision makers and residual claimants only for as long as they work at the firm, have little incentive to maintain the value of the capital they control, and they have some incentive to siphon some of that value into their own pockets. Thus, there is both motive and opportunity for the workers to exploit the owners of the cooperative's capital, namely, the state, and through it, society at large. Equity ownership, as it is found in capitalist society, eliminates both motive and opportunity, for the simple reason that those who are the ultimate decision-making authorities and the residual claimants are also the capital providers. A heretofore unnoticed advantage of equity ownership is that it forecloses opportunities for exploitation that must exist if equity ownership is in any way decomposed. If, as seems reasonable, exploitation is a form of injustice, citizens living under this version of market socialism would suffer systematic injustices that do not occur under capitalism, where the means of production have equity owners.

Notes

*The author would like to thank the Hoover Institution at Stanford University and the Social Philosophy and Policy Center at Bowling Green State University for their support. Work on this project was partially funded by the U.S. Department of State's

Discretionary Grant Program for Studies of Eastern Europe and the Independent States of the former Soviet Union based on the Soviet-Eastern European Training Act of 1983, Public Law 98-164, Title VIII, 97 Stat. 1047–50.

1. This list is not meant to be exhaustive. Following Marx, many socialists believe that systematic exploitation is also an evil of capitalism that a socialist system would eliminate; there may be other such evils, but for the purposes of this paper, this issue need not be decided. For a more elaborate discussion of the socialist vision of the good society as the polar opposite of the socialist vision of capitalism and its evils, see N. Scott Arnold, *The Philosophy and Economics of Market Socialism* (New York: Oxford University Press, 1994), 50–64.

2. Social democracy, especially as it has manifested itself in Western Europe, can be distinguished from socialism on just this point. Unlike socialists, social democrats are willing to live with a system of private ownership of the means of production. They believe that the evils of private property can be significantly ameliorated by collective bargaining and various forms of state action. Socialists, by contrast, deny this. They maintain that these evils can only be cured by a fundamental change in the structure of property rights.

3. This is not to say that corporate managers always act in the interests of shareholders. Sometimes they act in their own interests in ways that conflict with the interests of shareholders. The inefficiencies this occasions tend to be offset by the efficiencies that attend bringing together large amounts of capital under one decision-making roof. For more on this, see Oliver Williamson, *The Economic Institutions of Capitalism* (New York: The Free Press, 1985), chaps. 4 and 5 and a special issue of the *Journal of Law & Economics* 26 (June 1983).

4. See, e.g., Michael Jensen and William Meckling, "Rights and Production Functions: An Application to Labor-Managed Firms and Codetermination," *Journal of Business* 52 (1979), 485–88.

5. A similar point is made by Louis Putterman in his "Marx and Disequilibrium: Comment," *Economics and Philosophy* 4 (1988), 334. For a sophisticated discussion of this and related problems, see also Louis Putterman, "Exit, Voice, and Portfolio Choice: Agency and Public Ownership," forthcoming. For a survey of portfolio theory, see Michael Jensen, "Capital Markets: Theory and Evidence," *Bell Journal of Economics and Management Science* (1972), 357–98 and Eugene Fama, *Foundations of Finance* (New York: Basic Books, 1976).

6. David Ellerman, "Workers' Cooperatives: The Question of Legal Structure," in *Worker Cooperatives in America*, Robert Jackall and Henry Levin, ed., (Berkeley: University of California Press, 1984), 263.

7. David Schweickart, *Capitalism or Worker Control?* (New York: Praeger, 1980) and *Against Capitalism* (Cambridge: Cambridge University Press, 1993).

8. In what follows, I rely on an intuitive understanding of exploitation. A full analysis of the concept can be found in chapter 3 of *The Philosophy and Economics of Market Socialism*. Roughly, the idea is that the owner of an asset is exploited if and only if he or she is having some of the value of that asset appropriated (i.e., taken without compensation) by someone else without being in a position to do anything about it.

9. For a discussion of the accountant's conception of good will, see Donald Kieso and Jerry J. Weygandt, *Intermediate Accounting*, 4th ed. (New York: John Wiley and Sons, 1983), 572–74. For a discussion of complementarities of assets, see Benjamin Klein, Robert C. Crawford, and Armen Alchian, "Vertical Integration, Appropriable Rents, and the Competitive Contracting Process," *Journal of Law & Economics* 21 (1978): 297–326.

10. Jan Vanek, *The Economics of Workers' Management: A Yugoslav Case Study*, (London: Allen and Unwin, 1972), 220.

11. See Bayless Manning, *A Concise Textbook on Legal Capital* (Mineola, NY: Foundation Press, 1977), 33.

12. David Ellerman, *The Democratic Worker-Owned Firm* (London: Unwin and Hyman, 1990), 47.

13. These tasks are executed in chapters 6 and 7 of *The Philosophy and Economics of Market Socialism*.

14. For a critical evaluation of other models of market socialism along similar lines, see *ibid.*, chap. 8.

Liberal Obituary?*

Loren E. Lomasky†

For the second time in recent months, a notable exponent of libertarianism recants.[1] John Gray is best known for his Mill scholarship, culminating in *Mill on Liberty: A Defense*, in which he advances a strikingly original interpretation of Mill's advocacy of the liberty principle, finding it both consistent with the consequentialism of *Utilitarianism* and intrinsically well conceived.[2] His search for foundations adequate to a liberal order next focused on Hayek, whose work he characterized as an "attempt to restate liberal principles in a form appropriate to the circumstances and temper of the twentieth century [which] has yielded a body of insights wholly comparable in profundity and power with those of his forebears in the classical liberal tradition."[3] The twelve previously published essays of *Liberalisms* appraise the contributions to liberal thought of Isaiah Berlin, Karl Popper, Herbert Spencer, John Rawls, and Michael Oakeshott, as well as providing reexaminations of Mill and Hayek. In the first eleven of these, Gray extracts themes that he finds supportive of the institutions of a liberal polity. It is only in the twelfth, "Mill's and Other Liberalisms," originally published in 1988, that he begins to display serious reservations with the liberal project as such. That dissatisfaction is brought to a head in the volume's "Postscript: After Liberalism" in which he purports to "exhibit in a systematic and detailed way the failure of liberal ideology" (p. 240) and to sketch the contours of a viable postliberalism. Precisely because Gray's engagement with liberal thought has been so continuous and substantial, the capital sentence he now pronounces over it merits attention.

I

Its noteworthy "Postscript" aside, John Gray's *Liberalisms* is framed by two appraisals of Mill. In "J. S. Mill and the Future of Liberalism," originally published in 1976, Gray sums up the enduring relevance of Mill in this way:

> In at least three respects, I suggest that Mill's radical liberalism still has much to offer those in search of a reasonable radicalism. Mill's is a decentralist, antistatist radicalism, which, unlike orthodox socialism, addresses itself to the problems involved in meeting the widely acknowledged need for political devolution and the diffusion of power and initiative within the great entrenched institutions of our society. It is a radicalism which, while calling for a massive redistribution of property and therefore of incomes, offers an alternative conception of social justice to that of a levelling down egalitarianism. . . . Moreover, it is a radicalism which is well prepared to meet the challenges posed by an end to economic growth in the world's developed (or overdeveloped) societies. Mill's political thought should be a central inspiration of those who seek to modify the institutions and policies of liberal societies, while remaining faithful to the central ideals of the liberal tradition. [pp. 7–8]

But here is how Mill looks to him in 1988:

> In his distributionist theorizings, in his proposals for a competitive syndicalism of worker-managed enterprises and in his utterly Utopian schemes for the attainment of a stationary state in the growth of population and capital, Mill evinced a distance from the real and irresistible trends of his own age which condemned his thought to political impotence. . . . Mill's thought is infected with an anemic intellectualism which, in neglecting systemic and historical constraints on comprehensive social change, succeeds only in generating delusive images of a reformed state of things which were taken seriously, if at all, only by a few devout bands of rationalist sectarians. . . . The most distinctive features of Mill's revisionary liberalism, motivated as it was by an interest in addressing the dilemmas of the day, is its utter practical nullity in the nineteenth century and in our own. [p. 228]

Mill is Gray's barometer of liberalism; as the former sinks in his estimation, so does the latter. The project of *On Liberty* founders not simply because of the consequentialism and Eminent Victorianism with which it is burdened but also "because of crippling disabilities in the Principle of Liberty itself" (p. 218). Those disabilities are cataloged with staccato intensity in the final two essays of *Liberalisms* but are anticipated in the earlier pieces. In these the search for adequate liberal foundations is pursued with what seems to be a substantial measure of success, but Gray is too careful and conscientious an observer not to remark on the creakiness of the floorboards over which he steps. For example, Popper's fallibilism earns in "The Liberalism of Karl Popper" general approval as a tool to be wielded against the utopian fancies of centralized planning, but Gray notes the absence within Popper's thought of a theory of political development (p. 23). In "Spencer on the Ethics of Liberty and the Limits of State Interference," Gray offers a perceptive and largely persuasive corrective to the misapprehensions that have led to general neglect of Spencer's thought in the twentieth century. Gray's Spencer resembles to a remarkable degree Gray's Mill; each is exhibited as defending an indirect utilitarianism that provides layers of intermediate principles shielding individual liberty from the demands of an omnivorous maximization requirement. Nonetheless, Spencer's evolutionary naturalism is faulted as purveying a meliorism threatening to liberal civilization in virtue of its invocation of a monistic social entity taken to be a proper subject of moral attributions (p. 117). Yet more pronounced is the ambivalence of "Hayek on Liberty, Rights and Justice." Hayek's writings are duly praised for their scope and ambition, but Gray gives their components a good shredding. He faults Hayek for maintaining a positive conception of liberty, sees his excessively formalistic conception of law, lacking substantive rights, as potentially sanctioning tyrannous incursions on individuals, and deems his Darwinian utilitarianism incapable of differentiating between spontaneous orders in which freedom flourishes and stable systems of statist oppression.

Although Gray has oscillated under the sway of diverse influences, the two thinkers whose impact has been most pronounced and persistent are Isaiah Berlin and Michael Oakeshott. Gray fully subscribes to Berlin's understanding of moral life as necessitating a choice among incommensurable and incompossible values. Neither within an individual life nor within a political order is a frictionless harmony among all goods attainable. Berlin, of course, holds ineliminable value-pluralism to be supportive of liberal society; although liberalism is no more able than any alternative political structure to secure the totality of value, it is uniquely open and receptive to value-competition. That is, the preeminence of liberty, conceived as nonrestriction of options, does not represent an arbitrary privileging of the value of liberty vis-à-vis all others but rather the disposition at a political level to countenance rather than cut off competition among values. This disposition is sustained by an understanding that there can exist no synoptic height from which all contending forms of life can be neutrally and dispassionately evaluated. Rather, any alleged Archimedean point itself encapsulates a distinctive commitment to some virtues and principles at the expense of others. Liberal society is the repudiation of the moral monism of Plato's Form of the Good or a millinerianism in which all discord is ultimately swallowed up in a perfect and complete harmony.

Unlike Berlin, Gray does not accept the proposition that liberalism is the most appropriate political response to the plurality of incommensurable value. Already in the 1980 essay, "On Negative and Positive Liberty," he suggests, "It might be thought, for example, that the advocacy of value-pluralism and of the priority of liberty are not mutually supportive . . . but rather pull in different directions" (pp. 65–66). That will be so if sanctioning a perpetual competition among a diversity of values itself competes with the advocacy of other values as primary: that of communal solidarity, perhaps, or of equality.

This suspicion of liberal credentials deepens under the influence of Oakeshott.[4] For Oakeshott, as for Berlin, diversity among modes of human experience is the primary datum. But Oakeshott rejects as vain the attempt to formulate a principle of liberty that will definitively regulate the interplay of contending practices. That is not because of any disinclination on Oakeshott's part to prize liberty but is rather the consequence of an abiding conviction that the manufacture of commanding principles for the conduct of politics is an illicit trade: it is the intrusion of rationalism into politics. By "rationalism" Oakeshott refers to the view that only that which can be stated in explicit, theoretical terms merits recognition as genuine knowledge. It is the product of an imperialistic scientism (epitomized by the logical positivism of the 1930s) that condemns as irrational practices that do not hew tightly to the model of the natural sciences. Those institutions, customs, and ways of life unable to produce on demand a comprehensive justification of their fittingness are classified by the rationalist as superstitious recrudescenses meriting neither regard nor preservation.

For Oakeshott, all knowledge, including that contained within disciplines that have become theorized, is an outgrowth of practice. Their principles acquire whatever cogency they possess insofar as they express the tacit knowledge embodied in patterns of activity. Rationalism springs from an inversion of the proper precedential order between practice and theory. The consequences of according primacy to theory are far-flung, but it is within politics that the effects of rationalism have been most corrosive. The bolshevik revolution is its most disastrous fruit but, to a greater or lesser degree, each of the ideologies of the modern world has imbibed its poison.[5] An ideology claims universal scope and comprehensive validity for a set of ordering principles, but this theoretical rigor is achieved only at the cost of eviscerating from the body politic the knowledge preserved in its inherited particularities of circumstance. By construing political life as a goal-directed, planned activity, it denies the open-ended, inherently uncompletable nature of the craft of civil accommodation.

The Oakeshottian critique of rationalism is turned on Mill in *Liberalisms'* pivotal essay, "Mill's and Other Liberalisms." Gray there characterizes Mill as vacillating uneasily between two liberal doctrines. The strand predominant in *On Liberty* and *Principles of Political Economy*, culminating in the attempt to formulate "one very simple principle" for the regulation of liberty within civil society, is found to be bankrupt. It fails for at least three reasons. First, Mill's harm principle provides at best only necessary and not sufficient conditions for the restriction of liberty; it tells us that we may limit individual liberty only to prevent harm to others, but it neither indicates which circumstances constitute harms of the relevant sort nor does it specify how great an imposition on liberty is justifiable in order to preclude those harms. Thus it "tells us what we may not do, but not what we ought to do" (p. 221). Second, Mill's indirect utilitarianism presupposes our ability to make well-founded judgments concerning aggregate social welfare. That contention is notoriously troubled by the problem of interpersonal utility comparisons but, as argued by Berlin and Joseph Raz, it is impugned at an even more fundamental level by the existence of incommensurable and incompatible possibilities within an individual life. Third, the liberty principle is vulnerable to infiltration by claims of aggregate welfare. Where we have reason to believe that adherence to noninterference will generate a lesser sum of utility when more is attainable, it is difficult to provide a rationale for not acting directly to achieve maximum overall utility. This is a general disability of theories that attempt to erect rights as side constraints on a consequentialist foundation. The upshot of these three considerations is that "no 'one very simple principle,' of the sort Mill tried to state and defend in *On Liberty*, can possibly be derived" (p. 224).

Gray is more sympathetic to Mill's "other liberalism," characterized as those elements in his thought congruent with the philosophies of Scottish enlightenment thinkers and such French liberals as Tocqueville and Constant. Despite Gray's announcement in "Mill's and Other Liberalisms" that he will set out the contours of this alternate strain, that promise remains curiously unfulfilled in the essay. Instead, it is Rawls's theory that he presents as the preferable, yet still unavailing, alternative to Mill's dominant liberalism. Reprising the discussion of "Contractarian Method, Private Property and the Market Economy" (pp. 161–98), Gray credits Rawls with avoiding the pitfalls of a maximizing consequentialism, substituting for Mill's harm principle the greatest equal liberty requirement (and, in writings subsequent to *A Theory of Justice*, moving to a disaggregated listing of basic liberties), and with constructing a genuinely political doctrine that avoids moral provinciality. Nonetheless, claims Gray, "Rawls's move fails, and its failure carries with it the coherence of liberalism as that political philosophy devoted to the priority of liberty, however conceived" (p. 231).

It fails for three reasons. First, there is no reason to attribute fixity to

Rawls's list of basic liberties. Within any particular political culture, the importance of various liberties waxes and wanes; it is unduly conservative to privilege in theory those that enjoy predominance at some (inevitably arbitrary) one time. Second, the contents of basic liberties are underdetermined by the theory of justice as fairness; it provides no counsel for ascertaining whether, for example, pornography falls under the protection of freedom of expression. Third, it is disputable whether even for a societal time-slice, one may nonarbitrarily order liberties into the two exclusive categories of basic and nonbasic. In that case, claims Gray, "liberalism itself becomes indeterminate and barely coherent." This, he adds, is "a result that undermines liberalism in both its revisionary and its classical formulations" (p. 232).

Gray's winding journey from Mill to Mill is brought to provisional closure in the concluding, "Postscript: After Liberalism." Three liberal strategies, exemplified in the writings of more than a dozen theorists, are sketched and criticized. Each is held to fall short of justifying its pretensions of providing universally valid foundations for political practice. Gray diagnoses the upshot to be a liberal reason at the end of its tether, forced to recognize itself as no more than the outcropping of one ungeneralizable moment of the development of Western political life. It is, however, our particular inheritance, and were its products simply excised from a postliberal politics, the result would be a shambles. Instead, Gray commends what he calls a "Post-Pyrrhonian" mode of political inquiry, to be characterized by a finely grained "phenomenology of the forms of moral and political life we find among us" (p. 263), but minus recourse to the abstractions and counterfeit systematicness that have heretofore gripped liberal political culture. The prescription is a Humean (and Oakeshottian) attention to the conventions of primordial moral practice combined with a pragmatically Hobbesian quest for sustainable articles of peace that might modulate conflicts among inescapably plural conceptions of the good. Individual liberty is, of course, one of the moral ideals that infuse our inherited institutions, but it is not automatically to be assigned a lexical priority over all others. The task, to borrow Oakeshott's metaphor, is that of achieving ongoing balance so as to remain afloat among the perpetually shifting currents of political life rather than mechanically steering by a navigational chart into safe harbor.

II

Like a suitor finally grown disenchanted after a long courtship, Gray is inclined to magnify newly perceived flaws. For example, against the Hayekian claim that a liberal order is most conducive to the growth of welfare-enhancing knowledge, he responds, "It is far from clear that developments in medicine . . . have tended to enhance the quality of human life on balance" (p. 241). Such hyperbolic skepticism is both inherently unconvincing and tends to obscure his more interesting contention that growth of theoretical knowledge may be conjoined with, indeed encourage, a diminution of practical knowledge. Moreover, his newly found conviction that the liberal project is bankrupt prompts a string of off-handed dismissals of liberal variants. The force of these single-sentence verdicts is more epigrammatic than argumentative. Despite the frenetic pace of the "Postscript," Gray's second thoughts present what may reasonably be taken to be the single most serious contemporary challenge to liberal thought. Unlike communitarian nostalgia for a fabricated era of unquestioned moral certainty, Gray's postliberalism forthrightly acknowledges that it is our destiny to live amid a plurality of moral conceptions and that political life for us must be an exercise in accommodating diversity rather than a retreat to neo-medieval cloisters. If this is a form of conservatism, it is neither fideist nor supportive of a powerful central state apparatus, nor a doctrine of society as a hierarchically structured social organism. What it seeks to conserve are predominantly practices formed under the sway of liberal individualism, dispensing only with their illegitimate philosophical progeny.

The following four charges seem to be at the heart of Gray's indictment of liberalism:

1. *Spurious universality.* Liberalism represents itself as prescribing universally valid principles for the organization of political life when it is instead no more than the distillation of one localized form of civil life.
2. *Value pluralism.* Although liberal theory ostensibly embraces diversity, there exist intrinsically valuable forms of human life that can neither be accommodated by a liberal order nor accommodate it.
3. *Inversion of theory and practice.* Liberalism professes faith in the adequacy of a set of regulative principles for the governance of political life, but whatever cogency principles enjoy derives from particular practical judgments.
4. *Indeterminacy.* A liberty principle is inevitably indeterminate, unable to distinguish in nonarbitrary fashion between protected activities and those liable to curtailment.

The objections are mutually reinforcing. If all possible forms of human flourishing were able to coexist within a liberal order, then a claim on its behalf to universality would be plausible. It is because individuals have reason to value modes of life to which liberal sociality is necessarily antagonistic that they similarly have reason to reject the proclaimed bindingness of liberal principles. It is the perceived satisfactoriness of a family of practices that affords to it whatever warrant it may possess, and against the experience of successful sociality, objections grounded in a hostile ideology are unavailing. Modern Western individualism is one among a multitude of structures within which human beings have lived worthwhile lives, and so we have reason to preserve and extend its traditions. These, however, do not ascribe lexical priority to liberty but rather incorporate a diversity of moral goods that resist Procrustean theorizing. No "one very simple principle" can do justice to the internal complexity of civil association, and the strain of trying to adjudicate all conflicts in terms of such a monolithic maxim is palpable.

If these charges constitute an integrated package, they nonetheless are in tension with each other. Gray faults liberalism both for a hubristic universality and also for a lack of determinate application. It is hard to see how any political system could satisfy both demands. If the scope of normative standards is very broad, then it cannot reasonably be demanded of them that they provide an algorithmic decision procedure for the resolution of all possible conflicts. Whether or not liberalism should be understood as claiming to prescribe universally (a question to which I turn below), Gray correctly notes that it presents itself as considerably more than a synopsis of local procedures. What degree of determinateness can it be expected to display? If liberal principles were entirely neutral among competing moral demands, then they would indeed be a practical nullity. It does not follow that liberalism must ape a Benthamite felicific calculus to avoid vacuity. Principles can carry weight without uniquely prescribing. They do so in virtue of functioning as a normative filtering device that allows passage to certain considerations but not others. Such principles do not, however, obviate the need for prudence and fine-grained discrimination at the level of ground-floor decision making.

An example may help clarify the point. Gray faults liberal theory for its inability decisively to resolve disputed questions surrounding issues such as pornography, euthanasia, and abortion.[6] This is to misconstrue significantly the status of foundational normative principles. The priority of liberty does not, by itself, establish which actions are to count as illicit intrusions into individuals' protected spheres. What it does adjudicate with tolerable clarity is the admissibility of reasons submitted as bearing on the contended issue. The contention, say, that a taste for pornography is debased and therefore merits no protection, or that immersion in pornography harms its consumer, are summarily rejectable irrespective of whatever evidence can be gathered to support their truth, while a claim that pornography harms women and thus merits restraint is at least the sort of proposition that, if true, can be acknowledged in a liberal society as a justification for a ban on pornography. Nothing of course, is easier than simply to assert the existence of some vaguely specified harm, and I do not mean to suggest that every artful effort in that direction overcomes the liberal presumption against interference; the alleged harmfulness of pornography seems to me to be an instance in which that burden conspicuously fails to be satisfied. The point, though, is that such determinations cannot be made at the level of abstract theory, and it is unreasonable to take this lack of determinateness as in any way damaging to liberal credentials. Reflection on how the pornography debate actually tends to be framed within a liberal individualistic political culture illustrates quite clearly the error of Gray's claim that a principle of free expression is impotent. We observe that a premium is placed on construing the trade in pornography, however implausibly, as one in which specifiable harms are imposed on assignable consenting victims. That way one can be both liberal and a smiter of smut. The principle is not vacuous, but it does not adjudicate issues of who is harmed by what. There is, we might say, a division of labor in political life between high-level theory and particular application, and it is obtuse to expect the former to do the job of the latter. Liberal principles rule out paternalistic or perfectionistic appeals, but they neither can nor should be expected to sketch once and for all the boundaries of impermissible interference.[7]

I turn next to Gray's allegation that liberalism professes a universalism it is unable to substantiate. The cogency of the criticism varies depending on which liberal theorist is under consideration. There is, admittedly, a strain of Wilsonian optimism that commends always and everywhere the institutions of liberal democracy. Mill edges closer to this position than most political philosophers, but even he denies application of the liberty principle to "those backward states of society in which the race itself may be considered as in its nonage," leaving their governance instead to "an Akbar or a Charlemagne, if they are so fortunate as to find one."[8] Others, including Kant, Rawls, Hayek, and James Buchanan are yet more circumspect in their cautions concerning the prior buildup of social capital requisite for a stable liberal order.

Gray can, then, ascribe to liberal theory at most an avowal of conditional universality, the desirability of a liberal order for any society capable of instituting and maintaining it. A Weimar Republic, fatally riven with cancers rendering it unable to ward off the Brown Shirts, need not be accounted politically successful no matter how hospitable it may have been to liberty during its brief lifespan. This is not in any obvious sense to fall into Pollyannaish optimism. More plausible is the diagnosis that liberalism suffers from incurable valuational myopia, and that seems to be the gravamen of Gray's indictment:

> Liberalism, which in its applications to personal conduct aims for toleration and even [sic] pluralism, is in its political demands an expression of intolerance, since it denies the evident truth that many very different forms of government may, each in its own way, contribute to an authentic mode of human well-being. From the first, liberalism has always strenuously resisted this commonplace observation, since it cannot but undermine the claim to universal authority of liberalism as a political faith—a claim which exhibits the structural similarity of liberalism to the evangelizing Christianity of which it is the illegitimate offspring. [p. 239]

Gray finds liberalism hoisted by its own tolerationist petard insofar as it refuses to accord legitimacy to nonliberal or illiberal governmental forms. In at least three respects the accusation is contestable. First, as noted above, any universality claimed by liberalism is conditional. The analogy to evangelizing Christianity is, in that respect, inapposite.

Second, Gray cites no text exhibiting a denial of "the evident truth," and one may believe that the omission is not accidental. I am unaware of any credible liberal theorist who maintains that *no* authentic human good may be served by a nonliberal regime. Human beings need security of person and property, and the provision of these is not, of course, the monopoly of one form of government: a justification of *liberal* government is, simultaneously, a justification of liberal *government*. Nor is an ability to surmount the state of nature the only positive attribute of illiberal regimes. Tyrannies may address themselves, often more successfully than free societies, to patronage of the fine arts, sustenance of meaning-conferring religious faith, promotion of the martial virtues, and making the trains run on time. Although they thereby promote authentic human values, they nonetheless remain tyrannies. Advocacy of liberalism need not deny all value to these accomplishments. Indeed, to acknowledge rights that serve as side constraints is necessarily to commit oneself to forgoing valuable outcomes that might otherwise be attained (e.g., those that could be achieved via an exercise of paternalism). To suppose that liberals must be blind to goods that thrive under other forms of government is to misconceive the logic of liberal justification.

Third, and most fundamental, Gray fails to support his characterization of liberalism as a distinctive "faith" aiming to advance its own projects under the guise of a bogus tolerationism. Libertarianism, as well as most other liberal variants, explicitly withholds from the state an entitlement differentially to favor some rights-respecting projects at the expense of others. Individuals, acting severally or jointly, are, it goes without saying, free to do so. This is another respect in which liberal politics essentially incorporates a normative division of labor. It is not, of course, the case that liberalism maintains a studied neutrality among all projects: a display of impartiality between the would-be murderer and his intended victim is no part of the liberal prospectus. The positive role of the state is understood to be the protection of individual rights, primarily or exclusively understood as claims to noninterference within a morally protected zone in which individuals are at liberty to pursue those projects that are distinctively their own.

This is not an unfamiliar conception; indeed it is the one that Gray endorses in the early essays of *Liberalisms*. Evidently he now believes that the superficial hospitality liberalism extends to value pluralism conceals a deeper-seated intolerance. "It is obvious," he writes, "that many virtues and excellences are weak or absent from liberal societies. The virtues of a courtier, of a warrior, or of a pious peasant, presuppose a social order which cannot coexist with a liberal society" (p. 260). Whether or not those are the best examples that could have been selected,[9] Gray's point appears to be that professions of openness by a political culture to diverse manifestations of human flourishing are falsified if there are modes that fail to find accommodation within it.

Even restricting attention to forms of flourishing that do not inherently incorporate encroachments on the like flourishing of others—Carlos the Terrorist, Thrasymachus's splendid tyrant—the claim is unpersuasive. In free regimes as well as in free markets, some enterprises wax and others wane. Open entry is not rendered a sham even if it is largely predictable of various products that they will not enjoy sufficient market demand to prosper; the absence of a vibrant trade in buggy whips does not mean that the trust-busters ought to be on the lookout for a transportation cartel. Similarly, a shortage of pious peasants is not a reliable sign of intolerance to that form of life. (It would if the shortage were the consequence of a ban or prohibitive tax on piety, but that is not Gray's claim.) To shift the metaphor, an open society is not committed to making itself into a museum for the preservation of fragile social forms. Gray may have good arguments against Hayek's cultural Darwinism, but they do not support an Endangered Social Species Act.

Gray's point may at bottom be this: to individuals who are wedded to a mode of life that is unable to thrive within a liberal milieu, no argument concerning the universality of human rights or the knowledge enhancing attributes of civil society or the principles of justice to which individuals would assent behind a veil of ignorance will provide them sufficient reason to abandon the way of life that is theirs. Ever since Socrates launched himself into an extended answer to Glaucon's question, political philosophy has sought for the perfect reformatory argument, one capable of placing reluctant compliants in a logical armlock of Be Moral or Be Miserable! from which no egress is possible. However, notes Gray, "the spectacle of the retired torturer or well defended tyrant basking like a lizard in the sun of his self-esteem and the affection of his family tells another story." It is, he charges, "one to which the liberal mind is deaf" (p. 260). So construed, the charge of spurious universality accuses liberals of advertising their credo as one that provides to every rational person conclusive reasons for acquiescing to the set of principles or structure of basic rights that in fact characterizes what is no more than one localized moment of political life. The advertisement is deceptive; more than that, it is self-deceptive.

If this is indeed Gray's argument, it seems to me to be correct in every respect but one. He aptly diagnoses liberalism's susceptibility to the illusion that the form of civility it champions necessarily commends itself to all rational agents. It is a hard fact that the preferences of some individuals may simply afford no handle to be grasped by liberal reason. Against misanthropes within and Ayatollahs without, armaments offer better defense than arguments.[10] So far, so good. Gray is mistaken, though, in supposing that this spotlights a lacuna peculiar to liberalism. Normative justification cannot move the immobile, and every polity confronts the necessity of protecting itself against those who are deaf to appeals of reciprocal forbearance. A more realistic standard for justification is that it provide to each person with an interest in cooperating with those who are themselves amenable to cooperation terms each has reason to acknowledge as satisfying that interest. This is not the occasion to argue that liberal civil association satisfies this standard, or that illiberal forms of government necessarily fail to do so. I note only that Gray's charge of spurious universality is beside the point. Whatever may be the case for evangelizing Christianity, political philosophers need not accept as an article of faith that all souls are salvageable.

I turn finally to Gray's postliberal Pyrrhonism. Despite the presence of a few evocative remarks, these half dozen paragraphs of constructive political theory are too sketchy and impressionistic to support more than the most cautious critique. Clearly they are meant to be an elucidation of the Oakeshottian primacy of practice over theory, the negative half of which is to be accomplished by exorcising the myths that have heretofore sustained liberal institutions. The positive component is, as previously noted, a "phenomenology of the forms of moral and political life we find among us." Gray further characterizes this as a "return to history, in which we seek to uncover the genealogy or archaeology of our present forms of life and to understand them as historical creations" (p. 263).

Suppose that the archaeological project were carried off with virtuoso flair: How would that resolve the problem of political decision making? To catalog every nuance and wrinkle of the traditions we have inherited (and, in an era of free cultural trade, those that we have imported) does not inform us which of these have historically promoted welfare and which retarded it, let alone which today remain vital.[11] Protagonists on all sides of sharply disputed issues will be able to muster elements of tradition that may credibly be taken as supporting their case. Conservatism is one authentic response to tradition, but so also are reform and reaction. (And for societies that claim revolutionary antecedents, a return to history may take a distinctly radical shape.) This is indeterminacy with a vengeance!

Gray faults liberalism for its inability definitively to resolve debates surrounding pornography, abortion, and euthanasia, but is there reason to believe that a postliberal politics will enjoy more success in this regard? If anything, one might suspect, it will be more deeply enmired in perplexity. I argued previously that liberal principles can at least filter out inadmissible reasons, but moral phenomenology is unreservedly promiscuous. Thus it is normatively barren. To catalog everything is to adjudicate nothing. It is vain to hope that by bringing a microscope to traditions our quandaries will find themselves resolved. Rather, what is required are both high-level and intermediate principles through which assessments of relative justificatory weight can be made.[12] These need not be a priori constructs that deform the practices on which they impose themselves but may be grounded in both local and global human experience. A different phenomenology, one that scrutinizes the traditions of liberal theorizing, reveals a diversity of moral epistemologies. Even if the Oakeshott/Gray critique were able definitively to establish the poverty of one such strain, it would be far-fetched to generalize the result as a demolition of liberalism simpliciter.

III

What we have here, I believe, are the provocative yet unformed thoughts of a theorist very much in transition. Gray, after years of patiently winnowing libertarian themes, has come to despair of a successful consummation and leaps forthwith into a phenomenology from which principles have been exiled. His headlong rush in the "Postscript" through more than a dozen liberal formulations is laced with one-line summary verdicts that are elegantly barbed but quite resistible. I do not see that they do any lasting damage to liberal aspirations—though Straussians will feel themselves confirmed in their warning that the inevitable terminus of modernism is nihilism.[13]

Despite its too-precipitous verdicts, *Liberalisms* is a significant work of substantive political philosophy. Its previously published essays are subtle and searching treatments of important liberal thinkers and liberal motifs. Our understanding of Mill, Berlin, and Hayek in particular is notably enriched as a consequence of Gray's investigations. His concluding second thoughts are no less instructive. Although the proclamation of the bankruptcy of liberal theory in all its modes is overly ambitious and underly sustained, Gray has identified several junctures at which reconsideration is called for. In his critique of contractarian method Gray has supplied, I believe, a definitive demonstration of the limits of contractarianism. Contract may be a useful heuristic for fixing attention on the agent-relativity of value to which political prescriptions must conform themselves, but neither inside nor outside of an original position is it able in a non-question-begging way to establish generally binding principles of justice.

I have argued that Gray's charge of spurious universality misfires as an indictment of all liberal theory. Nonetheless, it has real bite against those who persist in the Plato/Kant tradition of seeking normative first principles that necessarily impose themselves on all rational agents. Gray's arguments here will force theorists to consider more carefully questions concerning the range over which liberal—or, indeed, any—political justification can reasonably be expected to extend. Similarly, his critique of liberal indeterminacy should motivate research aimed at establishing a satisfactory division of labor between high- and intermediate-level normative principles. For these and other reasons I am convinced that, despite the emptiness of his postliberal phenomenology of morals, Gray has given us the most trenchant critique of liberal theory that we possess.

Notes

*Review of John Gray, *Liberalisms: Essays in Political Philosophy* (London: Routledge, 1989). Citations are indicated by parenthetical page references in the text.

†I am indebted to John Gray for many conversations about issues in political philosophy. Needless to say, he is neither responsible for nor endorses the interpretative remarks and criticisms of this essay. Also not partaking in responsibility are Gerald Gaus and Stuart Warner, though each has helped me to see my way more clearly through various of the items discussed herein.

1. The other is Robert Nozick, *The Examined Life: Philosophical Meditations* (New York: Simon & Schuster, 1989).
2. John Gray, *Mill on Liberty: A Defence* (London: Routledge & Kegan Paul, 1983).
3. John Gray, *Hayek on Liberty* (Oxford: Basil Blackwell, 1984), 1–2.
4. In what follows I attempt to convey a sense of Gray's reading of Oakeshott rather than to offer my own, sometimes varying, assessment.
5. Oakeshott, in contradistinction to most other conservatives, does not locate the origin of contemporary vexations in the onset of modernity. Rather, he places the inception of the rot in the inheritances of the late Greco-Roman world and early Christian communal life (see "Oakeshott on Law," esp. 205–6).
6. See also in this regard Gray's review of *The Moral Limits of the Criminal Law*, by Joel Feinberg, *Times Literary Supplement (TLS)* (January 12–18, 1990), 31–32.
7. The above is presented as a schema for decision making within a thoroughly liberal society. Where, as in the United States, the civil constitution is imperfectly liberal, the filtering process generates a different result, so the U.S. Supreme Court admits "community standards" and the presence or absence of "redeeming social value" as factors legitimately entering into censorship decisions. Such incomplete liberalism complicates American pornography rulings, but it would seem to be a complication that Gray should find justifiable in terms of his postliberal phenomenology. See, however, his *TLS* review of Feinberg.
8. Mill, *On Liberty*, chap. 1.
9. Some would maintain that all too many fawning courtiers can be observed plying their trade inside the Beltway; nor is it obvious that the other two mentioned species are quite extinct.
10. "For as that stone which by the asperity, and irregularity of figure, takes more room from others, than itself fills; and for the harness, cannot be easily made plain, and thereby hindereth the building, is by the builders cast away as unprofitable, and troublesome: so also, a man that by asperity of nature, will strive to retain those things which to himself are superfluous, and to others necessary; and for the stubbornness of his passions, cannot be corrected, is to be left, or cast out of society, as cumbersome thereunto" (Thomas Hobbes, *Leviathan*, chap. 15).
11. It may be useful to imagine Mr. Gorbachev surveying the residue of Soviet history in search of guidance for how to move to the next stage of his policy of *perestroika*. If he finds—as indeed he would—that the gulags, Lubyanka executions, and Katyn forest massacres dominate whatever shreds of freedom may have briefly characterized Lenin's New Economic Policy, should that incline him toward a reaffirmation of Stalinist practice? Would a demonstration of the rarity of civil association within the Russian experience imply that liberalization is an illegitimate foreign import? (I hasten to note that a consistent theme of Gray's writings is an unqualified opposition to totalitarian barbarism. These queries are not meant to suggest otherwise, but neither is their ad hominem thrust entirely accidental.)
12. In his pamphlet *Liberal Government: A Positive Agenda* (London: Institute of Economic Affairs, 1989) Gray evaluates a wide mix of policy options for the Britain

of the 1990s. Perhaps not altogether surprisingly, his assessments appeal to just those high—and intermediate—level normative principles familiar from liberal discourse. He prefaces the investigation by noting that these "are not the 'unshakable first principles' of liberal doctrine" (p. 18), but peripheral questions of corrigibility aside, one is hard-pressed to find any basis for classifying the pamphlet as other than a pragmatically judicious exercise in bringing liberal considerations to bear on policy alternatives.

13. I owe this pleasantry to Gerald Gaus.

Community versus Liberty?

Douglas B. Rasmussen

> The primeval identification of the good with the ancestral is replaced by the fundamental distinction between the good and ancestral; the quest for the right way or for the first things is the quest for the good as distinguished from the ancestral.
>
> —Leo Strauss
> "Origin of the Idea of Natural Right,"
> *Natural Right and History*

Communitarianism[1] is a postliberal political view. Whatever unity is to be found in communitarian thought comes from its opposition to liberalism's claim that achieving and maintaining liberty should be *the central* and *primary* concern of the political order—that is, the value to be achieved and maintained before any other. Communitarianism is especially opposed to the division of ethics into two languages: a language of liberty for dealing with issues in the political order and a language of virtue for dealing with issues in the nonpolitical order, that is, for choices concerning oneself, family, friends, and acquaintances. Communitarianism holds that this division is not philosophically justifiable and cannot be maintained sociologically and culturally.

Since communitarianism is defined by its opposition to liberalism, it is, for the most part, a collection from various sources of diverse views that appear to be in conflict, in one way or another, with liberalism. Included among these are the following claims: that human beings are naturally social; that ethical subjectivism is not an adequate moral theory; that the individual human being is not the *only* thing of inherent moral worth; that a virtue ethics more successfully captures the nature of the moral life than any other; that practical reasoning is not merely instrumental reasoning and is crucial to ethics; that ethical rationalism is false because it fails to recognize the role of the particular and contingent in determining proper conduct and thus does not recognize how pluralistic the human good truly is; that impersonal moral theory is an inadequate and distorting way to achieve a vantage point from which to criticize the status quo; that liberty cannot be defined or understood without an ethical commitment; that any theory of rights capable of motivating human conduct must ultimately be based on a view of the human good; and that rights are not ethically fundamental or sufficient to maintain a liberal order. These views, loosely collected under the "communitarian" label, are not always advanced by people who see themselves as necessarily opposed to liberalism. Yet these views are used to challenge different tenets of liberalism often thought to be crucial for defending the claim that liberty should be the central and primary value for the political order.

Communitarianism challenges five interrelated tenets of liberalism. These are: (1) the individualistic conception of the person; (2) moral individualism; (3) moral universalism; (4) legal neutrality towards different views of the human good; and (5) the primacy of rights. By offering objections to each of these, communitarianism thereby seeks to show that liberalism is mistaken about the centrality and primacy of liberty for the political order.

There are, of course, different versions of liberalism, and some do not hold liberty to be as central and primary a value for the political order as others. Contemporary American liberalism has sought to modify its emphasis on liberty by bringing other values into the political order, especially when dealing with economic issues. Such modifications do not satisfy the communitarian, however; even liberalism in its American form accepts, when it comes to matters not directly concerned with economic life, the division of ethics into a language of liberty for the political order and a language of virtue for the nonpolitical order. It is this division at its very foundation that communitarianism rejects. This division is seen as destroying the ethical language of our culture and thus the institutions upon which a just and decent political community depends.

By providing a carefully specified and reconceptualized rationale for this division of ethical language, this essay will defend liberalism and thus the centrality and primacy of liberty for the political/legal order. This defense will consider some of the objections that have been made by communitarianism against the liberal tenets noted above. Not all forms of liberalism[2] will be defended, however, but only a particular kind—namely, "natural-rights classical liberalism" or what is today often called, with more or less accuracy, "libertarianism." Yet even in this case, it is only the approach and interpretation of the natural right to liberty presented in *Liberty and Nature: An Aristotelian Defense of Liberal Order*[3] that will be defended. Hence, this defense of libertarian liberalism will proceed from a perspective different in some respects from what is usually encountered, and this difference will become evident as each of liberalism's tenets is examined.

It should at the start be conceded that there is truth in many of communitarianism's claims about human nature and ethics. Accordingly, these claims will not be disputed, but instead will be shown not to lead to a rejection of liberalism in libertarian form. The understanding of the basic right to liberty that will be defended argues that such a right is due to the possession of certain natural attributes in virtue of which someone is said to be a human being. It is based on a normative understanding of human nature. It thus involves more than a mere appeal to "natural powers." Further, it does not require that people begin their lives in some original state of nature or at some time decide to join society. Indeed, it is argued that the natural right to liberty arises and is needed *just as the particular sort of ethical concept it is*[4] precisely because of our social nature. This right is needed to create, interpret, and evaluate a political/legal order.

1. Liberalism's Individualistic Conception of the Person

Communitarianism complains that liberalism in any form has a tendency to conceive of people in an asocial or atomistic manner. Human beings are viewed without any consideration of the relationships that are crucial to both their individuality and humanity. It is assumed that the needs, interests, wants, abilities, and beliefs of an individual are formed independently of a person's relationships with others. They are simply taken as abstractly given, with very little discussion of how they come about. Whether it be Hobbesian man and his cousin, *homo economicus*, or the famous "rational animal" of natural-rights theory, there is precious little discussion in liberalism of the important role social life plays in characterizing what it is that we call "human." The isolated individual is made the centerpiece of liberal theory, yet to argue for a political liberalism from such an assumption is to base that theory on a nonentity, the abstract individual. Liberalism thus ends up working only with abstractions and, like so much of modern philosophical thought, is caught in its own constructions, never dealing with real human beings.

There is truth in this complaint, and any conception of human beings that assumes that we, in fact, start or develop our lives apart from others will not be defended here.⁵ Human beings are social animals. In terms of natural origins we are not isolated entities in some state of nature. We are almost always born into a society or community, and it is in some social context or other that we grow and develop. Much of what is crucial to our self-conception and basic set of values is dependent on our upbringing and environment. Further, we are social in the sense that our moral maturation requires a life with others. We have potentialities that are other-oriented, and we cannot find fulfillment without their actualization. Living with and among others, having other-concern, is crucial to our moral maturation. Thus, it is fundamentally erroneous to attempt to conceive of human beings as *coming to maturity* apart from others and only later taking it upon themselves to join society. Contrary to Hobbes, we do not achieve our maturity like mushrooms, suddenly, all at once, with no engagement with one another. We are not abstract individuals; our lives are necessarily intertwined with others. The natural sociality of human beings cannot, and should not, be ignored.

Though human beings are indeed social animals whose moral maturation requires living with others, it is still the case that human beings are not merely cells in some social organism and that societies do not exist without the individuals who constitute them. Further, though we learn many of our values and beliefs from others, it is, nonetheless, the person, the individual, who does the learning. There is no social or collective mind that makes the connections needed to grasp a truth. Also, our dependence on others for many of our values does not prevent us from questioning, challenging, and replacing those values, if we judge it necessary. The crucial issue here is not whether human beings are social animals in the sense that has been discussed so far. Certainly, humans are social in that sense, and liberalism need not deny this. Rather, it is an issue of whether human sociality exhaustively accounts, at the most basic level, for what it is to be human.

Can *all* features of human nature be reduced without remainder to social relations? Our ordinary understanding of human sociality does not entail such an extreme claim. Clearly, the burden of proof rests on those who would advance this thesis. It seems very doubtful that the ontological discreteness of human beings, their uniqueness, their abilities to desire, choose, speak, and reason,⁶ as well as their possession of basic potentialities, can be explained entirely and solely by their relations with others. Sociological explanations are certainly necessary for understanding human beings, but they are not all that is needed.

To illustrate the problem in making such a reductionist claim, let us consider the role of culture and social tradition when it comes to understanding what is good for a person. Liberalism can agree that having a cultural and social tradition (CST) is a necessary condition for people to attain their good, but it does not follow that a CST constitutes or defines the good for persons. Further, the communitarian must be wary not to attempt to prove too much, for the communitarian does not want his position to amount to an argument for the conventionalist form of ethical relativism and, thus, ethical noncognitivism. If this were so, then one of communitarianism's reasons for rejecting liberalism—that it is based on ethical noncognitivism—would be disarmed. But the central point of this illustration, when generalized, is simply this: human nature, including the human good, must have some particular cultural and social manifestation but, abstractly considered, it can have any. Thus, the particular cultural and social manifestation of human nature or the human good should never be taken as defining or constituting human nature or the human good itself.

2. Moral Individualism

To the extent that liberalism holds each individual human being to be of ultimate moral worth, it is often charged with reducing moral values to mere subjective states or with upholding a version of ethical egoism that reduces all other values to mere instruments. Indeed, communitarianism holds that there is such a history of liberal thought. We do not need, however, to decide here whether this historical claim is accurate or not. We can for the sake of the argument grant that subjectivism and ethical egoism are not sufficiently powerful ethical theories upon which to base a defense of any form of the liberal regime. Again, our tack shall not be to defend a view that liberalism is accused of embracing but instead, to show that this view is not necessary to the support of a claim that liberalism seeks to make—in this case, the claim that each individual human being is of ultimate moral worth. This claim can be grounded in a version of value objectivism that will now be briefly described. (The full statement of how political liberalism in its libertarian form is to be grounded in value objectivism will not be made until later in this essay, and then it will only be in outline form.)

Holding that individuals are of ultimate moral worth does not imply that one is an advocate of subjectivism or, more generally, a desire-based ethics. Nor does it require that one accept mechanism, nominalism, or a view of the self as simply a bundle of passions for which all moral reasoning is merely instrumental. It is time for both critics and advocates of political liberalism to acknowledge that there are other conceptual alternatives for its foundation. In fact, one can uphold the supreme importance of the individual from a standpoint that shares many of the same ethical assumptions as communitarianism. In other words, one can endorse moral individualism from a more-or-less Aristotelian conception of the self, in which desires and passions, though present, do not rule. Rational desires are possible. Such a conception of the self can be the basis for a contemporary version of a self-perfectionist virtue ethics that holds the moral good is, indeed, objective and yet that individuals are of ultimate moral worth. Further, it can be understood as something more than just a species of ethical egoism.

For moral values to be objective, it is not necessary that such values be extrinsic or unrelated to the lives of individual human beings. Something is objectively valuable when its worth is not merely the result of its being desired, wanted, or even chosen, but rather is desired, wanted, or chosen because it has inherent worth—that is, because it is an end-in-itself. Furthermore, something can not only be *an* objective value and be related to the lives of individual human beings, it can actually be *the ultimate* objective value. In fact, this value can be the very fulfillment or flourishing of those lives themselves, as is the case in a self-perfectionist virtue ethics. In such an ethics the ultimate objective value is not something that competes with the good of individual human beings. Rather, the ultimate objective value for human beings—the human *telos*—just *is* their very self-perfection or flourishing.

Just as our humanity is not some amorphous, undifferentiated universal, so human flourishing is not something abstract and universal. Rather, it is individualized and diverse. One person's self-perfection is not the same as another's, any more than A's actualization of his potentialities is the same as B's actualization of his. There are individuative as well as generic potentialities, and this makes human fulfillment always something unique. Abstractly considered, we can speak of human flourishing and of generic goods and virtues, but concretely speaking, no two cases of human flourishing are the same, and they are not interchangeable. Thus, liberalism's claim that the individual is of ultimate moral worth is not only compatible with the objectivity of ultimate moral value, it can find strong support—possibly its strongest—in a view of ultimate moral value that is self-perfectionist.

The flourishing of an individual human being can, on this view, be conceived of as an "inclusive" (as opposed to "dominant") end. Instead of being a single end, which is the only thing of inherent worth and which makes everything else valuable only as a means, flourishing can be conceived as being constituted or defined by a number of virtues and goods, each of which is valuable in its own right. Such virtues as integrity, courage, and justice and such goods as friendship, health, and knowledge, for example, could be not only productive of flourishing, but expressive of it as well. Thus, it is possible that these virtues can be practiced and goods achieved for their own sakes and yet also promote and express one's self-perfection. Further, because of the social character of human beings, many values resulting from human relationships are valued for their own sake and not simply because they are means. Thus, this "inclusivist" view of individual human flourishing is not an ethical egoism that holds all things other than the individual self to have only instrumental value.

There is, then, no necessity for liberalism's espousal of the ultimate value of individuals to require that one adopt either a subjectivist view of human moral values or ethical egoism.[8] Liberalism's moral individualism can be based in a self-perfectionist virtue ethics.

3. Moral Universalism

Liberalism inherits from the Greeks the idea that the good is fundamentally distinguishable from the ancestral. Thus, according to liberalism, there is nothing necessarily morally sacrosanct about past practices or traditions. In fact, the status quo can constitute a systematic form of oppression and injustice. Further, persons may not even recognize or appreciate the injustice of their situations, because the possibility of a morally preferable state of affairs has never occurred to them. Thus, to evaluate the status quo, it is necessary that a certain amount of distancing take place. One needs to be able to view the practices of one's life and society not from a perspective that is one's own or that of any other particular person, but from an ideal perspective, a perspective that will consider what is the best that can be accomplished by human beings. In this way, one's life and the customs, traditions, and political arrangements of one's society can be dispassionately and objectively evaluated. This approach is often called "moral universalism."

To achieve the distancing needed for an ideal perspective, the use of the principle of universalizability is generally deemed to be necessary. This principle holds that in order for some course of conduct to be morally appropriate for one person, it must be morally appropriate for any other person in the same situation. Further, the principle of universalizability is thought to entail impersonal moral theory. An ethical theory is impersonal when all ultimately morally salient values, reasons, and rankings are "agent-neutral;" and they are agent-neutral when they do *not* involve as part of their description an essential reference to the person for whom the value or reason exists or the ranking is correct. "For any value, reason or ranking V, if a person P1 is justified in holding V, then so are P2-Pn under appropriately similar conditions. . . . On an agent-neutral conception it is impossible to weight more heavily or at all, V, simply because it is one's own value."⁹ Accordingly, when it comes to describing a value, reason, or ranking, it does not ethically matter whose value, reason, or ranking it is. One person can be substituted for any other.

Using impersonal moral theory to make judgments and guide conduct requires that one consider only values, rankings, and reasons that could be held by a rational agent, considered apart from all individuating conditions—be they social, natural, or cultural. By adopting the perspective of such a rational agent, a person could never use some value crucial to *who* he or she is as a reason to give extra weight or importance to that value when determining the proper course of action. For example, the fact that course of action A results in one's own personal project or family or friends or country being assisted, where non-A does not, provides no ethical reason for preferring A over non-A. These factors could perhaps explain how a person might feel about the situation, but when a person is acting from a properly moral perspective, they are irrelevant and should not weigh more heavily. The individual *qua individual* is not important in an impersonal moral theory. The individual only represents a locus at which good is achieved or right conduct performed.

Communitarians, as well as advocates of virtue ethics in general, do not challenge the desirability of being more adept at discerning moral failings in oneself and one's society, but they nonetheless do hold that liberalism's moral universalism, *as just described*, is unsound from root to branch. It is fundamentally erroneous for liberalism to assume that abstract ethical principles alone can determine the proper course of conduct. Such ethical rationalism fails to grasp that ethics is practical and that there are contingent and particular facts—which abstract ethical principles cannot *explicitly* capture and thus cannot be discovered a priori—that are crucial to determining what ought to be done. Thus, contrary to much of modern and contemporary ethics from which much liberal political theory formed itself, not all morally proper forms of conduct need be universalizable. Further, and what is even more important, the central intellectual virtue of ethics is practical reason. This is not merely means-end reasoning, however. Rather, it is the ability of the individual at the time of action to discern in particular and contingent facts just what is morally required. Without such a virtue, moral universalism, like so much of liberal theory, can only deal with ethical abstractions and not real questions of personal conduct and human life.

Particular and contingent facts are ethically important, and though some of these facts may be more important than others in achieving human moral well-being, this cannot be determined from the armchair. There is no great ontological divide between the facts that can and cannot be ethically relevant. Certainly, there is no basis for holding that individual, social, and cultural differences among people are ethically irrelevant. To the contrary, they are highly significant. Furthermore, there is no foundation to moral impersonalism's claim that values central to one's very conception of oneself may not be valued more than less central values. The fact that a value is crucial to some person's deeply held personal project, but to no one else's, does not make it morally irrelevant. In fact, it is just the opposite. Such value deserves even more careful consideration, precisely because of its relation to oneself. Liberalism's moral universalism tries to force all human moral valuations into a kind of ethical straightjacket that does not successfully capture the reality of both human individuality and sociality.

The communitarian rejection of liberalism's moral universalism need not be contested. Yet this does not mean that liberalism must give up the attempt to find an ideal perspective from which people can better discern whether their societies might be ethically improved upon. The way that this perspective might be achieved, however, will be surprising to some. Communitarianism's complaints about moral universalism will not only be accepted, but also made more precise and incisive. By showing the inadequacy of impersonal moral theory, we will ultimately be in a better position to appreciate liberalism's basic problem and thus the importance of the solution that is offered by the version of libertarian liberalism we are defending. In particular, we will be in a better position to understand the unique moral function of libertarianism's central ethical concept—the basic right to liberty (to be discussed in sections 4 and 5)—and thus the importance of a special ethical language for the political order. Our tactic, as before, will be to use a contemporary version of self-perfectionist virtue ethics, in this case to make our criticisms of impersonal moral theory and the usefulness of universalization. These criticisms are summarized as follows:

(1) It is not true that the principle of universalizability requires one to adopt an agent-neutral view, for it is possible to hold a moral theory that claims that a person's good is agent-relative and still universalize actions based on it. Let us say that the good, $G1$, for a person, $P1$, is agent-relative if and only if its distinctive presence in world $W1$ is a basis for $P1$ ranking $W1$ over $W2$, even though $G1$ may not be the basis for *any other* persons ranking $W1$ over $W2$. Further, let us say the same holds true of goods, $G2$-Gn, for persons $P2$-Pn, respectively. Conduct based on such agent-relative goods can be universalized as follows: just as the production of $P1$'s good is a reason for $P1$ to act, so is the production of $P2$'s good a reason for $P2$ to act. $P1$ cannot claim that $G1$ provides him with a legitimate reason to act without acknowledging that $G2$ provides $P2$ with a legitimate reason to act.

Agent-relative values can be universalized. Thus, being agent-neutral is not necessary for universalization.

(2) It should also be noted that the ability of a value to be the basis for universalizable conduct is not sufficient to establish common values or a reason for other-regarding conduct among persons. This is so because the universalization of agent-relative goods does not show P1's good to be P2's good, nor the production of P2's good as providing P1 with a reason for action, or vice-versa. Thus, if P1's good should conflict with P2's, universalizability could not provide a way out of this conflict.

(3) There is a widespread tendency to confuse an objective value with universality. But this is an error. As Henry B. Veatch has observed:

> If the good of X is indeed but the actuality of X's potentialities, then this is a fact that not just X needs to recognize, but anyone and everyone else as well. And yet given the mere fact that a certain good needs to be recognized, and recognized universally, to be the good of X, it by no means follows that X's good must be taken to be Y's good as well, any more than the actuality or perfection or fulfillment of X needs to be recognized as being the actuality or perfection of Y as well.[10]

It is not true that X or X-ing cannot be truly good for anyone unless it is truly good for everyone.

(4) Agent-relativity of values does not preclude them from being objective. That something is only valuable relative to some person does not necessarily make its value merely a matter of that person's attitude toward it, because its value may in fact result from what it is and not simply from its being desired, wanted, or chosen. It is, for example, perfectly consistent for flourishing of individual human beings to be an objective value and yet essentially related to persons. The weighting that is given by person A to his achievement of flourishing, Fa, is greater than what A gives to B's achievement of flourishing, Fb. In other words, Fa gives A the primary moral responsibility of achieving Fa without implying any such responsibility to A for B achieving Fb, and vice-versa. Thus, a commitment to the objectivity of the value of human flourishing does not imply that its value is something that can be exchanged or promoted regardless of whose flourishing it is. Agent-neutrality, then, is not necessary for upholding value-objectivity.

If these objections hold, how can liberalism ever justify the use of an ideal perspective in evaluating the status quo? The answer has three parts. First, there is a difference between "moral universalism" understood as a procedure by which we momentarily distance or put ourselves outside our current situation and attempt to determine the best that is possible for human beings, but then, so to speak, drop back in or return to our current situation, and "moral universalism" understood as requiring all morally proper courses of conduct to be universalizable. These are not the same, and our ability to do the former is all that is required to become more adept in evaluating our current situation.

Second, it is not necessary to accept an impersonal moral theory in order to take an ideal perspective from which to judge the status quo. People have the ability to take such a perspective without necessarily determining their values by or conducting themselves according to that perspective. Further, taking such a perspective does not require accepting the existence of agent-neutral values, because all values may in fact always be values *for some* person. An agent-relative conception of value could, for example, recommend that persons adopt an ideal perspective as a means to obtaining knowledge that would assist them in achieving agent-relative value. Adopting such a perspective would be a useful tool with which people could measure how well they are achieving human moral well-being. They look to what others have done and achieved or consider what is possible for human beings just as such.[11] This is what people sometimes mean when they speak of having their "consciousness raised." Finally, when dealing with others, it is quite often necessary to view things from a perspective that is not one's own. Sometimes one needs to take the perspective, as best as one can, of a friend; and sometimes it is even necessary to take a universal perspective, the perspective of *any* human being. In other words, adopting such perspectives is really nothing other than the central rational mechanism by which we relate to others.[12]

Third, communitarianism is correct to hold that people cannot flourish or morally mature without communities in which there are shared values, but this does not necessarily mean that they must accept the status quo. People may need to leave their community or change it. Yet this cannot be done if sociality is only possible with those with whom one has common values. It must be possible for persons to have relationships with others with whom no common values are yet shared and where all that is known is that one is dealing with another human being. Further, though human sociality is always manifested in some particular family, group, community, culture, and society, it is not thereby limited to those particular manifestations. It is not confined to some select group or pool of humans but is, in principle, open to *any* human. To claim, then, that one's flourishing or moral maturation is impossible without relationships with others does not mean that sociality is confined to only those relationships where there are shared values. It also allows for an openness to strangers or human beings in general. Human flourishing is possible only if people can be open to relationships with others with whom no values are yet shared.

The communitarian conception of human sociality so focuses on certain particular forms of human sociality that it tends not to appreciate its open-ended character. It is precisely because liberalism appreciates the open-ended character of the interpersonal dimension of human flourishing that it can justify taking an ideal perspective that applies to any and every human being. Further, in order to use this perspective, liberalism does not have to accept ethical rationalism or moral impersonalism, nor to make romantic assumptions about how the self-perfection of one person is somehow the same as, or cannot conflict with, that of others. "Moral universalism," in this sense, can be legitimately used by liberalism.

This is the good news for liberalism, and if human flourishing were simply monistic and uniformly the same for every person, there would be no problem with how to utilize this perspective politically. But human flourishing is not monistic. There is still a problem for liberalism.

Though there are "generic goods" and virtues that are universal in the sense of helping to define human flourishing, their particular form is given by the individual. Human flourishing is not an abstraction. It is individualized as well as agent-relative. Liberalism cannot simply appeal to what an abstract consideration of human flourishing entails in order to determine what should be used as the standard for evaluating the status quo. Such an abstract consideration is ultimately prejudiced against every concrete form of flourishing. This was the insight behind the foregoing critique of liberalism's use of universalizability and moral impersonalism. Liberalism cannot proceed as if human beings were simply noumenal selves. Ironically, it must realize the moral propriety of individualism.

Of course, it can be insisted that liberalism is a political theory, not a guide to human flourishing, and is only concerned with establishing, interpreting, and evaluating a political/legal order and thus does not need to consider the contingent and particular facts that are crucial to a person's self-perfection. Nevertheless, liberalism still cannot endorse a standard that does not take into consideration that human flourishing is individualized and agent-relative. Even though the human good, abstractly considered, involves the same generic goods and virtues, there is a problem when it comes to finding something that can be used for providing a standard of evaluation for the status quo that will not favor one form of flourishing over any other. In other words, liberal political theory has to address the problem of pluralism, and this means more than acknowledging the existence of many *views* of the human good. It means grasping that the human good is plural and complex, not monistic and simple, and hence that pluralism is morally appropriate. This is the problem that gives rise to the liberal political perspective. The following questions constitute what we shall call "liberalism's problem": How do we make possible relationships among humans, each of which has a unique form of human flourishing, ethically compossible? How do we find a principle that is concerned with the creation, interpretation, and evaluation of a political/legal context that will *in principle* not require that the human flourishing of *any* person or group be sacrificed to others? Serious consideration needs to be given as to how a self-perfectionist virtue ethics might solve this problem.

4. Legal Neutrality

Communitarianism argues that liberalism, especially in its libertarian form, is inconsistent in holding that the law should be neutral in relation to varying conceptions of the good life, neither favoring nor disfavoring any particular conception. That the political/legal context of a society should be confined to maintaining peace and order, understood in terms of an individual's basic right to liberty, is thought to be incoherent, because liberalism, in order to both define and justify itself, must make some ethical commitment. Yet once this is done, liberalism cannot claim that people have some ultimate right to live in ways that are contrary to liberalism's ultimate ethical commitment. There is not, and cannot be, "a right to do wrong." [OBJECTION]

This is a significant objection. It will be met by appealing, once again, to a contemporary version of self-perfectionist virtue ethics. However, it is important that we understand why this particular line of response will be taken, rather than ones used by other advocates[13] of libertarian liberalism. So we will briefly consider some other possible responses to this communitarian objection, before continuing our defense of liberalism in libertarian form.

There have been—indeed, are—versions of liberalism that do not think it necessary to make any ethical claim in defending the liberal vision of society. It is thought to be a type of category mistake to think that liberty is an ethical notion. It is contended that the scope and content of the concept of "liberty" can be specified without making an ethical commitment. It is amoral and can be defined as just the absence of external impediment. This is a mistake, however, and communitarianism is right to object to this amoralism. If liberty occurs only when one is able to do what one wants, then what can be said to resolve situations where there is, as frequently happens, a conflict between what people want to do? Whose wants are to be given free reign, and whose constrained? Whose liberty is to be preferred? Obviously, merely appealing to the maxim "promote liberty" will not suffice. When conceived in this amoral fashion, there is no way to even understand what it *means* to promote liberty. If our wants conflict, and if my wants are given legal protection and yours are thus constrained, then while it is the case that my liberty has been protected and your liberty denied, we still cannot say that liberty has been promoted. Liberalism, so viewed, becomes meaningless as a political ideal.

Putting aside the problem of what "liberty" could possibly mean without an ethical commitment, there is also the contention that liberty can be defended by upholding ethical noncognitivism. If no one knows what ought to be done, then no one can claim to know that someone ought to be required to live in a certain way or conduct themselves in a certain manner. This contention is, however, a two-edged sword: if no one knows that P ought to be done, then neither does anyone know that not-P ought *not* to be done. Thus, a defender of liberty could not justifiably claim that people ought *not* be required to live in a certain way or conduct themselves in a certain manner. Further, it is clearly contradictory for liberalism to advocate noncognitivism while seeking to uphold the claim that human beings *ought* to be free from the coercive interference of others. Denying that we can know what ought or ought not be done can hardly be a basis for such a claim. From the premise that no one can say any course of action is really morally better than any other, nothing follows regarding what ought or ought not to be done—including claims about trying to find a middle ground or compromise upon which to base an alleged social contract.[14] This would be the fallacy of *ad ignorantium*. Liberalism has no leg to stand on, if it tries to develop itself from a noncognitivist perspective.

Further, such an extreme position hardly seems necessary. To say that X-ing is morally right or good and ought to be done does not, *in and of itself*, imply that X-ing ought to be legally (coercively) required. Nor does saying that X-ing is morally wrong or bad and ought not to be done, *in and of itself*, imply that X-ing ought to be legally (coercively) prohibited. Something being right or wrong does not, by itself, carry any implications about what should be a concern of the political/legal order. Thus, it is not necessary for political liberalism to embrace noncognitivism in order to defend the primacy of liberty.

However, once it is admitted that liberalism must locate itself in the cognitivist metaethical camp to be meaningful or to have any chance of plausibility, communitarianism is ready with a most perceptive question: What is the justification for liberalism's strong distinction between the moral and the legal, the ethical and the political? Communitarians, together with many classical political theorists, simply deny that there is any fundamental difference between the principles used for ethics and those used for the political/legal order. For them, politics is simply a branch of ethics. Ultimately, political and legal principles are ethical principles, and both require a conception of the human good in order to operate. There is no reason why ethical principles concerned with establishing and evaluating political/legal orders should be different from ethical principles that give individuals guidance in achieving the good and doing right. In other words, there is no reason to assume that there is an ethical language—"rights-talk"—that is peculiar to discussing the political order and another ethical language appropriate for the nonpolitical order.

It can, of course, be replied that liberalism need not ground itself in a theory of the human good, but can instead base itself in an impersonal theory of right or duty. Yet we have already seen many of the problems that impersonal moral theory faces; and though we do not want merely to assume that there cannot be ways of basing the right to liberty in such a theory that somehow avoids these problems, there is still a fundamental problem anyone who uses impersonal moral theory must face. This problem can be summarized as follows:

> There seems to be nothing that can be said to those who ask why they ought to be moral in an impersonal sense. There is a perfectly ordinary, agent-relative sense of "ought" that can be employed in asking this question. Thus, using "ought" does not require the adoption of an agent-neutral view of values, reasons, and rankings, and as long as one is not asking for an agent-neutral reason, there is no self-contradiction in asking why one "ought" to adopt an impersonal moral theory. Further, there is, by definition, no way that an impersonal moral theory can give a reason that is not an agent-neutral reason. Thus, it cannot provide an agent-relative reason why one should be moral in an impersonal sense. Any rights theory based on such an impersonal view of morality can provide neither reason nor motivation for human conduct.

This is a major problem that must be addressed by anyone who bases the right to liberty on impersonal moral theory. So, if only for the sake of the argument, let us assume that the objections made against impersonal moral theory cannot be overcome and that morality or ethics—including any justification of the basic right to liberty—must ultimately be grounded in the human good.

If liberalism is to show that the law should be neutral toward varying conceptions of the good life—neither favoring nor disfavoring one conception over the other, but instead confining itself to maintaining peace and order (understood in terms of an individual's basic right to liberty)—it must make an ethical commitment; and this commitment must be based on an understanding of the human good. This situation, communitarianism contends, is an impossible one. Liberalism cannot base itself on the human good and yet argue that people have a right to conduct themselves in ways that do not achieve or promote this good. Is there not, then, a fundamental incoherence in liberalism?

Not really. There is available to liberalism a view of the human good that, in many respects, has already been presented. This view holds that the ultimate moral good for persons is their self-perfection, or flourishing. Self-perfection, or flourishing, is: (a) objective, (b) inclusive, (c) individualized, (d) agent-relative, (e) achieved with and among others, and (f) self-directed. This view can be used not only to justify the distinction between the ethical/moral and political/legal orders, but also to provide an answer to what we have called liberalism's basic problem—namely, finding a standard that can be used to create, interpret, and evaluate a political/legal context that will, *in principle*, not require the sacrifice of the human flourishing of *any* person or group to that of others.

Since human flourishing is individualized and agent-relative, practical reason must be employed in achieving the good and doing right. Practical reason is used to achieve, maintain, enjoy, and coherently integrate all the goods and virtues that constitute human flourishing. Such goods as, for example, health, friendship, and knowledge, and such virtues as, for example, integrity, courage, and justice, are essential features of human flourishing, not mere means. Yet each is only one of the features. Each, like all the other necessary features of human flourishing, must be achieved, maintained, and enjoyed in a manner that allows it to be coherently integrated with everything else that makes up human flourishing. No feature can be so heavily weighted that it requires eliminating any other necessary feature of human flourishing. This does not mean, however, that there is some specific weighting that can appropriately be imposed on all human beings merely by virtue of an abstract analysis of human flourishing. A priori universal rules that dictate the proper weighting of the goods and virtues of human flourishing are not possible. A proper weighting is only achieved by persons using practical reason at the time of action to discover the proper balance *for themselves*. They accomplish this determination in light of all the unique facts that pertain to them and through a consideration of the contingent circumstances in which they exist. The entire process of moral living is highly individualized and agent-relative.

Furthermore, the same process is also appropriate for determining how to deal with others. The more central the role a person plays in one's self-perfection, the more greatly valued that person will be. Nor does such valuing depend on some narrow interpretation of the "self." Persons who play a more central role in the activities, institutions, and relationships that help to define who one is are more highly regarded than those who do not. There is not an equal weighting or valuing of all persons.

This agent-relative view of the value of human relationships does not mean, however, that there is no role for an ideal perspective that applies to any and every human being. The particular social and cultural forms in which one's sociality is currently manifested do not necessarily exhaust the forms that can and should be taken. One's interpersonal relationships are not limited to only those with whom one shares values. They are open-ended. This feature of the interpersonal dimension of human flourishing allows for an openness to strangers and human beings in general. Thus, there is a need for a perspective that is concerned with what is required for possible relationships among human beings, regardless of their diverse forms of flourishing, to be ethically compossible. Measures need to be taken so that relationships can be ethically possible between persons with whom there are not, as yet, shared values. Otherwise, one's natural sociality is unnecessarily limited. In other words, a standard or principle is needed for establishing, interpreting, and evaluating a context or framework in which human beings in general (not merely those of some specific group, community, or culture) can go about that task of self-perfection. This context or framework is normally understood as a political/legal order.

However, since self-perfection is both individualized and agent-relative, one cannot establish an ethical basis for a political/legal context on some abstract understanding of human flourishing. That basis must be something that is common and peculiar to every act of self-perfection and something in which each and every person has a necessary stake. Otherwise, the pluralistic dimension of human flourishing will not be given its due, and liberalism's problem will not be solved.

It is time to consider the remaining feature of a contemporary version of self-perfectionist virtue ethics—namely, (f), the self-directed nature of human flourishing—and see how it fits into the solution of liberalism's problem. Human flourishing or self-perfection is not only an actuality, it is an activity. It is an activity according to virtue, and the central virtue of human flourishing is practical reason. Yet practical reason is not passive. It is fundamentally, at its very core, a self-directed activity. The functioning of one's reason or intelligence, regardless of one's level of learning or degree of ability, is not something that occurs automatically. It requires individual effort.

Self-direction is both central and necessary to the very nature of human flourishing. It is the only feature of human flourishing that is common to all acts of self-perfection and peculiar to each;[15] it is, thus, the one and only feature of human flourishing that everyone needs to have protected in the concrete case, if they are to have any possibility of flourishing. Self-directedness is the key to solving liberalism's problem. It is not amoral.[16] Its protection is something that, in principle, everyone can fulfill. Further, since it is not only common to, but required by, all forms of human flourishing (or their pursuit), regardless of the level of achievement or specificity, it can be used to create a political/legal order that will not require that the flourishing of any person or group be sacrificed to any other.

We should, however, make sure that we understand how we have come to this conclusion. Let us recall that to solve liberalism's problem, we need something consistent with each and all of the following requirements: interpersonal life in the open-ended sense; the moral propriety of pluralism; neutrality with respect to the various forms of human flourishing; being common to all acts of self-perfection and peculiar to each; and thus, regardless of circumstances, being something in which each and every person has a necessary stake. It must be something that expresses the fundamental core of human flourishing. Self-direction is the only feature of human flourishing that meets these requirements.

Yet, self-direction cannot exist when some people use others without their consent; and since the initiation of physical force is the single most common and threatening encroachment upon self-directedness, the aim of the right to liberty is to legally ban such activity in all its forms. By protecting the possibility of self-directedness, the right to liberty serves human flourishing, not in the sense of directly and positively promoting it, but rather by preventing encroachments upon the condition under which self-perfection can exist. The aim of the right to liberty is to secure the possibility of human flourishing, but in a very specific way: through seeking to protect the possibility of self-directedness. In this way, the right to liberty is justified by an appeal to the nature of human flourishing, and a libertarian solution to liberalism's problem is provided.

According to the self-perfectionist virtue ethics to which we have been appealing, all ethical principles are based on the human good, but they are not all reducible to the same type or function. Thus, it is possible for there to be a difference between ethical principles that provide guidance to people in achieving the good and doing right—let us call them "normative" principles—and ethical principles that are used to create, interpret, and evaluate a political/legal order or context in which people try to achieve good and do right—let us call them "metanormative" principles. We see, then, that the right to liberty is a metanormative principle, and we may now offer our reply to communitarianism's charge that liberalism's legal neutrality is incoherent if founded on an ethical commitment.

It is not incoherent for libertarian liberalism to base the right to liberty on the human good, because the view of the human good it employs requires that there be metanormative principles; and since the right to liberty is a metanormative principle, it need not and should not be concerned with whether people achieve good or conduct themselves rightly. Thus, there is nothing contradictory about a liberal political/legal system permitting people to act in ways that are not self-perfecting. Further, at the metanormative level, the legal system of a liberal political regime does not permit conduct that uses people for purposes to which they have not consented.[17] The right to liberty is the ultimate ethical principle at this level, and one does not have the right to violate this right. Such disrespect for the ultimate moral worth of individual human beings is not tolerated. The right to liberty is what makes liberalism in its libertarian form a meaningful political ideal.

5. Primacy of Rights

Communitarianism has two complaints about liberalism's advocacy of the primacy of rights. The first complaint is philosophical, and the second is cultural and sociological. The philosophical complaint has three aspects. First, rights are dependent on deeper ethical concepts and thus are not ethically primary. Second, to adequately handle the complexities of moral life, finer conceptual tools than rights are required. Rights have too much of an all-or-nothing character to be of very much use in dealing with moral subtleties and are thus not sufficiently precise. Third, a political regime based on the right to liberty is actually inimical to the self-perfection of most people. A regime that enforces the right to liberty destroys the various traditional forms of community life in which people's pursuit of their good is embodied.

The cultural/sociological complaint holds that liberalism and liberal regimes cannot make rights ultimate or primary and maintain themselves for long. The very things that have made liberal civilization possible—the intellectual, cultural, scientific, and moral prerequisites—cannot be maintained if the regime's ultimate moral message is simply liberty. More is necessary. Indeed, there are already signs of the demise of liberalism and its regimes. The current inflation of rights claims—that is, the tendency to think that everything one needs, or even wants, somehow creates a right—is cutting great swaths through conventional forms of life and impoverishing the taxpayer. Further, even if one sharply distinguishes negative from positive rights, it still seems that the liberal society, especially today's United

States, is losing the traditions and institutions that ultimately keep societies alive and functioning. Rights-talk has so invaded our ethical discourse and lives that we seem to think of lawyers whenever there is a conflict. Morals, manners, and other civilities that cannot be captured in such talk seem to have no role to play.

Given the character of the argument that has been advanced in this essay for defending a version of libertarian liberalism, it should not be surprising to learn that there is sympathy for some of these complaints. They contain, however, both a fundamental confusion regarding rights, as well as an overstatement of the role of social traditions in discovering and achieving the good. There is also an even deeper issue of how one understands human nature, which cannot be adequately dealt with in this essay but nonetheless will be commented on. We will begin by explaining how the concept of the basic right to liberty functions in the version of libertarian liberalism defended throughout this essay.

As should be clear by now, rights are metanormative principles. Their function is not to provide guidance in achieving the good or in conducting oneself properly, but rather to provide a means for establishing, interpreting, and evaluating a political/legal context. As such, rights do not aim directly and positively to secure self-perfection or human flourishing. Instead, their aim is to secure the possibility of self-perfection, and this is to be done only in a very limited way—specifically, by protecting the possibility of self-directedness. It must be remembered that rights are libertarianism's answer to liberalism's problem of how to find a standard that will allow interpersonal life in its widest sense to be possible, without at the same time requiring the sacrifice of the lives, time, and resources of any persons or groups to others.

Since sociality is not an option but a requirement for moral maturation, seeking a life of isolation, where one's self-direction could never be threatened by others, is not morally viable. Thus, it should be clear that the right to liberty is necessary to the possibility of self-perfection. However, it should also be clear that such a right deals with but one of the problems that human beings face in trying to find moral fulfillment—a crucial problem, one that is impossible to ignore, but still only one of the problems we face. Therefore, it should not be surprising to note that other moral concepts are needed to guide one toward human flourishing, and that the right to liberty provides little assistance in the task of directly and positively securing self-perfection. As noted before, even though all moral principles are based on human flourishing, this does not mean that they are reducible to the same logical type.

Communitarianism's philosophical complaint about liberalism's advocacy of the primacy of rights fails to consider that rights need to be the ultimate ethical concept only in regard to creating, interpreting, and evaluating political/legal contexts in which normative activities occur. As metanormative principles, rights do not provide people normative guidance in the conduct of their daily lives. They are not normative principles. They cannot replace the virtues, including interpersonal ones like charity and justice;[18] nor can rights replace the role of manners and etiquette in social life. Rights cannot replace all the other necessary moral activities that are needed to make human living more than mere survival. Liberalism has, however, not always been clear on the role or function of rights, so this complaint by communitarianism is not without some justification. Yet, once the metanormative character of rights is appreciated, the first two aspects of this complaint lose their force.

The third aspect of communitarianism's philosophical complaint is very serious. Its basic thrust is that the liberal regime, by enforcing the basic right to liberty, destroys traditional forms of community life that embody people's efforts to pursue their flourishing. A liberal regime acts as a detriment to the lives of people by allowing their basic institutions to be destroyed. Is this true? There is a difference, of course, between what a liberal regime allows and what it encourages or discourages. It is most certainly true that a liberal regime, by enforcing the right to liberty, allows people to decide for themselves whether they want to continue following traditional forms of community life or try other new forms. It does not, however, seek either to discourage traditional forms of community life or encourage new forms. Therefore, it is hard to see how a liberal regime, of the kind we have been defending throughout this essay, could be sensibly accused of destroying traditional forms of community life.

It might be argued, however, that, by allowing people to decide for themselves what forms of community life to pursue, the liberal regime in effect discredits the traditional forms of community life because it permits alternative forms to compete with them. Two points should be made here. (1) Allowing alternative forms of community life to compete with more traditional forms does not in and of itself mean or imply that the alternative forms of community life are as good for persons as the more traditional ones. To protect people's liberty to choose what form of community life they will adopt does not mean that any choice they make is as good as the next. Thus, it is not justifiable to claim that a liberal regime discredits traditional forms of community life. It is only by confusing a metanormative principle with a normative principle that such a claim could be plausibly made. (2) The need for community life is not something abstract or impersonal. It is, like all the other goods that make up human flourishing, an individualized and agent-relative good. Thus, it is not possible to know from our armchair whether a traditional form of community life is better for a person than an alternative one. Wisdom might suggest that one should only with great care and consideration reject a traditional form of community life for some alternative, but it is certainly possible that such a rejection could be morally appropriate for a person. If one's aim is for individuals to find community life that truly supports them in creating and fashioning worthwhile lives for themselves, it is important that they be allowed to use their practical reason, as best they can, in deciding what form of community life to adopt.

The communitarian might reply, however, that these two responses assume that people can make judgments about what form of community life is best for them from a perspective that does not consider the crucial role played by their community's traditions and practices in their very understanding of who they are and what their lives are *for*. This is never the case. People's understanding of what is best for them is always learned through and embodied in the customs, traditions, culture, and history of their community. Human moral judgments do not function autonomously apart from the traditions and social structures in which human beings live. Thus, there is no way that people can try to distance themselves from their influence. There simply is no abstract understanding of what is good for human beings over and above what is embodied in human communities. By allowing people the liberty to question the very workings of their community, the liberal regime destroys the only basis people have for discovering and achieving their good.

This reply deserves a long answer, but that is not possible within the confines of this essay.[19] The short reply is simply that, in order to evaluate how well a person's community promotes one's human flourishing, it is not necessary to deny that people's understanding of who they are, what their lives are *for*, and thus what is good for them is influenced greatly by their community's traditions and practices. To admit this, however, does not rule out the possibility that some aspects of what one has learned are false and that one can determine what they are. Though highly unlikely, it is even possible that one's community may have gotten things entirely wrong. The status quo can be judged.

Furthermore, one can have an abstract understanding of human flourishing that is not contentless. As we have noted many times, the virtues and goods that constitute human flourishing exist only in an individualized manner; nonetheless, it is true that we can, through abstraction, apprehend the constituents of human flourishing just as such. We can talk of the virtues and "generic" goods of human flourishing and thus have knowledge that, though it may be incomplete and reflect cultural influences, is sufficient for us to ask questions about and indeed evaluate what we have learned from our community. Indeed, such analysis of human flourishing can even provide insight for the solution to liberalism's problem. Though human flourishing must always be embodied in some form of community life, it is not necessarily limited to the ones with which a person is acquainted. Nor is human flourishing defined by merely the customs and practices of one's community. Communitarianism comes dangerously close to assuming that the customary morality of a particular society, *Sittlichkeit*, and impersonal moral theory, *Moralität*, exhaust all the possible conceptions of morality.[20] Yet we have seen in this essay an outline of a self-perfectionist virtue ethics that is neither. A virtue ethics is not simply customary morality.[21]

It seems, however, that we are returning to the issue of reductionism discussed in section 1: Does human sociality exhaustively account for, at the most basic level, what it is to be human? Though we are certainly not Cartesian egos or Kantian noumenal selves that operate in isolation apart from natural and social reality, are we to assume that who and what we are is something entirely and solely determined by our social relations? Is our capacity to reason, engage in abstract considerations of the nature of things, make moral judgments, and conduct ourselves accordingly something that is entirely and solely determined by the traditions and practices of our community? Or are there not features of who and what each of us is that exist and are what they are whether the traditions and practices of our community recognize them or not? It seems that the feature of natural-rights classical liberalism that communitarianism might be taking ultimate issue with is its *naturalism*.

We cannot take up a discussion of ontological and epistemological issues here. But if naturalism is rejected, if the nature of anything is totally explained by the traditions and practices of one's community, we cannot help but ask: How can communitarianism complain that the notion of "community" in liberal societies, infused with Enlightenment values, is somehow inadequate? To what can the communitarian appeal? Internal justification will not suffice, because people will adhere to these values despite inconsistencies, and they might ask why they should value consistency over their community's traditions and practices.[22]

It might, however, still be replied that this really misses the point that communitarianism is making. Granted that the liberal regime does not require the destruction of traditional forms of community life, is not this what generally happens in a liberal regime? What is life in a liberal regime actually like? In the real world, are not people in general so dominated by liberalism's emphasis on liberty that the institutions through which they endeavor to discover and achieve their moral well-being are destroyed? These questions cannot be answered here, for they involve more than philosophical considerations. Historical, cultural, and sociological studies are needed. Yet, if this is the level of inquiry at which communitarianism's concerns about liberalism are to be discussed, then there are questions that need to be asked about communitarian social orders: Assuming that we can get a clear understanding of what is meant by "community," what is real life in such social orders generally like? Are they for the most part blissful orders where everyone works in solidarity for a single common end, or do they tend to destroy all chances people have to flourish in their unique and diverse ways? How is the individualized and agent-relative character of human flourishing handled? Are some persons always and necessarily sacrificed for the common good of the community? In what manner, if any, is the open-ended character of human sociality allowed to exist? Can people choose to adopt a way of life with others that conflicts with the values of the community? How are conflicts between different forms of community life met? Are there different forms? It is, to say the least, not obvious that the real, everyday lives of most people in a communitarian political order are better than those in a liberal one.

These questions lead us to a further question: Is not the United States an example of a liberal order where diverse forms of community life, each with distinct traditions, have flourished? The answer seems to be "yes." Yet this answer may be premature, for we do not know how long such forms of community life will continue. Again, this question cannot be answered by philosophy alone, but it does bring us to communitarianism's cultural/sociological complaint—namely, that liberal regimes cannot make rights ultimate or primary and maintain themselves for long. This complaint has merit. A liberal regime cannot long maintain itself, if the only ethical message found in the society and culture that it protects is simply the right to liberty.

Indeed, many things need to be done to maintain a liberal regime, but first, liberalism needs to be clear about the function of the political/legal order. In the version of libertarian liberalism that we have been defending, this function has been made clear; but this has not generally been the case. Insofar as liberal theorists have not clearly recognized the difference between normative and metanormative principles, and insofar as they have thought that liberalism's political principles could be maintained without a deeper ethical commitment, theorists of liberalism have helped to create the very forces that are leading to its demise. Furthermore, the tendency in American liberalism to make a right out of every need (sometimes even a want) has made the concept of rights nearly otiose. Instead of rights being confined to basic issues about the nature of a political/legal order, they have been used to replace crucial moral concepts, like the virtues, which are primarily concerned with people achieving worthwhile moral lives. This has confused and damaged both forms of ethical language. In fact, to some people, it appears that the right to liberty is nothing more than a license to do whatever one wants, and that to call something a moral virtue is to demand a law compelling universal compliance with it. The ethical language of liberalism in the United States has been virtually deconstructed!

The solution to this problem is, however, not to deny the importance of rights-talk as something distinct from other ethical language. Rather, it is to clearly understand the rationale for liberal political institutions' being concerned only with the right to liberty. It has been the aim of this essay to provide such a rationale and thus defend liberalism in its libertarian form, and we need not reprise this argument here. It should be recalled, however, that the point of that rationale was to show that the very sociality of human flourishing, together with its individualized and agent-relative character, creates a profound need for a special kind of ethical language. When it comes to creating, interpreting, and evaluating political/legal orders, an ethical language is needed, not for the purpose of providing guidance to people in finding moral fulfillment, but rather for the purpose of providing a context in which all the diverse forms of human flourishing may exist together in an ethically compossible manner. The ethical language for this task is the language of metanormativity, as opposed to normativity. The natural right to liberty is the basic metanormative principle. Thus, there is an ethical justification for the liberal regime *qua political institution* to not extend its ethical message beyond respect for the basic right to liberty. It is morally necessary that there be a political theory that argues that not everything is or should be political, and this limitation on political action even applies to many of the activities that are socially and culturally necessary for the maintenance of liberal regimes.

It is precisely because there is a moral need for a division of ethical language that the liberal regime must do all that is necessary at the metanormative level to allow for the consistent and just implementation of a political/legal system based on the right to liberty. It should not allow the limitation imposed by its rationale to become so blurred that people believe the task of the political/legal system to be the direct and positive promotion of human flourishing. This matter must be understood to lie in the hands and minds of each person. By the liberal regime's remaining true to its proper function, the political/legal order will be seen as limited, and its ethical rationale will be more clearly discerned by the people. Both the importance of the right to liberty and its limitation will be more readily grasped. It will not be assumed that rights exhaust ethical language, and it will more likely be understood that there are other ethically important concerns. Specifically, it will be understood that the citizens are positively and directly responsible for the actual creation of social and cultural life conducive to the existence of a liberal regime and a morally decent society as well.

Many things need to be done. People need to care about the moral life, the role of virtue, and the importance of personal responsibility. They need to care about the ethical justifications of their social and political institutions. They need to better understand the nature of the arguments that can be used to defend the liberal regime. Further, they need to create institutions and traditions that explain and illustrate the importance of a political/legal system's being based on the right to liberty. These are very important matters.

The role of intellectuals here is not insignificant. They need to understand the difference between normative and metanormative principles. They need to appreciate how moral values can be both objective and yet highly personal and not universalizable. They need to understand the proper use of role models in ethical education. In general, intellectuals should be concerned with discovering theoretical and moral truths, exploring difficulties, and solving problems. Many of the items that communitarianism takes as evidence of the coming demise of liberalism and liberal regimes are themselves the result of various forms of ethical noncognitivism's taking root in our culture (to which it is hoped communitarianism is not contributing), and it is without a doubt impossible for a liberal regime to maintain itself in such a culture. Taking on the challenge of ethical noncognitivism and the nihilism it generates is a task that intellectuals need to undertake.

There is much to be done in maintaining liberalism and a liberal regime, but this is, in principle, no different from saying that there is much that persons need to achieve, maintain, enjoy, and coherently integrate if they are to self-perfect or flourish. Though it is a difficult task, this should not be news to anyone. That political liberalism and community life are not necessarily opposed is, however, news—news that needs to be spread. Indeed, political liberalism of the kind that has been defended in this essay is the result of a deep appreciation of our natural sociality as well as our individuality.[23]

Notes

1. Apologies are in order for the use of the term "communitarianism" in this essay; for it is not very well-defined. It is, however, a term that is developing greater

currency in ethical and political thought. See the following works: Markate Daly, ed., *Communitarianism: A New Public Ethics* (Belmont, California: Wadsworth Publishing Co., 1994); Stephen Mulhall and Adam Swift, eds., *Liberals & Communitarians* (Oxford: Blackwell, 1992); C.F. Delaney, ed., *The Liberalism-Communitarian Debate* (Lanham, Maryland: Rowman & Littlefield, 1994); Shlomo Avineri and Avner de-Shalit, eds., *Communitarianism and Individualism* (Oxford: Oxford University Press, 1992); Daniel Bell, *Communitarianism And Its Critics* (Oxford: Clarendon Press, 1993); and Amitai Etzioni, *The Spirit of Community* (New York: Crown Publishers, 1991); idem, ed., *Rights and the Common Good: The Communitarian Perspective* (New York: St. Martin's Press, 1995).

Much of the inspiration for the understanding of communitarianism that is found in this essay comes from the books listed above and from recent works of the following persons: Charles Taylor, *Sources of the Self* (Cambridge, Massachusetts: Harvard University Press, 1989); idem, *Philosophy And The Human Sciences: Philosophical Papers* 2 (Cambridge: Cambridge University Press, 1985); idem, *The Ethics of Authenticity* (Cambridge, Massachusetts: Harvard University Press, 1991); Alasdair MacIntyre, *After Virtue*, 2nd ed. (Notre Dame, Indiana: Notre Dame University Press, 1984); idem, *Whose Justice? Which Rationality?* (Notre Dame, Indiana: Notre Dame University Press, 1988); idem, *Three Rival Versions Of Moral Enquiry* (Notre Dame, Indiana: Notre Dame University Press, 1990); Michael J. Sandell, *Liberalism and the Limits of Justice* (Cambridge: Cambridge University Press, 1982); idem, (ed.) *Liberalism and its Critics* (Oxford: Blackwell, 1984); and Michael Walzer, *Spheres of Justice* (New York: Basic Books, 1983). It should be noted that not all of these authors consider their philosophy to be "communitarian," even though their philosophy is described as such by the works in the previous paragraph. Finally, mention should be made of Steven Lukes' helpful book, *Individualism* (Oxford: Basil Blackwell, 1973).

2. For a defense of liberalism more broadly construed, see Amy Guttman, "Communitarian Critics of Liberalism," *Philosophy & Public Affairs* 14 (1985): 308–322; and Jeffrey Paul and Fred D. Miller Jr., "Communitarian and Liberal Theories of the Good," *The Review of Metaphysics* 43 (June 1990): 803–830.

3. See Douglas B. Rasmussen and Douglas J. Den Uyl, *Liberty and Nature: An Aristotelian Defense of Liberal Order* (LaSalle, Illinois: Open Court, 1991).

4. See Douglas J. Den Uyl and Douglas B. Rasmussen, "Rights as MetaNormative Principles," in this volume.

5. See *Liberty and Nature*, 191–206 for a discussion of how social contract theory may be used in a limited and procedural way.

6. There are important issues regarding the nature of the relationship between human reason and language that cannot be handled here; but see Douglas B. Rasmussen, "Wittgenstein and the Search for Meanings," *Semiotics 1982*, ed. John Deely and Jonathan Evans (Lanham, Maryland: University Press of America, 1987), 577–590; and idem., "Rorty, Wittgenstein, and the Nature of Intentionality," *Proceedings of the American Catholic Philosophical Association* 57 (1983): 152–162.

7. In *After Virtue*, MacIntyre argued for social teleology and dismissed the possi-

bility of a naturalistic basis for a *telos*. In a more recent work, "Plain Persons and Moral Philosophy: Rules, Virtues and Goods," *American Catholic Philosophical Quarterly* 66 (Winter 1992): 3–19, MacIntyre seems to suggest that a theistically grounded account of teleology is the best hope. Yet for a discussion of how teleology might be naturalistically grounded in a scientifically respectable way, see *Liberty and Nature*, 41–46, as well as section 2, "Natural Teleology," of the concluding chapter in Fred D. Miller Jr., *Nature, Justice, and Rights in Aristotle's* Politics (Oxford: Clarendon Press, 1995).

   8. If one insists on holding that a self-perfectionist ethics of the type described here is, nonetheless, an ethical egoism, then it must be modified with the words "classical" or "Aristotelian." Tibor R. Machan and Henry B. Veatch, respectively, have used these terms in describing their own form of ethical egoism. Yet it does not seem that much is gained by using the term "ethical egoism."

   9. Douglas J. Den Uyl, *The Virtue of Prudence* (New York: Peter Lang, 1991), 27.

   10. Henry B. Veatch, "Ethical Egoism New Style: Should Its Trademark Be Aristotelian or Libertarian?" *Swimming Against the Current in Contemporary Philosophy* (Washington, DC: The Catholic University of America Press, 1990), 194.

   11. See *The Virtue of Prudence*, 213–223.

   12. *The Virtue of Prudence*, 223.

   13. See Tibor R. Machan, *Capitalism and Individualism* (New York: St. Martin's Press, 1990) for a discussion of some of the other ways to defend liberalism in its libertarian form.

   14. It might be argued that one can infer a procedural, not a substantive, "ought" from this ignorance—that is, that we should adopt a noninterference mode, because we have no basis or reason to do anything. Yet it can still be replied that we have no basis or reason to practice forbearance—that is, to *not* interfere. Further, no basis or reason can be given why one should accept the goal of a procedural "ought;" and if the procedural "ought" has no goal, then the distinction between procedural and substantive "oughts" we began with seems to have vanished.

   15. Formally self-direction is common to all acts of self-perfection, while its mode and means of expression is peculiar to each because each act of self-direction is unique at least in terms of its context. Moreover, each act of self-direction is manifested in an act of practical reason that seeks to achieve the unique reality, unity, and determinacy that is some individual's human flourishing.

   16. Simply stated, one needs to think. It is good to think; one ought to think. Before ever addressing questions about what one should think about, or how one should conduct oneself, it is the case that one should think and act for oneself—that is, be self-directed.

   17. The basic right to liberty is a "negative" right, not a "positive" one. For a discussion of this distinction and other important qualifications, see *Liberty and Nature*, 78–87.

   18. See the discussion of the normative and metanormative senses of justice in "Rights as MetaNormative Principles" as well as Douglas J. Den Uyl's essay, "The Right to Welfare and the Virtue of Charity" in this volume.

19. See T.H. Irwin, "Tradition and Reason in the History of Ethics," *Social Philosophy & Policy* 7 (Autumn 1989): 45–68. This is a careful examination of MacIntyre's *Whose Justice? Whose Rationality?*

20. See Alasdair MacIntyre, "Is Patriotism a Virtue?" in Daly, ed., *Communitarianism*, 307–318.

21. See Fred D. Miller, Jr., *Nature, Justice, and Rights in Aristotle's* Politics. Miller shows Aristotle's self-perfectionist virtue ethics not to be confined to mere community standards and that his politics is open to natural rights.

22. *Liberty and Nature*, 101.

23. This essay has benefited from the assistance of Douglas J. Den Uyl and Roger Bissell.

Liberalism and Libertarianism: Narrowing the Gap

Daniel Shapiro

At first glance, contemporary liberalism and libertarianism appear to have significantly different political implications. The former denies that there are any basic[1] rights to free exchange or robust private property rights[2]; the latter affirms it. The former maintains that the government is obligated to reduce or minimize certain social and economic inequalities; the latter denies it. This paper aims to narrow the gap between these political philosophies. My strategy is two-fold. First, I shall show that arguments that contemporary philosophical liberals[3] typically use to justify basic rights in the *noncommercial* realm—e.g., rights to freedom of speech, freedom of religion, privacy, etc.—support at least some basic rights in the *commercial* realm, that is, the realm of widespread exchange. Second, I shall show that liberal support for redistributive policies is compatible with the recognition of basic rights to free exchange. If my arguments succeed, then the gap between liberalism and libertarianism is *narrowed* in that they should agree that there are basic rights to free exchange. The gap is not, however, *bridged*: libertarianism rejects any governmental obligation to assist the disadvantaged. However, narrowing the gap is of some significance, for I suspect that one thing that contributes to a sense among many contemporary liberals that libertarianism is an unacceptable political philosophy is the view that libertarianism has *radically* different political implications than liberalism. This paper, I hope, will help to modify that view.

1. Respect for Persons, Diversity, and Basic Rights

In this section, I show how liberal arguments for basic rights apply to the commercial realm. In the following two sections, I derive two specific rights to free exchange.

Liberal arguments for basic rights are rooted in a notion of respect or concern for persons. Liberals understand this idea and connect it to arguments for basic rights in three different (and overlapping) ways. First, respect for persons involves allowing them the freedom to develop and exercise those capacities that are considered essential or important to being a person. Rawls, for example, justifies basic rights by arguing that they are necessary for the development and exercise of a person's capacity for a conception of the good (the capacity to form, revise, and act on beliefs about what ends are valuable and important), and a sense of justice (the capacity to apply, understand, and be motivated by principles of fair cooperation), which Rawls believes are the most important capacities of a person, as far as political philosophy is concerned.[4]

Another liberal view is that to show respect or concern for a person is, in part, to show respect or concern for that person's *good*.[5] Liberals think that the freedom and protection from coercive interference provided by individual rights is instrumental to and/or constitutive of a good life. It is instrumental because the successful achievement of most plans and projects requires the freedom to act in accordance with one's choices, and even if one's life-plan *at present* doesn't require this freedom, a rational person at some point needs to evaluate and possibly revise his conception of the good, and thus needs this freedom in order to discover or construct a life that is best for himself.[6] Such freedom is constitutive of one's good if a central aspect of a person's good is autonomy.[7]

A third liberal interpretation is that respect for persons is demonstrated by appealing to citizens' capacity for reason as well as their sense of fairness in order to decide or discover which principles of justice are legitimate.[8] We do this by determining what principles of justice rational persons who are aiming to find principles of fair social cooperation would or do unanimously consent to or find justifiable. Principles of individual rights would unanimously be agreed to or be found justifiable by such persons, since for the reasons just mentioned, the freedom provided by such rights is a means to and/or part of their good.

The respect-for-persons theme justifies standard basic rights in the noncommercial realm, such as freedom of speech, freedom of religion, and privacy, on the grounds that communication, religion, and private and intimate relationships are areas of choice that are central and/or necessary for projects and plans of life. Thus these areas of choice are means to and/or part of everyone's good (the second interpretation of the respect theme). Accordingly, each rational person would want protection for such choices (the third interpretation), and they would likely be involved in the exercise of one's capacity for a conception of the good (the first interpretation.)

Another liberal justification for basic rights stresses that individual rights provide the social conditions under which diverse and even incompatible conceptions of the good can peacefully coexist. One liberal justification of individual rights in terms of this idea of diversity is that if there are many alternative views of the good, then there will be a wide variety of organizations and associations, and being able to participate in organizations with people of complementary interests and values enables one to achieve a more comprehensive good than would otherwise be the case. A different liberal line of argument takes a brute fact of modernity to be the existence of divergent conceptions of the good—a "fact of pluralism"—and argues that given this, the only fair basis for social cooperation is to allow these conceptions to flourish (within the limits of justice.)[9]

Since the respect-for-persons and diversity themes support basic rights because they protect certain areas of choice that are central and/or necessary for a wide variety of projects and plans of life, the argument clearly has application beyond the noncommercial realm. One's choices as a seller or buyer are means to and/or constitute one's good as much as do one's noncommercial activities. Consumer choices, occupational decisions, the tradeoff between work and leisure, investment and entrepreneurial decisions, time-preference, etc., all clearly constitute and reflect a wide variety of conceptions of the good as much as do decisions about communication, religion, etc. Thus, liberalism supports basic rights in the commercial realm or the realm of free exchange.

One objection to my argument is that, in the commercial realm, inadequate resources often force one to make significant tradeoffs; thus one cannot achieve what one really wants or is of significant value. Accordingly, commercial choices are not means to and/or part of many people's conception of the good. This objection fails because making tradeoffs is not per se incompatible with pursuit and construction of a good life. Even if one's commercial choices are constrained to the point that one is not in an effective position to choose those options that would best reflect one's view of the good life, so long as there are some choices and different bundles of options, one's view of the good life can play a nontrivial instrumental or constitutive role in the commercial realm. Notice also that tradeoffs are ubiquitous in both the noncommercial and commercial realms, so if the existence of tradeoffs in a certain realm blocks a defense of basic rights on the grounds that the freedom they protect is a means and/or part of one's good, then rights in general cannot be defended this way.[10]

Another likely objection is that choices in the commercial realm only reflect and constitute a conception of the good in a narrow sense. Commercial choices have little to do with a *comprehensive* view of the value and significance of our ends and attachments to various groups or associations; nor do the values we pursue in the commercial realm reflect or constitute a *determinate* scheme of ends that we pursue for their own sake.[11] However, the same could be said about most noncommercial activities. Even religious activities, for many people in modern democratic societies, are not an essential part or necessary means to a comprehensive or determinate conception of the good. Admittedly, the notion of a conception of a good is vague, and it shouldn't include every view about value or preference. But if we broaden the notion so that only the unusually thoughtful have such a conception, then it's doubtful that any basic rights can be justified in terms of the connection between protected choices and the way in which such choices are means to and/or part one's view of the good life.

2. The Right to Exchange at Free Market Prices

I shall now derive the right to exchange at free market prices and in the subsequent section I shall derive the right to free entry, that is, the right to enter any (legitimate)[12] market. I focus on these two specific rights because they are so important to the concept of a free market. Free markets are networks of voluntary exchanges, and so the more that sellers and buyers are prevented from coming to mutually agreed upon terms of exchange, the less free the market. Probably the most important feature of a commercial agreement is the price, and so if the state sets the price of X, we don't have a free market in X. Also central to the notion of a free market is the idea of competition, of buyers and sellers being free to offer different terms of exchange from other participants in the market. Blocking people from entering a market obviously severely disrupts this process.

My derivation of specific rights to free exchange does not include any discussion of the precise scope and weight of these rights. Just as a derivation of a basic right in the noncommercial realm, such as the right to free speech, is not refuted if one can show that in hard cases, such as hate speech or the sale of violent pornography, the right can be restricted or overridden, the same point holds for basic rights in the commercial realm. Thus, I will not discuss here whether there might be special cases under which price controls or state barriers to entry might be justified. I will, of course, discuss objections to my arguments, but they will be objections that go to the heart of the derivation of the right.

My argument for the right to exchange at free-market prices proceeds in two stages. First, I'll argue that interference with free market prices, i.e., state imposed price controls, disrupt people's plans—as they produce shortages and surpluses—by blocking and/or distorting information that is necessary for the successful achievement of those plans. Next, I'll argue that this disruption of plans via blockage and/or distortion of information undermines the values or interests singled out by the respect-for-persons rationale for basic rights.

The first stage of the argument requires noting two facts. First, economic realities constantly change. Changes in consumer preference, changes in technology, changes in factors of production, etc., occur continuously in any sort of even moderately complex economic system. Second, information about these changes is scattered throughout society: different people know and/or believe different (and sometimes inconsistent) bits of it; most people have at best a kind of "specialty" vis-à-vis local, concrete, specific information, and so no one mind or group of minds can be aware of all the changes that are or will be occurring. Now one's success as an employee or employer, producer or consumer, depends on being aware of, alert to, or anticipating how the results of these changes will affect one's plans, and so some kind of system or mechanism is needed that will communicate the results of changes in economic realities to the countless people that need to be aware of them. Prices do this.[13] For example, suppose demand for a certain good has increased or a significant source of its supply has dried up. If some of the people who are aware of and "specialize" in such information act on their awareness of the change in demand and/or supply of that good, then the price will rise, sending a message: "use less." In this way, countless changes in production and consumption will occur throughout the economic system, affecting not only those who use the good, but those who use the substitutes for that good, the substitutes of the substitutes, and the supply of things made from that good. Thus, the price rise will let those who are unaware of the change in demand/and or supply—the vast majority—know what steps to take to adjust their plans to meet the result of the changes in economic realities.

Of course, those who initiate the price rise may be mistaken in their beliefs about changes in various parts of the economic system, and/or they may not anticipate these changes quickly enough so that the "message" can be gotten in a timely fashion to those who need to know. But in free markets, those who have the foresight or luck to recognize that production and/or consumption is proceeding on the basis of false beliefs relative to changes that are or will be occurring tend to make profits and avoid losses (thus giving signals to others to follow suit). In this way, changes in present prices tend to reflect future economic realities.

If, however, the government prevents prices from rising or falling beyond a certain point—which is what price (or wage or rent or interest) controls do—then the communication function of prices has been crippled in two senses. First, prices no longer let those who are unaware of changing economic conditions know that they must alter their plans to adjust to the result of these changes; second, as a result of blocking or not allowing this information, government prices have a significant potential to mislead vis-à-vis these conditions. For example, where a rise in the market price says, in effect, "use less," the fixed government price says, "no need to alter your present use." Since people do not make adjustments in their demand and/or supply relative to the conditions that are or will be changing, price controls produce shortages and surpluses, thus disrupting people's plans.[14]

We can now appreciate why price controls violate basic rights. Blocking and distorting information needed for the successful achievement of plans that merit the protection of a basic right manifests a gross disrespect for the fundamental interest that is central to many liberal arguments for basic rights—namely the interest that persons have in being able to pursue, revise, and evaluate, their plans and projects. One does not *respect* that interest if one fails to take seriously the importance of being able to pursue, revise, and evaluate one's conception of the good. When the government plays an active causal role in blocking and/or distorting an important factor (perhaps the most important) one needs in order to pursue, revise, and evaluate one's plans and projects—reasonably accurate information about the world, and others' intentions and actions—then this shows at the very least the lack of such seriousness.

One objection to my argument is that the basic right to exchange at free-market prices—or any basic right in the commercial realm—cannot be defended without *first* discussing the question of morally legitimate ownership. One does not have the right to exchange a resource unless one is the owner of that resource or has been delegated that right by the owner. Since I haven't provided any arguments concerning the right to the kind of exclusive use and control that ownership typically involves, I haven't shown that price controls violate anyone's basic rights.

This objection would be plausible if my argument purported to establish that a particular person A, as opposed to B or C, had the right to make pricing decisions about a certain resource. But that was *not* my argument. I argued that price controls violated basic rights because they disrupted people's plans via distortion and blockage of information—and this is a violation of the liberal respect for persons injunction, regardless of *who* should have the right to make pricing decisions. Even if some or many people are not morally entitled to use and control the resources that they legally own, price controls violate basic rights, for on liberal grounds, whatever the present distribution of resources, people are entitled to have the government not prevent them from basing their plans on reasonably accurate information. Of course, the information would be somewhat different if the distribution of resources were different; but that doesn't change the point about respect. Thus, when the government prevents A from exchanging X at the price that she and the buyer agree upon, this is a violation of A's (and the buyer's) basic rights—not because A is entitled to use and control X (though she might be), but because anyone who has the legal power to make decisions about exchanging X is denied respect due her as a person by a system that disrupts plans by distorting and blocking reasonably accurate information about changing economic realities.

Another way to put my point is that respect for persons requires a *system* of free-market prices. However, the argument for the system is independent of, and separate from, an argument about who within that system should have the right to make exchange decisions. Thus, my argument for a basic right to exchange at free market prices does not depend upon a prior argument about legitimate ownership.

My reply may generate the objection that the relevant options are not simply a free market system of prices versus a system with some controlled prices. There is also the option of a system with some controlled prices where government policies minimize the gaps between supply and demand caused by the controls, thereby minimizing the disruption of plans (via blocked and distorted information). For example, if rent control creates a shortage of rental housing, the government can subsidize builders to build more housing (either private or government owned) at below market rates. Thus, my argument is really that *either* there is a basic right to exchange at free market prices *or* a right that the state make up for the shortages and surpluses if it imposes price controls.

My response to this objection is three-fold. First, as a matter of fact, the shortages and surpluses produced by price controls are rarely made up by nonmarket means. That is, cities with rent controls have shortages of (nonluxury) rental housing that are not made up by subsidized or government housing.[15] Second, this isn't surprising: without a market price, it's very difficult for government planners or anyone else know how much supply or demand is needed to make up the gap between supply and demand. Third, the nonmarket methods used to make up the gap often reinforce the problem. For example, if a government tries to eliminate the shortfall in supply produced by a maximum price control by subsidizing suppliers and inducing them to provide more of the good, then—since this good will presumably be marketed at a below market price—this will lead people to demand more of it and once again demand can easily outstrip supply, thus maintaining the shortage. This example is an instance of a general problem, which is that prices are a far more reliable method for adjusting supply and demand than are political means such as subsidies.

Admittedly, I haven't shown that the gaps between supply and demand *couldn't* be made up by nonmarket means: it's just that it doesn't occur and it's unlikely it will occur. But that is sufficient in this context. Recall that the objection was that my argument did not establish a basic right to exchange at free-market prices, but rather established *either* (1) that right *or* (2) a right that the government make up for the shortages and surpluses if it imposes price controls. But since (2) entails an obligation that it is unlikely government could fulfill, while it is quite easy for government to fulfill the obligation entailed by (1)—it's easy for the government *not* to impose price controls—then for all practical purposes, the argument establishes (1).

3. The Right to Free Entry

Another systematic interference with free markets that liberals should condemn as basic rights violations are barriers that block the discovery/creation of new opportunities and innovation. Recall that a key liberal justification for basic rights is that they provide people with diverse views of the good life the freedom to pursue and revise their plans and projects, thereby helping them to discover what is really good for them or gives value to their lives. An economic system that is attuned to this freedom is one that provides a wide scope for the discovery/creation of new opportunities and innovation, that is, a *competitive* market system. This is because the best way to stimulate innovation and creativity in the marketplace is to allow consumers/employees to choose among a variety of goods, services, jobs, etc., and producers/employers to experiment with price, quality, quantity, organizational arrangements, techniques of production, etc. A principal way of blocking this competitive process is to erect state barriers to participation in or entry into markets. The state barriers that most clearly block free entry are restrictions on the type of work, occupation, or business one wishes to enter[16], since for most people decisions about what line of work to pursue are a central means and/or part of the process by which they pursue and/or revise their conception of the good. Thus, laws forbidding one to enter a certain business or offer a certain service—laws creating state monopolies—violate the basic right to free entry. Examples from the U.S. and Europe are delivery of first class mail, airlines, the generation of electricity, residential sanitation service, mass transit, local and long distance telephone service, and cable TV.

Licensing laws also clearly violate the right to free entry. These laws sharply restrict entry into certain occupations or businesses by criminalizing the offer of one's services unless one has taken a lengthy and costly state approved program of study. Licensing goes beyond certification, which is a method of indicating that a person has completed certain requirements or studies. Certification of certain professions allows noncertified people to practice in the field and is compatible with the right to free entry. Licensing is a violation of the right to free entry not because of the information-supplying feature it shares with certification, but because it goes beyond certification by making it a crime for nonlicensed practitioners to offer their services.

A likely objection is that state barriers *and* market barriers to entry harm the values or interests that underlie liberal arguments for basic rights. One commonly cited market barrier is structural constraints: some markets may be dominated by a few firms, which makes entry quite difficult for new competitors. A second is endogenous preference-formation: the idea here is that the preferences or plans that people express, pursue, or revise in free markets are largely a product of that market. Endogenous preference-formation seems to imply that it's false that free markets *allow* a wide variety of conceptions of the good to exist, because these markets in large part produce those conceptions (thus, in effect, creating barriers to conceptions of the good that are hostile to markets or capitalism). Structural barriers would seem to justify antitrust laws in order to limit firm size, and the endogenous preference formation would seem to justify restricting the extent to which preferences are shaped by the market, e.g., by restricting some kinds of advertising. Thus, the right to free entry does not simply require eliminating certain restrictions on voluntary exchanges that currently exist, it *also* requires restricting some voluntary exchanges, and so overall the right to free entry is not supportive of free markets in the way I have hitherto implied.

However, it's dubious that either of these alleged barriers can be used as liberal grounds for restricting voluntary exchange. That liberalism wants markets to be quite sensitive to the choices people make in designing their own plans and projects poses a serious problem for the structural barriers complaint. Usually, the best way to promote a variety of market arrangements is to allow people to arrive at mutually agreed upon terms of exchange. Even if structural barriers exist, restricting someone's options doesn't thereby give any excluded party an additional option. Since in a world of constant change and limited information we don't know what alternative structure might better promote someone's projects or plans, liberals should favor eliminating options only as a last resort. Thus, a liberal should favor a system of private property rights that has as much flexibility as possible, and be leery of restricting the right to exchange.

A second problem with the complaint about structural barriers is that the concept of a market structure is an end-state notion, that is, a description of a market at a certain time(s), as opposed to a description of the process by which an end state was achieved. However, liberal arguments for basic rights are not arguments for certain end states: rather, they are arguments that these rights *allow* a wide variety of peaceful conceptions of the good to coexist. Thus, it is improper to infer from the fact that a market arrangement seems to lessen diversity (e.g., a reduction in the number of firms in a given market) that liberals should support state restrictions on the right to transfer. Since success in a free market is due ultimately to success in meeting or anticipating consumer demand, and consumer demand does give important (though not the only) evidence about people's conceptions of the good, the apparent narrowing of options can plausibly be explained as the discovery or creation of products and services that are most compatible with people's plans, projects, and conceptions of the good life.[17]

The complaint about endogenous preference-formation also faces rough going. It's quite difficult to distinguish preferences that are allegedly largely a product of the system from preferences that are a result of learning.[18] In the case of advertising, some liberals have recognized that it is an important vehicle for communicating information to consumers about the price and quality of a product.[19] Perhaps even more important, advertising functions to let consumers know that a product exists or to grab consumers' attention—for in a dynamic market economy with millions of products (many of them new or changing), consumers' attention is likely to be difficult to obtain (which explains and to some extent justifies the nonrational methods that some advertisers use).[20] So to establish any claim that consumers' decisions to buy certain advertised products are due largely to advertiser manipulation, one must explain how one can know that these decisions aren't due to (or aren't also due to) consumers receiving information about products that turn out to further their plans and projects.

Perhaps an even more serious problem is that endogenous preference-formation in free markets is not really a threat to liberal values. Endogenous preference-formation is a feature of virtually all socioeconomic systems, or it's unique to systems where free markets predominate.[21] If it is the former, it is uninteresting; if it is the latter, it provides grounds for celebrating free markets! If a system where free markets predominate is the *only* socioeconomic system where the social and economic institutions in effect convince or persuade people to prefer or endorse the ways of life that flourish in those institutions, then this means that it is the only system that *generates* its own support. Of course, one might argue that these institutions don't convince but coerce or exploit, but in that case the complaint is not endogenous preference formation per se but injustice, which is a different issue.

The problems I have raised for the claim that the right to free entry should focus on state barriers *and* market barriers to entry are not decisive, but they suggest that a focus on the former was not arbitrary. Given the liberal bias against restricting free exchanges, and given that the evidence that purports to show market barriers instead may very well show that the market is competitive and generates its own support, there are good reasons why the right to free entry should not treat state and market barriers equally.

4. Liberal Egalitarianism and Basic Rights to Free Exchange

The arguments so far come to naught if liberal egalitarianism or support for redistributive policies is incompatible with any basic right to free exchange. I shall argue that they are compatible, by focusing on what I think is the best version of liberal egalitarianism, which stems from the work of Ronald Dworkin,[22] and then generalizing the argument.

This version says, roughly, that disadvantages or inequalities should be rectified if they are unchosen—that is, if they are not the product of, for example, voluntarily acquired tastes, ambitions, preferences, plans, or the development of persons' talents.[23] Now market exchanges are constituted by mixtures of unchosen disadvantages (e.g., disadvantages stemming from race, sex, family background, or genetics) and genuine choices. Since liberal egalitarianism calls for some kind of redress for unchosen disadvantages, it seems at least *permissible* to restrict market exchanges because they are partly constituted by such disadvantages. But if there are basic rights to free exchange, then this restriction wouldn't be permissible in cases where restrictions violated these rights.

However, it's not just market exchanges but life itself that is a mixture of unchosen disadvantages and genuine choices. Thus, if the permissibility of correcting for unchosen disadvantages undermines any basic rights to free exchange, it undermines any basic rights that liberals defend. For example, being inarticulate frequently depends upon unchosen circumstances and is usually a disadvantage, when one compares the ways in which the exercise of the right of free speech helps the articulate and the inarticulate achieve their goals. So if the permissibility of correcting for unchosen disadvantages shows that there can't be basic rights to free exchange, then we should conclude the same about basic rights to free speech (or any basic rights in the noncommercial realm).

One might respond that liberal egalitarianism is limited in *scope*: it applies only in the commercial realm or can be used only to restrict or void robust private property rights. The reason for the scope limitation is (1) unchosen disadvantages in the noncommercial realm are more likely to be rectified if one does *not* eliminate or restrict basic rights in that realm, while (2) unchosen disadvantages in the commercial realm are more likely to be rectified if one *does* limit or void robust private property rights. (1) is true because some of the disadvantages in the noncommercial realm are not rectifiable, while others are most easily rectifiable by economic means. For example, some of the disadvantages of the inarticulate are caused by genetic factors or personality traits that may be too deeply ingrained to correct, while others can be rectified without violating rights to free speech by giving the inarticulate greater economic resources so that they can obtain better education or speech lessons. (2) is true because economic inequalities or disadvantages are best addressed by limiting or changing the structure of private property rights.

This reply fails. (1) and (2) justify the refusal to violate basic rights in the noncommercial realm to satisfy the egalitarian requirement and the permissibility of restricting or eliminating *some* rights in the commercial realm to satisfy that requirement. In order for liberal egalitarianism to conflict with any basic right to free exchange, we would need not (2) but (2'): unchosen disadvantages in the commercial realm are more likely to be rectified by limiting or eliminating *any* (or *all*) robust private property rights. The reasons that were given for (2), however, do *not* transfer to (2'): that a certain *type* of inequality or disadvantage—economic—will most successfully be rectified by restricting or voiding a certain *type* of right—robust private property rights—hardly shows that economic disadvantages are rectified by restricting any or all robust private property rights. Furthermore, the arguments for the right to exchange at free-market prices and the right to free entry strongly suggest that (2') is false. Price controls, state monopolies, and licensing laws hardly seem necessary to help the involuntarily disadvantaged—quite the contrary. Restricting someone from making a certain exchange or entering a certain market can easily make the involuntarily disadvantaged even worse off, since it restricts the options of those who have limited options to begin with.

One other consideration might indicate a conflict between liberal egalitarianism and basic rights to free exchange. Though liberal egalitarianism supports some kind of redistributive policies, it is unclear which ones are most defensible. Since this is unclear, and since justice requires that we take serious steps towards minimizing involuntary disadvantages, then we should keep open the possibility of different kinds of redistributive policies. Since basic rights to free exchange will block at least some of these policies, one might question whether liberalism can accommodate such rights, as protection for them will limit experimentation with different redistributive policies.

Clearly, at some point a set of basic rights to free exchange could be so extensive or the protection they provide to private property rights could be so strong that there would be little if any room left for redistributive policies. That is one reason why there must remain a gap between libertarianism, with its very strong private property rights, and liberalism of the sort discussed here. But this point does not throw doubt on the derivation of *some* basic rights to free exchange. Notice also that to the extent that basic rights to free exchange, such as the ones derived in sections 2 and 3, are based on premises that are *well established* within liberalism, they take priority over claims that a particular redistributive policy *might* be the one most consonant with liberal egalitarianism.

I shall now generalize the arguments of this section. There seem to be three ways to set up a conflict between liberal egalitarianism and any basic right to free exchange. First, one could argue that since whatever disadvantages are singled out by liberal egalitarianism exist in the commercial realm, and since liberal egalitarianism makes it at least permissible to correct for those disadvantages, there can't be basic rights to free exchange that would rule out (in some cases) this correction. However, since these disadvantages exist in the noncommercial realm as well, this approach won't do, unless we want to reject all basic rights, period. Second, one could argue that economic disadvantages are best corrected by voiding robust private property rights, while noneconomic disadvantages are best corrected without touching basic rights in the noncommercial realm. But that argument doesn't rule out *all* basic rights to free exchange. Third, one could suggest that our ignorance about which redistributive policy is most consonant with liberal egalitarianism throws doubt on any derivation of a basic right to free exchange, since any such right limits experimentation with different redistributive policies. But a *well-grounded* basic right to free exchange cannot be defeated by a *speculation* that this right might block the most justified liberal egalitarian policy.

So it is dubious that liberal egalitarianism can block a derivation of any basic right to free exchange. The arguments in sections 2 and 3 remain standing, and thus there are good grounds for maintaining that contemporary liberalism must support basic rights to free exchange.[24] Both libertarianism and liberalism support basic rights to free exchange, and the gap between them has been narrowed.

Notes

1. A basic right has a considerable amount of moral weight, so that it usually defeats perfectionist claims or claims of societal or individual well-being.

2. A robust private property right is a right that constitutes or defines free markets in a capitalist society. It thus includes the right to exclude and the right to exchange, the latter being my primary concern here.

3. I have in mind liberals such as Bruce Ackerman, Ronald Dworkin, Will Kymlicka, Charles Larmore, Thomas Nagel, John Rawls, and David A. J. Richards.

4. John Rawls, *Political Liberalism* (New York: Columbia University Press, 1992), 303–4, 308. (Strictly speaking, Rawls views basic rights as specifying fair terms of social cooperation on the basis of mutual respect, but this is not relevant here.) See also Ronald Dworkin, *Taking Rights Seriously* (Cambridge: Harvard University Press, 1977), 272.

5. Dworkin, "What is Equality? Part 3: The Place of Liberty," *Iowa Law Review* 73 (1987): 7–9.

6. See, for example, Rawls, *A Theory of Justice* (Cambridge: Harvard University Press, 1971), 92; *Political Liberalism*, 312–13; and Will Kymlicka, *Contemporary Political Philosophy* (Oxford: Clarendon Press, 1990), 202–3.

7. For a valuable discussion of the complex concept of autonomy, see Joel Feinberg, *Harm to Self* (New York: Oxford University Press, 1986), 27–44.

8. For different developments of this idea, see Charles Larmore, *Patterns of Moral Complexity* (New York: Cambridge University Press, 1986), 64–66; David A. J. Richards, *Toleration and the Constitution* (New York: Oxford University Press, 1986), 84; and Thomas Nagel, *Equality and Partiality* (New York: Oxford University Press, 1991), 36. It is implicit in Bruce Ackerman, *Social Justice in the Liberal State*, (New Haven: Yale University Press, 1980), 3–4, and Rawls's model of the original position.

9. For the first line of argument, see Rawls, *Political Liberalism*, 320–23. For the second, see Rawls, *Political Liberalism*, 36–37, 303–4. (Rawls emphasizes not just the fact of pluralism but the "fact of reasonable pluralism," that is, that most of these doctrines are reasonable. This complication, however, is not relevant here.)

10. At some point, options become so narrow or few that it's fair to say that one has no choice. But this occurs in both the commercial and noncommercial realm.

11. I borrow this idea from Rawls, *Political Liberalism*, 13.

12. This qualification is necessary to exclude cases such as the buying and selling of persons (slavery) and the buying and selling of votes.

13. My explanation of the function of prices in a free market is taken from Friedrich Hayek. See "The Use of Knowledge in Society" in *Individualism and the Economic Order* (Chicago: University of Chicago Press, 1948), 181–208, and "Competition as a Discovery Procedure" in *New Studies in Philosophy, Politics, Economics, and the History of Ideas* (Chicago: University of Chicago Press, 1978), 179–90.

14. Since initiators of price changes in a free market do make mistakes, free market prices can also incorporate mistaken assumptions about future economic

realities, and this might seem to blunt the contrast between price controls and free market prices. The crucial difference, however, is that price controls prevent those who are aware of changing economic conditions from acting on that information, while free markets provide incentives to respond to or anticipate changing economic conditions.

15. For useful works on the effects of rent control, see Joel F. Brenner and Herbert M. Franklin, *Rent Control in North America and Four European Countries* (Washington D.C.: The Potomac Institute, 1972); Anthony Downs, *Residential Rent Controls* (Washington, D.C: The Urban Land Institute, 1988); and William F. Tucker, *The Excluded Americans* (Washington, D.C.: Regnery Gateway, 1990).

16. Some liberals, e.g., John Rawls, do discuss free choice of occupation, but as part of the requirement of equality of opportunity rather than as a basic right. Also, the requirement of free choice of occupation is only used to rule out compulsory labor, and is not applied to free markets in general. See *Political Liberalism*, 308 and *A Theory of Justice*, 272.

17. This point also applies to the claim that free market capitalism is not sufficiently responsive to a diversity of views about proper organizational arrangements. See my "Why Rawlsian Liberals Should Support Free Market Capitalism," *Journal of Political Philosophy* 3 (1995): 58–85.

18. As noted by Cass Sunstein, "Disrupting Voluntary Transactions" in *Markets and Justice: Nomos XXXI* ed. John W. Chapman and J. Roland Pennock (New York: New York University Press, 1989), 288.

19. Rawls, *Political Liberalism*, 364 and Richards, *Toleration and the Constitution*, 211-2.

20. See Israel Kirzner, *Competition and Entrepreneurship* (Chicago: University of Chicago Press, 1973), 146–163.

21. Another possibility is that endogenous preference-formation occurs in some societies, one of which is a free-market system. However, in that case, it's unclear why one would focus on free markets as having a so-called problem of endogenous preference formation.

22. "What is Equality? Part I: Equality of Welfare" and "What is Equality? Part II: Equality of Resources," *Philosophy & Public Affairs* 19 (1981): 185–262, 283–345. For recent refinements of Dworkin's version of liberal egalitarianism, see G. A. Cohen, "Currency of Egalitarian Justice," *Ethics* 99 (1989): 906–44, and Eric Rakowski, *Equal Justice* (Oxford: Clarendon Press, 1991).
Probably the main alternative to Dworkin's version of liberal egalitarianism is Rawls' difference principle, which requires that social and economic inequalities be to the greatest advantage to the worst off. The main problem with that principle is that it does not distinguish between inequalities that are to a significant extent the product of one's choices and those that are largely unchosen. Thus, the difference principle could easily justify subsidizing people's choices. However, since liberalism accepts that people have a right to act in accordance with their (peaceful) choices, it should accept that people are responsible for the costs of these choices—since it would be unfair for the right-holder to ask those who are under obligations to re-

spect her rights not to interfere with her peaceful choices *and* to require these others to bear the costs of those choices. For further elaboration, see Kymlicka, *Contemporary Political Philosophy*, 73–75.

23. Assuming that these plans, ambitions, etc., are not cravings or obsessions and that one had sufficient opportunity to develop alternative plans, ambitions, etc.

24. More detailed treatments of the arguments presented here occur in the following: for sections 2 and 3, see "Liberalism, Basic Rights and Free Exchange," *Journal of Social Philosophy*, 26 (1995): 105–28; for section 4, see "Liberal Egalitarianism, Basic Rights, and Free Market Capitalism," *Reason Papers* 18 (1993): 169–88. For discussion of Rawlsian liberalism, in particular, see "Free Speech, Free Exchange and Rawlsian Liberalism," *Social Theory and Practice* 17 (1991): 47–68, and "Why Rawlsian Liberals Should Support Free Market Capitalism," *Journal of Political Philosophy*, 3 (1995): 58–85.

The Right to Welfare and the Virtue of Charity*

Douglas J. Den Uyl

> As each individual abandons himself to the solicitous aid of the State, so, and still more, he abandons to it the fate of his fellow-citizens.
>
> Wilhelm Von Humboldt, *On the Limits of State Action*

Are the right to welfare[1] and the virtue of charity compatible? Consider this argument: *Since the right to welfare is an enforceable (not to mention enforced) duty, and since virtuous acts require uncoerced voluntary choice to qualify as virtuous, the extent to which welfare rights are exercised is the extent to which the virtue of charity is absent.* If "incompatibility" means that the presence of one thing requires the total absence of the other, then the right to welfare and the virtue of charity are not made incompatible by this argument. But the same thing cannot be both voluntary and compulsory at the same time, so it would seem that the right to welfare and the virtue of charity would be incompatible in the sense of "being incapable of simultaneous exercise."

The argument, nevertheless, has at least two obvious problems. The first is that some economic literature suggests that people will be less charitable if there is a total absence of coerced giving (e.g., due to a free-rider problem). Unfortunately, the *incentives* for and against giving cannot be a concern of this essay.[2] The second problem is that the argument seems to ignore what is central. Of course coerced action cannot count as virtuous, but the real problem is not establishing that compelled actions are virtuous, but rather showing exactly where the dividing line between justifiable coercion and noncoercion lies. The real problem, in other words, concerns finding that point at which we can no longer say that what is done is "up to us," but rather that what we do is *owed* to another as a matter of right and can accordingly be compelled if we fail to respect that right.

It might be argued that there is additionally a third obvious problem with the opening argument, namely, that the argument is logically uncompelling, since people might not have to exercise their right to welfare because of the prior, free, and uncoerced benevolence of the givers. In other words, although giving *could* have been compelled, those who transferred their resources did so willingly and without a thought to the compulsion that might have been brought to bear if they had failed to give. In such cases, the right to welfare would not seem to be in conflict with the virtue of charity. Yet despite appearances, there is a problem with this sort of analysis. For if one has a *right* to welfare, the provision of that benefit cannot be a virtue separate from justice (even if done with a "smile"), because the provider would only be offering to another what is the other's due. So although some commentators are quick to point out that justice and charity cannot be distinguished on the basis that one is owed while the other is not (since that begs the question about what is or is not owed),[3] it can still be said that if the benefit is owed to another, rendering it is not an act of charity. There is no virtue beyond that of justice in "rendering to each his due."

One of the purposes of this essay, then, is to indicate how arguments that attempt to blur or abandon the distinction between justice and charity end up dismissing charity altogether. This is because the normal frameworks, both moral and political, used for discussing aid to those in need are at odds with approaches that would be conducive to the virtue of charity. Consequently, charity gets relegated to the dustbin of the supererogatory and becomes increasingly unimportant. To resuscitate this virtue we need to understand something of its historical meaning and context, the conceptual framework in which it is likely to be significant, and the ways in which it has been dismissed by other theories.

I. Adam Smith, Liberalism, and the Distinction between Justice and Charity

Allen Buchanan writes that

> [t]he view that duties of justice are always negative, while those of charity are (generally) positive, is perhaps the least satisfactory attempt to distinguish

justice from charity since it simply begs one of the most hotly disputed questions in the theory of rights, the question of whether there are positive as well as negative (general) rights.[4]

Buchanan seems to understand the issue of distinguishing justice from charity as a dispute about rights. Yet in the history of liberal political theory the distinction was forcefully asserted by Adam Smith without any mention of rights and presumably with an appeal to some standard of evaluation other than rights (i.e., sentiment). Consider these passages from Smith's *Theory of Moral Sentiments*:

> Beneficence is always free, it cannot be extorted by force, the mere want of it exposes to no punishment; because the mere want of beneficence tends to do no real positive evil. It may disappoint of the good which might reasonably have been expected, and upon that account it may justly excite dislike and disapprobation; it cannot, however, provoke any resentment which mankind will go along with.[5]
>
> There is, however, another virtue, of which the observance is not left to the freedom of our own wills, which may be extorted by force, and of which the violation exposes to resentment, and consequently to punishment. This virtue is justice: the violation of justice is injury: it does real and positive hurt to some particular persons, from motives which are naturally disapproved of. It is, therefore, the proper object of resentment, and of punishment, which is the natural consequence of resentment. . . . The person himself who meditates an injustice is sensible of this, and feels that force may, with the utmost propriety, be made use of, both by the person whom he is about to injure, and by others. . . . And upon this is founded that remarkable distinction between justice and all the other social virtues, . . .that we feel ourselves to be under a stricter obligation to act according to justice, then agreeably to friendship, charity, or generosity; that the practice of these last mentioned virtues seems to be left in some measure to our own choice, but that, somehow or other, we feel ourselves to be in a peculiar manner tied, bound, and obliged to the observation of justice. (TMS, II.ii.I.5)

In Smith's system, justice and beneficence are motivated by the corresponding sentiments of resentment and benevolence. These are entirely different sentiments that attach themselves to what must as a consequence be rather different virtues. But in pointing this out I do not mean to suggest that the move from the language of rights to that of sentiment solves Buchanan's problem. For a possibility that Smith himself may not have adequately considered is that the sentiments of resentment and benevolence could attach themselves to rather diverse (even contradictory) sorts of circumstances. The person of little means raised under a Marxist ideology could possess every bit the resentment towards his capitalist "exploiters" as the libertarian may show towards the leaders of the redistributive state. In this respect, sentiment begs all the same questions that Buchanan claims the rights perspective does. Nevertheless, Buchanan's way of presenting the issue *is* indicative of a problem of moral reductionism to be discussed momentarily.

In any case, it does not follow from the fact that a line is difficult to draw, that there is therefore no line to be drawn at all. For however relative or difficult it may be to determine the line between justice and charity, the passages from Smith indicate that such problems are not sufficient to remove the distinction itself. For surely, the fact that some things are freely given to others, while other things are given because they are owed or due, marks a distinction that can be maintained in spite of any difficulties there may be in deciding the exact dividing line. . . .

[A]ppreciating the role of virtues other than justice may require that we see ethics as concerned with more than the prevention of harm or the promotion of utility.[6] There is no hope, for example, for a virtue like charity when morality is understood as, "fundamentally (though not exclusively) concerned with avoiding states of affairs that are harmful for individuals."[7] The avoidance or prevention of harm is some distance from the promotion or exhibition of virtue, which, even if not "excluded" from morality, would nevertheless require the sort of proactive and perfecting conduct that is not adequately captured by issues of harm or avoidance. Further, such a conception of ethics makes every ethical issue a matter of some form of justice; for the prevention or avoidance of harm (justice), while necessary, is neither ennobling nor always laudatory, though it may be, at least with respect to avoidance, always due. And this problem is not overcome by expanding "justice" to include so-called "positive" rights. For whether one respects another's rights by forbearance or by positive action, one still renders only that which is due and thus exhibits no virtue but that of justice.[8]

It should be no surprise, then, that Buchanan can plausibly claim at the end of his article that the distinction between justice and charity plays no significant role in the prominent moralities of our era (e.g., in utilitarianism and contractarianism) and that nothing important is lost by the absence of this distinction.[9] Maybe so; but it is patently false to claim that the avoidance or prevention of harm is the essence of ethics,[10] or that such a view represents the bulk of the history of this subject. Moreover, it is equally problematic to suppose that all virtues can, in quasi-Platonic fashion, be reduced to one form of the good, namely justice. That sort of moral reductionism is, in effect, what the willingness to abandon the distinction between justice and charity amounts to when otherwise charitable acts are said to be owed to someone as a matter of right. . . .

All this raises the more general and deeper problem of whether the reductionist tendency is inherent in liberalism itself, and whether liberalism in the end has any place for virtue at all.[11] For if we can generate the sort of conduct we want by first reducing all moral virtues (or their appropriate parts) to justice, and then using the enforcement power such a reduction now renders morally permissible, what need (or room) could there be for an appeal to the types of exclusively self-directed actions virtue requires? But what is at issue here is not just whether liberalism has any role for virtues like charity. It may be that liberalism has actually succeeded at the *expense* of such virtues! Smith tells the following story about the impact of commerce, a central feature of liberal orders, on the institution of charity:

> In the antient state of Europe, before the establishment of arts and manufactures, the wealth of the clergy gave them the same sort of influence over the common people, which that of the great barons gave them over their respective vassals, tenants, and retainers. . . . Over and above the rents of those estates, the clergy possessed, in the tythes, a very large portion of the rents of all the other estates in every kingdom of Europe. The revenues arising from both those species of rents were . . . paid in kind . . . . The quantity exceeded greatly what the clergy could themselves consume; and there were neither arts nor manufactures for the produce of which they could exchange the surplus. The clergy could derive advantage from this immense surplus in no other way than by employing it, as the great barons employed the like surplus of their revenues, in the most profuse hospitality, and in the most extensive charity . . . . They not only maintained almost the whole poor of every kingdom, but many knights and gentlemen had frequently no other means of subsistence than by travelling about from monastery to monastery, under pretence of devotion, but in reality to enjoy the hospitality of the clergy. . . . The hospitality and charity of the clergy . . . increased very much the weight of their spiritual weapons. . . . Every thing belonging or related to so popular an order . . . necessarily appeared sacred in the eyes of the common people, and every violation of them, whether real or pretend the highest act of sacrilegious wickedness and profaneness. . . .
>
> The gradual improvements of arts, manufactures, and commerce, the same causes which destroyed the power of the great barons, destroyed in the same manner, through the greater part of Europe, the whole temporal power of the clergy. In the produce of arts, manufactures, and commerce, the clergy, like the great barons, found something for which they could exchange their rude produce. . . . Their charity became gradually less extensive, their hospitality less liberal or less profuse. Their retainers became consequently less numerous, and by degrees dwindled away altogether. . . . The ties of interest, which bound the inferior ranks of people to the clergy, were in this manner gradually broken and dissolved. . . . The inferior ranks of people no longer looked upon that

order, as they had done before, as the comforters of their distress, and the relievers of their indigence. On the contrary, they were provoked and disgusted by the vanity, luxury, and expence of the richer clergy, who appeared to spend upon their own pleasures what had always before been regarded as the patrimony of the poor. (WN, V.i.g.22–25)

If the charity of the clergy is more a function of their economic opportunities than their moral character, one cannot help but wonder what role the virtue of charity could possibly play in a well-ordered liberal economic system. For although there may still be some who possess that virtue as a quality of their character, they would be few in number and not of any significance to the workings of the economic system. And although there may also be those who are too weak, infirm, or otherwise distressed to function in this type of economy, these groups could be easily handled by a rather minimal provision of welfare. The bulk of the population in a well-ordered liberal society would conduct their affairs in a market system where the real standard of living for the lower classes would be improving and the wealth of the upper classes would always be subject to market tests that tend to keep that wealth employed in ways that benefit society at large. This was certainly Smith's picture of the effects of the "system of natural liberty" as described in *The Wealth of Nations*. And if this is really how the picture looks, why should we care about the virtue of charity? After all, people are much better off than they were under the medieval order of systematic "charity and hospitality" offered by the barons and clergy. And if the charity that will exist will only be present at the margins anyway, why not join Buchanan and simply be done with the whole issue by making it all a matter of justice? Given the relatively low cost of maintaining marginal members of society, it would seem that only the pedantry of some philosophers stands in the way of conceding that in liberal regimes everyone has the right to a certain form of minimal subsistence.

We have now reached a point where we need to take stock of where we are. On the one hand, it would seem that we require some sort of distinction between justice and charity to help us separate what is owed from what may be freely given, and possibly also to enliven the virtues generally. On the other hand, liberalism seems to incline towards moral reductionism or the division of the moral landscape into issues of justice on one side and matters of personal preference or supererogatory conduct on the other. Thus, the further question was raised as to whether liberalism has room for virtue at all. For after getting desirable conduct under the rubric of justice, and after designing appropriate incentive systems (i.e., the market) to handle that which we do not presently compel, there seems to be no need for classical virtue, except as a form of moral heroism.

It is undoubtedly the case that the issues we have raised are too vast to be dealt with fully here. It is not just the relationship between justice and charity that is now before us, but the role of virtue in general. It may be, for example, that the loss of virtue is not to be lamented, especially if all the goods we want are provided in its absence. But let us at least understand something of what is being lost if virtue is to be abandoned. The remaining sections of this essay should provide at least some of the understanding. I believe, however, that the choice we face is not so exclusionary. Consequently, I wish to draw a provisional conclusion that can serve, when applied to charity in particular, as a kind of thesis for the rest of the essay: *For virtues to have a significant chance of flourishing in liberal orders where all persons are morally equal, every effort must be made to distinguish those virtues from the virtue of justice.* The first step in lending some support to this thesis is to see charity in its historical context. Indeed, one of my conclusions, which is only partially supported in this essay, is that the classical (self-perfective) paradigm in ethics can offer us a way of conceiving of virtue as being significant while also being compatible with the principles of ("classical") liberal order. This may have been Smith's insight as well.

II. The Roots of the Virtue of Charity

The virtue of charity has its roots in the Christian era. Although such Aristotelian concepts as "friendship" are at least partially incorporated into charity, this virtue was regarded as one of the three great "theological" virtues (along with "faith" and "hope") in the Christian Middle Ages and beyond. These theological virtues were superior to the so-called "four cardinal virtues" of "prudence," "justice," "courage," and "temperance." The four cardinal virtues were, nonetheless, the four basic moral virtues that all others were either derived from or subordinated to.[12] For the purposes of this essay, the fact that charity was a theological and not a moral virtue is of little significance. The philosophical aspects of the virtue are easily identified, and it is the philosophical heritage that interests us here. In this respect, it seems only natural that my remarks focus on Aquinas's discussion of charity in the *Summa Theologiae* (II-II). The concept of charity presented there is most certainly the understanding that was carried forward, modified, or abandoned by later thinkers.

"Charity" is a translation of the Latin *caritas*, which broadly means "love."[13] *Caritas* is a theological virtue for two reasons. First, because as Aquinas notes citing Augustine, " 'by charity I mean the movement of the soul towards the enjoyment of God for His own sake.' "[14] We may love self or neighbor, but the love that is charity ultimately issues in the love of God. Second, *caritas* is a theological virtue in Aquinas because it is an inclination *added* to our natural will. Presumably then, if left to nature alone, we would not have an inclination to charity. This in turn raises the interesting question of just how different charity could be from what nature would presumably have given us, namely, benevolence and beneficence.

For the moment, however, the point to be recognized is that the cardinal virtues must be *infused* with the theological virtues (*ST*, II-II, Q23, A4; Q24, A1–3), for the list of cardinal virtues is not especially Christian. Indeed, these are the same four virtues (prudence, justice, courage, temperance) that seemed to rule the theories of pagan antiquity. Consequently, for the four cardinal virtues to be manifestations of, and consistent with, Christianity, they must be exercised in a context already laid out by the theological virtues. Presumably, then, we could check the difference between an infused and noninfused virtue by comparing the description of the virtue in Aristotle with a description of the same virtue in Aquinas. This is not always easy or even possible to do, since Aquinas is concerned to follow Aristotle as closely as possible and to reconcile reason and faith rather than separate them. Still, we shall see below how infusion may be a partial explanation of the differences between what Aquinas says about one virtue (liberality) and what Aristotle says about it.

Now charity for Aquinas is an act of self-perfection that is not essentially concerned with the sentiment of benevolence or even our relations towards others. Rather, charity involves perfecting our own capacity to love by directing it towards that which is perfectly lovable (God) and by devoting our time to divine things and habituating our heart to God (*ST*, II-II, Q24, A8). In practice, this means that we begin by "avoiding sin and resisting [our] concupiscences" and then progress to pursuing the good as much as possible. In the end, we seek the union and enjoyment of God that these first two stages make possible, but that cannot be fully realized in this life (*ST*, II-II, Q24, A9). The foregoing represents a progression of self-perfection, with others entering into the process as a component of that perfection, but not as its driving principle. We have charity towards others because we love God (*ST*, II-II, Q25, A1), and Aquinas even tells us that charity requires that we love ourselves more than our neighbor (*ST*, II-II, Q26, A4). Moreover, because our neighbors can be sinners, or enemies, charity only requires that we love their human essence, that is, their general capacity for improvement and salvation. As individuals, they may be appropriately the objects of hate (*ST*, II-II, Q25, A6, 8, 9).

From this all too brief summary of the elements of charity, a couple of points are worth our attention. First, charity turns out to be a kind of general openness to the good. The love that is charity is one that disposes us in all our actions and thoughts to seek the good and promote it as much as possible. In this respect, then, charity is loving the good for its own sake and keeping that as a general attitude in all one's endeavors. But charity is not simply attitudinal or dispositional in nature. As a form of love it requires an object. As we noted, that object is God, but that in effect means everything, since God is master and creator of all. Consequently, the charitable person does not approach any situation with an attitude of suspicion or distrust, nor does such a person do so opportunistically, selfishly, or instrumentally. Instead, one enters into any circumstance with the recognition that this situation too is an opportunity to do good. It is this general positive, even optimistic, approach that gets transformed by later thinkers into such things as universal benevolence. What one is therefore impressed with when considering classical charity is its scope. Not only is it not limited to transferring resources, it is not even limited to one's dealings with others. Charity encompasses everything. But what does that mean once the virtue is secularized? We shall return to that question in a moment.

The other point that needs to be made is that charity is not a *means* to self-perfection but a constituent of it. Consequently, one is not charitable so that one may become self-perfected, but rather charitable conduct is the very expression of one's self-perfection. More importantly, it is self-perfection that defines the context for the classical conception of charity (and indeed the classical conception of all virtues) in the first place. This is because virtue in general is the disposition to perfect the powers of the agent as those powers relate to their appropriate objects or ends, e.g., reason and knowledge (*ST*, II-II, Q55, A2). Man's end for Aquinas was God, for Aristotle happiness or *eudaimonia*. These ends served as standards of success, and defined for the classical world (both pagan and Christian) the most important and foundational concern of ethics, namely, what is the good and how should one achieve it? This is an approach quite different from that of the modern period, where the central question of ethics concerns what duties one may have towards others.[15]

In a very real sense, the ethics of antiquity is characterized by self-realization, and this in turn is due to the teleological metaphysics that stood behind it. In contrast, modernity abandoned teleology, and consequently the question of achievement was replaced by the issue of adherence to duty, understood either in terms of deontic rules or in terms of maximizing some form of social utility. In either case, the agent was asked to constrain self-interest in response to some pressing moral principle that was almost always social in nature. So-called "duties to self," if they existed at all, were relegated to the back burner in modern ethics.

Because of the central idea that the good is brought into being by the achievements of the self, it might be said that the classical model of ethics was "supply-sided." The more modern approach—whereby ethics is viewed as fulfilling certain duties towards others—might be termed "demand-sided." There were, of course, elements of demand-sidedness in classical ethics, just as one can find some elements of supply-sidedness in modern ethics. But as archetypes and designators of the central focus of approaches to ethics, these labels will serve us nicely.

In a significant sense, classical virtue ethics is *inherently* supply-sided, since it places the bulk of its attention on the agent's own character, defines moral goodness in terms of the agent's nature, and expects that goodness to be the direct product of the agent's own actions. Moreover, the "beneficiary" of the conduct is the agent himself. The exception to this seems to be, once again, the virtue of justice, which appears to be exclusively other-oriented. The perception that justice is the exception to the supply-sided character of classical virtue is, in fact, a misperception. One need only recall Plato's definition of justice as "having one's soul in proper order," and Aristotle's description of justice in Book V of the *Nicomachean Ethics* (1129a6; hereafter *NE*) as being a state of character, to realize that justice, like the other virtues of antiquity, is still within the self-perfective context.[16] The *object* of justice may, of course, be other-oriented, but not its ground or justification.

Christianity, however, may have brought some ambivalence into the picture by its *infusion* of theology into ethics. Aquinas, for example, when discussing the virtue of liberality claims it is closer to justice than charity (ST, II-II, Q117, A5).[17] Although liberality is not a *species* of justice, because it does not involve something that is owed to another (thereby indicating Aquinas's commitment to the distinction between justice and charity), liberality is, nonetheless, closest to justice because of its interpersonal nature and its concern with material things (i.e., money). It is only like charity in its "particular regard to the recipient." Oddly enough, when "beneficent" and "merciful" giving is directed to a particular individual (and is *not* concerned with money) it fits under the rubric of charity for Aquinas. In contrast to contemporary understanding, charity is thus the "perfect" duty (i.e., one where the recipient of the duty is specified) and liberality the "imperfect" duty. Yet Aristotle mentions justice only once during his discussion of liberality (*NE*, IV, 1120a20) and then only in a way that would separate it entirely from liberality. There is no problem for Aristotle in deciding whether liberality is a species of justice or charity, as there is in Aquinas. This is not just because there is no exact equivalent for charity in Aristotle's list of virtues (elements of friendship and magnanimity are closest), but because those virtues are not infused with anything outside themselves.

If God's love for us is the paradigmatic form of charity, then our own charity will be more perfect the more it imitates God's. Since God's love extends to everyone, our own charity must also. But this means that the interpersonal realm is now dominated by *two* significant virtues: justice and charity. Which one governs which minor virtue becomes increasingly difficult to determine in interpersonal cases, as we just saw. This is so evident that at least one commentator has claimed that Aquinas explicitly "argued against the separation of charity and justice."[18] In one sense, of course, that claim is true—none of the virtues are *separated* from charity, since all are infused with it. The basic distinction in Aquinas, however, is the one I have already elaborated in Section I, namely, that justice deals with what is owed to another while charity does not. The problem of the distinction between justice and charity arises for the modern mind because Christian charity makes such things as almsgiving obligatory (*ST*, II-II, Q32, A5).[19] But it is critically important to understand that we have this obligation for Aquinas not because we owe it to the other, as in justice, but because we owe it to ourselves; that is, such actions are a sign of our self-perfection (i.e., of our love of God).[20] It is from mercy that we give alms, and not out of a sense of justice (*ST*, II-II, Q32, A1).[21] The self-perfectionist or teleological character found in Aristotle is still dominant in this model, but the infusion of Christian charity has been more insistent about our obligations to others, especially the needy.

Suppose now that we de-theologize the doctrine and remove God from the picture. Only two of the three possible ultimate objects of charity would remain: self or others. As long as God was present, it could be argued that self and others were nicely balanced, because our obligations to both had to be understood through God. And although teleological metaphysics (ethics) gave the self precedence over others, the infusion of charity was thought to keep that precedence from lapsing into an egoism. But if we remove teleology as well, the self would lose its standard of perfectibility. This would be especially true if the self were conceived as a bundle of passions without a *summum bonum*. For now there could be no end to serve as a standard of perfection by which to measure one's achievements, leaving the satisfaction of desires to constitute the good for the self. Yet the satisfaction of desire is something one pursues anyway. Consequently, our relations with others would have to come to claim the central focus of normative theory and become the object of charity (since God and self no longer have any claim). This line of reasoning should have brought to mind a particular individual, namely the father of all modern social and normative theorizing—Thomas Hobbes.

Hobbes is quite explicit about the object of charity being others.[22]

> Moreover, that moral virtue, that we can truly measure by civil laws, which is different in different states, is justice and equity; that moral virtue which we measure purely by natural laws is only charity. Furthermore, all moral virtue is contained in these two. . . . Nor in truth, should one demand that the courage and prudence of the private man, if useful only to himself, be praised or held as a virtue by states or by any other men whatsoever to whom these same are not useful. So condensing this whole teaching on manners and dispositions into the fewest words, I say that good dispositions are those which are suitable for entering into civil society; and good manners (that is, moral virtues) are those whereby what was entered upon can be best preserved. For all the virtues are contained in justice and charity. (*De Homine*, ch. 13, sec. 9)
>
> It is also a law of nature, That every man do help and endeavor to accommodate each other, as far as may be without danger of their persons, and loss of their means, to maintain and defend themselves. For seeing the causes of war and desolation proceed from those passions, by which we strive to accommodate ourselves, and to leave others as far as we can behind us: it followeth that the passion by which we strive mutually to accommodate each other, must be the cause of peace. and this passion is . . . charity. (*Elements of Law*, pt. 1, ch. 16, sec. 8)

Notice that the purpose of charity is now social cooperation. It is still broader and prior to justice, for it represents the sort of attitude needed to escape the state of nature or solve the Prisoner's Dilemma, namely, good will towards others and a willingness to cooperate. Justice, in contrast, is adherence to the rules of order established by the sovereign for the maintenance of the sought-after peace and security. In neither case is what is "useful only to[one]self" to be counted for anything. The self-perfectionist ethics has been traded for an ethics of social cooperation. Altruism in the *normative* sense has now been placed at the center of modern ethics, although it has been removed by Hobbes as a *descriptive* category of human action. In any case, for Hobbes as for Aquinas, the term "charity" is still broader than and logically prior to "justice." But if justice is what the sovereign commands, then the two can and should be merged in practice. Consider:

> And whereas many men, by accident unevitable, become unable to maintain themselves by their labour; they ought not to be left to the Charity of private persons; but to be provided for, (as far-forth as the necessities of Nature require), by the Laws of the Commonwealth. For as it is Uncharitableness in any man, to neglect the impotent; so it is in the Sovereign of a Commonwealth, to expose them to the hazard of such uncertain Charity.[23]

If one wishes, however, to see justice and charity collapsed together in a thoroughly demand-sided approach to ethics, one must look elsewhere.

It may seem surprising, but a most explicit reduction of charity to justice, and a narrowing of charity to the question of aiding the poor, is contained in the following passage from John Locke:[24]

> But we know God hath not left one Man so to the Mercy of another, that he may starve himself if he please: God the Lord and Father of all, has given no one of his Children such a Property, in his peculiar Portion of the things of this world, but that he has given his needy Brother a Right to the Surplusage of his Goods; so that it cannot justly be denied him, when his pressing Wants call for it. And therefore no Man could ever have a just Power over the Life of another, by Right of property in Land or Possessions; since 'twould always be a Sin in any Man of Estate, to let his Brother perish for want of affording him Relief out of his Plenty. As *Justice* gives every Man a Title to the product of his honest Industry, and the fair Acquisitions of his Ancestors descended to him; so *Charity* gives every Man a Title to so much out of another's Plenty, as will keep him from extream want, where he has no means to subsist otherwise; and a Man can no more justly make use of another's necessity, to force him to become his Vassal, by with-holding that Relief, God requires him to afford to the wants of his Brother, than he that has more strength can seize upon a weaker, master him to his Obedience, and with a Dagger at his Throat, offer him Death or Slavery.

Notice that not only can those in need lay title to the "surplusage" of others, but those others cannot *justly* refuse. Notice also that the perspective here is from the standpoint of those in need rather than the person supplying the benefit. In other words, nothing is said about the perfective qualities of such actions with respect to the benefactor.

We have seen over the course of this historical sketch that the context for understanding the virtue of charity has been dramatically altered. We have also seen that the exact relationship between justice and charity has been problematic for some time. By the same token, our account has made it clear that charity and altruism (the moral primacy of others) are not necessarily bedfellows, and that if one looks for that partnership, one is more likely to find it in the modern than the premodern or classical world.

The problematic nature of the relationship between justice and charity is not, as Edward Andrew has argued, a reason to claim that early modern liberalism sought to separate justice from charity in order to remove the barriers to commercialization.[25] If anything, the matter almost seems the reverse. Modern liberals are keen on making some sort of charity a right, if for no other reason than to avoid the whimsy and uncertainty of leaving it to individual choice.

It may nevertheless be correct to suppose that liberalism essentially calls for distinguishing, even separating, justice from charity (now understood in the narrow sense of aiding the poor). It may do so not, as neo-Marxists might suggest, to protect selfishness and allow one to avoid charitable conduct, but rather because liberalism conceives of itself as an inherently classless system unable to institutionally recognize certain members of society as the class from which charity should flow and others as its perpetual recipients.[26] The best it can do is speak in terms of rich and poor, but these are fairly amorphous and (for any individual) unstable categories compared to pre-liberal class systems with defined multigenerational hierarchical orders. As we saw from Smith in Section I, it was part of the promise of liberalism to remove the system of charity that depended upon alms from the clergy or aristocracy. Those who then came to occupy the ranks of the rich and poor would have no particular occupation or class association, because various individuals of differing occupations and social status would cycle through these ranks. Consequently, no one under liberalism would be identifiably born into or inherit the role of almsgiver or receiver. Another way of putting this point is to suggest that the rise of commercialism and the middle class transformed charity from a "perfect" to an "imperfect" virtue.

Critics of liberalism charge that liberalism has no place for charity. This would seem to mean that if charity is not a right, people are free not to be charitable. And this in turn is interpreted to imply that liberalism does not care about charity. Perhaps. But we have seen that *thinkers* who are liberal certainly care. These same thinkers, however, did not believe it was the role of the state to manage the entire moral landscape. Indeed, the state was only really fit to manage one virtue—justice. But therein lies our opening problem: either everything that matters gets reduced to justice (e.g., formulated in terms of rights) or liberalism seems indifferent to virtues distinct from justice. Since the *cultural* inheritance of liberalism is predominantly Christian, and Christianity does not permit indifference about aid to the poor, liberalism would appear indifferent if it failed to institutionalize some right to charity. Yet doing that may run counter to other features inherent in liberalism.

The problem just stated can be characterized in another way: liberalism has no systematic procedure for determining whether conduct is virtuous or not. This is because liberalism was founded on the idea that the state is concerned with outward conduct rather than with inner states of being. But if that is so, liberalism may permit confusing the appearance of virtue with its real expression. The various aspects of this problem were first noticed by Bernard Mandeville.

III. The Mandevillian Problem of Charity

To appreciate Mandeville's discussion of the appearance/reality problem as it applies to the virtue of charity, we must first understand something of how Mandeville conceived of charity. He defines charity in the following way:

> Charity is that Virtue by which part of the sincere Love we have for our selves is transferr'd pure and unmix'd to others, not tied to us by the Bonds of Friendship or Consanguinity, and even meer Strangers, whom we have no obligation to, nor hope or expect any thing from. If we lessen any ways the Rigour of this Definition, part of the Virtue must be lost.[27]

With regard to our historical sketch of the last section, this definition still shares many of the characteristics of the classical view: it is broad in scope, supply-sided in nature, and does not reduce charity to the giving of alms. It also clearly supposes that charity is freely given and directed towards those "whom we have no obligation to." Yet although this definition provides a context for our discussion, it is not its components that concern us, but the ways in which its "rigours" might be lessened.

Charity manifested itself in three distinct aspects for Mandeville: (1) when we interpret the actions of others in the best possible light ("and if a Man sleeps at Church . . . we ought to think he shuts his Eyes to increase his Attention"); (2) when we "bestow our Time and Labour for nothing" on behalf of others; and finally (3) when we give away what we value ourselves, "being contented rather to have and enjoy less, than not relieve those who want" (p. 254). Most of Mandeville's essay is spent on the third manifestation of charity, but the particular "Mandevillian" problem that concerns us is applicable to all three. Now the basis for the Mandevillian problem of charity is brought to light directly after the three aspects of charity are identified:

> This Virtue is often counterfeited by a Passion of ours, call'd *Pity* or *Compassion*, which consists in a Fellow-feeling and Condolence for the Misfortunes and Calamities of others: all Mankind are more or less affected with it; but the weakest Minds generally the most. It is raised in us, when the Sufferings and Misery of other creatures make so forcible an Impression upon us, as to make us uneasy. . . . [A]nd the nearer and more violently the Object of Compassion strikes those Senses, the greater Disturbance it causes in us, often to such a Degree as to occasion great Pain and Anxiety. (pp. 254–55)

Following this description of the confusion of pity or compassion with charity, Mandeville gives a particularly gruesome account of an infant being devoured by a swine as one looks on helplessly. He notes in this connection that "there would be no need of Virtue or Self-Denial to be moved at such a Scene; and not only a Man of Humanity, of good Morals, and Commiseration, but likewise a Highwayman, a House-Breaker, or a Murderer could feel Anxieties on such an Occasion" (p. 256). The passion or sentiment of pity or compassion, then, is nearly universal in scope and capable of great power. These sentiments are not, however, the end result of sophisticated moral education or habituation.

The essence of the Mandevillian problem can now be stated quite simply: *Acting to relieve or satisfy the sentiment, desire, or passion of pity or compassion is no different in principle from the relief of any other sentiment, desire, or passion.* There is no virtue here. Easing the anxiety one feels in the face of a pitiable circumstance is no different from easing the anxiety one feels in the face of a good one wishes to possess, or a sexual opportunity one wishes to exploit. Remember Mandeville's definition stated that we must transfer "sincere Love" "unmix'd" to others. The endeavor to relieve the anxieties accompanying compassion is, on its face, more like self-gratification than pure unmixed love. . . .

It is tempting at this point to start accusing Mandeville of what he was accused of in his own day and beyond—namely, rigorism (the view that virtue is inseparable from self-denial). Mandeville believes that people are moved by self-interest and yet holds a theory of virtue that entirely excludes the presence of self-interest. It is then easy to mock the virtues and show their absence from everyday life, and to claim that those who preach them are being hypocritical. But, so the argument goes, we need not accept such a rigoristic conception of virtue. Yet one must not be too quick here, for the Mandevillian problem is precisely the one Kant employed to reject the whole course of sentimentalist ethics from Hobbes through Hume to Smith. No matter how one twists and turns and otherwise obfuscates the issues, there is no way, according to Kant,[28] to transform passion or sentiment into principle. Morally speaking, Mandeville is right: one no more acts out of principle in the relief of the anxiety of compassion than in the relief of sexual lust, and conduct must be principled for it to qualify as moral or virtuous.

In this respect, it is not simply the *distance* between virtue and practice that makes Mandeville's problem of the appearance versus the reality of virtue worthy of consideration, but the problematic character of virtue itself. For a typical sort of response would be to suggest that as long as the "good" gets done, what difference does the motive make? In other words, as long as the hospital gets built, what does it matter that the chief donors were moved by pride and vanity? In many respects this is the utilitarian response to the Kantian challenge—to focus on effects. But this response only points to the dichotomous nature of modern ethics (between deontologists and utilitarians) and not to the nature of virtue. Indeed, the very conflict over effects versus motives reflects the abandonment of classical virtue, which involved both.

Mandeville's point, then, is that the virtue of charity (like any other virtue) requires something well beyond an expression of concern for the plight of the poor. But suppose, in any case, we wanted a system to assuage our feelings of compassion and pity in the efficient manner in which many of our other desires are relieved. What would such a system look like? First, we would expect such a system to maximize the relief in the least costly way to us personally. Second, if we could relieve our desires, then we could increase the efficiency of relief. And finally, if we could feel like we have done a great deal with little effort, the very confusion between compassion and charity mentioned by Mandeville can go on unmasked.

We do have a system that meets these criteria quite well; it is the modern welfare state. Unlike the less fortunate Mandeville, who had to face beggars daily, we can effectively relieve our consciences by mail. Through the system of paying taxes to support welfare programs, we may never actually confront the spectacle of a person in need. They are swept from our streets and institutionalized out of sight. One simply mails in one's "contribution" in the form of taxes[29] without much interference with the pursuit of one's other projects or desires. Indeed, one can clamor for more relief on a regular basis through political action and thus demonstrate one's compassion even further. When those who might otherwise qualify for welfare *do* confront us—and this is increasingly the case on the streets of large cities—we regard this as a *failure* of the system and something to be corrected. The welfare state, in other words, does not just provide the needy with benefits; it also provides a comfortable and convenient way to relieve one's conscience or satisfy one's duty to the poor.

It is not my view that compassion should be relieved privately rather than publicly because private systems would somehow better accord with people's interests. I do not think the welfare state is a plot foisted on the freedom-loving masses by an elite group of maniacal socialists. We have welfare states because people want them; we want them so that in a relatively easy and convenient way, we can do our part for the poor at little cost to ourselves. Provided we never do what Mandeville did and question the equation of acting out of compassion with charity, we can (in a manner that seems less possible in a system where all charity is private) contribute to the betterment of the poor without having to make such betterment an actual part of our personal projects. Compassion may be relieved under any system, but in the welfare state, where "charity" is impersonal, institutional, and professional, the only required inconvenience to us personally is the tax rate—and that is supposed to be, in the name of justice, graduated. Consequently, the welfare state, in which everyone has a right to welfare if need be, makes it convenient to trade on the confusion between compassion and charity. A private system, in contrast, would tend to make charity much more a matter of personal responsibility.[30] But then making something a matter of personal responsibility may be the first step one takes to avoid the confusion between compassion and charity and to move from sentiment to virtue. For the welfare state appeals to one's compassion, the private system to one's obligations.

IV. The Right to Welfare and the Virtue of Charity

Among the theses I have sought to support is the idea that in a society of moral equals, the virtue of charity most accords with that system that does not sanction it with coercive force. As we have seen, we can abandon the assumption that we are all equal, which might allow the provision of welfare by the state on "paternalistic" grounds, or we can abandon classical virtue altogether. The first alternative seems unacceptable to the modern mind, while the second runs contrary to what amounts to an operating assumption of this essay, namely, that classical virtue is a viable candidate in moral discourse.

In addition, one of my motivations has been to contrast the self-perfective framework of classical virtue with more modern approaches. It could not, of course, be my purpose here to show the superiority of the classical conception over its competitors, for that is a project that extends well beyond the confines of this essay.[31] But modern discussions of welfare seem to take for granted that the moral worth of the right to welfare can be justified independently of any mention of the virtue of charity. It is necessary therefore that we examine some of the broad parameters of defenses of the right to welfare, if for no other reason than to identify just how absent the virtue of charity is from these discussions. . . .

But leaving aside antiquity for the moment, defenses of the right to welfare tend to fall into three main types: reciprocity arguments, agency arguments, and (for lack of a better name) it's-really-not-your-property-after-all arguments (henceforth "RNY" for "really not yours"). Of course, some arguments combine elements of each of these basic categories,[32] while others do not seem to fit neatly into any.[33] And as with any effort to categorize, oversimplification is inevitable. Nevertheless, my reading of the literature does suggest these as the main types of defenses.

To take the last first, the RNY arguments essentially regard all property as conventional, and thus no one has any absolute claim to his possessions or resources.[34] Sometimes people are regarded as trustees of the resources of society,[35] which would make it a relatively easy matter to transfer those resources if the trustees were not using them wisely, or if society had more pressing needs elsewhere. By themselves these arguments can only stand as negative defenses of the right to welfare. In other words, they might be marshaled to defeat arguments against welfare that depend on an absolute natural right to private property. Beyond this, they can only grease the wheel of more positive arguments for welfare, since the notion that property is conventional does not of itself make the case for transferring it.

We can put all contractarian arguments in the RNY category, because property rights for contractarians are either all, or for the most part, the product of the social contract. So if there were a contractarian case for the right to welfare[36] then the agreed-upon contractual rules would include the legitimacy of redistribution, since that would be nothing other than living up to the bargain struck by the contractors. Yet it is for this very reason that contractarianism can be rejected, for purposes of this essay, as being necessarily incompatible with an explanation derived from the virtue of charity. The redistribution that occurs takes place because of the terms of the agreement, so the sanctions involved are there to enforce that agreement. In this respect, then, contractarian redistribution is all a matter of justice, not charity, since keeping or enforcing agreements are matters of justice. Of course, contractarians may individually care about "charity" and make agreements with each other such that it has a large place in their social system. This may give charity some practical leverage, but it does not give it any theoretical footing; for the final appeal of the argument is not to the virtue of charity itself, but to the terms or process of the agreement. Charity comes out looking like one among a number of possible preferences held by the contractors. It is, in other words, instrumental to the terms of the agreement and not itself the moral basis for the defense of welfare.

The essence of agency arguments is perhaps best and most succinctly summed up by Loren Lomasky:

> Individuals have reason to value the maintenance of a regime of rights because they value their own ability to pursue projects. Should that ability be placed in jeopardy by a system of rights such that one can *either* continue to respect others' rights *or* be able to pursue projects *but not both*, then one would no longer have a rational stake in the moral community established by that system of rights.[37] (*Persons, Rights, and the Moral Community*, p. 127)

When individuals are put in the position of having to either respect rights or pursue projects, they have reached the point where they can no longer effectively function as agents in the community; for the central feature of agency—pursuit of personal projects within a human community—is no longer available. It is this aspect of the argument that seems common to all agency positions, namely, that (potential) loss of agency calls for rectification to bring the individual back to the level where agency is again functional. Differences would then be over what does or does not threaten agency and over the various means that might be employed to recover it.

Lomasky himself, like Locke, goes on to argue that the agent in these dire circumstances has a residual claim to the surplus property of others. We do not have an absolute claim to our "surplus," because it is possible for each of us to fall prey to agency-removing circumstances. When that happens, we too would not value any system of rights that failed to restore our agency. Consequently, the only system that would be valued would be one in which individuals did not have absolute entitlement to their surplus property, even when that property was legitimately obtained. "Surplus" here means something like "that which goes beyond what is necessary to maintain agency." Lomasky seems to interpret what is necessary for agency in fairly minimalist terms, so that the right in question entitles one to sufficient but not extensive or necessarily continuous aid. However, the questions of what constitutes a surplus, when agency has been restored, and what is necessary to maintain agency would all seem open to interpretation and dispute.

Agency arguments are structured in terms of the agent in need and not the one giving the aid. In this respect they all trail off into general abstract conclusions about how "someone" must provide the benefit "owed" to the recipient. This may seem analogous to all rights arguments, where some indefinite "others" are bound to respect the right in question. Yet unlike, for example, the right to negative liberty, which each and every individual is bound to (and can) respect at all times, the right to welfare (or the restoration of agency) could not be taken this way without thereby thrusting the recipient(s) into riches. Instead, the right seems to be understood to mean that anyone *may* be called to contribute and that all should be prepared to meet the obligation, but that only so much will be demanded as is necessary for the restoration of agency. Nevertheless, like the negative right to liberty, the right to welfare based on an agency approach considers nonrecipients only to the extent that they may be in a position to respect the right. Otherwise, the entire focus is on the claimant, making these sorts of arguments thoroughly demand-sided.

In Lomasky's case, for example, the argument at best establishes that the agent in need no longer has reason to value the system that does not restore his or her agency, not that perhaps hundreds of millions of others have a reason to disvalue that same system. One can respond to this either with some sort of contractarian argument ("No one would agree to such a system . . .") about which I have already had my say, or one can suppose that agency is the *sine qua non* of morality, such that failure to rescue the (presumably) involuntary departure from it on the part of some is tantamount to rejecting morality altogether.[38] This latter alternative still suffers, however, from what might be called the "problem of engagement"; that is, it fails to provide a direct *personal* reason for taking the action. Even if we grant, for the sake of argument only, that the indirect impersonal case has been made—where the individual's own membership in the class of agents commits that individual in some way and on "pain" of inconsistency to a concern about the agency status of others—what does the argument say to each person individually about the action and his own project?

Notice that if our appeal is to the virtue of charity, instead of the right to welfare, the problem of engagement is immediately met, for the focus then is on the one(s) who will provide the benefit, not the recipient. Yet unlike the agency argument, which ignores the provider altogether, this focus does not preclude the person in need from being a part of the nature of the virtue of charity, and not just abstractly. Indiscriminate or impersonal giving would be unconcerned with those specifics (e.g., how much, how long, to whom, why) necessary for making charity an integral part of one's own projects. Doing so becomes increasingly difficult the more the projects are impersonally conceived and universally required.

It is worth noting at this point that there is nothing especially self-perfecting about aiding those in need,[39] except perhaps for those positive feelings that naturally result from our propensity for benevolence. Yet as part of a more broadly conceived charity such actions may indeed be perfective. For as premodern philosophers seem to have seen more correctly, the general outlook of cooperation, good will, or moral optimism is what is self-perfecting—the particular manifestations (such as giving aid to those in need) are but the sign of moral accomplishment. Consequently, we can say that the failure to render appropriate aid signifies one's moral defectiveness, but that the giving of aid is not itself necessarily a sign of one's self-perfection or possession of the virtue of charity. If, on the other hand, the concept of charity is narrowed to the act of giving aid to those in need, is it really surprising that the recipient is the object of analysis and the provider entirely ignored? After all, under this way of looking at things, what more is there to say to the donor about the act of transferring resources to those with less, except that one will "feel good" afterwards?[40]

It may still be possible, however, to get a less one-sided perspective on welfare out of reciprocity arguments. In general, reciprocity arguments take the form of returning "good for good" (or "evil for evil"). This would suggest that both the benefactor and recipient would be given at least equal consideration.[41] Indeed, it is precisely because one may play either role that reciprocity arguments do not seem as demand-sided as agency arguments might be. As Lawrence Becker has noted in his book *Reciprocity*, if a system of reciprocity cycles correctly, the benefits should tend to equal out without too much domination or exploitation.[42] This continues to make it look as though both benefactors and recipients are given equal consideration and as though the middle ground between the right to welfare and the virtue of charity has finally been discovered.

Yet we have it on the same authority that

> [r]eciprocity is a *recipient's* virtue. It is the way people ought to be disposed to *respond* to others. It says nothing about how people ought to behave, or feel, when they *give* a gift. (p. 93; emphasis in original)

This clearly indicates that the focus of reciprocity arguments is again not on the benefactor, but on the recipient. But why should this be the case? After all, if reciprocity is truly reciprocal, it would seem that the conduct of the benefactor is of equal concern to that of the recipient.[43] In Becker's case, however, the recipient is the focus of the theory because virtue is itself justified in terms of increasing aggregate goal satisfaction (pp. 87 and 125). So although the argument is conducted in terms of dispositions necessary for flourishing as a moral agent (e.g., pp. 74–75), the final justification of that flourishing is social rather than self-perfective. This is demonstrated at the critical juncture where the most controversial of Becker's maxims of reciprocity is being defended: to wit, reciprocation should be made for any good received, not just those we seek or accept. The other maxims (p. 74) are quite compatible with the more ordinary notion that reciprocal arrangements are voluntary and that one is not obligated to reciprocate for positive externalities that one has not sought or accepted.

We get locked into the stronger claim, however, by the argument that certain social goods will not be as forthcoming if we do not make the disposition to reciprocate for every good received obligatory. Aggregate goal satisfaction, in other words, will be diminished without this obligation (p. 125). Apart from any empirical doubts one may have, this claim immediately makes the virtue in question instrumental in a way that the self-perfective qualities of classical virtue were not. The flourishing moral agency that seems to be the focus of the theory is itself secondary to a social good (*aggregate* goal satisfaction) that serves as its measure or standard. Classical virtue, in contrast, was exercised for its own sake, which means that its self-perfecting qualities were realized through the very performance of the virtue itself. Social benefits were expected, and were sometimes even the object of the virtue, but they were not its ground or measure.

It is important to realize that Becker's own argument is not about charity, welfare, or many of the other themes we have been talking about. These topics are left largely undiscussed in this book. But reciprocity is given fundamental status by Becker and is rivaled only by justice as a basic virtue (pp. 149–50). Consequently, accepting the maxim mentioned above is likely to have important welfare implications. This is because we all are most certainly the beneficiaries of positive externalities we do not seek, and with something as vague and impersonal as aggregate goal satisfaction as our standard, each of our lives could be perpetually mortgaged to whatever someone's conception of our obligation to reciprocate might be.[44] In practice at least, that is likely to translate into entitlement or rights claims by recipients. The benefit of focusing primarily on the morality of the benefactor, as the virtue of charity does, is that individuals can vary both the degree and object of their charity to better fit the pursuit of their own projects. This seems to accord more directly with the pluralism assumed and encouraged by classical liberalism.

It has not been my claim here that the reciprocity or agency arguments may not be compelling in some practical sense. No doubt social goods are more likely to be produced under a strong ethic of reciprocity and we should not fail to be moved in the face of a possible loss of agency. But apart from any doubts we may have about these arguments establishing a positive *right* to welfare, the arguments clearly say nothing about the moral context in which traditional virtues such as charity arose. It is likely, though, that we knew all that going in. What we may have established even more clearly here is the nonaltruistic and noncommunitarian character of virtue within the self-perfective framework. Virtue theories, under the rubric of self-perfection, tend to appeal to self-initiated and proactive sorts of arguments. Reciprocity, then, would be more compatible with a virtue like charity if it could include self-initiated action. Apart from the question of whether self-initiation is precluded from reciprocity on definitional grounds (since reciprocity is always *responsive*), Becker's controversial maxim virtually wipes out self-initiated nonresponsive action. In other words, the right to welfare is destructive of the virtue of charity because it alters the character of virtue from its classically proactive posture into a reactive one.

V. Conclusion

My argument in this essay has *not* been that the right to welfare is destructive of the virtue of charity because the virtue of charity cannot exist if the state provides any form of welfare. Even if "bad welfare" drove out the "good," it is unlikely that a modicum of state support to the truly needy would in practice threaten the virtue of charity, although some empirical evidence suggests that more extensive aid may do so.[45] That some welfare is a legitimate function of the state is a basic tenet of classical liberalism (as opposed to libertarianism). Instead, my argument was about the theoretical threat to the virtue of charity posed by the right to welfare. Perhaps "threat" is too mild a term; for while the virtue of charity may still be alive among private individuals, it is moribund among theoreticians. If charity is mentioned at all, it is simply as a synonym for "welfare," or it is mentioned critically as part of a larger effort to guarantee the final triumph of the welfare state, namely, the obliteration of the distinction between charity and justice.

While there are clearly many parameters to this debate and many facets of it to consider, I might conclude by suggesting that the debate nonetheless seems to me to be another version of a more common discussion in our era over public activities versus private ones. The virtue of charity is essentially private, while the right to welfare is essentially public. Classical liberalism and libertarianism put their trust in private approaches, whereas the "new" liberalism and socialism seek more public or socialized measures. It is therefore no accident that as our culture continually sheds its classical-liberal heritage in politics, it comes to focus less upon an ethics supportive of private measures. I have suggested both that charity is being forgotten and that it might be worth our further attention. Perhaps more importantly, I have suggested that certain theoretical foundations that predate liberalism itself may be necessary to resurrect charity. It is, after all, in an evolved state of liberalism that this discussion is being conducted. If charity has gotten lost as liberalism has evolved, then perhaps we need to look carefully at where it was lost, the reasons for its departure, and what might be done to reestablish its importance in liberal orders. We may even discover that virtue is best served when classical ethics is allied with classical liberalism.

Notes

*I wish to thank Stuart Warner, Loren Lomasky, Susan Feigenbaum, and Neil DiMarchi for preliminary help on this essay. I am especially grateful to Douglas

Rasmussen, to the other contributors to *Social Philosophy & Policy* 10 (Winter 1993), and to its editors for their extensive critical comments.

1. I am using the term "right" very loosely here to mean any claim of justice coupled with a correlative duty that is coercively sanctioned by the state. There may be rights without duties but they would have little bearing on our problem here since we are concerned with legitimate redistribution of resources in response to a right claim. More importantly, not all defenses of redistribution are formulated in the language of rights. I have tried to keep the notion of "rights" loose enough to include those normative proposals that require state-sanctioned redistribution, but that for some reason prefer not to defend that redistribution by using the language of rights. In these cases, "rights" is a shorthand expression.

2. For a discussion of some of the issues and literature on this problem, see Susan Feigenbaum, "The Case of Income Redistribution: A Theory of Government and Private Provision of Collective Goods," *Public Finance Quarterly* 8, no. 1 (January 1980), 3–22.

3. See Allen Buchanan, "Justice and Charity," *Ethics* 97, no. 3 (April 1987), 573.

4. *Ibid.*, 559.

5. Adam Smith, *The Theory of Moral Sentiments*, ed. D. D. Raphael and A. L. Macfie (Indianapolis: Liberty Classics, 1982), II.ii.I.3. I shall refer to this work hereafter as *TMS*; references will be given parenthetically in the text.

6. It is worth noting that for Smith, as reported by John Millar to Dugald Steward (introduction to the Oxford edition of *TMS*, 2), questions of utility or benefit were categorized under the heading of "expediency" and came after the subjects of natural theology, moral theory, and jurisprudence.

7. Buchanan, "Justice and Charity," 561. A number of the points I am making here and below seem to parallel those made elsewhere by Loren Lomasky in "Justice to Charity," unpublished manuscript.

8. This is true even of Jeremy Waldron's unique approach to the problem of charity. The adoption of his principle "Q" ("Nobody should be permitted even to use force to prevent another man from satisfying his very basic needs in circumstances where there seems to be no other way of satisfying them") in no way takes his solution out of the realm of justice and into a defense of some other virtue, for Q still describes what is owed to others. See Jeremy Waldron, "Welfare and the Images of Charity," *Philosophical Quarterly* 36, no. 145 (October 1986), 463–82.

9. Buchanan, "Justice and Charity," 574–75.

10. I have argued for this point at length in *The Virtue of Prudence* (New York: Peter Lang, 1991), ch. 1 and *passim*.

11. In this connection, Leo Strauss has noted: "The soul of modern development, one may say, is a peculiar realism, consisting in the notion that moral principles and the appeal to moral principles—preaching, sermonizing—are ineffectual, and therefore that one has to seek a substitute for moral principles which would be much more efficacious than ineffectual preaching." Strauss, "Progress or Return,"

in *The Rebirth of Classical Political Rationalism*, ed. T. Pangle (Chicago: University of Chicago Press, 1988), 242.

12. The virtue of prudence, however, was technically an *intellectual* virtue, not a moral one. This distinction need not detain us at the moment, for it would only serve to confuse matters further. If interested, see Den Uyl, *The Virtue of Prudence*, ch. 1 and *passim*.

13. It is worth consulting in this connection the Oxford English Dictionary, which discusses the etymology of the term. In general, it notes that the *Vulgate* (the Latin version of the Bible prepared by St. Jerome in the fourth century) distinguished *dilectio* (love) from *caritas* (charity), but *caritas* was used more often. The English version of the Bible translated the terms this way until the sixteenth century, when "love" was sometimes used where "charity" normally would have been used. By 1881, however, "love" was used for everything, thus eliminating the distinction between *dilectio* and *caritas*.

14. St. Thomas Aquinas, *Summa Theologiae*, ed. Timothy McDermott (Westminster, Maryland: Christian Classics, 1989), II-II, Q23, A2. I shall refer to this work hereafter as *ST*; references will be given parenthetically in the text.

15. For a further discussion of this distinction between ancient and modern ethics, see Douglas Den Uyl and Lee C. Rice, "Spinoza and Hume on Individuals," *Reason Papers* no. 15 (Summer 1990). In the meantime, one of the best contemporary statements about "love" (and thereby "charity") in the classical sense is given by David L. Norton in *Democracy and Moral Development* (Berkeley: University of California Press, 1991), 40.

> [L]ove is not exclusively or primarily interpersonal; it is first of all the right relationship of each person with himself or herself. The self to which love is in the first instance directed is the ideal self that is aspired to and by which random change is transformed into the directed development we term growth. When the ideal of the individual is rightly chosen, it realizes objective values that subsisted within the individual as innate potentialities, thereby achieving in the individual the self-identity that is termed "integrity" and that constitutes the foundation of other virtues.

16. Aquinas notes that justice is exclusively concerned with others (*ST*, II-II, Q58, A2), and Aristotle suggests something similar (*NE*, V, ch. 11). But my point is not to suggest that supply-sided virtues cannot have others as their object, but only that their ultimate justification is grounded in the person's own good or character development, and that is the focus of classical ethics, but not modern.

17. But the Dominican fathers believe this has roots in some Roman authors (e.g., Cicero) whom Aquinas is looking to in *ST*, II-II, Q117, A5, when he says that "liberality is listed by some authors as a part of justice."

18. Edward Andrew, *Shylock's Rights* (Toronto: University of Toronto Press, 1987), 7–9.

19. I am not, however, saying that the mere fact that something is obligatory renders it a matter of justice, but rather that when something is conceived of as obligatory outside of the self-perfective framework and within the strictly social or

modern framework, the problem of the conflation of justice and charity would be likely to arise. It is also worth noting that this article in Aquinas is also cited by Andrew along with Q58, A12 and Q66, A7–8. How he misinterprets Q32, A5 is explained above in the text. The other citations also do not support his contention that Aquinas does not want to separate justice from charity, assuming again that "separate" means something close to "distinguish" (for if it did not, Andrew's point would be trivial).

20. One should not now assume that therefore others are simply instrumental to one's own self-perfection. Giving alms for "God's sake" is another way of saying that one's love of God causes one to recognize the love of others *for their own sake*. Aquinas would argue that it is in the absence of that sort of love that we treat others as instruments.

21. Elsewhere (*ST*, II-II, Q66, A7–8, noted by Andrew and cited in n. 19 above) Aquinas does seem to say that those in need have a "right" to the surplus of others and that this has something to do with justice. Moreover, he says (*ST*, II-II, Q58, A2) that justice is exclusively other-oriented and (*ST*, II-II, Q58, A12) that justice is the supreme moral virtue. But this should not be interpreted to mean that justice and charity collapse into one another. In the first place, charity as a theoretical virtue is obviously the broader notion. Secondly, we have already seen at least one case where they are distinguished, and we have observed the manner in which their distinction was the basis for the problem of categorization. Finally, as I have already noted, the fact that something is the object of a virtue does not necessarily make it the ground of the virtue. So even if others were the exclusive object of justice, it would not necessarily be the case that justice must be understood exclusively in terms of others. That would be like saying we must understand courage solely in terms of risky circumstances, without reference to the agent. It would still not be accurate, then, to say that for Aquinas one owes the other the goods as a matter of justice, although other Christian thinkers do hold that position.

22. Both of the following quotes are drawn from Thomas Hobbes, *English Works*, 11 vols., ed. W. Molesworth (Evanston, Illinois: Adlers Foreign Bks., 1966).

23. Thomas Hobbes, *Leviathan*, ed. Richard Tuck (Cambridge: Cambridge University Press, 1991), ch. 30.

24. John Locke, *Two Treatises of Government*, ed. Peter Laslett (Cambridge: Cambridge University Press, 1988), Book 1, ch. 4, sec. 42. It is not my intention to imply that Locke was the first to look at matters in the way described below. Pascal, for example, favorably cites St. Gregory (*Provincial Letters*, 12): "When we give the poor what is necessary to them, we are not so much bestowing on them what is our property as rendering to them what is their own; and it may be said to be an act of justice rather than a work of mercy."

25. See Edward Andrew, *Shylock's Rights*, 5. Later in chapter two (p. 58) Andrew cites the same passage from Locke that I do above. Nevertheless, he refuses to believe it, asserting instead that his thesis about early liberals separating justice and charity must be correct so we should not read this in terms of what it says but in terms of something else. No further textual evidence, however, is provided, and

from my point of view it is because Andrew has at least partially misconstrued the problem that he cannot read the texts correctly.

26. Recall the early liberals such as Smith saw commercial societies *not* as a means of entrenching a wealthy class, but of closing the gap between rich and poor that older systems had solidified. The rise of the *middle* class was thought to be the great product of liberal orders.

27. Bernard Mandeville, "An Essay on Charity and Charity-Schools," in *The Fable of the Bees* (Indianapolis: Liberty Classics, 1988), 253. All references to Mandeville will be to this edition. Hereafter, page numbers will be given in the text.

28. Cf., e.g., Kant, *Foundations of the Metaphysics of Morals*, sec. I. Kant shares with the classical moral tradition a recognition of the importance of principle and a rejection of social utility as the foundation of ethics. Nevertheless, Kant's formalism, rule orientation, and impersonalism are antithetical to the classical virtue of charity as I have described it here. Moreover, attempts to turn Kant into a virtue ethicist are unconvincing (see Den Uyl, *The Virtue of Prudence*, ch. 5). Nevertheless, the second formulation of the Categorical Imperative does share something of the basic spirit of classical charity. I thank Thomas Hill for showing me this.

29. This is not to suggest that taxes cannot be onerous, but the degree of the burden is a separate issue from the replacement of charity as a virtue with charity as a commodity.

30. This is not to say individuals in this system might not also confuse compassion and charity. A critic might be more likely to respond that the private system allows "charitable" deeds to be done more from motives of "pride" and "vanity" than a public system which, in a sense, removes motives altogether. But part of the issue here is whether having to occasionally appeal to those vices is worse than systematically abandoning the possibility of charity being a question of personal responsibility.

31. Some attempt to begin such a defense is contained in my two books: *Liberty and Nature* (with Douglas Rasmussen) (La Salle, Illinois: Open Court, 1991), and *The Virtue of Prudence*.

32. Loren Lomasky's argument, for example, seems to be a combination of the agency and the RNY arguments. See Loren Lomasky, *Persons, Rights, and the Moral Community* (Oxford: Oxford University Press, 1987), especially 125–28.

33. An example here might be Baruch Brody in "Redistribution Without Egalitarianism," *Social Philosophy & Policy* vol. 1, no. 1 (Autumn 1983), where "redistribution programs . . . are forms of compensation for the violation of rights" (86). This view, however, would be closest to a type of reciprocity argument.

34. Gerald F. Gaus correctly notes that this is the Rousseauian perspective on political philosophy, where property cannot be antecedent to political society but is itself the product of convention, law, and politics. See Gerald F. Gaus, "A Contractual Justification of Redistributive Capitalism," in *Markets and Justice*, ed. John W. Chapman (New York: NYU Press, 1989), 90.

35. This seems to be the view of Jeremy Waldron in "Welfare and the Images of Charity" (see n. 8 above).

36. And of course there are contractarian cases. See, for example, Gaus, "A Contractual Justification of Redistributive Capitalism"; and Christopher W. Morris, "A Hobbesian Welfare State?" *Dialogue*, vol. 4, no. 27 (Winter 1988): pp. 653–73.

37. *Person, Rights and the Moral Community*, p. 127.

38. A better argument, and one more consistent with other things that at least Lomasky says in his book, is to say that agency is a necessary condition of human communities. To let anyone's agency lapse without taking action is equivalent to a lack of commitment to a necessary condition for a human community which, in quasi-Hobbesian terms, puts one in a state of nature with respect to the community. So one's property can be taken either because one is an enemy of the community or because as a member one is committed to doing what is necessary to maintain the conditions of community. So far as I know Lomasky does not make this argument, but this argument may represent his own view, since his approach often seems to me to be at least partially contractarian. Incidentally, this is an argument I would accept, though not as a foundational argument, but rather as one that has force within a self-perfective context. It would not, in my view, imply a *right* to welfare, although it might at least partially establish an obligation to aid. For further information on my own position, see Douglas Rasmussen and Douglas Den Uyl, *Liberty and Nature*, pp. 144–51.

39. At least in the absence of a theology which promises eternal rewards for such conduct, there is nothing especially self-perfecting about the mere act of aiding those in need.

40. Indeed, the appeal to "good feelings" is just the Mandevillian problem all over again.

41. A classic example of a reciprocity argument outside a teleological ethical context is Kant's famous position in the *Foundations* that we all have a duty to aid others because we would will such aid for ourselves. One problem here, though, is that if we specify "will" in any concrete way, the argument may take on a contractarian character. Kant himself, of course, was making the case that we would somehow contradict ourselves if we did not will for others what we will for ourselves. Consistency therefore is the main ingredient in reciprocal willing for Kant; but as is well known, this tends to give more formal than substantive results. Contemporary thinkers, such as Alan Gewirth, who use the same sort of strategy, try to obviate the formalism by referring to what is implied by the *actions* of agents rather than their "wills." But then these arguments look less and less like reciprocity arguments and more like agency arguments. And like the agency approach just discussed, these arguments tend to regard persons impersonally and thus suffer from the problem of engagement.

42. Lawrence Becker, *Reciprocity*, p. 133. Subsequent page reference in the text refer to this book.

43. In saying this, I am temporarily ignoring a possibility that may lie unstated in the background of Becker's argument and perhaps all reciprocity arguments, namely, that there are *only* recipients. In other words, benefactors are nothing but recipients paying off their debts. In the end (see below) this is the conclusion I finally arrive at about these sorts of arguments.

44. I find it strange that a sustained argument on reciprocity exists anyway. As Adam Smith points out, it is virtually a natural sentiment. If there is virtue in it, it would come from transforming the sentiment into a "moral sentiment," but that has less to do with reciprocity than it does with the other features of a moral outlook for Smith, such as impartiality. But other than Becker's maxim 7 ("returns should be made for goods received, not merely for goods accepted"), and insofar as we are no longer speaking of simply natural inclinations, the rest of the maxims would have been captured under the traditional virtue of charity or the pagan virtue of magnanimity. This is also a way in which the discussion would be less likely to get confused with justice. I am by no means suggesting that Becker's project is a failure. Indeed, the discussion is often brilliant and always sensitive, and since I have forced the argument in a direction Becker himself does not take, I should be circumspect about criticism. Becker's discussion is, as far as I know, the only position that gives a central and fundamental place to reciprocity.

45. See Wolfe, *Whose Keeper?*, pp. 89–94 and 168–77. Wolfe himself, however, regards the evidence as mixed. In addition, one could make the case that our current bankrupt and ineffective system of welfare—where the numbers of poor keep increasing despite no real lessening of welfare expenditures—can have the effect of *encouraging* the virtue of charity. More and more people are realizing that the state is so inept at actually relieving suffering that, if individuals do not help on a private basis, no relief will be forthcoming! In such a case we have an uneasy tension between the welfare paradigm and the charity paradigm as they both try to exist together.

Against Moral Minimalism

Gregory R. Johnson

The two most popular ways of making a case for libertarianism are the *moral* and the *technical-scientific* strategies. The moral strategy starts from the idea that libertarian and nonlibertarian social theories differ ultimately on *moral* grounds, whether these be differing conceptions of the good, of rights, or of both. The technical-scientific strategy begins from the idea that libertarianism and nonlibertarianism differ ultimately on *scientific* grounds, primarily on differing *economic* conceptions of the nature of society and of the politically possible. These differing scientific visions lead to differing *technological* recommendations for the creation and reform of institutions.

The technical-scientific strategy comes in two forms, which I shall dub *positivism* and *moral minimalism*. Positivism denies or ignores the necessity of moral considerations in political philosophy, reducing all political issues merely to technical-scientific questions. The problem with such a value-free approach to political theory is that it can only lay out differing political options—cataloging their costs and benefits, their capacities and incapacities—but it cannot recommend which options we should *prefer* without appealing to the kinds of moral considerations that it excludes. In short, positivistic political science can tell us what *is* and what is *possible*, but it cannot recommend what *ought* to be—unless it smuggles in value judgments, which operate tacitly and are therefore immune to rational reflection and criticism.[1]

Because of this problem, no serious libertarian theorist avows outright positivism. Most technical-scientific libertarians do not altogether deny the necessity of a moral dimension of political theory. Instead, they seek merely to *minimize* or *neutralize* the moral dimension by denying that there are any significant moral differences between libertarians and nonlibertarians. The real differences, they argue, are scientific and technological. Nonlibertarians, they claim, are simply ignorant of the superiority of voluntary over coercive social arrangements in achieving such allegedly common goals as freedom, equality, prosperity, environmental cleanliness, and the elimination of arbitrary discrimination on the basis of religion, race, gender, ethnicity, sexuality, etc. All of these goals are said to follow from allegedly common values. The moral minimalist credo is well-expressed by F.A. Hayek:

> . . . not only I, but I believe also the majority of my contemporary libertarian fellow-economists, were originally led to economics by the more or less strong socialist beliefs . . . which we felt in our youth, and the study of economics turned us into radical anti-socialists. . . . my concrete differences with socialist fellow-economists on particular issues of social policy turn inevitably, not on differences of value, but on differences as to the effects particular measures will have.[2]

Other prominent moral minimalists include Milton Friedman, David Friedman, and Leland B. Yeager.[3]

The first question we must ask the minimalists is: What precisely is the content of the moral consensus they claim exists among libertarians and nonlibertarians? The moral consensus has at least three elements: (1) individualism, by which I mean the view that each and every *individual* has an innate dignity or value that commands our respect and concern; (2) egalitarianism, by which I mean the view that *each and every* individual—regardless of accidental differences of race, religion, class, or gender—has an innate dignity or value that commands our respect and concern; and (3) altruism, by which I mean the sentiment of moral respect, concern, and solidarity elicited by the dignity of the other, whether this be manifested as active solicitude or simple forbearance from transgressing the rights of the other. Again, Hayek provides an admirable statement of the consensus. On the origins of altruism and solidarism, he claims that:

> Our instincts and emotions have been shaped by something like a million years in which the human race lived in small bands of thirty to fifty people in a hunting and gathering life in which all their emotional attitudes, still embodied in our physical constitution, were gradually developed. Our instincts tell us, first, that out duty is to serve the visible needs of our known friends; and, second, that the activity that gives us most satisfaction is to join in a common effort for common ends.[4]

Over time, these altruistic and solidaristic sentiments were extended beyond particular societies to apply equally to each and every individual, creating the basic moral code that Hayek claims is shared by socialists, interventionists, and libertarians alike.[5]

In sum, on the moral minimalist model, the task of social theory is, in the words of one advocate, "... not denying the force of our moral obligations to others, but analyzing the extent to which the welfare state actually fulfills them."[6] Since the argumentative thrust of moral minimalism depends upon technical-scientific accounts of the *consequences* of different social institutions and reforms, it is properly dubbed a form of moral consequentialism.

The appeal of moral minimalism is easy to understand. First, it gives the decisive role in political theory to economics, which is a libertarian forte. Second, by downplaying moral disagreements, it helps to avoid the emotional denunciations and academic ostracism endured by libertarians who stand on moral grounds, particularly those who, like Ayn Rand, argue for capitalism on the basis of ethical egoism. A third, more psychological motivation is an academic version of the Stockholm syndrome: Many libertarian students and academicians find so unbearable the anxiety of having their careers and ambitions held hostage by intolerant ideological opponents that they begin to identify with and seek the approval of their captors. However, in spite of its many temptations, I shall show that there are serious problems with moral minimalism.

1. The Wreckage of the New Consensus

Does the moral consensus claimed by the moral minimalists really exist? Are there really no moral differences between libertarians on the one hand and communists and welfare statists, communitarians and deep ecologists, fascists and religious, racial, national, and ethnic chauvinists on the other hand? Can their differences be reduced ultimately to scientific and technological questions?

There are, it seems, striking moral differences between libertarians and those deep ecologists who eschew moral "humanism." Moral humanism is the view that human beings are the primary object of moral concern. Humanistic moral philosophy is concerned with discovering the good life *for man*. Other kinds of beings fall within the scope of moral concern only to the extent that they are instrumentally related to the good life for man. Libertarianism, because it is premised upon individualism, egalitarianism, and respect for the integrity and rights of other human beings, is deeply humanistic. Deep ecology, however, can be radically anti-humanistic. Some deep ecologists claim that moral humanism, because it enthrones man and reduces the natural world to a mere stockpile of resources for the satisfaction of human desires, is the root of an environmental crisis so overwhelming that it cannot be solved by mere technology. Instead, it requires a fundamental moral transformation: the adoption of an ethic that makes life *as such* and the earth *as a whole* the center of moral concern, and if this requires a severe curtailment of human flourishing, then so be it.[7] These moral differences cannot be reduced to differences of scientific opinions and technological recommendations about the environment, for what is in question is precisely the legitimacy of a technical-scientific approach to these issues.

There seem, furthermore, to be equally striking moral differences between libertarians on the one hand and welfare statists and Communists on the other. Although in the abstract both sides evoke elements of egalitarianism, individualism, and altruism, when these abstractions are made concrete, a vast moral difference appears: libertarians treat each individual as an end in him- or herself, not merely a means to the ends of others. Consequently, libertarians hold that generosity, charity, persuasion, and exchange for mutual advantage—not force, fraud, and exploitation—are the only legitimate ways by which individuals can derive benefits from one another. Communists, socialists, and welfare statists hold—in theory, in practice, or both—that each individual is not an end in him- or herself; instead, all individuals, to the extent that they have resources and ability, can be used as means to the satisfaction of the needs of others. This is the meaning of Marx's principle "From each according to his ability, to each according to his need." Consequently, the use of force, fraud, and exploitation is licensed by communists, socialists, and welfare-statists if individuals of ability cannot be persuaded to sacrifice themselves voluntarily to the needy.

It is important to see that communists, et al., do not use force out of simple paternalism, for paternalism is the attempt to use force on a person *in that person's own interest*. Rather, they use force to subordinate one person's interests to another's.

Although many communists, socialists, and welfare statists often complain that capitalism is an impediment to individual self-realization, their individualism is superficial, for their political practice requires that some individuals be sacrificed for others; they are, in short, better described as moral collectivists rather than individualists.

The great Russian liberal Alexander Herzen prophetically expressed the moral difference between liberal individualism and socialist and communist collectivism as follows.

> If progress is the goal, for whom are we working? Who is this Moloch who, as the toilers approach him, instead of rewarding them, draws back; and as a

consolation to the exhausted and doomed multitudes, shouting *"morituri te salutant,"* can only give the mocking answer that after their death all will be beautiful on Earth. Do you truly wish to condemn the human beings alive today to the sad role of caryatids supporting a floor for others someday to dance on, ... or of wretched galley slaves who, up to their knees in mud, drag a barge ... with the humble words "progress in the future" upon its flag? ... The end of each generation is itself.[8]

This is a moral difference that cannot be reduced to technical-scientific questions, for what is in question is precisely whether individuals belong in the category of ends or of means.

A moral minimalist might object to this argument along the following lines. Granted, communists, socialists, and other statists are collectivists in practice. But when libertarians criticize them for their collectivism, they are pointing out the incompatibility of their collectivist practices with their individualistic moral commitments; they are, in short, pointing out the inappropriateness of using collectivist means for the achievement of individualist ends; it is a dispute about means, not ends; therefore, it is a technical argument, not a moral one. There are two problems with this response. First, it assumes what is actually in question: the depth or genuineness of the individualist commitments of communists, socialists, etc. Libertarians may not be calling their opponents *back* to individualism. They may be calling them to individualism in the first place. And this is an inescapably moral project, not a technical one. Second, even if the libertarian critique only amounted to the attempt to call wayward individualists back to the fold, the demand that one's actions be consistent with one's principles is the demand for moral integrity, which is a form of moral suasion, even though it might appeal to the concrete historical consequences of collectivist practices.

Another possible strategy for criticizing libertarian individualism is to attempt to force libertarians to admit some collectivist elements into their own theory. For instance, one could argue that even libertarian societies might sometimes come under attack; therefore, it might become necessary for their citizens to risk and even lose their lives in defense of freedom. And if even libertarian societies sometimes require the sacrifice of individual citizens for the preservation of society, then there is only a difference of degree, not a difference of moral kinds, between libertarianism and communism, and it is merely technical-scientific questions that determine their different places on the moral continuum. The main problem with this response is that it ignores a crucial moral distinction between kinds of self-sacrifice, a distinction drawn strikingly by Rousseau:

> If someone were to tell us that it is good that one person should perish for all, I would admire this saying when it comes from the lips of a worthy and virtuous patriot who dedicates himself willingly and out of duty to die for the welfare of his country. But if this means that the government is permitted to sacrifice an innocent person for the welfare of the multitude, I hold this maxim to be one of the most despicable that tyranny has ever invented.[9]

The objection, in short, presupposes that there is no moral distinction between the Spartans fighting to the last man at Thermopylae and forced labor in Soviet death camps—between voluntarily risking one's life for one's freedom and being involuntarily immolated for the sake of the next five-year plan.

Finally, there seems to be a vast moral gulf between libertarians and advocates of various forms of racial, religious, ethnic, and national chauvinism—which, along with the mixed economy and the welfare state, is the dominant form of politics in the postcommunist age. These forms of chauvinism are neither egalitarian nor individualistic, stressing instead the superiority of the group to the individual and of one group to all others. Chauvinism is altruistic only in a delimited way, demanding intragroup altruism and solidarity and promoting intergroup egoism, exploitation, and strife. Consequently, tribalist chauvinism is no friend of limited government, free markets, and international peace. No more striking contrast to libertarianism could be imagined.

Nor could clearer evidence of the bankruptcy of moral minimalism be provided. Moral minimalism seems to thrive on a form of myopic academic parochialism. Surrounded by left-wing academicians, most of whom espouse simply another form of liberalism, it is easy for libertarian moral minimalists to think that there is a fundamental moral consensus and that all debates can be reduced to technical-instrumental questions. However, when one glances outside the academy—and even into certain nooks inside the academy—one soon encounters radically different perspectives. Nobody could seriously claim that there are no moral differences between libertarians on the one hand and fascists, Nazis, Islamic fundamentalists, Christian Reconstructionists, and various kinds of militant nationalists on the other. Nobody could seriously claim that the differences between Adolf Hitler and Milton Friedman are on matters of means, not ends. Nobody could seriously claim that the Ayatollah Khomeini and Ludwig von Mises merely held different ideas about how to achieve common goals. Thus it is amusing (and it would be especially amusing from the point of view of a Popperian falsificationist) to see one moral minimalist claiming that, "the once-controversial ideal of equal individual liberty now has no universally plausible competitors" (as if the competitors *had* to be "universally plausible" to upset the consensus thesis), and then—with a nervous glance outside the academy—observing (in parentheses) that, "One might even contend that the spread of authoritarian Islam shows that ideological history has not ended at all," but then, having touched that base, proceeding blithely forth with his minimalist argument for another 72 pages.[10]

In sum, the moral minimalist "consensus thesis" suffers from what we can call, following Hegel, the "night in which all cows are black" problem. If someone declares that all cows are black, this could follow from the fact that all cows are indeed black, or from the fact that the observer himself is in the dark and therefore cannot see what color the cows really are. Likewise, the minimalist claim that the moral underpinnings of all competing social theories are the same *could* follow from the fact that they really are the same, but—as I have shown—it actually follows from the minimalists' inability to make moral distinctions. This inability to make moral distinctions is evident in such hyphenated minimalist constructions as "egalitarian-individualism," which seem to refer to a moral code common to libertarianism and the left, but do so only by abstracting away and ignoring the moral differences.

2. The Question of Bourgeois Liberalism

Another serious problem with moral minimalism is that it leaves out significant moral ideals and cultural practices that most libertarians—minimalists included—would like to defend, and indeed might *have* to defend in order to make capitalism and limited government work. As Edith Efron pointed out many years ago, there are few libertarians who would defend negative liberty if it meant that they would have to live in caves.[11] Efron's point is that negative liberty is not valued purely as an end in itself. Nor is it valued as a purely neutral instrumentality, without regard to its broader moral and cultural context and the ends to which it is conducive. Rather, negative liberty is valued because it is one of the essential elements of modern civilization, specifically modern *bourgeois* civilization:

> To an overwhelming degree our lives, our actions, our goals, and our very identities are functions of our civilization. And when we speak of liberty, we actually mean: liberty to function freely within *this* civilization. . . . Individual Liberty and modern civilization are *interlocking* values.[12]

Libertarians are not, therefore, merely advocates of abstract liberty; they are advocates of concrete *bourgeois* liberalism.

This is not, moreover, simply the cultural prejudice of some libertarians for, as Hayek has argued, capitalism and limited government do not and cannot rest simply upon the minimalist morality of egalitarianism, individualism, and altruism. They also depend upon the spontaneously evolved institutions and practices characteristic of bourgeois civilization and upon the virtues required and instilled by these institutions and practices to ensure their survival. Hayek describes the bourgeois ethic as follows.

> They [the early *bourgeoisie*] . . . esteemed the prudent man, the good husbandman and provider who looked after the future of his family and his business by building up capital, guided less by the desire to consume much than by the wish to be regarded as successful by his fellows who pursued similar aims. . . . Its [the market order's] mores involved withholding from the known needy neighbours what they might require in order to serve the unknown needs of thousands of unknown others. Financial gain rather than the pursuit of a known common good became not only the basis of approval but also the cause of the increase of general wealth.[13]

Such institutions as the family and the business firm and such virtues as hard work, self-restraint, fair dealing with strangers, and capital accumulation are as much parts of the moral fabric of libertarianism as are negative liberty and the protection of rights, and their destruction is just as fatal to libertarianism as the destruction of negative liberty and rights. Furthermore, according to Hayek, these bourgeois institutions and virtues are not only *different* from the principles of moral minimalism, they are actually to some extent *incompatible* with them. For instance, from the point of view of pure egalitarianism and altruism, the preference to take care of one's self and one's immediate family before one takes care of more distant relations, friends, or strangers is irrational, but such a preference is a cornerstone of bourgeois society. Thus, the survival of bourgeois society requires the repression and sublimation of our more solidaristic and altruistic sentiments.

According to Hayek, liberal society was viable so long as the traditional bourgeois virtues underlying it remained unquestioned. But unfortunately, the spirit of modern Cartesian rationalism is inimical to all spontaneously evolved institutions, practices, and virtues because most of them cannot offer rational justifications for themselves and are thus condemned as irrational superstitions and prejudices. Thus, the rationalist spirit, by paring away all traditional morality, arrives at what Hayek calls the innate "instincts" of solidarity and altruism. And because any merely personal and parochial limitations on the extent of the applicability of these instincts cannot be rationally justified, rationalism absolutizes them into a minimalist moral code at war with the leading institutions, practices, and virtues of bourgeois civilization. The left, in short, represents the truest form of moral minimalism, while libertarians are committed—largely, in spite of themselves—to a much thicker bourgeois conception of the good life.

It is here that another moral gulf opens up between libertarians and their opponents on the left, for although it might be possible to reach a consensus in terms of moral generalities—so long as they are sufficiently abstract—this consensus soon evaporates when one raises the question of what kind of culture one's political system requires and is conducive to. This is so because the left—no matter how bourgeois the lifestyles of many of its members may be—is characterized by distrust, distaste, and even active hostility toward bourgeois culture. Indeed, it is not entirely unfair to characterize today's disillusioned postcommunist left as driven in large part, not by the pursuit of vanished utopian ideals, but simply by the cultural anxiety that they might wake up someday in the world of *Ozzie and Harriet* and *Leave it to Beaver*. The left is, furthermore, largely correct in its suspicion that libertarianism, in spite of the bohemianism of many of its practitioners, is "objectively" culturally conservative, for capitalism and limited government require and therefore tend spontaneously to inculcate bourgeois virtues. Furthermore, although libertarianism would leave dissenters and oddballs free to opt out of mainstream society, it would also privatize the public educational system, which is the left's chief means of reproduction. By giving parents greater control of their children's education, libertarianism would make '50s-style bourgeois conformism much more likely than '60s-style alienation and radicalism, an intolerable option for the left. There are, in short, vast *concrete* moral and cultural differences between libertarians and the left, differences that are merely papered over by minimalist attempts to build a consensus in abstract terms.

Hayek, to his credit, is aware of this problem. Thus, while he is fully willing to admit that he shares the minimalist moral instincts of the left, he is also aware that libertarianism rests upon and is conducive to a much thicker bourgeois conception of morality, which he seeks to defend from its rationalistic critics. Thus Hayek, in spite of his excellent statements of the moral minimalists' credo, does not ultimately belong on their rolls.

3. Beyond Consequentialism and Deontology

If both the positivist and moral minimalist versions of technical-scientific libertarianism are unviable, does that imply that we must embrace what one might call "moral maximalism" or "hypermoralism"? In other words, is the only alternative to a technical-scientific case for libertarianism the kind of moral argument that would make absolutely no reference to scientific knowledge and technical concerns? In short, is the only alternative to minimalist consequentialism a maximalist "deontology"? Given this question, I believe that the moral minimalist would be inclined to answer "yes."

This, at least, is the case with one moral minimalist, who rests the plausibility of his own form of minimalist consequentialism largely on a caricature of "moralistic," "deontic" libertarianism, an approach that allows him to dismiss the entirety of nonconsequentialist libertarianism from Locke down to Nozick, Rothbard, and Rand in five-and-a-half pages.[14] The kernel of this argument's plausibility—such as it is—is that many deontic and rights-based forms of libertarianism are problematic, largely because they tend to be morally minimalistic in their premises (starting from a few initially plausible intuitions or assumptions, such as Lockean property-appropriation or Kantian dignity) and rationalistic in their method (deducing morally implausible conclusions from morally impoverished premises, and shrinking from no absurdity in the process). The most egregious example is Murray Rothbard's *The Ethics of Liberty*, in which he argues from Lockean property-appropriation to such conclusions as the advocacy of anarchism; a laissez-faire attitude toward child-pornography, child-prostitution, and running away from home; and a position on abortion that sidesteps all questions of moral personhood by arguing that unborn children may be killed at their mothers' convenience, *even if they are moral persons*.[15] Needless to say, Rothbard's approach to politics is not only indifferent to but actually hostile towards the bourgeois *Sittlichkeit* that capitalism and limited government both depend upon and encourage.[16] It is indeed hard to square this principled, moralistic radicalism and Olympian disregard for consequences with the fact that most libertarians—Rothbard included—are economists and policy analysts, for given this approach to moral philosophy, economics and policy analysis are completely irrelevant to political philosophy.[17] Given that rights theories like Rothbard's seem to be hermetically sealed off from history, social science, common sense, and moral intuitions so widespread that they should be considered more than mere prejudices—in a word, given that they are sealed off from *reality*—it is tempting to conclude that the only way of getting some empirical input into libertarian social theory is to adopt a form of moral consequentialism, tracking the outcomes of differing proposals with the tools of economics, sociology, history, and policy analysis.

However, while morally and intellectually stultifying forms of rights theory and deontology may give libertarianism a bad name, they do not thereby give minimalist consequentialism a good name. The chief problem with minimalist consequentialism is that it is just as intellectually stultifying as deontology, although in a different way. Minimalist consequentialism is an essentially piecemeal, empiricist approach to politics, condemned to nit-picking each and every policy proposal that comes down the line because it is not allowed to rule out entire classes of policy *in advance, on moral grounds*. Thus, while the consequentialist may be able to show that the costs of oil industry regulation outweigh the benefits—at least at *this particular time*, as proposed *in this particular plan*—tomorrow is always another day, with new circumstances and new plans. Is plan X un-economic? Well, then, how about plan Y? Is it uneconomical to regulate the steel industry? Well, how about the coal industry? Is it harmful to give welfare to unwed mothers? Well, maybe we can phase it in gradually.

So long as there are no deontic or rights-based side-constraints on the kinds of policies the state can pursue, the minimalist consequentialist cannot rule out tout court the kinds of policies that sacrifice the interests of one group for the benefit of another. All the consequentialist can do is argue that this particular proposal has costs higher than its benefits—*in this particular case*, as proposed *in this particular plan*. But maybe "our" human resources can be deployed and disposed of more efficiently at another time, with another plan.

If asked to identify what is wrong with slavery, the deontic or rights-based libertarian would reply that it is a gross violation of human dignity and human rights, and that it should never, ever be permitted again. All the consequentialist libertarian could answer is that it is inefficient at producing utility—but he must remain open to considering happier, more efficient forms of slavery. If asked to identify what is wrong with Soviet-style labor camps, the deontic or rights-based libertarian would again answer that they are gross violations of human dignity and human rights—no matter what their alleged utopian goals—and that they should never, ever be permitted again. The consequentialist libertarian could only say that they are inefficient—but he must remain open to considering happier, more efficient models. The only objection that the consequentialist libertarian seems to have to Stalinism is that Stalin didn't get away with it.

The insidious political "conservatism" of this approach is clear. By surrendering rather than trying adequately to secure the moral high ground, libertarian consequentialism becomes no different *in principle* from any of the other forms of liberalism, Republican or Democratic, Tory or Labour. Libertarianism loses any distinct moral identity and becomes at best a free-market "tendency" within the general welfare-state consensus. But, in fact, it is not even accurate to call consequentialist libertarianism a vague ideological "tendency," for a tendency has to tend *toward* some determinate goal that stands above the flux of events, whereas the consequentialist regards all such goals as endlessly renegotiable in light of shifting circumstances. With everything up for grabs and open to revision, the consequentialist drifts rudderless and compassless in the currents of political expediency—currents created by those who *do* have ideals and principles. The promise of even this sort of access to the intellectual mainstream and the political policy process—the chance to be a "player"—might be appealing, even intoxicating, to some, but it is ultimately self-defeating. The minimalist consequentialist, like the courtier journalists of the Washington press corps, gains "access" to the corridors of power—but only by surrendering all critical distance from "business as usual" and consequently any ability to propose radical alternatives to it.

Fortunately, though, there is a third option besides an Olympian deontic disdain for reality on the one hand and slaving in the galleys of consequentialist policy-wonkery on the other. Although an entire approach to moral philosophy could never be set forth in the narrow compass of this essay, one can at least point to Aristotle and Hegel as models for a third approach, which combines the valuable features of both deontology and consequentialism but leaves behind their intellectually stultifying limitations.

Aristotle's moral philosophy is neither consequentialistic nor deontic, but it comprises both consequentialism's openness to experience and deontology's robust, principled normativity because it derives its standard of value—*eudaimonia*, human flourishing, the good life for man—from the study of human nature, which is conceived in teleological and thus inherently normative terms. The root and essence of the Aristotelian alternative is this teleological and normative understanding of nature. For Aristotle, what truly *is* is also what truly *ought* to be. Thus, Aristotelian moral and political philosophy is not only open to, but actually requires, the use of the best available scientific knowledge of what *is* in order to know what *ought* to be. In keeping with this, the method of Aristotle's ethical treatises is richly empirical and even historical and anthropological. He does not simply intuit the human essence, formulate it in terms of a few impoverished axioms, and then deduce a set of moral rules. Instead, on the assumption that time-tested experience reflects the reality of nature, he carefully works through long-standing and widespread reputable opinions about the good life, probing and testing them, eliminating some and marshalling the remainder into a maximally consistent and unified but also richly variegated whole.[18] Aristotle's *Politics* likewise combines a robust normativity with political realism and a wealth of historical experience.

Aristotle, unfortunately, did not and could not conceive of the human good in light of the more than 2,000 years of scientific progress and historical experience since his passing. Christianity and, to a lesser extent, Stoicism have brought us the idea of the equality and innate dignity of each and every human being. Furthermore, the Christian understanding of creation elevated unrecompensed generosity to a basic metaphysical fact, and the life of Christ similarly elevated self-sacrifice. These changes required a deepening and revision of Aristotle's moral philosophy in light of new experience, a task that fell to Aquinas. Likewise, the Reformation and Counter Reformation, the scientific revolution, the European exploration and conquest of the globe, the American and French revolutions, the industrial revolution, and modern economic science all throw further light on the nature and concrete social and political requirements of human flourishing, requiring again the deepening and revision of Aristotelian moral and political philosophy.

Hegel's *Philosophy of Right* provides an excellent model for such a project. Hegel's account of concrete ethical life (*Sittlichkeit*), with its emphasis on the character-forming functions of concrete institutions and practices, can incorporate those features of Aristotelian ethics that make it superior to modern alternatives—for instance, the teleological definition of value, the emphasis on the primacy of practical reason, the accounts of virtue and vice, of strength and weakness of the will, and of the role of education into tradition and concrete ethical institutions and practices. But Hegel's *Sittlichkeit*, unlike the Aristotelian *polis*, incorporates as moments not only the family and the state, but also modern civil society, i.e., the realm of voluntary interaction. This realm includes the market economy, for which Hegel had a profound appreciation—not as a morally "neutral" framework for the individual pursuit of differing conceptions of the good life, but as an ethical institution that forms a particular kind of character in accordance with a particular conception of the good life for man. Hegel also incorporates modernity's hard-won appreciation of religious tolerance and constitutional government. Furthermore, he provides a more rigorous articulation of the kind of holistic and dialectical method used by Aristotle.

A similar deepening and revision of an Aristotelian approach to moral and political philosophy in light of the economic discoveries and political experience of the twentieth century—particularly the horrors of communism and fascism and the failure of the welfare state—now falls to libertarians. Of all contemporary libertarians, F. A. Hayek and Michael Oakeshott come closest to fulfilling this task and thus stand as exemplars, but much work remains to be done. And it can be done only by those who recognize that a consequentialistic moral minimalism is as much an impediment as a deontic moralism to the creation of a libertarianism for the twenty-first century.[19]

Notes

1. For a sustained critique of positivistic economism, see Tibor R. Machan, *Capitalism and Individualism: Reframing the Argument for the Free Society* (New York: St. Martin's Press, 1990).

2. F. A. Hayek, "Socialism and Science," in *New Studies in Philosophy, Politics, Economics, and the History of Ideas* (Chicago: University of Chicago Press, 1978), 296. Although Hayek gives an excellent statement of moral minimalism, his inclusion among its ranks is, as we shall see, somewhat problematic.

3. Milton Friedman has at times expressed a purely positivistic position. See Tibor R. Machan's "An Interview with Milton Friedman," *Reason* 6 (December 1974): 4–7. In his more popular works, however, Friedman soft-pedals moral distinctions and emphasizes economic issues. This is the essence of the minimalist strategy. See, for instance, his *Capitalism and Freedom* (Chicago: University of Chicago Press, 1962). David Friedman's main minimalist statement is *The Machinery of Freedom*, 2nd ed. (LaSalle, Illinois: Open Court, 1990). Leland B. Yeager's distinctive minimalist strategy is to argue that all of his opponents are really utilitarians at heart. See, for example, his "Rights, Contracts, and Utility in Policy Espousals," *Cato Journal* 6 (1985): 259–94. See also Tibor R. Machan's response, "Are Teleological Rights Theories Utilitarian?" *Cato Journal* 7 (1987): 255–58. In the vanity press, we find Geoffrey Friedman's epic manifesto of "post-libertarian" moral minimalism, "The New Consensus, Part I: The Fukuyama Thesis," *Critical Review* 3 (1989): 373–410 and "The New Consensus, Part II: The Democratic Welfare State," *Critical Review* 4 (1990): 633–708. I myself have bought into a version of moral minimalism in my essay "A Friend of Reason: Jose Guilherme Merquior," *Critical Review* 5 (1991 [appeared 1992]): 421–46, esp. 440–42. I would like to take this opportunity to repudiate that position.

4. Hayek, "The Reactionary Character of the Socialist Conception," in *Knowledge, Evolution, and Society* (London: The Adam Smith Institute, 1983), 38.

5. See, for example, "The Reactionary Character of the Socialist Conception," 40–41, where Hayek ascribes the generalization of altruism and solidarity to the rise of modern mass society and modern Cartesian rationalism. Although these surely do play a role, it is a serious oversight for him to ignore the role of Stoicism and Christianity in the promulgation of the idea of fundamental human equality. Modern radical egalitarianism is largely a rationalistic and secularized abridgement of Christian egalitarianism and altruism.

6. G. Friedman, "The New Consensus, Part II," 659.

7. On the critique of humanism and its connection to deep ecology, see George Sessions, "Anthropocentrism and the Environmental Crisis," *Humbolt Journal of Social Relations* 2 (1974): 1–12; David Ehrenfeld, *The Arrogance of Humanism* (New York: Oxford University Press, 1978); Arne Naess, "The Shallow and the Deep, Long-Range Ecology Movement," *Inquiry* 16 (1973): 95–100; and William C. Devall, "The Deep Ecology Movement," *Natural Resources Journal* 20 (1980): 299–322. A good overview of the field is provided by George Sessions, "Shallow and

Deep Ecology: A Review of the Philosophical Literature," in *Ecological Consciousness: Essays from the Earthday X Colloquium,* ed. Robert Schultz and Donald Hughes (Washington, D.C.: University Press of America, 1981).

8. Alexander Herzen, *From the Other Shore,* quoted by Isaiah Berlin in "Herzen and Bakunin on Liberty," in his *Russian Thinkers,* ed. Henry Hardy and Aileen Kelly (New York: Viking, 1978), 92.

9. Jean-Jacques Rousseau, *Discourse on Political Economy,* in *The Basic Political Writings,* ed. and trans. Donald A. Cress (Indianapolis: Hackett, 1987), 122.

10. G. Friedman, "The New Consensus, Part II," 635–36.

11. Edith Efron, "The Petr Principle," *Reason* 10 (May 1978): 62, 71.

12. Efron, "The Petr Principle," 62.

13. Hayek, *Law, Legislation and Liberty,* vol. 3, *The Political Order of a Free People* (Chicago: University of Chicago Press, 1979), 164–65.

14. G. Friedman, "The New Consensus, Part II," 661–66. See also the replies to Friedman by Jan Narveson, Antony Flew, Tibor Machan, and Donald N. McCloskey and Friedman's rejoinder in *Critical Review* 6 (1992) *and* the replies by David L. Brooks, W. William Woolsey, Ingrid Harris, and Raphael Sassower and Joseph Agassi, with Friedman's rejoinder, in *Critical Review* 8 (1994).

15. Murray N. Rothbard, *The Ethics of Liberty* (Atlantic Highlands, N.J.: Humanities Press, 1982).

16. To his credit, in recent years, Rothbard has moved toward a more probourgeois, culturally conservative position, which he calls "paleolibertarianism."

17. G. Friedman, "The New Consensus, Part II," 663.

18. There is a large literature on Aristotle's method of ethics. A good introduction to the issues is J. Donald Monan, "Two Methodological Aspects of Moral Knowledge in the Nicomachean Ethics," in Suzanne Mansion, ed., *Aristote et les problemes de Methode* (Louvain: Beatrice-Nauwelarts, 1961).

19. The author wishes to thank Glenn A. Magee for his assistance with this paper.

Political Legitimacy and Discourse Ethics

Douglas B. Rasmussen

> He who dares to undertake the making of a people's institutions ought to feel himself capable, so to speak, of changing human nature, of transforming each individual, who is by himself a complete solitary whole, into part of a greater whole from which he in a manner receives his life and being; of altering man's constitution for the purpose of strengthening it; and of substituting a partial and moral existence for the physical and independent existence nature has conferred on us all. He must, in a word, take away from man his own resources and give him instead new ones alien to him, and incapable of being made use of without the help of other men. The more completely these natural resources are annihilated, the greater and the more lasting are those which he acquires, and the more stable and perfect the new institutions; so that if each citizen is nothing and can do nothing without the rest, and the resources acquired by the whole are equal or superior to the aggregate of resources of all the individuals, it may be said that legislation is at the highest possible point of perfection.
>
> —Jean-Jacques Rousseau, "The Legislator," *The Social Contract*

In the wake of the apparent collapse of orthodox Marxism, Marxian intellectuals have been in pursuit of an alternative theoretical basis from which to critique capitalism. One influential standard-bearer is Jürgen Habermas. Habermas has set out to correct what he sees as a serious flaw in Marxist theory, the lack of a firm normative foundation from which to legitimate the struggle against capitalism. Habermas proposes his theory of "discourse ethics" as the way to assess the validity of a conception of justice and in turn the legitimacy of the political institutions and public policies based upon it. This essay seeks to explain the exact character of Habermas's "discourse ethics" and to show that it not only does not succeed in establishing a normative basis from which to assess conceptions of justice, but fails to express one of modernity's central values—the moral propriety of pluralism and individualism.

I

1. The Problem of Political Legitimacy

Legitimacy claims pertain to a political regime or order, and Jürgen Habermas holds that "legitimacy means that there are good arguments for a political order's claim to be recognized as right and just; a legitimate order deserves recognition. *Legitimacy means a political order's worthiness to be recognized.*"[1] Habermas thus distinguishes between a legitimate political order and what is held to be a legitimate political order.

Jürgen Habermas is a cognitivist regarding social and political ethics. He does not believe that the differences between theoretical and practical discourse are sufficient to exclude argumentation about social and political matters from the realm of rationality. Yet, he does not believe that normative claims can be justified by any appeal to the nature of a human being—no matter what form it may take.[2]

According to Habermas, there are different levels of justification—for instance, myths of origin, religious/cosmological world views, philosophically argued ontologies, and the formal conditions of justification itself (which Habermas calls "reconstructive" justification).[3] Habermas views these levels of justification as hierarchically ordered such that the myth stage of justification is superseded by the religious/cosmological stage which in turn is superseded by "ontological modes of thought," and so forth. Habermas does not believe that this hierarchy is ordained or that all societies must go through this process. Rather, he conjectures that the process of providing reasons for claims of legitimacy is a social-evolutionary process which renders certain kinds of reasons once thought sufficient in a society to establish legitimacy now no longer so, e.g., descended from a certain family would not in a Western democracy be a sufficient reason for a claim to political power. "Modernity," he claims, "can and will no longer borrow the criteria by which it takes its orientation from models supplied by another epoch; *it has to create its normativity out of itself.*"[4]

Habermas holds that as the ontological foundations for natural law became more and more problematic, the problem of legitimating political regimes in post-conventionalistic,[5] modern times became more reflective. "The procedures and presuppositions of justification are themselves now the legitimating grounds on which the validity of legitimations is based. The idea of an agreement that comes to pass among all parties, as free and equal, determines the procedural type of legitimacy of modern times."[6] The social contract theories from Hobbes to John Rawls and the transcendentally oriented theories from Kant to Karl Otto-Apel[7] represent traditions in which "it is the formal conditions of possible consensus formation, rather than ultimate grounds, which possess legitimating force."[8]

Habermas's "discourse ethics" is "formalistic" in the sense that he seeks to show that norms which are used as guides for human action can be justified only if they are universalizable and that it is rational for anyone who argues about norms to accept the principle of universalizability. Showing why Habermas believes that it is rational to accept the principle of universalizability as well as what he thinks this principle involves will be the object of analysis in the following sections of part I of this essay. Part II will confine itself to a criticism of Habermas's understanding of the principle of universalizability. It will be argued that Habermas fails in terms of his own account of human action and rationality to show that it is rational to accept the principle of universalizability *as he understands it.*

Habermas's account of human action and rationality as well as his "consensus theory of truth" will not, however, be intensively examined or directly challenged. Such an examination and challenge are well beyond the scope of this essay. It should suffice to note that Habermas rejects the model of an isolated individual actor who can on his own relate to the world either cognitively or practically. Rather, Habermas upholds as fundamental the model of human beings interacting for the purpose of reaching an understanding. He calls this "communicative action." Truth, for Habermas, is not the correspondence between the contents of the mind of an isolated knower and some independently existing reality but instead "the possibility of *argumentative corroboration* of a truth claim that is falsifiable in principle."[9] Karl Otto-Apel, a colleague of Habermas and also an advocate of a discourse ethics, has noted that truth understood as consensus "cannot be attained by finite individuals and that, for this reason, membership in the argumentative community of scholars incorporates a basic transcendence of the egoism of finite beings—a kind of self-surrender in terms of [what Peirce called] a 'logical socialism.' "[10]

Discourse occurs for Habermas when the participants in communicative action take up the issue of whether a contested claim of truth, normative legitimacy, or authenticity (called a "validity claim") can be vindicated or criticized through arguments. Discourse does not necessarily occur in a formal way but is continuous with the everyday questioning, puzzling, interpreting, and clarifying that make up social life. Practical discourse is the form of argumentation "in which we can hypothetically test whether a norm of action, be it actually recognized or not, can be impartially justified."[11] "Discourse ethics" is concerned with reconstructing the procedural norms that are implicit in the communicative process.

2. Discourse Ethics

Regarding Marxian social theory, Habermas claims that "from the beginning there was a lack of clarity concerning the normative foundation."[12] He further claims that such a foundation is possible "only if we can reconstruct general presuppositions of communication and procedures for justifying norms and values."[13] He thus aims to provide a normative foundation for Marxian critical social theory and to do so by means of a discourse ethics.

Three general features of Habermas's discourse ethics should be initially noted. First, it is not concerned with questions of prudence or the good life but only with so-called questions of morality, and, in true Kantian fashion, the latter are differentiated from the former because they are answered from the standpoint of universalizability. The function of a discourse ethics is to justify norms that will determine the legitimate opportunities for the satisfaction of needs.[14] It deals primarily with questions of institutional justice. Second, it is a proceduralist ethics. It does not offer any substantive theory of goodness or principles of justice. Rather, it provides a procedure that ought to be followed in determining the validity of a norm. In other words, it tells us how the practical discourse which seeks to adjudicate between conflicting norms ought to be conducted. In this regard, it is important to understand that Habermas sees the principle of universalizability as a rule of argumentation that belongs to the logic of practical discourse which enables moral actors to generate rational consensus whenever the validity of a normative claim is in dispute. As such, it should not be confused with the content of any abstract normative principle.[15] Just as there is a difference between the concept of justice and a conception of justice for Rawls, so for Habermas there is a difference between the principle of universalizability as the principle upon which the process of discourse is based and the content of the norms which real discourse determines. Third, and unlike Rawls, the discourse is actual, not merely hypothetical. It is something that is carried out by real people.[16]

Habermas believes that a valid norm for answering moral questions has the quality of impartiality, that impartiality is expressed by some version of the principle of universalizability, and that this principle can be rationally defended.[17] He seeks to defend a version of the principle of universalizability by means of a transcendental argument or, at least, a transcendental argument of sorts.[18]

Before describing this kind of argument, some idea of Habermas's version of the principle of universalizability should be gained. Habermas holds that a norm is justified only if it fulfills the following condition (hereafter "U"): "The consequences and side-effects which would foreseeably result from the universal subscription to a disputed norm, and as they would affect the satisfaction of the interests of *each* single individual, could be accepted by all without *constraints*."[19] Habermas endorses Thomas McCarthy's summarization of the difference between the discourse ethics' account of the principle of universalizability and Kant's: "The emphasis shifts from what each can will without contradiction to be a universal law, to what all can will in agreement to be a universal norm."[20]

As already said, Habermas seeks to defend his version of the universalizability principle by means of a transcendental argument. A transcendental argument seeks to show that something, call it X, cannot be rejected and must be accepted as true because the very process of rejecting X depends on something else, call it Y-ing, and Y-ing could not exist unless X were the case. For a transcendental argument to work two things must be true: (1) Y-ing is something unavoidable; and (2) X is indeed necessary for the very possibility of Y-ing—that is, the universal negative proposition, "No Y-ing is possible unless X is the case," must be true. A transcendental argument, then, attempts to show that anyone who rejects "X is the case" is caught in a contradiction. For Habermas this is specifically a "performative contradiction." The rejection of X (where X is "U") is inconsistent with the existence of the activity Y-ing (where Y-ing is argumentation), the only way in which the rejection of X exists. The contradiction is between the existence of the *activity* of rejecting X and the necessary conditions for that activity existing. Thus, the contradiction that is involved is not semantic, but practical in nature.

The history of philosophy, as well as contemporary philosophy, is full of complicated uses of transcendental arguments,[21] and Habermas's "discourse ethics" adds another page to this history. A transcendental argument, however, is no better than the unavoidability of Y-ing and the truth of the universal negative proposition it implicitly affirms. In Habermas's case, (1) is argumentation (Y-ing) something that is unavoidable and (2) is there no possible way to engage in argumentation other than through the acceptance of the truth of "U" and all that it involves? An answer to question (1) cannot be provided here, because determining whether argumentation is truly unavoidable depends on the overall adequacy of Habermas's "consensus theory of truth" and account of communicative action and rationality. For the sake of the argument, it will be assumed that argumentation is indeed something unavoidable. Regarding question (2), a more detailed consideration will occur below in part II. For now, we shall confine ourselves to grasping Habermas's position regarding question (2).

3. *The Rules of Argumentation*

In response to question (2), Habermas claims that "everyone who participates in the universal and necessary communicative presuppositions of argumentative speech, and who knows what it means to justify a norm of action, must assume the validity of a principle of universalizability (either in its above form or in some other equivalent formulation)."[22] He insists that "one who seriously makes the attempt to redeem normative validity claims *by way of discourse* engages intuitively in conditions of procedure which are equivalent to an implicit recognition of 'U.' "[23] Habermas thus has no doubt about the claim that anyone who engages in argumentation accepts the truth of "U." Yet, just what are the universal and necessary presuppositions of argumentation?

The answer to this question can be found in unpacking the following lengthy description of discourse from Habermas's *Legitimation Crisis*.

> Discourse can be understood as that form of communication that is removed from contexts of experience and action and whose structure assures us: that the bracketed validity claims of assertions, recommendations, or warnings are the exclusive object of discussion; that participants, themes and contributions are not restricted except with reference to the goal of testing the validity claims in questions; that no force except that of the better argument is exercised; and that, as a result, all motives except that of the cooperative search for truth are excluded. If under these conditions a consensus about the recommendation to accept a norm arises argumentatively, that is, on the basis of hypothetically proposed, alternative justifications, then this consensus expresses a "rational will." Since all those affected have, in principle, at least the chance to participate in the practical deliberation, the "rationality" of the discursively formed will consists in the fact that the reciprocal behavioral expectations raised to normative status afford the validity to a *common* interest ascertained *without deception*. The interest is common because the constraint-free consensus permits only what *all* can want; it is free of deception because even the interpretations of needs in which *each individual* must be able to

Political Legitimacy and Discourse Ethics   357

recognize what he wants become the object of discursive will-formation. The discursively formed will may be called "rational" because the formal properties of discourse and of the deliberative situation sufficiently guarantee that a consensus can arise only through appropriately interpreted, *generalizable*, interests, by which I mean needs *that can be communicatively shared*.[24]

The universal and necessary presuppositions of argumentation or discourse can be stated in terms of rules.[25] These rules constitute discourse—that is to say, they determine just what it is for someone whose interests are possibly affected by the adoption of a certain norm to consent to it, without constraint and only through the force of the better argument. These rules express for Habermas what "U" as a rule of valid argumentation belonging to the logic of practical discourse requires.

The first rule is simply that if one is a participant in communicative action, then one is under the obligation to provide a justification for the different sorts of claims one makes and to apply any norms one proposes equally to oneself as well as to others. This obligation is regarded as the minimal normative content inherent in communicative action.[26]

The remaining rules result from reconstructing our intuition of what it would be like to resolve conflicting claims to normative rightness[27] by the force of the better argument alone. This reconstruction is called the "ideal speech situation,"[28] and these rules provide the formal properties of a situation in which rationally motivated agreement could be reached. These rules are:

(a) everyone who is capable of speech and action ought to be allowed to participate in discourse;
(b) everyone ought to be allowed to question any proposal;
(c) everyone ought to be allowed to introduce any proposal into discourse;
(d) everyone ought to be allowed to express his attitudes, wishes, and needs; and
(e) no one ought to be hindered by compulsion—whether arising from inside the discourse or outside of it from making use of the moral claims implied by (a)–(d).[29]

Since discourse is something actual and not merely hypothetical, that is, as noted earlier, since it is something that real people carry out, rule (e) implies a general obligation with respect to the context of action from which the discourse is taken up—namely, that this context have moral features similar to those of the ideal speech situation. In other words, it should be a situation in which everyone affected by a proposed norm has free access to all the discourse activities, and opportunities to participate should be equally distributed. Further, it should be a situation in which everyone can openly express their true feelings and intentions. Indeed, it should be so open that a person's very interpretation or understanding of his needs can be examined and questioned. "Only at the level of a universal ethics of speech [*Sprachethik*] can need interpretations themselves—that is, what each individual thinks he should understand and represent as his 'true' interests—also become the object of practical discourse."[30] Only when needs or interests can be communicatively shared is there a possibility of reaching a more truthful interpretation of an individual's particular needs. Negatively stated, the situation should not be one in which there are hidden agendas or motives or where there are any obstacles to discourse created by deception, power, and ideology.

Finally, since the argumentation process by which norms are evaluated is dialogical and not monological and thus requires the consent of all affected by a proposed norm, Habermas holds that each individual's interpretation of his needs or interests must be something that is generalizable. The interpretation must express a need or interest that can be common to all concerned. Indeed, it must in principle be possible for every participant in the argumentation process to exchange roles with the other when it comes to the expression of a need or interest which a proposed norm affects. As Habermas states: "The point of discourse-ethical universalization consists . . . in this, that only through the communicative structure of a moral argumentation involving all those affected is the *exchange of roles* of each with every other forced upon us,"[31] and "impartial formation of judgment is expressed in a principle that compels *each one* in the circle of those affected to assume in the weighing of interests the perspective of *every other*."[32] Further, he notes that "argumentation is expected to test the generaliz*ability* of interests, instead of being resigned to an impenetrable pluralism of ultimate value orientations (or belief-acts or attitudes). It is not the fact of pluralism that is here disputed, but the assertion that it is impossible to separate by argumentation generalizable interests from those that are and remain particular."[33]

This final rule shall be called the "generalizability of interests" rule (hereafter, "G"). "G" is an important rule for practical discourse because without it, it is doubtful that consensus could ever be achieved or the context for legitimate compromises determined. Habermas claims that insofar as anyone takes up practical discourse, he unavoidably "suppose[s] an ideal speech situation that, on the strength of its formal properties, allows consensus only through *generalizable* interests."[34] "G" does not require special justification, Habermas claims, because the expectation on the part of others that one will offer reasons for one's normative claims is contained in the intersubjective character of discourse, and for Habermas the only principle in which practical reason expresses itself is one that obliges each participant in discourse "to transfer his subjective desires into generalizable desires."[35] Karl Otto-Apel states that "this necessary readiness to justify personal *needs qua interpersonal claims* represents an analogy to the 'self-surrender' demanded by Peirce in that the 'subjectivity' of the egoist assertion of one's interests must be sacrificed in favour of the 'transsubjectivity' of the argumentative representation of interests."[36]

To summarize then: Habermas holds that argumentation or discourse is something that is unavoidable and that argumentation cannot exist unless "U" is true, and "U" is expressed in the rules of discourse (the major ones having been presented above). Anyone who argues against these rules or in favor of norms that fail to meet these rules is guilty of a performative self-contradiction and is thus rationally defeated. Habermas thus offers a non-naturalistic, cognitivist, proceduralist account of morality which can be used to assess the validity of proposed conceptions of justice.

II

1. Generalizable Interests: A Critique

Of the many aspects of Habermas's view of what "U" requires that might be challenged, his claim that "G" is one of the rules required by "U" seems particularly vulnerable. Let us see how "G" enters into Habermas's discourse ethics by considering the following proposed justice norm: "Wealth is to be equally distributed unless unequal distribution is to the advantage of the least well-off members of society." We shall call this norm the "difference principle" (hereafter, "DP").

"U" is only a necessary condition for the legitimation of any proposed justice norm and so cannot be used to justify the "DP", but it can be used normatively to reject it. According to "U," the "DP" should be rejected (and the political institutions and policies which implement it are illegitimate) if it is not the case that it can be accepted without constraint by each individual whose interest satisfaction is foreseeably affected by its universal adoption. Since discourse for Habermas must be real and not hypothetical, "DP" is not evaluated from behind some Rawlsian "veil of ignorance." Yet, if this is so, how can the "DP" avoid rejection? Why would someone who possesses more so-called "natural assets," e.g., Michael Jordan, be inclined to agree to a principle whose implementation would foreseeably affect the satisfaction of his interests adversely? Indeed, how can the acceptance of any proposed norm "be accepted by *all*"?[37] And if the "DP," which from a neo-Marxian perspective is an anemic principle of social justice, cannot avoid rejection, what political "punch" does Habermas's discourse ethics really offer?

One might reply that this objection assumes that one's understanding and commitment to the satisfaction of certain interests or needs[38] are privileged, and, as already noted, Habermas does not grant this assumption. One's understanding of his interests or needs is something that must be tested by the discourse process, because it is only through discursive testing of one's understanding of his interests or needs that a truthful understanding of them might be achieved. Thus, when one considers how a proposed norm will affect the satisfaction of his interests or needs, it must ultimately be the case that this consideration be something dialogical, not just monological—that is to say, these interests must be capable of being discussed with others. One cannot merely assert without providing reasons to others that one has an interest or need with which a proposed norm, e.g., the "DP," conflicts and then justifiably refuse to accept the norm. One's understanding of his interests or needs must be "communicatively shared."

Let us grant the thrust of Habermas's "consensus theory of truth" when it comes to determining whether an understanding of one's interests is correct and thus not suppose that any individual's understanding of his interests or needs is privileged. Further, let us even suppose that no interest can be "real" unless it can be "communicatively shared." There is still, however, a logical gap between all members of the discourse process being able not only to communicate to each other that "E is an interest of Smith" but also to agree that E is indeed an interest of Smith, and E being a generaliz*able* interest, that is, an interest not only of Smith but also an interest Jones and everyone else could have. It seems perfectly possible for Smith to have an interest or need that is uniquely his and for this to be acknowledged by everyone, that is, for consensus regarding "E is an interest of Smith" to be achieved and thus communicatively shared, and it still not be the case that this interest is generalizable. There seems to be a conflation of the mode in which an interest for Smith is known—in Habermas's case, the operative term is "discussed"—and the mode in which the interest for Smith exists.

Though Habermas is quite insistent that his discourse process is a real one which has no need of hypothetical constructs like the "veil of ignorance," it is instructive to consider how he envisions the discourse process actually working:

Practical discourses are always related to the concrete point of departure of a disturbed normative agreement. These antecedent disruptions determine the topics that are up for discussion. This procedure, then, is not formal in that it abstracts from content. Quite the contrary, in its openness, practical discourse is dependent on contingent matter being fed into it from the outside. In discourse this content is subjected to a process in which particular values are ultimately discarded as being not susceptible to consensus.[39]

Habermas thus does not deny that there is a pluralism of interests, but the point of the discursive process is to separate those interests that are generalizable from those that are not, and it is only the former that are regarded as capable of rational justification. Thus, Habermas's conception of discourse already has a principle for filtering out interests that are unique to individuals and not capable of being shared by everyone. Though not materially the same, "G" has a function in Habermas's discourse ethics which is not unlike the function that the "veil of ignorance" has in Rawls's theory of justice.[40]

Yet, why must a discursive consideration of the foreseeable consequences of the universal adoption of a proposed norm to the satisfaction of interests of individuals confine itself only to those interests that can be shared by all? Having "G" as the rule by which to separate generalizable interests from particular ones does not seem to be warranted by "U."

Habermas does not, however, see any need for a special justification of "G." As noted before, he states: "In taking up a practical discourse, we unavoidably suppose an ideal speech situation that, on the strength of its formal properties, *allows consensus only through generalizable interests.*"[41] He even goes so far as to describe "U" as "a rule that eliminates as nongeneralizable content all those concrete value orientations with which particular biographies and forms of life are permeated."[42] What is it, however, about the formal properties of the ideal speech situation that places this limitation on what interests may be used in attempting to achieve consensus?

Since the very activity of proposing a norm is a communicative act and thus establishes an interpersonal relation which requires of its participants the abilities to be open to consensus and willingly to take the perspective[43] of the other person and not confine themselves merely to their own point of view, and since the rules of discourse require participants to reflect sincerely on their understanding of their interests, Habermas believes that one is obligated to consider only those interests which are generalizable in determining whether a norm is to be accepted. As Habermas notes, "Only the claim to *general* validity confers on an interest, a volition, or a norm the worth of moral authority."[44] Concretely, this means that any discourse participant ought to be flexible and modify his understanding of his needs if they are not as generalizable as alternative ones. Yet, this is but another instance of the very reasoning that has already been called into question. For even if anyone who communicatively acts must have the ability to take what Habermas calls a "decentered understanding of the world,"[45] and thus can look at the world in an agent-neutral manner, this by no means shows that only generalizable interests ought to be used in trying to form a consensus regarding a proposed norm. Neither the moral superiority of "G" nor the obligation to follow it is established.

2. Alternative Interpretations of "G"

At this point in the argument, one might reply that the foregoing criticism misses its mark, because "G" has been misinterpreted. "G" could be construed in at least two ways different from the previous interpretation.

(1) "G" does not require that E be an interest everyone can have but rather that E be found acceptable by everyone. In other words, it is not enough that everyone recognize that "E is indeed an interest of Smith" and then determine whether E could be an interest had by all. Instead, E must also be acceptable from the perspectives of everyone else. To say that an interest is acceptable is, however, to say either that it is normatively acceptable or that it is not. If it is not, then "acceptable" means nothing more than "an interest others judge they could have," and we remain with the interpretation that has already been given to "G." If "acceptable" means "normatively acceptable," then there is the problem as to what the discourse participants are to appeal in order to determine whether someone's interest is acceptable. Given Habermas's assumptions, there can be no appeal to any substantive understanding of human interest. Rather, the discourse process, and that alone, must be the basis for determining what is an acceptable interest. "G" is, therefore, not defined by some normative understanding of what is acceptable but is, instead, one of the rules of a process which determines whether an interest is normatively acceptable. So, the interpretation given "G" stands, and we return to the question of the justification of "G."

(2) Yet, might it not be that we see a need for a justification of "G" because we have interpreted "G" too strongly? Instead of holding that "G" requires that only interests which could be shared by all be used in trying to form consensus regarding a proposed norm, one should understand "G" as merely requiring that we assume the perspectives of other affected parties. It is not necessary personally to subscribe or adhere to the interests of

others or even to try and find out what it feels like to have those interests. All that is necessary is that one come to understand what the interests of others mean for them. This procedure is similar to what George H. Mead called "ideal role taking" where, in Habermas' words, "any morally judging subject put[s] itself in the position of all who would be affected if a problematic plan of action were carried out or if a controversial norm were to take effect."[46] According to Habermas, "practical discourse can be viewed as a communicative process *simultaneously* exhorting *all* participants to ideal role taking. Thus, practical discourse transforms what Mead viewed as *individual, privately enacted* role taking into a *public* affair, practiced intersubjectively by all involved."[47]

According to this weaker interpretation of "G," one assumes or tentatively adopts the interests of others so as to achieve ideal communication—where everybody knows the interests and evaluations of everybody—and this shared knowledge is used to provide the context in which consensus regarding proposed norms is sought. Yet, on this interpretation of "G," there is nothing to prevent one from treating his interests and evaluations as of more importance to him than those of others. "G" thus does not provide any basis for resolution of normative dispute, and, given that discourse begins when there is a disruption of normative agreement, it is difficult to see how, on this interpretation of "G," there could ever be any proposed norm that a discourse ethics using "U" would not reject. But there could be more to this weaker interpretation of "G"; Habermas states:

> Repairing a disrupted consensus can mean one of two things: restoring intersubjective recognition of a validity claim after it has become controversial or assuring intersubjective recognition for a new validity claim that is a substitute for the old one. Agreement of this kind expresses a *common will*. If moral argumentation is to produce this kind of agreement, however, it is not enough for each individual to reflect in this way and then to register his vote. What is needed is a "real" process of argumentation in which the individuals concerned cooperate.[48]

For Habermas, a "real" process of argumentation goes beyond every discourse participant merely coming to understand the value perspectives of every other and then still consenting only to those norms which best promote his needs or interests. The process of argumentation requires that the discourse participants not give greater weight or importance to their own interests or needs than to anyone else's interests or needs when it comes to consenting to a proposed norm, e.g., the "DP." Thus, even if "G" does not require discourse participants to forsake their personal interests or needs for generalizable ones, this weaker interpretation of "G" still requires every discourse participant to adopt a disinterested or impartial perspective when it comes to determining whether to consent to a proposed norm. Yet it can and should be asked: Why should someone engaged in communicative action adopt such a perspective? Whether "G" be interpreted weakly or strongly, the logical gap in Habermas's argument remains.

3. *The Moral Point of View Versus the Personal Point of View*

Despite his vast theoretical machinery, Habermas does not produce any satisfactory answer to the question: What justifies "G"? It might be, however, that "G" is, in effect, nothing other than Habermas's version of *the moral point of view*,[49] and Habermas assumes that the moral point of view is implicit in communicative action. "The moral point of view cannot be found in a first principle, nor can it be located in an ultimate justification that would lie outside the domain of argumentation. . . . The sought-after moral point of view that precedes all controversies originates in a fundamental reciprocity that is built into action oriented towards reaching understanding."[50] This certainly seems to be the reason why Habermas does not provide any explicit justification of "G." The moral point of view provides the justification for "G."

The moral point of view is, for Habermas, the one and only view point from which moral reasoning occurs. This point of view requires one to consider the satisfaction of his needs or interests not from a personal point of view—that is to say, from a view that gives extra weight or importance to one's needs or interests because they are one's own needs or interests—but from an impersonal point of view—that is to say, from a view that treats the fact that some interests or needs are *uniquely* yours as of no *moral* consequence. Accordingly, the moral point of view could allow one's needs or interests to become part of *moral* deliberation only insofar as they could be shared by others or if they were given no more weight or importance than those of others. It could not allow unique interests and needs or greater weighting of them to become part of moral discourse.

There are, however, four problems with invoking the "moral point of view" as a justification for "G":

(1) It is simply not true that the moral point of view, at least as described above, is the only view from which moral reasoning occurs. Moral reasoning can appeal to needs or interests, let us simply call them "values," that are agent-relative.[51] "A state of affairs S_1 is valuable relative to an agent A_1 if and only if S_1's distinctive presence in [world] W_1 is a basis for A_1 ranking W_1 over W_2 even though S_1 may not be a basis for any other agent ranking

W_1 over W_2."[52] The value of S_1 to me provides me, and possibly only me, with a reason for action. Thus, neither the value of S_1 nor the reason it provides me is something that must be shared by others.[53] They are not impersonal or agent-neutral. S_1 could, however, be the basis for the reason why I, and no one else, ought to help my brother or why it should be me, and only me, who picks out my gift for my spouse. The very moral obligation to act in certain ways toward my brother or my spouse could stem from a value which is not generalizable or impersonal. In fact, the possible examples of moral obligations that are based on agent-relative values are by no means limited: my obligation to tend to my children before those of others; my obligation to keep my promises before assisting others in keeping theirs; and, in general, my obligation to act in a manner that upholds my integrity.

(2) Even if we appeal to a different understanding of the principle of universalizability from the one Habermas uses[54] and understand this principle to hold "that if a consideration of so-and-so sort is a reason for person A to act, then a consideration of the same sort is *ceteris paribus* also a reason for person B to act," the moral point of view is not implied. This understanding of the principle of universalizability says nothing about the character of the values or reasons for actions that are universalized. The principle of universalizability operates even in the case of agent-relative values or reasons. For example, if the production of *his* own well-being is a reason for A to act, then the production of *his* own well-being is a reason for B to act. A cannot claim that his well-being provides him with a good reason for acting without acknowledging that B's well-being provides him with an equally good reason. Yet, this does not mean that A's well-being is B's well-being or that A's well-being provides B with a reason for action or vice versa. There is, then, nothing about the principle of universalizability that requires the adoption of an impersonal point of view regarding values or reasons for acting.

(3) The moral point of view is, in fact, not even compatible with the moral reasoning of real persons in real situations. One cannot even recognize his own life as his and his own reasoning as his very own if in order to play the moral game one must forego all special attachments to ends that are uniquely one's own. Personal projects with the partial attachments they entail are an important way of understanding what it is to be a person. As Loren E. Lomasky writes, "when we wish to understand or describe a person, to explicate what fundamentally characterizes him as being just the particular purposive being that he is, we will focus on his projects rather than his more transitory ends."[55] Yet,

> Project pursuit . . . is partial. To be committed to a long-term design, to order one's activities in light of it, to judge one's success or failure as a person by reference to its fate: these are inconceivable apart from a frankly partial attachment to one's most cherished ends. An individual's projects provide him with a *personal*—an intimately personal—standard of value to choose his actions by. His central and enduring ends provide him reasons for action that are recognized as his own in the sense that no one who is uncommitted to those specific ends will share the reasons for action that he possesses. Practical reasoning is *essentially differentiated* among project pursuers, not merely contingently differentiated by the various causal constraints that each person faces from his unique spatiotemporal location. That end E_1 can be advanced by B and may provide B overwhelmingly good reason to act; that C could be equally effective in advancing E_1 may merit vanishingly little weight in C's deliberations concerning what to do.[56]

Being a project pursuer and adopting the moral point of view, as described above, are incompatible, and to the extent project pursuit characterizes how real people conduct their lives, the moral point of view is not something that is relevant to their moral reasoning.

(4) Despite what has been said, if the previous account of the moral point of view does in fact capture the nature of moral reasoning, then the classic question "Why be moral?" appears. It should be recognized that this question is not merely a motivation-request but rather a validation-request. It is specifically an agent-relative validation request—that is, it is asking what agent-relative value, and thus reason, is there for adopting the moral point of view. As long as the agent-relative point of view is maintained, there is nothing self-contradictory about this request or anything the advocate of the moral point of view can reply.

Further, this request can be made not merely by the moral skeptic but by a participant in communicative action, who is thus capable of taking an impersonal point of view, but who sincerely does not see why this viewpoint must be superior to the agent-relative view when it comes to determining what values are to be consulted or what weighting of them is to be used in evaluating proposed norms. Thus, Habermas's recent claim that "to know the right answer to a moral problem means that nobody has good reason to act otherwise, . . . [and] that moral judgments do possess just the degree of motivating force which the reasons possess on which they rest"[57] does not suffice, because it is Habermas's assumption that the moral point of view exhausts moral reasoning which is the point at issue.

In fact, if we consider what Lomasky notes about the foregoing characterization of the moral point of view—namely, that it "renders ends perfectly socialized, the completely common property of all active beings" and that "the price to be paid for this evaluational socialism is . . . the metaphysical breakdown of the person"[58]—then morality seems, to say the least, something one can do without. Indeed, "if all ends *qua* ends are impersonally determined and impinge on agents equally, then no agent is individuated as the particular purposive being with just those projects to pursue. Agents are dissociated from their ends because the ends are no longer, in any significant sense, theirs."[59] If destruction of personal identity is the price of morality, then it seems irrational[60] not to avoid morality.[61]

4. Personal Identity

One might reply, however, that the preceding objections fail to consider Habermas's views regarding personal identity. As a result, these objections make the discursive testing of a person's needs or interests appear as something alien to him. Habermas holds, on the contrary, that a person has an incentive to participate in discourse; for discursive testing of one's needs or interests is part of the process by which one establishes a sense of identity.

According to Habermas, there are three basic stages of individual identity development: "natural identity," "role identity," and "ego identity."[62] "Natural identity" is formed when a child can distinguish himself from his environment. "Role identity" is formed when an adolescent can distinguish himself from physical objects and understands himself as a member of a social group—family at first and then wider groups. "Ego identity" is formed when a person can distinguish himself and his obligations from particular social roles and from the norms of action they involve, and understand himself as someone who can think according to principles and overcome identities that are tied to concrete roles and particular systems of norms.

> This ability is paradigmatically exercised when the growing child gives up its earlier identities, which are tied to familial roles, in favor of more and more abstract identities secured finally to institutions and traditions of the political community. To the extent that the ego generalizes this ability to overcome an old identity and to construct a new one and learns to resolve identity crises by reestablishing at a higher level the disturbed balance between itself and a changed social reality, role identity is replaced by ego identity.[63]

The notion of "ego-identity" primarily refers to the ability to integrate an old identity into a new identity; for what is currently the new identity may later be old. "Ego identity proves itself in the ability of the adult to construct new identities in conflict situations and to bring these into harmony with older superseded identities so as to organize himself and his interactions—under guidance of general principles and modes of procedure—into a unique life history."[64] Thus, it is not the specific content of a person's self-concept that is crucial to "ego-identity."

Further, a person's understanding of who he is, for Habermas, is necessarily related to how others recognize them. "No one can construct an identity independently of the identifications that others make of him.... [I]n communicative action the participants must reciprocally suppose that the distinguishing-oneself-from-others is recognized by those others. Thus, the basis for the assertion of one's own identity is not really self-identification, but intersubjectively recognized self-identification."[65]

When faced with changing social and cultural traditions and the problems this creates for one's self-concept, that is, when one's social environment undergoes a change which causes the intersubjective identification of one's identity to conflict with one's own, there is a disequilibrium which requires the exercise of one's "ego-identity." In this situation, a person develops a flexible and reflective attitude toward his need interpretations and an awareness of how future fulfillment of his needs might be frustrated by the new environment. As part of the process by which the integration and construction of a new self-concept takes place, a willingness to test discursively and even to revise one's need interpretations develops. Discursive testing of one's need interpretations is thus part of the very process by which one constructs a new identity and is not alien to the person. Rather, it is the very process by which a person tries to meet the concrete difficulties the new situation presents.

Assuming that this account of how one forms a sense of personal identity is true and assuming that a person does indeed have an incentive to test discursively his need interpretations in order to construct a self-concept during times of social and cultural turmoil, can one thereby establish the claim that the only needs or interests that ought to be used in assessing a proposed norm are those that can be shared by all or that their evaluation should be treated in an impersonal or agent-neutral manner? Has "G" been established? The answer is clearly, "No." Further, even if it is the case that many of the unique interests or needs which one holds dear turn out not to be crucial to the understanding of who one is, and even if a person must, through the many twists and turns of his life, abandon certain central understandings of himself for new ones, it does not follow that discursive assessment ought to eschew consideration of needs or interests unique to a person or to refrain from giving them extra weight. Nor does "G" follow from Habermas's account of "ego-identity;" for as we have seen, the ability to take a universal perspective is consistent with values and reasons being agent-relative and does not require one to adopt an impersonal point of view.

One might, however, still object that the central point of Habermas's account of personal identity has been missed—namely, that there simply are no needs or interests that are unique, but only need interpretations that are considered unique and, as has been shown, that are by no means fixed. Yet, even if all one's unique needs or interests are culturally shaped, this does not mean that there are not needs and interests that are regarded as unique and of special importance at the time of discourse. Indeed, Habermas introduces "G" precisely because he recognizes this fact. If there were no needs or interests that were regarded as unique or of special importance, there would be no point to "G." But if this is granted, then the problem of what justifies "G" remains.

No matter how you analyze it, there is a *non sequitur* at the very heart of Habermas's discourse ethics. His discourse ethics does not provide an adequate procedure of legitimating proposed conceptions of justice.

5. Morality and Modernity

One should recall that Habermas understands his discourse ethics as exemplifying the type of normativity that is appropriate to modernity. The openness to criticism, the willingness to challenge any and all beliefs and, when warranted, reflectively to reconsider one's most cherished ones, and to do so in a manner which excludes no one and allows only the force of the better argument to prevail are certainly values that are associated with modernity. There are, however, other values that are also associated with modernity: pluralism, diversity, self-directedness, and above all the inherent dignity and worth of the *individual* human being. Indeed, the Lockean idea that there are no natural moral slaves or sovereigns and the more contemporary "libertarian" claim that "no one's purposes or goals take moral precedence over the purposes and goals of any other person in a way that would justify the complete or partial subordination of any individual to any other individual or any group of individuals"[66] are expressions of a deeply held moral value and are not merely expressions of "possessive individualism." These values are also part of what a post-conventionalist, modern world view values. Such a modern view, then, does not call for theoretical attempts to paper over the real and legitimate differences among the values and projects of individuals by attempting artificially to induce consensus through a generalizability of interests rule or by appealing to the so-called "moral point of view." Rather, it requires that one accept the moral propriety of pluralism and individualism, and from this starting point attempt the difficult task of constructing a theory of justice.[67] Despite his desire to exemplify theoretically the norms that are inherent to modernity, Habermas misses one of modernity's central values. This is ironic, to say the least, in a thinker who sees himself as trying to capture in theoretical form modernity's expression of itself.[68]

Notes

1. Jürgen Habermas, "Legitimation Problems in the Modern State," *Communication and the Evolution of Society*, trans. Thomas McCarthy (Boston: Beacon Press, 1979), 178.

2. Paul Schuchman has suggested that this claim is too strong. Habermas's "discourse ethics" might be understood as making an appeal to the social nature of human beings—not, to be sure, an appeal which tries to discover theoretically norms in this nature, but instead one which tries to see what norms are implied in the active, intersubjective expression of this nature. Given Habermas's adamant rejection of all "philosophically argued ontologies," however, such a characterization does not seem to be one which he would endorse.

3. "Legitimation Problems in the Modern State," 183–85 and 203–205. See note 18 below for an account of the "reconstructive" process.

4. Jürgen Habermas, *The Philosophical Discourse of Modernity*, trans. Frederick Lawrence (Cambridge, Mass.: MIT Press, 1987), 7.

5. "Post-conventionalistic" refers to moral claims that are not based on the tribe, tradition, or social mores but on the argumentation process itself. See Jürgen Habermas, "Moral Consciousness and Communicative Action," *Moral Consciousness and Communicative Action*, trans. Christine Lenhardt and Sherry Weber Nicholsen (Cambridge, Mass.: MIT Press, 1990), 116–94.

6. "Legitimation Problems in the Modern State," 185.

7. Karl Otto-Apel, a colleague of Habermas, is also a neo-Marxist and an advocate of "discourse ethics." See note 10 below.

8. "Legitimation Problems in the Modern State," 184.

9. Jürgen Habermas, "A Postscript to *Knowledge and Human Interests*," *Philosophy of the Social Sciences* 3 (1973), 166 (emphasis added).

10. Karl Otto-Apel, *Towards a Transformation of Philosophy*, trans. Glyn Adey and David Frisby (London: Routledge & Kegan Paul, 1980), 262.

11. Jürgen Habermas, *The Theory of Communicative Action*, vol. 1, trans. Thomas McCarthy (Boston: Beacon Press, 1984), 19.

12. "Historical Materialism and the Development of Normative Structures," *Communication and the Evolution of Society*, 96.

13. "Historical Materialism and the Development of Normative Structures," *Communication and the Evolution of Society*, 97.

14. Discourse ethics does, however, involve a moral-transformative process in which a participant's understanding of his needs is changed. See section entitled

"Personal Identity" of this essay for a discussion of this process as it relates to a person's conception of himself.

15. Jürgen Habermas, "Diskursethik—Notizen zu einem Begründunsprogramm," *Moralbewusstsein und kommunikatives Handeln* (Frankfurt: Suhrkamp, 1983), 103–4.

16. Jürgen Habermas, "A Reply to my Critics," *Habermas: Critical Debates* ed. John B. Thompson and David Held (Cambridge, Mass.: MIT Press, 1982), 257. Also, "Diskursethik," 104.

17. "Diskursethik," 75.

18. Habermas sees philosophy as collaborating with the empirical sciences, especially those which make strong universalistic claims resulting from attempts to reconstruct intuitive knowledge that competent judges, actors, and speakers reveal. Reconstruction is the process of taking what is implicit—the know-how of competent judges, actors, or speakers—and turning it into explicit rules—a theoretical knowledge, a knowledge-that. Unlike classical transcendental analysis, the theoretical account of the implicit know-how that the reconstructive process provides is hypothetical, empirical, and fallible. Thus, Habermas's claim that certain norms are "always-already" present in communicative action is defeasible. Whether this undercuts his discourse ethics and whether the notion of reconstructive science is tenable are crucial questions which cannot be answered here. Yet, see C. Fred Alford, "Is Jürgen Habermas's Reconstructive Science Really Science?" *Theory and Society* 14 (1985): 321–40.

19. "Diskursethik," 103.

20. "A Reply to my Critics," 257. Thomas McCarthy, *The Critical Theory of Jürgen Habermas* (Cambridge, Mass.: MIT Press, 1978), 326.

21. John Finnis's *Natural Law and Natural Rights* and Allan Gewirth's *Reason and Morality* are two contemporary examples of this way of arguing.

22. "Diskursethik," 97.

23. "Diskursethik," 103.

24. Jürgen Habermas, *Legitimation Crisis*, trans. Thomas McCarthy (Boston: Beacon Press, 1975), 107–8.

25. These rules are discussed in "Diskursethik," 97–99. It will not be necessary to discuss the logical-semantical rules.

26. Habermas holds that when the illocutionary force of a speech act is examined, one finds that the speaker is implicitly offering to redeem his claim of truth or normative rightness or sincerity and is thus under an obligation to provide a justification to the listener. See "What Is Universal Pragmatics?" *Communication and the Evolution of Society*, 63–65. Also, see "Diskursethik," 68.

27. This applies to claims to truth and authenticity as well.

28. Habermas claims that the concept of communicative rationality "carries with it connotations based ultimately on the central experience of the unconstrained, unifying, consensus-bringing force of argumentative speech, in which different participants overcome their merely subjective views and, owing to the mutuality of rationally motivated conviction, assure themselves of both the unity of the objective

world and the intersubjectivity of their lifeworld." *The Theory of Communicative Action*, 10.

29. "Diskursethik," 98.

30. Jürgen Habermas, "Moral Development and Ego Identity," *Communication and Evolution of Society*, 90. Also, "Diskursethik," 77–78.

31. "A Reply to my Critics," 257.

32. "Diskursethik," 75.

33. *Legitimation Crisis*, 108.

34. *Legitimation Crisis*, 110.

35. *Legitimation Crisis*, 109.

36. *Towards a Transformation of Philosophy*, 277.

37. Habermas does consider the situation where the participants in discourse have not been able to find needs or interests that they all share. Habermas holds that in this situation a compromise is called for, and a compromise is defined as follows: "A normed adjustment between particular interests . . . [which] takes place under conditions of balance of power between the parties involved." (*Legitimation Crisis*, 111). He further notes that "compromises stand under restrictive conditions because it is to be assumed that a fair balance can come about only with the participation by equal right of all concerned." ("Diskursethik," 83). A compromise, then, cannot be achieved between persons in unequal bargaining positions, and the burden of proof is on the person whose bargaining position affords him greater power to demonstrate that his advantage can be discursively justified. See Stephen K. White, *The Recent Work of Jürgen Habermas* (Cambridge: Cambridge Univ. Press, 1988), 75–77.

38. Habermas uses these terms interchangeably.

39. "Discourse Ethics: Notes on a Program of Philosophical Justification," *Moral Consciousness and Communicative Action*, 103. Also, to repeat a statement that was previously quoted: "Argumentation is expected to *test* the generaliz*ability* of interests, instead of being resigned to an impenetrable pluralism of interests of apparently ultimate value orientations (or belief-acts or attitudes). It is not the fact of pluralism that is here disputed, but the assertion that it is impossible to separate by argumentation generalizable interests from those that are and remain particular." (*Legitimation Crisis*, 108, first emphasis added).

40. After noting the conditions that characterize practical discourse, Habermas observes that "like Rawls's original position, it [practical discourse] is a warrant of the rightness (or fairness) of any conceivable normative agreement that is reached under these conditions. Discourse can play this role because its idealized, partly counterfactual presuppositions are precisely those that participants in argumentation do in fact make. That is why I think it unnecessary to resort to Rawls's fictitious original position with its 'veil of ignorance.'" ("Morality and Ethical Life: Does Hegel's Critique of Kant Apply to Discourse Ethics?" *Moral Consciousness and Communicative Action*, 198).

41. *Legitimation Crisis*, 110 (some emphasis added).

42. "Moral Consciousness and Communicative Action," 121.

43. "Moral Consciousness and Communicative Action," 122, 163. Also, see *Communication and the Evolution of Society*, 88.

44. "Diskursethik," 59. Habermas makes this claim while explaining and endorsing P.F. Strawson's claim that we can explain such moral phenomena as guilt feelings only if we have damaged a normative expectation that is valid for not only one person but all persons.

45. See "Moral Consciousness and Communicative Action," 168–70.

46. "Morality and Ethical Life: Does Hegel's Critique of Kant Apply to Discourse Ethics?" 198.

47. "Morality and Ethical Life: Does Hegel's Critique of Kant Apply to Discourse Ethics?" 198.

48. "Discourse Ethics," 67.

49. See *The Theory of Communicative Action*, 19. Also, see "Diskursethik," 54, 75–77.

50. "Moral Consciousness and Communicative Action," 163.

51. It should be noted that to say X is an agent-relative or personal value is not necessarily to say that X is merely a subjective value—that is, valuable solely because it is desired or chosen—and to say that X is an agent-neutral or impersonal value is not necessarily to say that X is an objective value—that is, something which is desired or chosen because it is valuable.

52. Eric Mack, "Moral Individualism: Agent-Relativity and Deontic Restraints," *Social Philosophy & Policy* 7 (Autumn 1989), 84. Also, see Douglas B. Rasmussen, "Liberalism and Natural End Ethics," *American Philosophical Quarterly* 27 (1990), 153–61 for a discussion of the concept of agent-relativity in natural end ethics and the limitations this concept sets on theories of justice.

53. This is not to say that it could not be understood by others.

54. Habermas does endorse this understanding of the principle of universalizability. He wants to understand it to involve more than this, however.

55. Loren E. Lomasky, *Persons, Rights, and the Moral Community* (Oxford: Oxford Univ. Press, 1987), 26.

56. *Persons, Rights, and the Moral Community*, 27–28.

57. Jürgen Habermas, "Kohlberg and Neo-Aristotelianism," 1988, 20 of manuscript which is forthcoming in *New Directions for Child Development*. This statement is cited by David M. Rasmussen, *Reading Habermas* (Oxford: Basil Blackwell, 1990), 70.

58. *Persons, Rights, and the Moral Community*, 34.

59. *Persons, Rights, and the Moral Community*, 34. Cf. "It is only in so far as you can identify your own motive and actual end with the common good that you reach the moral end and so get to moral happiness. As human nature is essentially social in character, moral ends must also be social in their nature." George H. Mead, "Fragments of Ethics," *Mind, Self, and Society* (Chicago: Univ. of Chicago Press, 1934), 385.

60. Despite Habermas's division of evaluative judgments into judgments of prudence and morality, it is by no means obvious that "irrational" should be understood here to mean merely instrumentally or strategically irrational.

61. Seyla Benhabib in *Critique, Norm, and Utopia* (New York: Columbia Univ. Press, 1986), 327–43 argues that the discursive process can be expanded to include a consideration of an individual's unique interests and needs by having discourse participants adopt the standpoint of the "concrete other"—that is, recognize the very individuality of each other. It is hard to see, however, how this form of communicative action could ever be accomplished. It seems as difficult as trying to plan an economy centrally. Putting aside this doubt, this expanded form of discourse still faces other difficulties. According to Benhabib, solidarity, friendship, love, and care are the norms of such interaction. By knowing that one will be treated in accordance with these norms, one will feel "recognized and confirmed as a concrete individual with specific needs, talents, and capacities" (*Critique, Norm, and Utopia*, 341). But, this still falls short of truly recognizing the individuality of the other. We do not give or receive solidarity, friendship, love, and care in the abstract but in the concrete. For each individual, the worth of the values which these norms call us to create is found only in how they meet and fit with his concrete needs or interests. The problem for this expanded discourse ethics is, then, not merely that such ethical/moral norms allow for great diversity in these values; rather, it is that these values become determinate—fully real—only in the concrete, in relation to and through the judgment and conduct of an individual human being. There is an ineliminable pluralism and individualism to the ethical/moral life, and this puts severe limitations on what can be interpersonally achieved. This is, however, to call into question the whole model of communicative action that we said we would not question, but would assume in this essay. So, it will have to suffice to note that this pluralism underscores the importance of *phronesis*, and the importance of the individual determining for himself how to achieve, maintain, and coherently integrate his values. See Douglas J. Den Uyl, *The Virtue of Prudence* (New York: Peter Lang, 1991), especially chapters 7 and 8; and "Teleology and Agent-Centredness," *The Monist* 75 (January 1992).

62. See "Moral Development and Ego Identity" and "Historical Materialism and the Development of Normative Structures," in *Communication and the Evolution of Society*.

63. *Communication and the Evolution of Society*, 110.

64. *Communication and the Evolution of Society*, 90–91.

65. *Communication and the Evolution of Society*, 107.

66. Eric Mack, "The Ethics of Taxation: Rights Versus Public Goods," *Taxation and the Deficit Economy* (San Francisco: Pacific Institute for Public Policy, 1986), 489–90.

67. See Douglas B. Rasmussen and Douglas J. Den Uyl, *Liberty and Nature: An Aristotelian Defense of Liberal Order* (La Salle, IL: Open Court, 1991) for one such attempt.

68. The time to do research for this essay was made possible by the support provided by the Earhart and Heritage Foundations. Douglas Den Uyl, Tibor Machan, Eric Mack, James Marsh, Martin Schwab, Jeremy Shearmur, Paul Schuchman, and Henry Veatch provided helpful comments on earlier versions of this paper.

Recommended Readings

Anderson, Terry and Leal, Donald, R., *Free Market Environmentalism* (San Francisco: Pacific Research Institute for Public Policy and Westview Press, 1991).

Arnold, N. Scott, *Marx's Radical Critique of Capitalist Society* (New York: Oxford University Press, 1990).

Boaz, David and Crane, David, *Market Liberalism* (Washington, D.C.: The Cato Institute, 1993).

Conway, David, *A Farewell to Marx* (New York: Penguin Books, 1987).

Den Uyl, Douglas J., *The Virtue of Prudence* (New York: Peter Lang, 1991).

——— and Rasmussen, Douglas B., *The Philosophic Thought of Ayn Rand* (Urbana, Illinois and Chicago, University of Illinois Press, 1984).

Engelhardt, Tristram, Jr., *The Foundations for Bioethics* (New York: Oxford University Press, 1986).

Epstein, Richard A., *Takings* (Cambridge, Massachusetts: Harvard University Press, 1985).

———, *Forbidden Grounds* (Cambridge, Massachusetts: Harvard University Press, 1992).

Friedman, Milton, *Capitalism & Freedom* (Chicago: University of Chicago Press, 1962).

Glenn, Kelly V., *The Free Market Environmental Bibliography*, 3rd ed. (Washington, D.C. Competitive Enterprise Institute, 1994).

Gordon, David, *Resurrecting Marx* (New Brunswick, New Jersey: Transaction, 1990).

Green, David B., *Working-Class Patients and the Medical Establishment* (New York: St. Martin's Press, 1985.)

Hayek, F. A., *The Road to Serfdom* (Chicago: University of Chicago Press, 1944).

———, ed., *Capitalism and the Historians* (Chicago: University of Chicago Press, 1954).

———, *Law, Legislation and Liberty*, 3 vols. (Chicago: University of Chicago Press, 1973–1979).
Hospers, John, *Libertarianism* (Los Angeles: Nash, 1971).
Johnson, M. B., and Machan, T.R., eds., *Rights and Regulation* (Cambridge, Massachusetts: Ballinger, 1983)
Johnson, Paul, *Modern Times* (New York: Harper & Row, 1983).
Kirzner, Israel M., *Competition and Entrepreneurship* (Chicago: University of Chicago Press, 1973).
———, *Perception, Opportunity, and Profit* (Chicago, University of Chicago Press, 1979).
Lomasky, Loren E., *Persons, Rights, and the Moral Community* (New York: Oxford University Press, 1987).
Machan, Tibor R., *Human Rights and Human Liberties* (Chicago: Nelson-Hall, 1975).
———, *Individuals and Their Rights* (LaSalle, Illinois: Open Court, 1989).
———, *Capitalism and Individualism* (New York: St. Martin's Press, 1990).
———, ed., *Commerce and Morality* (Totowa, New Jersey: Rowman & Littlefield, 1988).
———, ed. *The Main Debate* (New York: Random House, 1987).
———, *Private Rights, Public Illusions* (New Brunswick, New Jersey: Transaction, 1994).
McGee, Robert W., ed., *Business Ethics & Common Sense* (Westport, Connecticut: Quorum Books, 1992).
Miller, Fred D., Jr., *Nature, Justice, and Rights in Aristotle's* Politics (Oxford: Clarendon Press, 1995).
von Mises, Ludwig, *Human Action* (New Haven, Connecticut: Yale University Press, 1949).
Murray, Charles, *Losing Ground* (New York: Basic Books, 1984).
———, *In Pursuit of Happiness and Good Government* (New York: Simon and Schuster, 1988).
Nardinelli, Clark, *Child Labor and the Industrial Revolution* (Bloomington, Indiana: Indiana University Press, 1990).
Narveson, Jan, *The Libertarian Idea* (Philadelphia: Temple University Press, 1988).
Norton, David L., *Personal Destinies* (Princeton: Princeton University Press, 1976).
Nozick, Robert, *Anarchy, State, and Utopia* (New York: Basic Books, 1974).
Paul, Ellen Frankel, *Equity and Gender* (New Brunswick, New Jersey: Transaction 1989).
Poole, Jr., Robert W., ed., *Instead of Regulation* (Lexington, Massachusetts: D.C. Heath, 1984).

Rand, Ayn, *Capitalism: The Unknown Ideal* (New York: New American Library, 1967).
Rasmussen, Douglas B. and Den Uyl, Douglas J., *Liberty and Nature* (LaSalle, Illinois: Open Court, 1991).
——, and Sterba, James, *The Catholic Bishops and the Economy: A Debate* (New Brunswick, New Jersey: Transaction, 1987).
Rothbard, Murray N., *America's Great Depression*, 4th ed. (New York: Richardson & Snyder, 1983).
——, *Man, Economy, and State*, rev. ed., (Auburn University, Alabama: Ludwig von Mises Institute, 1993).
——, *The Ethics of Liberty* (Atlantic Highlands, New Jersey: Humanities Press, 1982).
Schmidtz, David, *The Limits of Government* (Boulder, Colorado: Westview Press, 1991).
Siegan, Bernard H., *Economic Liberties and the Constitution* (Chicago and London: University of Chicago Press, 1980).
Sowell, Thomas, *Knowledge and Decisions* (New York: Basic Books, 1980).
Veatch, Henry B., *Human Rights* (Baton Rouge, Louisiana: Louisiana State University Press, 1985).
West, E. G., *Education and the State*, 3rd ed. revised and expanded (Indianapolis: Liberty Fund, 1994).
Williams, Walter, *The State Against Blacks* (New York: Mc-Graw-Hill, 1982).

Index

Acton, Lord, 71
advertising, business ethics and, 151; preference formation, 298
affirmative action, business ethics and, 153; education and, 180; objections to, 121–123
altruism, charity and, 316, 317; moral minimalism and, 336
American West, conflict resolution, 93–94
Americans with Disabilities Act (1992), 127
Ames, Bruce, 161
anarchism, 77–95; conflict resolution, 85–95; game theory and, 85–87, 89; in America, 78; versus statism, 81
anarchists, American, 78; individualist versus collectivist, 77–78; versus statists, 85
Anarchy, State, and Utopia (Nozick), 78, 79
Anderson, Terry, 93–94, 95
Andrew, Edward, 317
Aquinas, Thomas, 28, 175, 311–16, 347
argumentation. *See* discourse
Aristotelian ethics, 72, 73–74, 145, 175, 312, 313, 314, 346–47
Augustine, 175, 311
autonomy, just war defense and, 112
Axelrod, Robert, 86–87, 89, 90, 92–93, 94

Bakunin, Mikhail, 77–78
Barnett, Randy, 85, 88, 89, 90–91, 92–93, 95
basic liberties, 248
basic negative rights, defined, 3
basic rights, commercial realm, 289–292; conception of the good and, 290, 291–92; liberalism versus libertarianism, 289–92; price controls and, 294–96; sense of justice and, 290
Bastiat, Frederic, 13
Becker, Lawrence, 326–27
Benson, Bruce, 85, 91–92, 94–95
Berlin, Isaiah, 243, 245–47, 256
Bill of Rights, 11
Biodiversity (Wilson), 68
Bolick, Clint, 123, 124, 132–33
Brave New World, 131
Buchanan, Allen, 306–8, 310
Buchanan, James, 251
business, defined, 146
business ethics, 143–54; advertising, 151; affirmative action, 153; classical individualism, 144, 147–48, 149; defined, 146; employees, 152–53; implications of classical individualism in, 150–53; insider trading, 151; international laws and customs, 152; nepotism, 153; racial discrimination, 150–51
Butler, Bishop, 32

Cameron, David, 167
Capaldi, Nicholas, 126, 127
capitalism, classical firm and modern corporation compared, 228–29; social ills and, 228; versus socialism, 227–40
Carson, Rachel, 169, 170, 171, 172
charity, 33; altruism and, 316, 317; as function of economic opportunity, 309–10; justice and distinction between, 306–11, 314–18; Mandelvillian problem of, 319–22; as openness to the good, 312–13; origins of the word, 311–12; self-perfection and, 312–13, 314, 315, 325; versus pity, 319–20; versus right to welfare, 305–28
Christianity, virtue of charity, 311–15
citizenship, education and, 181–85
civil rights, 121–40; affirmative action, 121–23; libertarian agenda, 132–39; original vision versus revised agenda, 123–24, 139–40
Civil Rights Act (1991), 127
Clague, Christopher, 194
classical individualism, business ethics and, 144, 147–48, 149, 150–53; defined, 145; moral sovereignty, 149–50; professional ethics and, 148–49. *See also* individualism
coercion, 41, 42; financing of public goods and, 103
collectivism, argument against, 128–30; social engineering and, 125
Commoner, Barry, 170
communitarianism, defined, 259–60; versus liberalism, 259–84
Comte, Auguste, 126
conflict resolution, American West and, 93–94; anarchism and, 85–95; free-riding and, 93
conscription, impermissibility of, 103–4
consequentialism, 43–44, 344–46
conservatism, in moral theory, 28

contractarian proposal, 30
contractarianism, 19–38; defined, 25; libertarianism and, 25–26; limits of, 256; non-tuism and, 32; practicality of, 30; recent views of, 31; welfare and, 35–38
contracts, nature of, 24; social, 23–25
Contrat Social, Du (Rousseau), 124
Cornuelle, Richard, 138
crime prevention, commonly held resources and, 90–91

Darwinian utilitarianism, 245
Darwinism, cultural, 253
Declaration of Independence, 3, 8, 11, 59
defense, broad, 105; financing, 102; just war, 105–7, 109, 111–14; limitless, 107–8; necessary force, 107; permissible, 109, 110–14; strategic, 114–16; strict, 105. *See also* strategic defense
deontology, 344–46
Den Uyl, Douglas J., 221
determinism, problems of, 130–31; social engineering and, 125
discourse, defined, 356–57, 353–54; Habermas's rules of, 356–59
discourse ethics, 351–70; as formalistic, 353; difference principle and, 359–60; features of, 354; generalizable interests and, 357, 358–64; modernity and, 369–70; moral point of view, 364–67; personal identity, 367–69; process of argumentation, 363; truth and, 353
discrimination, reverse, 127
diversity, education and, 180
Dworkin, Ronald, liberal; egalitarianism, 299

Earth in Balance (Gore), 162
economics, Austrian school of, 188–90; discovery process, 188–89; egalitarianism, social engineering and, 127;

neoclassical model of perfect competition, 189
education, 175–85; advances in technology, 178; aims of, 179–80; affirmative action and, 180; citizenship and, 181–85; communist versus free society, 183–85; compulsory, 177, 181; diversity and, 180; outcomes of, 176, 180–81; problem of the poor, 177–78; standards in, 175–76, 178–80; universal, 175, 176–78
Efron, Edith, 341
egalitarianism, economic, social engineering and, 127; moral minimalism and, 336
egoism, ethical, 263–65
Ehrlich, Paul, 158, 159, 160, 171
Ekins, Paul, on resource economics, 159
Elements of Law (Hobbes), 316
elitism, social engineering and, 126–27
Ellerman, David, 231
End of Nature, The (McKibben), 166
Endangered Species Act (1973), 166; underlying science, 167–68
Engels, Friedrich, 217
Enlightenment, 59, 72
Environmental Defense Fund, DDT and, 161
Environmental Protection Agency, 166; DDT and, 161
environmentalism, 157–73; evaluation of risk from industrial or natural chemicals, 161–63; global climate issues, 163–66; historical context of, 169–72; human right to thrive and, 168–69, 173; as inherently destructive, 171–72; philosophic perspective of, 157–58; replacement of, 172–73; values and, 166–67
equity ownership, 228–240
ethical theory, 43–44
ethics, as relates to virtue and justice, 308; classical versus modern approach, 313–22; choice and, 149–50;

noncognitivism and concept of liberty, 272; normative versus metanormative principles, 276–77, 282, 283; professional, 148–49; defined, 146; versus politics, 68, 271–77. *See also* discourse ethics
Ethics of Liberty, The (Rothbard), 344
Evolution of Cooperation, The (Axelrod), 86
exploitation, market socialism and, 236–40

fallibilism, Karl Popper's, 244
free market prices, state interference with, 292–96
free-riding, conflict resolution and, 91, 93; public defense and, 103
free will; social spontaneity, civil rights and, 133, 135
freedom, defined, 11
Friedman, David, 336
Friedman, Milton, 336, 340; criticism of, 148; social responsibility of corporations, 144, 145, 146, 148; versus classical individualist position, 148–49

game theory, anarchism and, 85–87, 89
Gauthier, David, 24
generalizable interests; discourse ethics and, 357, 358–64
good, human flourishing and self-perfection as, 274; practical reason and, 274–75
Global 200 Report to the President, 158
Gore, Albert, environmental position, 162
government, as fee-for-service agency, 80; intervention on drug use, 188; justification of, 80; as protector and violator of rights, 14–16; roles in conflict management and humanitarian intervention, 108–9, 116–18; scope of, 99–100; social spontaneity, civil rights and, 133, 136–37. *See also* state

Graber, David, 166
Gray, John, 243–56; indictment of liberalism, 249–55
Gulf War, justification of U.S. involvement, 117–18

Habermas, Jürgen, 351–70; problem of political legitimacy, 352–54
Haeckel, Ernst, 170
Hansen, James, on global warming, 164
Hart, H.L.A., 217
Hayden, Tom, 170
Hayek, F.A., 67, 125, 126, 128–29, 243, 245, 248–49, 251, 253, 256, 336–37, 342–43, 347
Hegel, George, 170, 341, 346–47
Herzen, Alexander, 338–39
Hill, P.J., 93–94, 95
Hitler, Adolf, 340
Hobbes, Thomas, 24, 29, 31, 87, 124, 125, 134, 262, 315–16, 320, 353; First Law of Nature, 26; Laws of Nature, 20; Rothbard's parody of, 90
Homine, De (Hobbes), 316
Human Exposure Rodent Potency Index (HERP), 161–63
human flourishing, 61–65, 264–65, 268, 269–71, 274–76, 278–84, 346–47; deep ecology and, 338; liberty and, 184; as ultimate moral good, 274
human sociality, 262–63, 269–70, 278, 281
Human Rights and Human Liberties (Machan), 83
Hume, David, 24, 248. 320
Hutt, W.H., 188

independent sector, social spontaneity and civil rights, 133, 138–39
individual as end-in-himself, 101
individualism, moral minimalism and, 336; social spontaneity, civil rights and, 133–35. *See also* classical individualism

Individuals and Their Rights (Machan), 79, 217
insider trading, business ethics and, 151
insurance, welfare and, 36–37
interests, inherently conflicting, 32–33; liberal, 33. *See also* generalizable interests, discourse ethics and
international relations, as being in an Hobbesian state of nature, 87–88
interventions, prohibition and, 188–90
Iverson, Ken, 172–73

Jefferson, Thomas, 8
just war defense, 105–7, 109, 111–14; implications of, 114–18
justice, 68–71; and charity, distinction between, 306–11, 314–18; ethics and, 73; as metanormative principle, 68, 69–70; as normative principle, 70; relation to ethics and virtue, 308

Kant, Immanuel, 144–45, 251, 256, 320, 321, 353, 355
Kaplan, John, 194
Khomeini, Ayatollah, 340
knowledge, as outgrowth of practice, 246; theoretical versus practical, 249
Kropotkin, Peter, 78

Lane, Rose Wilder, 14
Lao Tzu, 4
Law of Equal Freedom, 7, 16
LeCarre, John, 147
Legitimation Crisis (Habermas), 356
Leviathan (Hobbes), 124
Levin, Michael, 12
liberal egalitarianism, right to free exchange and, 299–301
liberalism, 74; as atomistic, 261; bourgeois, 341–43; charity and, 318; communitarian objections to, 259–61, 266–67, 271, 272–73, 274, 277–78; death of, 72; Gray's indictment of, 249–55; moral theory, 28; political theory, 270–77; radical, 244; reduc-

tionist tendency, 309, 310; rights versus needs, 282–83; traditional community life and, 279–81; versus communitarianism, 259–84; versus libertarianism, 282–301
liberalism's problem, 271, 274, 276
Liberalisms (Gray), 243–56
Libertarian Idea, The (Narveson), 79
libertarianism, arguments in support of, 4; Declaration of Independence and, 3; defined, 3, 28; Lockean, 209, 210, 211, 212, 213, 214; moral defense, 335; relationship to conservatism and liberalism, 28; relationship to contractarianism, 25–26; technical-scientific defense, 335; versus deep ecology, 337–38; versus liberalism, 282–301; versus tribalist chauvinism, 340; versus welfare, statism, and communism, 338–44
liberty, as amoral concept, 271–72; defined, 26, 42; erosion of, 73; ethical noncognitivism and concept of, 272; human flourishing and, 184; positive versus negative, 5–6, 26; problem of normative basis for, 71–72; self-direction and right to, 278; social, defined, 26
Liberty and Nature: An Aristotelian Defense of Liberal Order (Den Uyl and Rasmussen), 59–60, 261
licensure laws, 137–38; as violation of right to free entry, 296–97
Lincoln, Abraham, 209
Locke, John, 3, 10, 27, 209, 217, 317, 324, 344
Lockean libertarianism, 209, 210, 211, 212, 213, 214
Lomasky, Loren E., 323–25, 365–67

Machan, Tibor, 79, 90, 220; on the justification of government, 80, 83–85
Mandeville, Bernard, 318–22
Mandevillian problem of charity, 319–22

market socialism, 227–40; in Yugoslavia, 238
Marx, Karl, 78, 124, 145, 170, 212, 218, 219, 338, 351–52
Marxism, 124, 126; and anarchy, 77
materialism, reductive, 125
McCarthy, Thomas, 355
McKibben, Bill, 166
Mead, George H., 363
metanormative/normative distinction, 73–74; as rights of equal liberty, 64; justice as, 68, 69–70; money as, 66–68; versus normative principles, 276–77, 282, 283, 284
military, alliances, 114–16; conflict management and humanitarian intervention, 108–9; roles in local intervention and humanitarian expeditions, 116–18
Mill, John Stuart, 20–21, 46, 175, 199, 243–56; harm principles, 247; indirect utilitarianism, 247; liberty principles, 247
Mill on Liberty: A Defense (Gray), 243
Mises, Ludwig von, 126, 128–29, 199, 340
money, as metanormative principle, 66–68
Montaigne, Michel de, 191
Moore, Mark H., 194
moral humanism, 337–38
moral impersonalism, 266–70, 273
moral individualism, 42, 444, 48, 50, 263–65
moral minimalism, argument against, 335–47
moral sovereignty, classical individualist ethics and, 149–50
moral universalism, 265–71; defined, 24
morality, defined, 24
morals and modernity, 369–70
More, Thomas, 124
Muir, John, 167

Narveson, Jan, 79; on pacifism, 109, 110
National Alcohol Prohibition, 192

natural law, 20
natural rights, 7–9, 101–2; to liberty, 261; as negative rights, 101–2
needs versus rights, 211
nepotism, business ethics and, 153
New Deal, 122
Newton, Isaac, 125
Nicomachean Ethics (Aristotle), 314
Nock, Albert Jay, 78
nonequity ownership, 234–40; exploitation of the state and, 236–40
nonunanimity, 15–16. *See also* unanimity, lack of
normative/metanormative distinction, 73–74
normative principles, justice as, 70; versus metanormative principles, 276–77, 282, 283, 284
Nowak, Martin, on the prisoner's dilemma, 86–87
Nozick, Robert, 62, 78, 79, 88–89, 344; concept of state as inevitable, 81–83
nuclear weapons, strategic defense and, 114–16
Nucor Steel, 172–73

Oakeshott, Michael, 243, 245–47, 248, 254, 255, 347
On Liberty (Mill), 244, 247
oppression, poverty and, 216–17
ozone depletion, 164–65
Otto-Apel, Karl, 353, 359

pacifism, critique of, 109–10; just war defense and, 112; principled, 104–5
Paine, Thomas, on natural and civil rights, 123–24
Peltzman, Sam, 189
personal identity, discourse ethics and, 367–69
Persons, Rights, and the Moral Community (Lomasky), 323
Philosophy of Right (Hegel), 347
Plato, 66, 124, 175, 210, 245, 256, 314

political legitimacy, defined, 352; problem of, 352–54
Politics (Aristotle), 346
politics versus ethics, 68, 271–77
Popper, Karl, 243, 244–45
Population Bomb: Population Control or Race to Oblivion?, The (Ehrlich), 158
population growth, resource use and, 158–59
portfolio problem, 231
positive rights, 101–2; as acquired rights, 102; versus negative rights, 11–14, 209–21; weakness in concept of, 12
positivism, 335
Possibility of Cooperation, The (Taylor), 87
poverty, oppression and, 216–17
Power and Market (Rothbard), 89
practical rationality, defined, 21
practical reason, and achieving the good, 274–75
Preston, Richard, 172
price controls, as violation of basic rights, 294–96
prisoner's dilemma, 85, 316; game theory and, 85–87
prohibitionism, alternatives to, 188, 193–95; argument against, 191–93; crime and, 190; extended free market solution, 197–98; free market solution, 195–98; interventionism and, 188–90; moral case for legalization, 199; pragmatic case against, 188; rights and, 187
property rights, 8, 44, 212–13, 214, 215, 216, 219; as extension of self-ownership rights, 55–56; as fundamental, 10–11, 27, 56–57; free speech and, 9–10
protection of rights. *See* defense
Proudhon, Pierre, 77
prudence, virtue of, 147

racial discrimination, business ethics and, 150–51

Rand, Ayn, 7, 8, 16, 128, 129, 210, 337, 344
Rasmussen, Douglas B., 221
rationalism, defined, 246
Rawls, John, 211, 243, 247, 48, 251, 290, 353, 354; veils of ignorance, 29, 31, 34
Raz, Joseph, 247
reason, as basis for political theory, 19–20
Reciprocity (Becker), 326
reductionist tendency, as inherent in liberalism, 309, 310
relationship, exclusive versus nonexclusive, 68–69, 70–71
Republic (Plato), 124
resources, laws of thermodynamics and, 160; problem of commonly held, 90–91; use of, 158–60
responsibility, personal, social spontaneity and civil rights, 133, 135–36; professional versus social, 148–49
rights, 6–14; acquired, 102; contractual, 12; exchange at free market prices and, 292–96; free entry and, 296–99; free exchange, 299–301; free speech, 8; function of, 60; individualism, 42, 44, 47–57; liberty, 8; life, 8; as metanormative principles, 60, 278–79; negative, 101–2, 11–14, 209–21; primacy of, 277–84; pursuit of happiness, 8; relationship to morality, law, politics, 59–60; self-ownership, 44; versus entitlements, 122–23, 124, 136–37; versus needs, 211, 282–83; welfare, 209–21, 305–28. *See also* basic rights, basic negative rights, natural rights; positive rights; property rights.
Roosevelt, Franklin, 170
Rothbard, Murray, 89–90, 91–92, 93, 94–95, 344; anarchist society, 78–79; definition of state, 80; lack of justifiable government, 83–85; parody of Hobbes's argument, 90

Rousseau, Jean-Jacques, 124, 169–70, 339–40
Ruckleshaus, William, on DDT, 161

Schmidtz, David, on free-riding, 93
Schneider, Stephen, 163
Schweickart, David, market socialism, 234–40
self-direction, 61–65, 275–76; and right to liberty, 278
self-ownership, as negative right, 54–55; prerogative argument, 48–50; prerogative versus recognition argument, 54; property rights, 55–56; recognition argument, 50–54
self-perfection, 62–65; charity and, 312–13, 314, 315, 325; classical individualism and, 145; rights of equal liberty and, 64; as ultimate moral good, 274
self-perfectionist virtue ethics, 264–65, 267, 271–77, 281
Sigmund, Karl, on the prisoner's dilemma, 86–87
Silent Spring (Carson), 169, 170
Simon, Julian, 158–59, 160
Smith, Adam, 3, 175, 307–11, 318, 320
social atomism, 134
social engineering, philosophy of, 132–39
socialism versus capitalism, 227–40
society, as distinct from the state, 79–80
Socrates, 254
Soviet Union, relations with U.S., 114–15
Spencer, Herbert, 7, 8, 16, 212, 243, 245
Spooner, Lysander, 78
Spy Who Came in From the Cold, The (LeCarre), 147
standards, as inherent inactivities, 179
state, defined, 80; as distinct from society, 79–80; as inevitable, 81–83
state of nature, 28–30
state ownership, 230, 233–34
statism versus anarchism, 81, 85

strategic defense, nuclear weapons and, 114–16. *See also* defense
Sterba, James, basic rights, 209–21
Stirner, Max, 78
Sweeney, Edmund, 161

Taoism, 4
Taylor, Michael, 87–88
Theologiae Summa (Aquinas), 311
Theory of Justice, A (Rawls), 247
Theory of Moral Sentiments (Smith), 307
Tocqueville, Alexis de, 247
transcendental argument, defined, 355
Trotsky, Leon, 10
truth, consensus theory of, 353–54, 360
Tucker, Benjamin, 78

unanimity, lack of, 31. *See also* nonunanimity
United States, relations with Soviet Union, 114–15
United States Supreme court, civil rights and, 127
universalizability principle, 353–69; alternative understanding, 365; defense of, 355–56
utilitarianism, 34, 245
Utopia (More), 124

value, agent relative versus agent-neutral rankings, 46–47, 49–50; nature and, 166–67; objective, 263–65, 268; normative pluralism versus normative monism, 50–51; subjective, 263–65
value individualism, 42, 44, 45–47
Vanek, Jan, Yugoslav market socialism, 238
victimization, historical social engineering and, 126, 131–32
virtue, classical versus modern approach, 313–22; effect versus motive, 320–21; prudence, 147; relation to ethics and justice, 308; role of, 311
voluntarism, social spontaneity, civil rights and, 133, 137–38

war, defense doctrines and, 104–8; vindication of, 104; *See also* defense
Warburton, Clark, 192
Warren, Josiah, 78
Wealth of Nations, The (Smith), 310
welfare, 35–38; agency argument for, 323–25; as means of relief of conscience, 321–22; reciprocity argument, 326–27; RNY argument, 322–23
welfare rights, nonexistence of, 209–21
well-being, 61–63; value individualism and, 45–46
Weyerhauser, and forest management, 159, 160
Wilson, Edward, 168
Wiseman, Clark, on waste disposal, 162
Wurster, Charles, on DDT, 161

Yeager, Leland B., 336

About the Contributors

John Hospers is Professor Emeritus at the University of Southern California.
Jan Narveson is Professor of Philosophy at the University of Waterloo, Canada.
Eric Mack is Professor of Philosophy at Tulane University.
Douglas J. Den Uyl is Professor of Philosophy at Bellarmine College, Louisville, Kentucky.
Douglas B. Rasmussen is Professor of Philosophy at St. John's University, New York.
Aeon J. Skoble teaches philosophy at the University of Central Arkansas.
Steven Yates teaches philosophy at the University of South Carolina.
Tibor R. Machan is Professor of Philosophy at Auburn University.
Mike Gemmell is a freelance writer on environmental policy.
James E. Chesher is Associate Professor of Philosophy at Santa Barbara City College.
Mark Thornton is O.P. Alford, III, Assistant Professor of Economics, Auburn University.
N. Scott Arnold is Professor of Philosophy at the University of Alabama at Birmingham.
Loren E. Lomasky is Professor of Philosophy at Bowling Green State University, Ohio.
Daniel Shapiro is Associate Professor of Philosophy at West Virginia University.
Gregory R. Johnson teaches philosophy at Morehouse College in Atlanta.